THE SPANISH
BORDERLANDS FRONTIER

THE

SPANISH

BORDERLANDS

FRONTIER

1513–1821

Δ

JOHN FRANCIS BANNON
Saint Louis University

Maps researched and drawn by
Ronald L. Ives
Northern Arizona University

HISTORIES OF THE AMERICAN FRONTIER
Ray Allen Billington, General Editor
Howard R. Lamar, Coeditor

UNIVERSITY OF NEW MEXICO PRESS
Albuquerque

FOREWORD

For a generation after 1893 when Frederick Jackson Turner announced his "frontier hypothesis," he and his disciples pictured the population stream that peopled the continent as flowing from east to west, advancing relentlessly from the Atlantic to the Pacific. Its source, they taught, was the British Isles, whence came the Anglo-American pioneers who established their beachheads at Jamestown and Plymouth and Boston, then began their march westward across the Appalachian barrier, over the interior valley, and through the Great Plains to plant their settlements in the valleys of California and the Oregon country. They were joined at times by other European migrants, the Germans especially, but their cultural baggage was basically English and the civilization they planted was a British civilization, modified only by the environmental forces operating on the frontier.

That Turner should evolve this provincial interpretation by observing conditions in his native Wisconsin, and that it should be perpetuated in that day of the Anglo-Saxon myth, is easy to understand. Yet in stressing this viewpoint, to the exclusion of all others, he and his followers seriously distorted the truth. Actually four migratory streams contributed to the population of the United States during the era of settlement. The principal flood tide was, as Turner saw, moving from east to west, and carried with it the Anglo-American culture that laid the foundation on which the nation's civilization rested. But the superstructure built on this foundation was significantly altered as it was joined by lesser population streams during the eighteenth and nineteenth centuries.

One of these originated in Canada and advanced upon the present United States from the northeast; French Canadians during the seventeenth and eighteenth centuries occupied much of Michigan and the Illinois country, pushed their posts southward along the Mississippi River to St. Louis and beyond, and spread their fur-trading operations across the northern Great Plains as far as the Rocky Mountains. Throughout this vast area vestiges of the French occupation can be observed today. A second migratory stream had its source in the Caribbean Islands. From there Spaniards advanced upon the mainland from the southeast, establishing themselves in the Floridas, and planting their outposts as far north as the Carolinas and Virginia. The third and most important subsidiary migration began in Mexico. From that Spanish stronghold a northward-moving frontier advanced steadily during the seventeenth and eighteenth centuries, filling the plateaus of northern Mexico, and pushing on into Texas, New Mexico, Arizona, and California. By the dawn of the nineteenth century New Spain's mission stations, ranches, and presidios swept in a giant arc from eastern Texas to the Bay of San Francisco. Half a century later these holdings were to be absorbed by the relentless drive of the westward-moving Anglo-American pioneers. But this conquest could not erase the cultural tradition planted there by the Spaniards; Spanish culture remains a significant force in the civilization of the Southwest today.

The importance of this heritage was first fully realized by Herbert Eugene Bolton. During a fruitful career of teaching at the University of Texas, Stanford University, and the University of California at Berkeley, Bolton evolved the concept of the Americas, North and South, as a single geographic unit, to be viewed as a continent, not as a multiplicity of nations. In this perspective, the United States became not simply an outpost of England, but a complex region understandable only in terms of the Anglo-French and Anglo-Spanish intrusions that had altered its behavioral patterns. This concept Bolton strengthened by a lifetime of research in the archives of Spain, France, and Mexico, as well as in the extensive Latin-American manuscripts of the University of California's own Bancroft Library.

The result was not only a shelf full of books, monographs, and edited tomes from Bolton's prolific pen, but the emergence of a new school of historical interpretation. Its concern was with the peopling of the continent, but particularly with the cultural conflicts and adaptations that occurred when two frontiers met, as they did in the southwestern United States where the northward-moving Spaniards and the westward-moving Anglo-Americans joined in conflict during the early nineteenth century. Bolton set the guidelines for the study of these areas in 1921 when he published a small volume in the "Chronicles of America" series which he called *The Spanish Borderlands*. Here he sketched in broad outline the story of the clashing frontiers and suggested the importance of a study-in-depth of a phase of frontier history that had been virtually neglected.

The Spanish Borderlands was a germinal book, for it stated rather than solved a problem. In it Bolton demonstrated the significance of the Borderlands in American expansion; years of research would be needed to show how those Borderlands were occupied and to appraise their exact role in the history of Mexico and the United States. This was a challenge to the dozens of disciples trained by Bolton in his seminars; over the years they and their academic children and grandchildren studied the Borderlands with an avidity that their master could only admire. The result was a flood of books and monographs and articles, mounting into the thousands, that shed light on every phase of the Borderlands story.

Until this time, no one has seen fit to weld this mountain of information into a new synthesis, comparable to Bolton's own *Spanish Borderlands* in scope and purpose, but enriched now with the findings of the half-century of scholarship since his book was published. That this task has fallen to Dr. John Francis Bannon is both fitting and fortunate. It is fitting because Dr. Bannon learned the historical trade with Bolton and is one of his most prominent students; he has edited a volume of the most significant Bolton writings and is currently preparing a biography that promises to rank among the major works in American historiography. It is fortunate, for Dr. Bannon is one of the nation's foremost scholars in the field of Border-lands history and the author of a number of books and articles that demon-strate his thorough mastery of the field.

His volume follows the broad outlines of that by his teacher, but goes far beyond. Its pages are spiced with evidence of his own research, as well as by his knowledge of the sources, published and unpublished, that touch on every phase of the vast subject that he treats. But—and more important—they reveal his skill in synthesis, for within them are compressed the results of hundreds of investigators who have studied aspects of the Borderlands story in the half-century since Bolton's volume appeared. Rich in color and brimming with excitement (as must be any well-told tale of the *conquista-dores* and mission fathers), the pages of this volume contain a wealth of detail and interpretation to be found in no other book. Indeed Bannon's *Spanish Borderlands Frontier* promises to serve coming generations as effectively as Bolton's *Spanish Borderlands* served scholars over the past fifty years.

This volume is one of eighteen in the Holt, Rinehart and Winston "Histories of the American Frontier" series. Like other books in the series, it tells a complete story; it may also be read as part of the broader history of American expansion told in connected form in these volumes. Each is written by a leading authority who brings to his task an intimate knowledge of the period that he covers and a demonstrated skill in narration and interpretation. Each will provide the general reader with a sound but readable account of one phase of the nation's frontiering past and the specialized student with a documented narrative that is integrated into the general story of the nation's growth. It is the hope of the authors and editor that this full history of the most American phase of the country's past will help its people to understand themselves and thus be better equipped to face the global problems of the twentieth-century world.

The Huntington Library   Ray Allen Billington
March 1970

PREFACE

THIS WORK, in a sense, is a golden jubilee volume. Just short of half a century ago, in 1921, there appeared a little study in the "Chronicles of America" series entitled *The Spanish Borderlands*, also a synthesis. Herbert Eugene Bolton for the previous two decades had been working on the history of the Spaniards in North America, teaching about them in the classroom, producing a variety of short studies, editing significant pieces on two great figures of the Spanish frontier (Athanase de Mézières and Eusebio Francisco Kino), compiling a guide to the archives of Mexico, and drawing on those of Spain. The opportunity to contribute a volume to the series in progress offered him the challenge to pull together his own researches and insights and to incorporate those of predecessors and contemporaries—Hubert Howe Bancroft, Adolph Bandelier, Charles Lummis, Frederick Webb Hodge, and his own graduate students—into a short popular account of Spanish colonial enterprise in the northern continent.

During those two decades, the first of the twentieth century, and for the next two as well, Bolton continued to interest and inspire graduate students —at Texas first, then at Stanford, and finally at California-Berkeley. His own further studies and theirs, since 1921, have piled up. His students researched and wrote; their students, and sometimes their students' students, as well as other scholars have broadened and deepened knowledge of the Spanish Borderlands. The accumulation has become considerable.

The time is ripe, so thought the editors of the "Histories of the American Frontier" series, to do another synthesis, and in the process to recognize that North America had frontiers other than the more familiar ones of Anglo making. Here is the attempt to retell that story of the Borderlands, or, as someone has facetiously suggested, of the "Boltonlands." This one runs a bit beyond the chronological limits imposed on Bolton and tries to carry the story to the end of the Spanish regime. But this one, too, has limits and has designedly left the Mexican years in the Borderlands to others. Also not attempted herein is the story of the culture clash that ensued when two American frontiers collided in the second quarter of the nineteenth century, in Texas, New Mexico, and California. Even with these limitations, the area covered is so vast and the time span so great that little more than the highlights of the total story can be touched. It is hoped that these have been properly modernized, by notice of the research and writing of the past half century.

In a work of synthesis, such as this, the author owes thanks to many scholars, too numerous to mention individually. The spot references will indicate the author's indebtedness and tell from whose researchings he has borrowed. Very special thanks are due Professor Ronald L. Ives, Department of Geography, Northern Arizona University, for so generously putting his great and often on-the-spot knowledge of the Borderlands into the maps—these could very well be more valuable than the text. Professor Ives would wish to acknowledge with gratitude the assistance given him by the U.S. Coast and Geodetic Survey, whose base maps he used, and by the Flagstaff office of the U.S. Geological Survey, which was always ready to help in the solution of knotty problems tormenting the cartographer. Abigail Solomon, an art editor at Holt, Rinehart and Winston, has assembled fine and anything-but-shopworn illustrations. The series editor, Ray Allen Billington, and the editorial readers, outside of and at Holt, have been patient, helpful, and constructive. In assembling the bibliography students in the author's seminars have contributed more than he—special thanks in this matter to Russell M. Magnaghi, Warren L. Barnhart, and Anne Louise Mooney Day. The author is very grateful to his assistant, Dr. Rita G. Adams, for sharing many of the chores attendant on bookmaking once the manuscript goes into production—writers know these only too well.

Saint Louis University   John Francis Bannon
March 1970

CONTENTS

MAPS

◁ **1** ▷

The Spanish Borderlands, Another Kind of Frontier

*T*he farther the Anglo-American frontier edged toward the heart of the continent and the closer it came to the Mississippi River, the less true it became that the frontier was moving into a so-called virgin wilderness. Of course, even in its first stages of advance away from the Atlantic seaboard the frontier was never really confronting a virgin wilderness. Many, many centuries before the English came, the North American continent as a whole had lost its virgin character. Other men peopled the continent's vast reaches, east to west and north to south. But too often in the thinking of the frontiersmen and their interpreters the Indians really did not count. They, so to speak, went with the land. Only other Europeans, and rather specifically Englishmen, seemed to have the power to take American territory out of the wilderness category.

There were areas in the trans-Allegheny and more in the trans-Mississippi which could and did qualify as wilderness, by these standards, and in which the westward-moving Anglo-Americans were pioneers. But there were also many other regions in which these Anglo-Americans were late arrivals.

The French had been in mid-continent a good century and more before

1

there was, officially at least, a United States of North America. Not a great many of them it was true, but there were enough Frenchmen to have pre-empted the pioneer laurels in the Mississippi Valley. English predecessors of the Anglo-Americans had driven the French from the Forks of the Ohio right after the middle of the eighteenth century. But victory in the French and Indian War had only effected a change of sovereignty in the rest of the trans-Allegheny. It had not eliminated the Frenchmen from around the Great Lakes or on the Wabash River or in Wisconsin or in the Illinois country or in the lead belt around Sainte Genevieve (Missouri) or in the other lead mines of northern Illinois and Iowa. Even less had the Peace of Paris (1763) ousted the French from the lower Mississippi Valley or around the Gulf Coast eastward to Mobile.

When American boundaries were expanded, in 1803, to include the Louisiana Purchase Territory, and the Anglo-American frontier crossed the Mississippi, at its middle point was Saint Louis, downstream at the mouth of the Arkansas was the very old, though never large, Poste des Arkansas, and farther south, on the Red River, was Natchitoches, tracing its foundations back to 1713. Mid-continent to both sides of the Mississippi was French long before it became American, even on the paper of international treaties.

The farther the Anglo-Americans pushed westward, especially into the southwestern quadrant of the United States, the more they found them-selves latecomers and the less they encountered the challenge of a wilderness. Rather they were confronted with the challenge of another frontier, stretching on an uneven but well-defined line from Texas through New Mexico and Arizona and on to California. This was the Spaniards' Borderlands frontier, the outer ring of their Provincias Internas, the farthest advance of their northward movement, begun almost as soon as Hernán Cortés and his fellows completed their conquest of the capital of the Aztec empire, back in 1521.

This Spanish frontier in North America has been known as the Borderlands since the appearance, in 1921, of the little volume of Herbert Eugene Bolton in the Chronicles of America series, which bore that title—*The Spanish Borderlands: A Chronicle of Old Florida and the Southwest*.[1] The term Spanish Borderlands[2] has never been clearly delimited. Some authors use it as inclusive of all the territories within the limits of the United States which Spain once held, from Florida to California. Others make it apply in a more restricted sense to the Spanish provinces from Texas to California —in a word to the Greater Southwest or the Spanish Southwest. At times Spanish Louisiana has been included, and very particularly so-called Upper Louisiana, or the Spanish Illinois. Louisiana and Florida are less secure as to their inclusion, since both Spanish provinces, administratively, depended on the Islands and have their histories more intimately bound to the Caribbean than to the northern frontier of New Spain (Mexico). There are not a few historians who broaden the concept of the Borderlands so as to encompass the north Mexican provinces—Nuevo Santander, Nuevo León, Coahuila, Chihuahua (which was the Nueva Vizcaya of colonial days), Sinaloa, Sonora, and Baja California, most of which Spain itself included in its late reorganization of the frontier into the Provincias Internas. The broadest concept has its merits, even though prime emphasis may go to the frontiers of New Spain, from Texas westward.

It was in these western Borderlands that the Spanish expansionist movement worked itself out most effectively. Here the Spanish frontier philosophy developed typical and often distinctive institutions, attitudes, and policies, all the while retaining many common denominators with the forward surges of the other colonial powers, and in the case of the English, of their American successors. Here two frontiers collided, sometimes violently. Here a fusion began, which is still in process.

A study of the Spanish frontier, the Borderlands, will show that the Anglo-American experience, magnificent and thrilling though it was, actually was not quite as unique as it is sometimes pictured and chauvinistically thought to be. The Anglo-American frontier can be better understood and more properly evaluated by process of comparison.

If, as is so often asserted, one of the marked characteristics of a frontier is the advance of civilization into the wilderness, then the Spanish frontier in North America fully met that requirement and was, perhaps, even more outstanding on that score than was the Anglo-American westward movement. The northern reaches of New Spain constituted a formidable natural challenge to the Spanish pioneers who advanced slowly northward from Mexico City, to plant their outposts along a great arc stretching from eastern Texas to the Bay of San Francisco. The land was rugged and treacherous, arid and forbidding. The climate was seasonal: parching droughts alternated with long months of chill and often drenching rain. Mountains were almost everywhere, and the plains now parched and next swampy. Rivers, until the frontier edged north into Texas, were few and dry for many months out of the year; they were no help for transportation and barely ran enough water for year-round irrigation. Not until the Anglo-American frontier reached onto the Great Plains or into the mountain cordilleras of the West did it bring the Americans into lands with comparable problems. The Spaniards knew of nothing to compare with the prairies of Indiana and Illinois or the grasslands of Kentucky or the rich alluvial soils of the Old Southwest or the potential breadbasket stretches of the double tier of states lining the Mississippi. Texas and California had areas which might compare, but almost without fail the Spaniards passed them by—for example, they did not even explore the great San Joaquín Valley of California thoroughly, let alone try to people or exploit it. Their northern borderlands more than qualified as a wilderness into which they introduced civilization.

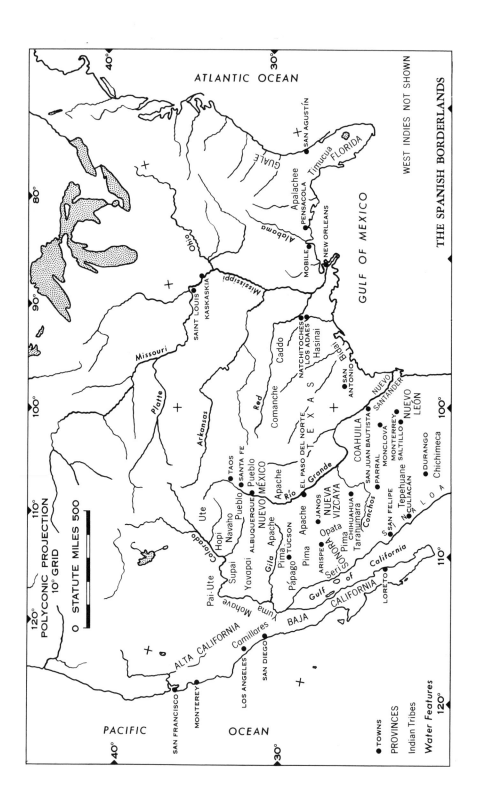

THE SPANISH BORDERLANDS

WEST INDIES NOT SHOWN

ATLANTIC OCEAN

PACIFIC OCEAN

GULF OF MEXICO

POLYCONIC PROJECTION
10° GRID

0   STATUTE MILES 500

● TOWNS
PROVINCES
Indian Tribes
Water Features

Sometimes the Indians of the north were an even greater challenge to the pioneers than was the land. The Spaniards, as they moved beyond the edge of the Aztec empire, first met the wild tribes whom they lumped together under the generic designation of the "Chichimeca." For long decades they contrived to slow the Spanish advance through the north Mexican silver country or, at very least, made it precarious; at times they became so troublesome that the Spaniards thought seriously and debated long as to whether a war of extermination might not be in order. The Franciscans and other churchmen at the Third Provincial Council, in 1585, managed to fend off such a harsh decision.[3] Beyond were other nations, quite as fierce and intractable, until the missionaries were able to tame them. But even then there were the Apache, almost omnipresent from western Texas into the Gila Valley of Arizona. In New Mexico the Pueblo peoples proved not so peaceful on occasion, as in the damaging Revolt of 1680. And beyond the frontier lines were the Seri and the Yuma, the Navaho and the Ute, and on the southern plains the Comanche, fiercest, perhaps, of them all. The Indians taxed the ingenuity of the Spanish pioneers and policy-makers who came up with two interesting frontier institutions, the presidio and the mission.

The military post on the Spanish frontier was not wholly distinctive as an institution on the path of expansionist advance.[4] The Anglo-Americans had their forts, and so did the French. The Spaniards, with a much more extended frontier line, had to multiply their presidios and had much greater expense in manning them and greater trouble in provisioning and supplying them.[5]

The mission, on the other hand, was very distinctive.[6] Counterparts to the friar and the padre rarely figured prominently in the story of the Anglo-American westward movement. They were, however, "standard equipment" on all Borderland frontiers, which were frequently, in their earlier stages, primarily mission frontiers. This was true in New Mexico, on the western slope of the Sierra Madre, and in both the Californias—Baja first and then Alta. Conversion and, if possible, assimilation of the native American was a Spanish aim of almost equal importance to wealth-gathering and other secular advantage. And this aspiration was very regularly shared by the civilian as well as the clerical frontiersman.

On one point the two frontiers showed a marked disparity—in the area of governmental control of the expansionist urge. The shadow of Spanish absolutism, extending even to the farthest reaches of the Indies, allowed the Spanish frontiersman little chance to develop a sense of self-expression or a feeling of self-reliance. The Spaniards in the Americas at no time and in no area enjoyed the boon of salutary neglect. The frontier, as all else, was carefully planned, minutely organized, and regularly oversupervised. The Spanish practice of the *residencia*—the official checkup to which major officers were liable at the end of their term of appointment—was applicable to frontier governors, as well as to viceroys and captains-general. This prospect was a serious deterrent to anything bordering on independent action; the safer course for all, and particularly for the ambitious official, was to wait for notification of the royal will and then to follow it with scrupulous exactness. All this waiting took time, even when the orders did not have to come from the court but might be issued by the viceroy, who was still hundreds of miles and more than one or two weeks away.

The two frontiers differed markedly, too, in the relative freedom enjoyed by the frontiersmen. The Anglo-American was aggressive and acquisitive: the hope of gain, broader opportunity, and personal advantage drove him westward. He was rarely motivated by anything other than individual aggrandizement. But most of all, he was free to go or come, to stay or withdraw; he was, in general, answerable to no one but himself. At times the laws of his country bothered him little or not at all. The Spanish frontiersman was regimented, closely governed, and restricted. He might be free to go or not to go onto a far frontier. But, once there, he was committed. Unauthorized withdrawal was equivalent to desertion and rendered the frontiersman liable to punishment. Even the way he could make a living and where he could try was very often dictated by royal officials. To the end he was much like the first English settlers in Virginia, with the sole exception that he was the servant of the crown, not of the company.

The Borderlands frontiersman was more regularly a miner or a rancher. He did farm, but not as extensively as his Anglo-American counterpart; the lands he occupied were less well adapted to agriculture. Often much of the farming was done at and around the missions. For that matter, so was much of the stock raising, at least in the earlier years. In fact, he might have been hard pressed to feed himself had it not been for the friar and the padre and their mission Indians.

Ethnographically, the Borderlands frontier was far less homogeneous than that of the Anglo-Americans. The crossbreeds were numerous, especially the mestizos. So, too, were the Indians, who figure so insignificantly in the westward movement, save as the opposition and the "bad guys." The Spaniards not infrequently sent colonies of Christianized Indians northward to help to hold a difficult frontier or to serve as an example to Indians still unconverted or recently baptized. The Christianized Indians were an integral part of the Borderlands frontier, and this made the fusion process quite difficult and painful following the American take-over at mid-nineteenth century.

Finally, the Spanish Borderlands frontier was in many instances a defensive frontier, something which was rarely characteristic of the Anglo-American frontier. The American rush into the Oregon country in the 1840s to forestall Great Britain's ambitions for the Columbia River basin stands as a solitary exception. Two of the Borderland provinces were established for the primary purpose of holding back the enemies of New Spain—Texas against the French in the Mississippi Valley and California as protection against the Russians, pushing down the coast from Alaska for bases.[7] New Mexico in time developed into a far northern defensive outpost; and even in the days of its occupation strategic considerations contributed to the decision to settle there.

So here is an American frontier, sometimes like but more often unlike familiar Anglo-American patterns. It is a frontier that is historically on a collision course with the more aggressive and more successful Anglo-American westward movement. Its background will be important when the two meet. And, even apart from the confrontation, its history has interest in itself as an example of man's pioneering enterprise.

◁2▷

The Conquistador Explorers,
1513-1543

*T*he story of the American frontier began, it has often been asserted, when
the first Englishmen stepped ashore on the Jamestown site or when the
Pilgrims landed at Plymouth. If we properly qualify the statement by the
addition of a national prefix, the statement is correct: the story of the Anglo-
American frontier does open in those early years of the seventeenth century.
However, if we wish to talk of the American frontier, even limiting consideration to the northern of the two continents, then we must go back a
full century, and more, to pick up the tale at its historically correct beginning, with the first Europeans who were, or at least represented, the
Spaniards. Even the history of the American frontier, if confined only to
lands that in time became part of the United States, must antedate 1607
and 1620 by many, many decades. There, too, the first hyphenated Americans
were Spaniards, and the starting date was 1513.

Juan Ponce de León, when he first touched Florida, in 1513, formally
opened the history of the Spanish Borderlands frontier. The Spaniards had
been on Española, or Santo Domingo as it is better known to moderns, for two
decades. Five years before, in 1508, they had started their expansion.[1] The
same Juan Ponce de León branched out to look over the neighboring island

of Puerto Rico, and Juan de Esquivel led other Spaniards to Jamaica. Two patentees, Alonso de Ojeda and Diego de Nicuesa, crossed over to Tierra Firme and the Isthmus of Panama in the next year, to begin the occupation of the continental mainland. Two years before Vasco Núñez de Balboa trekked across the isthmian strip, and Ponce de León went out from Puerto Rico to touch Florida, Diego de Velásquez had landed in Cuba, in 1511, to begin the subjugation of that largest island of the Antillean chain.

From Cuba went forth the first expedition, as well as the next two expeditions, which gave the Spaniards their New Spain, as they quickly named Mexico. Hernández de Córdoba and his fellows, in 1517, came upon the Maya in Yucatan and saw that the mainland to the west held much more promise than anything seen or reported to date. Next, the governor's nephew, Juan de Grijalva, followed, coasted the shoreline of the Gulf of Campeche, went northward beyond the site of the soon-to-be-established Villa Rica de la Vera Cruz, heard the first reports of the empire inland, and, even before he returned with the first evidence of Mexican treasure, sent word back to Governor Velásquez. Hernán Cortés landed on the Mexican coast in 1519. The conquest of the Aztec empire kept him and his Spaniards very busy for the next two years.[2] But before 1521 was gone, the conquistadores were firmly established in Tenochtitlán (Mexico City) and lieutenants of Cortés were fanning out, northward along the Gulf Coast from Vera Cruz, westward toward the Western Ocean, and southward into the

Cortés marching on Tenochtitlán. Sixteenth-century Mexican codex. (Bibliothèque Nationale)

lands of Zapotec and Mixtec of Oaxaca. There was movement northward, too, which in time would lead the Spaniards into the Borderlands.[3]

Francisco Buenaventura, nephew of Cortés, pushed out as far as Sinaloa; but his reports on the country and its Indians were far from encouraging and aroused little immediate interest. Gonzalo de Sandoval went into the Huastec country, north of Vera Cruz and along the Gulf of Mexico; his reports were equally drab and unencouraging. There seemed to be nothing to the north to compare with what the Spaniards were learning about the lands of the Tarascans, to the west, or about the peoples of Oaxaca or what they guessed to be the promise of the empire of the Maya, back on the Yucatan peninsula, which they had not yet had time to investigate. Pedro de Alvarado pushed on to Guatemala and, ultimately, Cortés himself took a look at Honduras, after a quick thrust to the northeast into Huastec-land to check the trespass of Francisco de Garay, sailing along the Gulf coast, seeking to extend his land of Amichel as far as the Vera Cruz corridor into the highlands of Anahuac.

After Honduras, Cortés hurried back to Spain, to counter the charges made against him by the corrupt First Audiencia, the body of four judges named by the crown in 1528 to supervise and, if possible, to control the Conqueror of Mexico, whose rumored ambitions had begun to disturb young Charles Habsburg (Charles I of Spain and Charles V of the Holy Roman Empire). Most of the charges, which ranged from treason through cruelty and rapacity to wife murder, were flimsy, concocted out of the jealousy and the envy of associates less capable than Cortés. But with the great man away, the field was open, temporarily at least, for lesser men. Before he returned to New Spain, vindicated and free to deal with his detractors, the *presidente* of the Audiencia, one Nuño de Guzmán, realized that he must post a record of achievement which might divert the not unlikely wrath of King Charles and distract attention from some of the blunders and the graft of himself and his fellow judges.[4] Accordingly, he set out to conquer the northwest and, hopefully, to carve out a domain for himself. He thus became the next figure in the background to the Borderlands story.

In these late years of the 1520s—when Guzmán and his men were leaving a bloody mark on Nayarit, Jalisco, and southern Sinaloa and thus moving toward the western Borderlands—other Spaniards under Pánfilo de Narváez were trying to establish Spain in the eastern Borderlands, which were the Floridas. Their adventures will be noted later; but it is worthwhile to mark the contemporaneity of the two northward thrusts—one out of the Islands and the former out of Mexico City. A like time parallelism occurred in 1521 when Ponce de León was back in his Floridas and Cortés was completing the conquest of the Aztecs.

When Guzmán and his band moved into southern Sinaloa, they were beyond the northern edge of the area of effective Aztec control; they were really beyond the Aztec Borderlands and opening the first one of Spanish

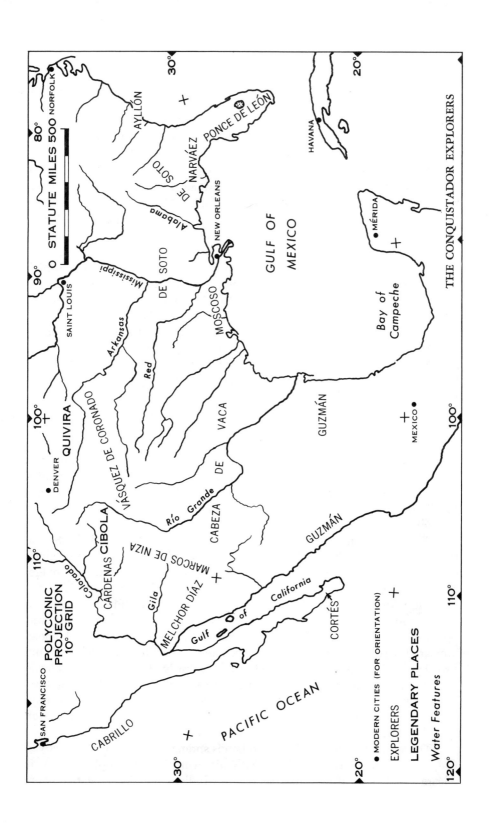

THE CONQUISTADOR EXPLORERS

POLYCONIC
PROJECTION
10° GRID

STATUTE MILES 500

0

LEGENDARY PLACES

Water Features

EXPLORERS

• MODERN CITIES (FOR ORIENTATION)

PACIFIC OCEAN

GULF OF
MEXICO

Bay of
Campeche

CABRILLO

CORTÉS

MELCHOR DÍAZ

Gulf of California

Gila

CÁRDENAS CIBOLA

Colorado

VÁSQUEZ DE CORONADO

QUIVIRA

MARCOS DE NIZA

Río Grande

CABEZA DE VACA

GUZMÁN

GUZMÁN

MÉXICO

MÉRIDA

HAVANA

MOSCOSO

Mississippi

Red

Arkansas

DE SOTO

DE SOTO

Alabama

NARVÁEZ

PONCE DE LEÓN

AYLLÓN

NEW ORLEANS

SAINT LOUIS

DENVER

SAN FRANCISCO

NORFOLK

30°

20°

80°

90°

100°

110°

120°

20°

30°

100°

110°

variety. The town of San Miguel de Culiacán, which they founded in 1531, was destined to be a northwestern outpost for the next half century. From this town, Guzmán and his companions carried their explorations, and their depredations, eastward toward the Sierra Madre Occidental, which cut them off from the central plateau, on which another northward movement would soon be under way. They also pushed northward along the Gulf of California coast. Their first quest was the Isle of the Amazons, rumored to be in those parts; and there were the fabled Seven Golden Cities, or Cíbola, to spur them forward. They found neither, but they were tracing paths. The bellicose ladies and their fabled wealth did not show; and only the haziest information on Cíbola could be gleaned.

In this context we should be aware of the very important role which myth and fable played in Spanish exploration of the Americas. Once the Spaniards had uncovered the riches of the Aztecs in North America or the equally fantastically wealthy empire of the Incas in the southern continent, they were only too willing to believe that the fairy tales of their younger days might really have substance in actuality. The Indians were quick to sense the greed-inspired gullibility of their unwelcome guests and they fed this credulity with consummate skill. What the Spaniard sought was regularly "just a little farther on"—*poco más allá*. And the very interesting aspect of this whole matter is that the native Americans—north, south, east, and west—on both continents and on either seaboard, seem to have the almost identical answer. Whether it was El Dorado or the Amazons or the White King, the Land of Chicora or Cíbola or Quivira, the Mountain of Silver or dozens more, the Indians fitted their misinformation to tantalize Spanish hopes and to keep alive Spanish get-rich-quick dreams. First contacts with the Borderlands of the future sprang from the incurable optimism of the conquistadores.

When Guzmán and his men turned in their search toward the Sierra, they were, unwittingly, moving off the "road to Cíbola." The next men along would stay closer to the Gulf coast. But these successors had an advantage; they, so to speak, had "road maps" at least for part of the way.

On a March day in 1536 a band of Guzmán's slavehunters, trying to make up for lack of gold and silver booty by collecting human treasure, was operating in the valley of the Río Sinaloa. Suddenly on the trail ahead appeared a strange company of thirteen men—a white man, bearded and browned, naked save for a breech cloth, a burly dark man, and eleven Indians. Alvar Núñez Cabeza de Vaca and Estevánico had at last found the white men of whom Indian friends had been telling them for some days past.[5] Two more Europeans, Andrés Dorantes and Alonso del Castillo Maldonado, with other Indians, were coming a day or two behind.

The joy of the leaders of the two bands sprang from very varied motives. Cabeza de Vaca was again back with his own kind of people; Diego de Álcaraz, of the scouting party, seeing the Indians and learning that more were on the way, congratulated himself on a fortunate human windfall. Here were Indians who did not have to be hunted and chased; they were ready to be taken. After much argument Cabeza de Vaca won safe conduct for his friends and sent them back to their northern homeland. A few days later a very strange quartet, escorted by the Spaniards, came into Culiacán, where Melchor Díaz was in charge. Díaz treated the wanderers well and listened with high interest to their story.

These days at Culiacán and those which followed some few weeks later in the capital, when they retold their exciting tale to the new viceroy, Antonio de Mendoza, were of great importance for the future of New Spain. Their accounts of the north did much to reawaken Spanish hopes and to launch the movement into the western Borderlands.

It was a fantastic story that the four had to tell. In 1527 they had come out of Spain with Pánfilo de Narváez and his company. They had paused in Santo Domingo, had gone on to Cuba, hoping there to recruit replacements for the hundred or more men who had deserted in Española, and, in the spring of 1528, had headed for Florida. Wealth and the rumored Kingdom of Apalachee, supposedly in northern Florida, had not materialized. Their women in the ships had sailed back to Cuba—the party had come with elaborate plans for full-dress settlement on the peninsula; hence, the female complement. Stranded on an inhospitable shore, worn and disillusioned, the men constructed makeshift boats and set out westward across the Gulf of Mexico; they felt that they had a better chance of making Pánuco (Tampico) than of fighting winds and tides along Florida's west coast. Most of the men were lost along the way; but several of the craft made the Texas coast. Gradually the survivors, who at first probably numbered close to a hundred in all the scattered groups, dwindled to four. United, Cabeza de Vaca, Dorantes, Castillo, and the Moor, Estevánico, wandered for several years through western Texas—now as slaves, now as traders, sometimes in great honor as medicinemen, moving from tribe to tribe, holding all the while to the hope of one day reaching the Río Pánuco and their Christian brethren in New Spain.

It was probably sometime in the late summer of 1535 that they reached the Río Grande. In search of Indians with food, they were directed up that stream into modern New Mexico. They worked their way through a gap in the Mimbres Range and came out on the upper waters of the Gila, in Arizona. Turning southwestward, through the pass between the Dos Cabezos and the Chiricahua, they passed through Opata and Pima country and ultimately came to the site of Ures, on the Río Sonora. There the Indians "gave Dorantes over 600 opened deer hearts, which they always kept in great supply for food; so we named this place the Town of Hearts." This Pueblo de los Corazones was to become an early northern landmark.

It was at this Pueblo de los Corazones, or in the neighborhood, that the Pima gave Dorantes five "emerald arrow heads" (probably malachite).

When Cabeza de Vaca inquired whence they came, the Indians "said from lofty mountains to the north, where there were towns of great populations and great houses, and that the arrowheads had been purchased with feather bushes and parrot plumes," which came from their own country. This is the segment of the travelers' report, which seems to have made the deepest impression, both on the men at Culiacán, who first heard it, and very particularly on the viceroy. Cabeza de Vaca and his companions told of the many Indian nations whom they had met and of the "shaggy cows" (buffaloes) which they had seen in such numbers; but the Spaniards of the day were much less interested in anthropology and zoology than in the possibility that these towns in the north might be the Seven Cities of Gold. Maybe there really was an *otro México* in the north. If there was, Viceroy Mendoza was determined that his men, not those of his rival Cortés, would be the conquerors.[6] There were a few formalities, such as the necessary permission from the crown and the choice of a captain to represent him; but the wheels were already set in motion, almost as soon as Cabeza de Vaca left the viceregal palace. As of 1536 the north country was a target.

Mendoza originally suggested to Cabeza de Vaca that he return to the

The "shaggy cow." From Francisco López de Gómara, *History*, sixteenth century. (Rare Book Division, New York Public Library)

north, this time with a full company of Spaniards, to run down the rumor of those cities of which he had heard. The traveler, having other plans for the future in which he featured himself as nothing short of the *adelantado* in the north, begged off and headed for Spain, to plead his own cause at the court. Mendoza, then, made other plans, intent on being the main agent in opening the north.

About this time—the spring of 1537—the Bishop of Mexico, Juan de Zumárraga, brought an interesting visitor to the viceregal palace. A fellow Franciscan, Fray Marcos de Niza, had recently come in from Guatemala with tales which the bishop felt that Mendoza should hear. Fray Marcos had been in the Americas for the past half-dozen years. Experience had acquainted him with Santo Domingo; then he had crossed over to Guatemala; next he had gone with Pedro de Alvarado to the new kingdoms which Francisco Pizarro was winning for the crown of Spain. He had met the conquistador of the Inca empire, possibly had even witnessed the execution of Atahualpa; but, when Alvarado had made the bargain with Diego de Almagro, Pizarro's partner, and for a handsome consideration had agreed not to press claims to the Kingdom of Quito, Fray Marcos had returned with his patron to Guatemala. Having come to New Spain at the invitation of Zumárraga, the much traveled Franciscan was anxious to work among the Indians there, possibly in the new province of Nueva Galicia to the northwest of the capital which was being opened in those years of the 1530s. From this interview developed the involvement of Fray Marcos in the viceroy's schemes for the north country.[7]

Proper permissions, royal and that of the Franciscan superior, obtained, Fray Marcos, in late 1538, was handed the viceroy's instructions and the commission "to find a way to go on [beyond Culiacán] and penetrate the land in the interior." The friar was to make careful observations on the people, the land, the rivers, the flora and the fauna of the farther regions. And "if God, our Lord, should will it that you find some large settlement which you think would be a good place for establishing a monastery and for sending friars who would devote themselves to conversions, you are to send a report by Indians, or return yourself to Culiacán. Send back reports with the utmost secrecy so that appropriate steps may be taken without disturbing anything. . . ." Mendoza most probably meant "anybody" and had Cortés in mind. At any rate this was to be Mendoza's own official reconnaissance of the north. Further, Estevánico, whom Mendoza had arranged to borrow from Dorantes, would be guide for Fray Marcos in this scouting venture.

The instructions for Fray Marcos had been entrusted to the young governor of Nueva Galicia, Don Francisco Vásquez de Coronado, and were delivered to the Franciscan on November 20, at Tonalá. Almost immediately the governor had to hurry north to Culiacán, to deal with a threatened Indian revolt. Fray Marcos went with him, and it was at this outpost town that the expedition was assembled. Besides a Franciscan companion, Fray Onorato, and Estevánico, there were some Indians detailed by the viceroy and others, former friends of Cabeza de Vaca who had settled closer to the Spaniards, instead of returning to their own country.

In March 1539, the little band left Culiacán on what was to be the first official exploration of the Borderlands. Passion Sunday (March 21) found them on the Río Mayo. Here what proved to be a fatal decision was made: Estevánico, restless over the slow progress of the larger party, was to push on ahead, as an advance scout; he was to send back, in the form of varying sized crosses, information about what he found; then he was to wait, in the neighborhood of the cities, for the arrival of Fray Marcos so that all might proceed into "Cíbola" together. Fray Marcos never saw Estevánico again. But crosses came back and each time they were larger and larger. Increasingly excited by these reports, Fray Marcos pushed on as swiftly as he and his companions could. However, their progress was not rapid; they were proceeding on foot and, more than that, Fray Marcos according to his instructions had to gather what information he could about the country through which he was passing and, particularly, had to inform himself about the proximity of the "road to the sea." It should be noted here that the Spaniards were still not clear on the coastal geography, unaware that the "ocean" to the west in those more northerly latitudes was really a gulf.

The friar had pushed up the Valle de Sonora and onto the "Despoblado," in southeastern Arizona, when the news of the disaster at Cíbola (identified with the Zuñi pueblo city of Hawikuh) came back through several Indian refugees. Estevánico was dead; so were many of his companions, probably Opata and Pima, who had joined his suite as he moved north. Although most of his own Indian companions deserted at this news, Marcos pushed on and, probably, got within sight of Cíbola. There has been much discussion in modern times concerning the veracity of the friar's report; some writers label Fray Marcos a prevaricator (a milder name than liar), while others hold that his statement is to be taken at face value:

> . . . I told them that, in any event, I was going to see the city of Cibola, and they told me that no one would accompany me. Finally, seeing me so determined, two of the chiefs said that they would go with me. Accompanied by them and by my own Indians and interpreters, I proceeded on my journey until coming within sight of Cibola, which is situated in a plain at the base of a round hill.
>
> The pueblo has a fine appearance, the best I have seen in these regions. The houses are as they had been described to me by the Indians, all of stone, with terraces and flat roofs, as it seemed to me from a hill where I stood to view it. The city is larger than the city of Mexico. . . .
>
> When I told the chieftains who were with me how well impressed I was with Cibola, they told me that it was the smallest of seven cities, and that Totoneac is much larger and better than all the seven, that it has so many houses and people that there is no end to it.

On his return to the south Fray Marcos reported his findings and the details of his *entrada* (expedition into a still unconquered area) first to Governor Francisco Vásquez de Coronado at Compostela and subsequently to Mendoza, on his arrival in Mexico City, September 2, 1539.

Mendoza's fuller plans had, meanwhile, matured. He was now determined that Coronado was his man, and preparations for the formal *entrada de conquista* were well advanced.[8] Sanction from the king came on January 6, 1540, and the viceroy's nomination of the young governor of Nueva Galicia was fully approved. Feeling certain of this permission, Mendoza already had Coronado making elaborate preparations to go north. The viceroy went out to Compostela, in February, to review the company and to firm up all the details.

A magnificent company it was.[9] So numerous was it that the viceroy had to reply to the charge which was being circulated that "the city of Mexico and New Spain were left with but a few people, which may result in serious difficulties." Cristóbal de Oñate, spokesman for the viceroy, noted rather interestingly, that not only were the charges untrue, but that "many of the young gentlemen and other persons living in the said city and in other parts of New Spain who were going on the said expedition will do more good than harm by going away, for they are all idle and had no means of support."

The expedition set out in late February 1540. Mendoza waved them good-bye. He had great hopes and was confident that the previous fame of Cortés was about to be definitely and forever eclipsed, and for this reason the viceroy had put a good deal of his own fortune into the enterprise. There were more than 230 mounted men, many of them the cadet sons of noble families; the infantry detachment numbered 62. A small party had gone on ahead; and there were still more men to come, who had not been present for the gala review of the main body. The Spaniards were flanked by upwards of 800 Indians. Three women, wives of the men, were in the company. Fray Marcos was with the army, and he was accompanied by Fray Juan de Padilla, destined within a few years to have the distinction of being the first missionary to be killed by the natives on future United States soil. The expedition carried much of its own food, on the hoof; it picked up more during its stop at Culiacán. Further, the viceroy had arranged that the army, until it turned inland, would also be supplied by the ships of Hernando de Alarcón, which were being dispatched from Acapulco.

This last aspect of the overall plan failed. Alarcón went north, touched the Gulf of California coast at several points but never succeeded in making contact with the land force. At one point he waited several weeks. The letter which he left for his fellow Spaniards and which they later dug up from beneath the foot of a marked tree, two months too late, read in part: "Hernando de Alarcón reached this place in the year '40 . . . and after waiting many days without news, he was obliged to depart, because his ships were being eaten by worms." Alarcón did, however, add some bits to the Spaniards' knowledge of the Borderlands. His ships reached the mouth of the Río Colorado (of the West), just as had Cortés' man, Francisco de Ulloa, the year before. But then Alarcón in two small boats edged past the sandbars at the river's mouth, went upstream some distance, and made the first contacts with the Yuma Indians. Ulloa had earlier rounded the head of the Gulf and then proceeded down the eastern shoreline of the peninsula. In these days there was no doubt in the minds of the Spaniards concerning the geographic character of Baja California. It is one of the curiosities of American historical geography how later in that sixteenth century and through the whole of the seventeenth the conviction persisted that California was an island, albeit a large one; and the map makers were led into that same error. The Jesuit missionary and explorer Padre Kino, as will be seen later, set the record straight in the early years of the eighteenth century.

Arrived as far as Culiacán, Coronado recognized that the pace of the whole army was much too slow—it had taken over a month to make the 350 miles from Compostela to the Sinaloa outpost. Therefore, he decided to take about a third of the force and to push on more rapidly. His group set out on April 22. Don Tristán de Arellano was left in charge of the main body, since the original *maestro de campo*, Lope de Samaniego, had been killed shortly before in a skirmish with the Cáhita Indians near Chiametla. A short time later the expedition lost another fine captain. Melchor Díaz, a veteran of the northern frontier, lost his life in a freak accident shortly after having returned from a foray to the coast in search of Alarcón—he had thrown a lance at a bothersome canine which was upsetting the horses; he missed the dog, the spear stuck in the ground, and Díaz was run through as he rode by.

Coronado and the vanguard band, with Fray Marcos showing the way, hurried up the coastal "trail," across the Sinaloa, the Fuerte, the Mayo, the lower Yaqui, and into the Valle de Sonora, out onto the Despoblado, and on July 7 came to Hawikuh, the first of the seven "golden cities of Cíbola." Intense was their disappointment on seeing this Zuñi town at close range— adobe was hardly gold or silver, no matter what the brightness of the sun or the moon. The natives showed no signs of hospitality, and the Spaniards had to fight their way into the town. This in itself was an ill omen for the future.

Exploration soon showed that the "Seven Cities were seven little villages, all within a radius of four leagues." Having reached the Land of Cíbola, disillusioning though the reality turned out to be, hope still lived in the hearts of the conquistadores. Word went back to Tristán de Arellano to proceed with the main body of the army, from the temporary camp at Corazones on the Río Sonora. Don Pedro de Tovar, with a score of soldiers and Fray Juan de Padilla, was dispatched to learn something of the province of Tusayán. They were the first white men to see the Hopi towns of north-eastern Arizona. The Hopi, regularly called the Moqui by the Spaniards, were minded to resist the intruders; but a short and fierce skirmish convinced the Indians that they were facing a new kind of force. They thought better of their original inclination and came forth in peace: "the natives of the land assembled and came to offer their obedience; they offered their towns openly, permitting the soldiers to go there in order to buy, sell, and trade." It was while in these Hopi towns that Tovar heard of the great river to the west. On his return to Cíbola with such information, Coronado dispatched García López de Cárdenas to investigate. His band was the first to witness the majesty of the Grand Canyon of the Colorado. But none of these groups brought back any evidence of great wealth.

Meanwhile, at Cíbola the Spaniards were picking up reports on the

Zuñi in the land of Cíbola. Photo by J. K. Hillers, 1879. (The Bettmann Archive)

country to the east, and these were rather encouraging. A delegation had come in from Cicuye (Pecos). Hernando de Alvarado and a band of twenty went off to explore. En route they passed the famous "sky city" of Ácoma; thence they advanced into the province of Tiguex, the future Albuquerque area. At that point they were in the heart of the Pueblo country. They pushed on to Cicuye and next ventured beyond the mountains toward the Texas Panhandle, where they got their first look at that amazing creature, the American buffalo—the "shaggy cows" of the Cabeza de Vaca story. At Cicuye they met the Indian whom they dubbed "The Turk," who was to influence their lives and those of their companions for the next ten or so months—and profoundly. His was the story of Quivira, a land lying to the north and east whose riches made former dreams of the Seven Cities conservative by comparison.

When Hernando de Alvarado was off to the east, the main army had come up from Corazones. The whole band was readying to settle down at Cíbola for the winter; but the Alvarado report changed the plans. The decision was to move eastward into the valley of the Río Grande in order to be in better position to march off to Quivira the following spring. Headquarters, accordingly, were established at Alcanfor, in the province of Tiguex—"a province with twelve pueblos on the banks of a large and mighty river." This description of the Río Grande seems a bit ridiculous, until one remembers that many of Mexico's rivers with which the conquistadores had become acquainted were regularly little more than dry ditches through which water ran when it rained, and the climate was seasonal. Rivers were going to play a very minor role on the Spanish Borderlands frontier as avenues of communication and transport; certainly their importance would be nothing like that of the waterways on other American frontiers.

The winter of 1540–1541 came early and was quite severe, with only the dream of Quivira to make it bearable. And the inconveniences of the cold were compounded by a series of unpleasantries with the Indians. Vexed by the inconsiderate demands of their "guests" for blankets, warm clothing, and food, and with other vexations thrown in for good measure, the Pueblo peoples revolted. The winter months saw petty wars, raids and counterraids, sieges and reprisals.

Spring of 1541 came none too soon, for either Spaniard or Indian. The Turk embroidered still further the glowing tales of Quivira's riches. As he admitted later, this was a carefully contrived plot to rid the valley of the white men, who would be lured onto the plains to die or to return so broken that they could be wiped out with ease by the embattled and waiting natives.

In April 1541, the entire army moved eastward. Nine days beyond Cicuye the Spaniards reached the edge of the "buffalo plains" and encountered Indians of a different stamp from those of the Pueblo country. The Plains people were nomad hunters, whose lives were conditioned by the buffalo. Beyond was the unknown. Spurred by hope, the Spaniards ventured into the rugged Panhandle country. Movement was exasperatingly slow. A conference of the captains was called, and it was decided that the main body of the army should return to the Río Grande valley, while Coronado and a smaller detachment would push northward to find and hold Quivira.

Skepticism, born of hardship, was growing; the Turk, now suspect, was in chains; but hope still drove the little band northward. On the Arkansas in mid-summer the adventurers reached a group of Indian encampments, straw huts and buffalo-skin tepees, with nothing golden about them save the yellow dust which the relentless winds raised in choking clouds. The Turk was made to confess the hoax and was unceremoniously garroted. At this point the Spaniards were in the neighborhood of Wichita (Kansas).

The party remained at Quivira for about a month, weary, disappointed, and increasingly disgruntled. Further exploration of the plains, to the valley of the Smoky Hill, uncovered nothing of promise. With the fall season coming on, the decision was made to return to the main base on the Río Grande, reluctantly on the part of a few incurable optimists.

Before another winter struck, the adventurers were back. The season 1541–1542 was not as severe as its predecessor, and there was some talk of possible further exploration in the spring. Many of the men, however, thoroughly disgusted, were hankering for the comforts of New Spain and were becoming very, very unwilling pioneers. An injury to Coronado, the result of a riding accident, clinched the decision to return home. Early in 1542 the army broke camp and headed south. Two of the Franciscans remained behind. Fray Juan de Padilla went back to Quivira, and to his death. Fray Luis de Ubeda was destined for a similar end among the Indians of the Cicuye province. Within months all the white men had left the north. The first chapter of Borderland history in the farther north closed.

The road-weary Spaniards straggled into Culiacán by early summer, with little good to say about the country they had seen. In July 1542 Coronado was reporting to the viceroy, in the capital. The lands which he and his men had traveled held little of interest to a generation of swash-buckling conquistadores—no great cities, no new empire, no signs of gold-and-silver wealth, only cantakerous Indians, whom only the most devoted and saintly missionaries might love, buffalo, prairie dogs, rattlesnakes, burning summers and freezing winters. The veil had been torn from the "mystery of the north," and all were agreed that it might have been better left untouched. It would take time and other considerations to overcome this initial "bad press" for the western Borderlands.

During the year 1539 and the several following, when Fray Marcos de Niza and Coronado and his band were ranging through the western Border-lands, another conquistador was looking over the more easterly portion of the Borderlands, the southeast.

Hernando de Soto, fresh from exploits in Peru and loaded with his share of the Inca's ransom, some few years before had returned to Spain, with more ideas of adventure and more ambitions centering around the New World. As early as April 1537 he had been named governor of Cuba and *adelantado* of the Floridas.[10] Even the failures of Ponce de León and Narváez had not put to rest the lure of those lands.

Juan Ponce de León had touched and named the Florida peninsula back in 1513. He had applied for and received the patent to conquer that land, and also the supposedly rich Island of Bimini, as early as 1514. But affairs in Puerto Rico kept him occupied for the next seven years. Finally, in 1521, he sailed out with several hundred hopeful conquerors and colonists. The Indians of the west coast were belligerently inhospitable; Ponce de León was mortally wounded; he and the party returned to Cuba. This was the first Florida failure.

The next attempt of the Spaniards in the eastern Borderlands was the short-lived venture of Lucás de Ayllón along the Atlantic side and as far north as the future South Carolina. This, too, was a settlement attempt. He led a group of some 500 potential colonists, men, women, and children, and even several Dominican friars, to the "northern Floridas," in 1526. Within two years the leader was dead, and the colonists were quarreling among themselves; this Land of Chicora had proved a disappointment. In 1528 the survivors, reduced to fewer than 200, abandoned the land and returned to Santo Domingo.

Pánfilo de Narváez was the next to try. Conquest and settlement of the Floridas proper was his aim—no one could really give limits to "the Floridas," proper or otherwise, in those years. Narváez had lost an eye in the skirmish with Cortés on the east coast of Mexico, in 1520, when he came on orders of Velásquez of Cuba, to arrest Don Hernán. In 1526 King Charles had rewarded his loyalty to authority by granting him the patent which had led Ponce de León to his untimely death. Again, the aim of Spain was colonization. His party of some 600 was off the west coast of the peninsula in 1528. The men landed to explore. Their quest for the Kingdom of Apalachee, as noted earlier in this chapter, led them, fruitlessly, northward to the neighborhood of modern Tallahassee. There, realizing that they had been abandoned by their ships, they built makeshift boats and headed for the Río Pánuco. Cabeza de Vaca and his several companions were the only survivors of this newest attempt in the eastern Borderlands. But the story is not yet finished.

De Soto was the next patentee. No one at that time knew the westward extent of "Las Floridas," the lands which had been granted to him, and it is wholly possible that De Soto may have considered that the rumored Cíbola might well fall within the limits of his jurisdiction. This seems to have been the reason why he was so anxious to talk with Cabeza de Vaca, when the latter returned to Spain, in 1537. He even seems to have propositioned the Borderlands veteran to join his forces. Cabeza de Vaca declined, for he had

De Soto in the Floridas. From Garcilaso de la Vega, *L' Histoire de la conquête de la Floride*. (Rare Book Division, New York Public Library)

other plans of his own, which, hopefully, would include the right to conquer the Cíbola country himself. De Soto had the more powerful friends at the court.

Preparations, at home and then in the islands, took De Soto two years to complete. It was not until May 1539 that his expedition sailed from Havana, with about 600 colonists. The landing was on the western coast, near Tampa. The operations of 1539 were almost exclusively in the west; the party spent their first winter in the unrewarding Land of Apalachee. But the Indians were true to form and filled the Spaniards full with tales of riches, *poco más allá*. In 1540 the army pushed northeastward through Georgia and as far as the Carolina Piedmont. It is possible that one of the scouting parties may have touched Tennessee. In Carolina they came upon the only wealth which was found, in the domain of the chieftainess Cuti-fachiqui, who had a store of not-too-perfect pearls. Thwarted in that quarter the Spaniards moved back toward the Gulf, hoping to make contact with the ships that had been sent back to the Islands for badly needed supplies. At Mabilla (to the north of the modern Mobile) the Indians enticed the Spaniards into a fortified town and very nearly destroyed the entire party.

A new spring (1541) found them moving out of Alabama and into

Mississippi. In May they came to the great river which they named Río del Espíritu Santo, somewhere in northern Mississippi and probably not too far south of Memphis; the point of crossing has been a matter of much debate. They built rafts and crossed to the Mississippi's right bank, which put them into Arkansas. Their quest in the trans-Mississippi was for a golden city; but riches eluded them in the west, as they had in the Floridas. Pacaha, at the mouth of the Saint Francis River, was a disappointment. The two sisters of the chief may have been "dolls," as the Gentleman of Elvas seems to hint in his chronicle; but De Soto wanted something other than two more wives. An expedition went northward to find a town called Chisca, where, Indian assurance had it, "there was gold in plenty and a copper foundry." The men did not find it, nor did they turn up any gold. This band got as far as a town called Coluça, located somewhere between the White and the Saint Francis rivers, and this was the most northerly advance of the De Soto party. Recent scholars quite unanimously reject the earlier claim that the expedition reached into Missouri. Another scouting party may have penetrated into Oklahoma, but not very far, certainly not to the buffalo range. De Soto's men were well enough acquainted with the processed hides of the American bison; but they do not seem to have seen that animal live. Moving up the Arkansas the Spaniards hardly reached beyond Little Rock, at least not as an army. The Quiguate of their narratives was in the neighborhood of that point. They may have reached Hot Springs. After these northward and westward probings the season was advanced. De Soto went into winter quarters on the upper Washita, at Autiamque.

The following spring (1542) found De Soto moving southeastward toward Guachoya, near the mouth of the Red River. Still in the dark as to his distance from the sea and still hoping that he might make contact with Cuba, he sent Juan de Añasco southward. The return of this scout and his horsemen, after eight futile days of wandering and wallowing in swamps and bayous, seems to have plunged the ailing De Soto into a state of despair. He could not shake the fever that was burning through his system and on May 21 (1542) Hernando de Soto died, alongside the river with whose discovery his name was to be forever linked. The Spaniards first buried him in their camp. Then, when the Indians became suspicious, fearing they might be emboldened to attack with the leader gone, the men wrapped the body in a marten-skin shroud, placed it in a hollowed-out log, and lowered the conquistador into "his" river, the Mississippi.

De Soto was gone, and so were over half of the 600 men who had set out with him three years before, so full of enthusiasm and hope. Luis de Moscoso had been named by De Soto as his successor in command. The new leader and the great majority of the several hundred survivors had had their fill of the American wilderness. There was little opposition to the decision to head for New Spain, specifically Pánuco.

At first they thought that they might reach Pánuco by land, and a small party went forth to check for a possible overland trail. Cutting westward across northern Louisiana, these men crossed the Red River and possibly got as far as the Trinity.[11] However, the going was too rugged and the way too uncertain, so they retraced their route to the Mississippi, agreed now that they must construct boats and venture out onto the Gulf. The building operations took the winter of 1542–1543.

In June 1543 they were ready to embark. Three months later, after running face to face with disaster time and again, they finally put into the Río Pánuco. After resting some weeks in the town, where they were most hospitably and cordially received, with strength restored the majority pushed up the Sierra Madre of the East, climbed onto the Central Plateau, and went southward to Mexico City. Their expedition into the north came back empty-handed, with nothing but a tale of disenchantment to tell. That "other Mexico," if one there was, still eluded the Spaniards. But their northward probings were not yet done. The story of one more expedition belongs to this period.

Eternal hope in 1542–1543 sent other Spaniards on another quest, this time by sea but again northward into the future Borderlands. Rich kingdoms had not been discovered inland. But there remained the haunting hope that farther north than men had been able to penetrate by land an empire might be awaiting discovery. Haunting, too, was the hope that there might be a strait running through the northern landmass which could give easy access from the Atlantic to the Pacific, to send the Spaniards on their way to the Orient. As far back as 1524 Cortés, when writing to the emperor, had voiced this hope for a shortcut, "less by two-thirds than the route now followed."

Very early, Cortés had been interested in the shoreline along the ocean to the west of his Mexico. He had sent his lieutenant Cristóbal de Olid westward, first to Michoacán and then to Colima, where in 1524 he had founded a town on the Pacific, Colima by name. In 1535 Cortés himself had sailed off to found a colony on the California peninsula. The attempt was abortive. When excitement over Cíbola was rife in New Spain, Cortés had sent his man, Francisco de Ulloa, up the coast to scout the north—Cortés in those days was preparing to use his rights to explore at will and to become the conqueror of the Seven Cities. Ulloa, in 1539, sailed to the head of the Gulf of California and then down the coastline opposite, rounding the tip of land and proceeding up the Pacific side to a point about 30 degrees latitude, thereby proving California to be a peninsula.[12]

Now that Mendoza had Coronado en route to Cíbola, in 1541, impetuous Pedro de Alvarado, back from the Land of the Incas and with pockets bulging, thanks to his having been paid off to withdraw from the Kingdom of Quito, decided to invest in Pacific exploration, "in the west toward China or the Spice Islands."[13] He readied a fleet in Guatemala and sailed his four ships up the coast to Mexico. An untimely death, in 1541, brought his career to an end. With Coronado in the north, the Indians of Nueva Galicia thought the time ripe for a revolt. This is known as the Mixton War. Alvarado, unable to resist a good fight, but more especially because he and his men were sorely needed to restore peace in the temporarily undermanned province, agreed to postpone his Pacific plans. When he was killed, his four ships were left behind.

Mendoza inherited them through a deal which he had made with Alvarado, by which the two partners contracted to share, mutually, the profits of their two enterprises—Mendoza's to the Seven Cities and Alvarado's to the Orient. In 1542 Mendoza sent two of these ships, captained by López de Villalobos, across the Pacific to learn more about those Philippine Islands, where Ferdinand Magellan had lost his life twenty-one years before. Although Villalobos also met death there, this voyage reinforced Spain's claims to the Philippines. In 1564 Miguel López de Legazpi would begin their conquest and occupation and, in a broad sense, make them a distant borderland. The Philippines were to have their role in the Borderlands story, very particularly after the Spaniards turned Manila into the entrepôt in the trade between Mexico and the Orient.

Mendoza took the other pair of Alvarado's ships and sent them northward along the outer edge of the continent, to find out what secrets the Pacific coastline might hold—great wealth, new kingdoms, a transcontinental strait? Juan Rodríguez Cabrillo was in charge of this reconnaissance, with Bartolomé Ferrelo as his chief pilot.[14] The *San Salvador* and the *Victoria* sailed out of Navidad, the west coast predecessor of Acapulco, in June 1542. The two ships would return nine months later, without their captain, left dead on San Miguel Island in the Santa Barbara Channel, and with little promise and even less information to support the dream of a transcontinental strait.

The expedition ran the Pacific coastline as far north as Oregon's Rogue River. The original thrust northward, with Cabrillo in command, probably did not reach much beyond Point Reyes. After the captain's death, Ferrelo went north again, from the winter base on San Miguel Island, and this time got to a point beyond 42 degrees latitude.

This Cabrillo-Ferrelo expedition turned up San Diego Bay; but in its four runs along the shoreline missed both Monterey Bay and the Golden Gate. Each time, when in the neighborhood of those two famous landmarks, rough weather forced the ships to hold to a course far out from the shore. The Spaniards did see the Farallon Islands, probably were in Drake's Bay, which they called Bahía de Los Pinos, and seem to have spotted the Santa Cruz and also the Santa Lucía Range from the sea.

The expedition was quite remarkable as a feat of navigation, carried out under great difficulties, with inadequate ships and rather continual unfavorable weather, neither of which proved of much assistance to men who were charting unknown coasts. At the very least, later explorations along the Pacific shoreline would benefit. But for long even these later men would find little of an encouraging character to report. Thus, another sector of the continent proved disappointing.

This year 1543 can be said to close the Age of the Conquistadores in North America: the Coronado band had been back for some months; the De Soto survivors reached Mexico; the Cabrillo-Ferrelo expedition returned to the home port. Far-ranging exploration was at an end. Actually, the age of the Spanish northward movement was about to open.

The Spaniards had seen much of the north country and had been in all of the future Spanish Borderlands, even though only in passing. The Floridas, as far north as Carolina and west to the Mississippi, were on the map; so, too, were Louisiana and Texas, New Mexico and Arizona and California; and on the Mexican side of the later international boundary, Coahuila and Chihuahua, Sinaloa and Sonora, and Baja California. One after another of the great dreams had burst in the hot heat of reality. The hopes which the surprise discovery of Tenochtitlán had kindled two dozen years before were now all put to rest. There was no "other Mexico," no Isle of the Amazons, no Seven Golden Cities, no Strait of Anian connecting the Atlantic and the Pacific.

The north was vast, often forbidding, almost always inhospitable: its peoples many and varied but none comparable to the strong Aztec or the cultured Maya, or the Mixtec, or the Zapotec, or even the Tarascans, its fauna interesting yet sometimes ferocious, its valleys occasionally lush, but its plains dusty, arid, and betimes almost unending, its mountains frequently too rugged and forbidding, and its rivers rarely navigable. Had the men of Coronado or De Soto been naturalists or anthropologists, or even agricultural-minded, the north country might have delighted and enthralled them with its almost limitless potential. But the Spaniards of the second quarter of the sixteenth century were none of these. They sought riches, quick and easy wealth, especially what had already been gathered by the native Americans. The Borderlands had their full share of Nature's bounty, but she had left much of it hidden. In time the Spaniards would discover some of it. But, when and as they did, humbler, more prosaic, more pedestrian folk than the colorful conquistadores would be the agents.

◁ **3** ▷

First Settlements in the Borderlands

*T*he early disappointments in the north, by the middle 1540s, had the Spaniards revising their dreams and resetting their sights. Their hopes for quick and easy wealth, such as had come to them with the conquest of the Aztec empire, were dashed as the expeditions, one by one, came back empty-handed to report no other rich kingdoms to be conquered or raided. They were certain, however, that the great treasure in gold and in silver which the Mexicans had amassed came from somewhere in the land. The conquerors geared themselves to locate that "somewhere" and at the same time resigned themselves to the more painful and much less glamorous task of extracting future treasure from Mexico's subsoil. They turned to prospecting. Before the decade of these 1540s was gone, their efforts had been rewarded. The rich silver lode of Zacatecas was uncovered in 1548, and North America had its first boom town.[1] Others followed in quick succession —some along the eastern face of the Sierra Madre, such as Guanajuato and Aguas Calientes, and farther to the east on a line northward from Querétaro, such as San Luis Potosí and Mazapil.[2] The province of Nueva Galicia began to be dotted with mining camps and little towns. As exploration and prospecting carried farther north, a new province, Nueva Vizcaya, was established in the early 1560s beyond Nueva Galicia. Francisco de Ibarra was named the governor in 1562 and the next year he founded the town of Durango, long destined to be the military capital of the north country.[3]

From Durango the Spaniards pushed along the Sierra into southern Chihuahua, to Indé, San Juan, and Santa Bárbara. This last outpost, on the headwaters of one of the tributaries of the Río Conchos, was the center from which several expeditions to the farther north pushed out in the 1580s, expeditions which set the stage for the occupation of New Mexico, the first of the western Borderlands.

During these later sixteenth-century decades the first American frontier movement was in progress. In this instance it was a northward movement, and the Spaniards were the first American frontiersmen. These were what can be called "learning decades." The Spaniards received an introduction to a whole series of new problems, which in one form or other they would meet on each expanding frontier.[4] For some of them they found, by process of trial and error, workable solutions; others would continue to dog them to the very end; and there would be still others in the future for which northern Mexico did not prepare them.

Heading the list was, in terms of Spanish experience, a new kind of Indian. This search for mines quickly took the Spaniards beyond the confines of effective domination of the Aztec empire. The wilder Indians of the nearer north, the Chichimeca as the Spaniards dubbed them, had never been conditioned to a regime of personal service or to tribute paying, as had the Aztec and their subject peoples. The Spaniards found, to their dismay, that practices, the *repartimiento* and the *encomienda*, which had worked tolerably well among the subjects of Montezuma, had little or no applicability. The arrival of the conquering white man in the north was not simply a change of masters, as had been the case, to all practical purposes, in the imperial areas of Old Mexico. The Chichimeca had bowed to no imperial masters; they were not accustomed to answering a call for forced labor; they had never been dominated to the point that they would, without a fight, bend to the payment of tribute. Further, they did not live in large population concentrations which might facilitate easy conquest and subsequent subjection. They existed in small groupings, were hunters rather than farmers, and were fierce and independent. Any humans proposing to take over their country were in for trouble, as the Spaniards quickly learned. They harassed the mining camps, disrupted the lines of communication, made themselves quite generally troublesome and dangerous. In time the Spaniards seriously considered a war of extermination as the solution to their new Indian problem. But the churchmen in the capital and the Franciscan missionaries on the frontier strenuously opposed such a policy, and in the end won their point.[5] Ultimately, the Spaniards had to trade their former control practices, the *repartimiento* and the *encomienda,* for reliance on the mission as a means of pacifying and holding this Chichimeca frontier.

Another problem which the Spaniards had to solve was that of keeping lines open between the frontier and the edge of advancing civilization farther to the south. The matter of getting food and supplies to the miners was important; the safe return of the silver output of the mines was of even greater concern. Communication had to be maintained quite exclusively overland, without benefit of convenient waterways, through rugged country, which the Chichimeca knew well, and this by packtrains, so vulnerable to surprise attack, or by wagons, over roads which hardly merited the name. The Spaniards developed a type of armored wagon, built strong houses (*casas fuertes*) as shelters along the way, and tried to minimize distances by spotting strategically placed presidios and little armed towns on frontier trails. This first frontier taught them many valuable lessons.

In that last quarter of the century the Spaniards tried an interesting experiment, namely that of sending colonies of civilized and Christianized Indians to settle in key locations. The Tlascalans, friends since the days of Cortés, were brought north. Saltillo, on the right side of the advancing frontier, was the site of one of these Indian settlements, which were meant to serve both a defense purpose and also as an advertisement to the unconverted of the benefits of cooperation and of Christianity.[6] This is an aspect of what has been called the "Indian conquest of America." All of the colonial powers used friendly Indians to further imperial ambitions—there were the famous girls, Marina in Mexico and Pocahontas in Virginia, the Huron-Algonquin friends of the French and the Iroquois allies of the British, the Creek on the Anglo-American southern frontier, and the list could go on and on.

These lessons, learned on the first Mexican frontier, were applied in the next northward advance. The Coronado party had seen and reported on the Pueblo country, but the existence of precious metal indications had not figured in those reports. The Spaniards, accordingly, had given the farther north little thought since those days, preferring to concentrate manpower and resources on the lands of the nearer north, their mining frontier. However, tales of the large towns in the Río Grande Valley, heavily peopled, still had currency. The Franciscans, who had been moving northward with the frontier and who were not realizing Christianizing results commensurate with their apostolic ambitions, kept missionary dreams alive, even though they received scant encouragement and less promise from officialdom. But they nurtured their hopes, and probably seconded these with many a prayer.

A captive Indian from the north country, brought into Santa Bárbara in 1579, told exciting stories of his homeland. The civilians were less interested than was Fray Agustín Rodríguez. He went into action and was off to the capital to obtain the requisite permissions, official and ecclesiastical, to make a missionary reconnaissance into the farther north. Clearance given, Rodríguez hurried back to Santa Bárbara and in June 1581 he and his companions ventured forth.[7] In the little band were 2 other Franciscans,

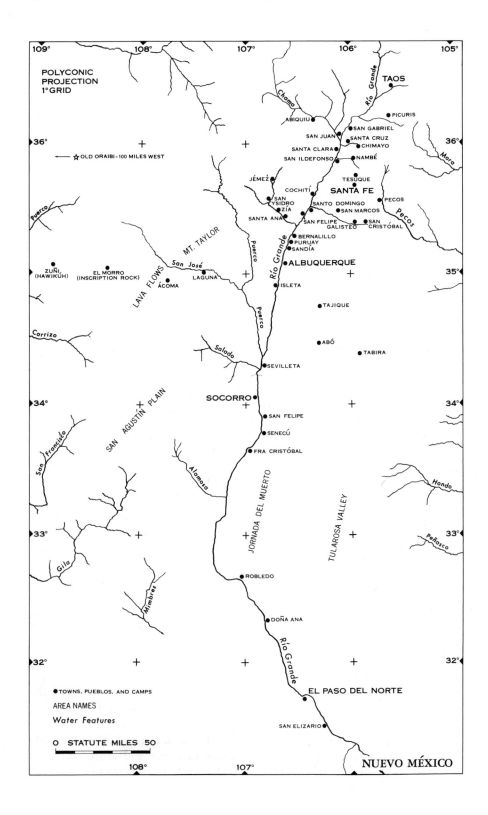

POLYCONIC
PROJECTION
1° GRID

★ OLD ORAIBI - 100 MILES WEST

Chama

TAOS

Río Grande

PICURIS

ABIQUIU

SAN GABRIEL
SAN JUAN
SANTA CRUZ
CHIMAYO
SANTA CLARA
SAN ILDEFONSO
NAMBÉ

Mora

JÉMEZ
TESUQUE
COCHITÍ
SANTA FE
SAN
YSIDRO
ZÍA
SANTO DOMINGO
SAN MARCOS
SANTA ANA
SAN FELIPE
GALISTEO
SAN
CRISTÓBAL

Pecos

PECOS

Puerco

MT. TAYLOR

San José

LAGUNA

Río Grande

Puerco

BERNALILLO
PURUAY
SANDÍA
ALBUQUERQUE

ZUÑI,
(HAWIKÚH)
EL MORRO
(INSCRIPTION ROCK)
ÁCOMA

ISLETA

TAJIQUE

Corrizo

ABÓ

Puerco

TABIRA

Salado

SEVILLETA

San Francisco

SAN AGUSTÍN PLAIN

SOCORRO

SAN FELIPE

SENECÚ

FRA CRISTÓBAL

Alamosa

Hondo

JORNADA DEL MUERTO

TULAROSA VALLEY

Gila

Peñasco

ROBLEDO

Mimbres

DOÑA ANA

Río Grande

TOWNS, PUEBLOS, AND CAMPS
AREA NAMES
Water Features

0   STATUTE MILES   50

EL PASO DEL NORTE

SAN ELIZARIO

NUEVO MÉXICO

Fray Francisco López and Fray Juan de Santa María; there were 9 soldiers captained by Francisco Sánchez Chamuscado; 16 Indians went along as carriers and helpers. Their route of advance was down the Conchos to the Río Grande, thence up that river to the Pueblo country. Arrived in the north, they ranged to the east of the valley, toward the "buffalo plains," and to the west they visited Ácoma and Zuñi.

Fray Juan de Santa María preceded the main band southward, to report their findings. It was later learned that he had been killed by the Manga Indians as he proceeded downriver. Not aware of this untoward development at the time, the rest of the party continued their explorations. When they did turn back toward home base, the other two friars remained among their recent hosts. This decision was to prove a mistake, but it also was the circumstance that ultimately led the Spaniards into New Mexico permanently.

Chamuscado and his men told of their findings. The viceroy, now the Conde de Coruña, was mildly interested. However, when Franciscan superiors learned that the three friars had been left behind, without military protection, they were greatly disturbed. Their concern was shared by other folk on the frontier. Out of this anxiety came the next move.

Fray Bernaldino Beltrán volunteered to organize a rescue party. At the moment the wealthy and pious Antonio de Espejo was in Nueva Vizcaya and, hearing of the project, came forward to finance the rescue mission. Requisite permissions were obtained—here is one of the marked characteristics of the Spanish frontier movement: advances were never the whim or the desire of individual enterprise; each was always part of an officially sanctioned scheme; no one went out without proper authorization, secured clearly and beforehand.

The so-called Espejo-Beltrán expedition into New Mexico set out in early November 1582.[8] By this date word had come back to Santa Bárbara that Fray López, too, was dead; a bit earlier news of the murder of Fray Santa María had filtered back to the northern outpost. But there was still Rodríguez; so the mission had a valid reason to proceed. On arriving in the Pueblo country they learned that Rodríguez, too, was dead. It was then decided that even though the first object of the expedition, the rescue of the friars, was unattainable, the Spaniards might stretch their instructions and do a bit of exploring in the far north. Espejo, particularly, was in favor of this, hoping that some overlooked wealth might be uncovered. He had his own ambitions to win fame and fortune.

To the east, in the country of the Manga Indians, they verified the report of the death of Santa María. They pushed on to the valley pueblos; next, they, too, visited Ácoma and Zuñi, to the west of the Río Grande; thence they pushed farther westward into Hopi-land and farther still into western Arizona. They found some evidence of mines and heard stories of others, supposedly located still farther to the west. They were heartened by this information, even though they had little in the way of proof. Back at Zuñi, Espejo and some of the men agreed to push north and east from the valley of the Río Grande, while Beltrán and the others returned to Santa Bárbara. Espejo and his band came back some months later, after having opened a new route on their return; they had gone south down the Río Pecos and through the lands of the Jumano. As of 1583 data on New Mexico were beginning to accumulate, and some interest was rising.

Reports were duly filed with the viceroy, and with them a request from Espejo to be allowed to return for the conquest of the country which he had recently traversed. This opportunity was to go to another; but the Espejo-Beltrán expedition had really set the stage for the first move of the frontier into the Borderlands. Tales of mines were now added to the earlier stories of populous towns and many natives, much more advanced culturally than the Chichimeca and their northern fellows among whom, for the moment at least, the Spaniards' lot was cast.

As this interest was building on the frontier, a new factor had appeared to influence official thinking about the vast north. Francis Drake had recently returned from his surprise foray into the Pacific, into what the Spaniards felt to be *their* Mar del Sud (the original Spanish name for the Western Ocean). The daring sea dog of Elizabeth, late in the decade of the 1570s, had carried the war against Spain out of the Caribbean and around to the farther side of the two American continents.[9] Clearing the Strait of Magellan, he had caught the Spaniards off guard at Valparaíso, Arica, and Callao, along the coast of Chile and Peru; he had given them a scare at Guatulco, on Mexico's Pacific side; he had spent some time at the bay above San Francisco which bears his name, before pointing his *Golden Hind* homeward by the long-way-round. Intelligence coming out of England concerning his activities and findings north of Mexico worried officials at the court of Spain. There was even the hint that he had discovered the western outlet of a transcontinental strait, in the land of New Albion which he had claimed for England and Elizabeth. This rumor was disturbing to the Spaniards and by the early 1580s they were seriously considering the possibilities of the future if the strait turned out to be a reality. Should they anticipate the English by moving a base into the farther north, from which they might occupy that transcontinental waterway or, at the very least, be in a position to challenge English use of it?

Therefore, possible mines, potentially successful missions among reputedly advanced Indians, and a base from which to harass the English, all these, entered into the decision to drive a salient of the frontier far into the north country. True, this outpost settlement would be, for a time at least, rather dangerously removed from the farthest edge of the effectively held frontier; but imperial considerations seemed to demand that the risk be assumed. If nothing more, the new province could serve as a buffer against potentially worrisome rivals.[10]

Following various viceregal reports to the crown concerning the farther north, as early as April 1583, a royal cedula came into New Spain, authorizing the viceroy to take steps looking to the conquest and occupation of the land recently explored. There was one proviso in the instructions to the viceroy, one already familiar in such instances of new conquests; this was to the effect that no royal funds might be expected and that the future patentee would have to undertake the conquest with his own resources. Even so, there were several men of New Spain who professed immediate interest.[11]

First in the line of applicants was Cristóbal Martín, wealthy, ambitious, but much too exacting in the demands which he made of the crown as his price for undertaking the venture. Espejo was also very much interested. When the viceroy failed to react to his first hint, he decided to bypass that officer and go directly to the crown; but his proposal, too, was thumbed down by the Council of the Indies, in whose hands Philip II left such decisions. An official of Puebla, Francisco Díaz de Vargas, also was rejected by that august body of royal advisors. Several years went by before Juan Bautista de Lomas y Colmenares, a Nueva Galicia millionaire, came forward with the next bid. The new viceroy, the Marqués de Villamanrique, recently arrived, was much impressed, approved the Lomas proposition in March 1589, and sent the papers to Spain for final confirmation. Nothing happened, and the matter hung undecided.

During these years of official indecision the stories of mines in the farther north were still very much alive on the frontier. In 1589 and again in 1593, two unauthorized or "bootleg" expeditions set out for New Mexico; in each instance the leaders seemingly were gambling that actual conquest might win the royal nod of approval *post factum*. Gaspar Castaño de Sosa went north in the summer of 1589, with a party of some 170 men, women, and children. Informed, the viceroy sent a squad of soldiers into New Mexico to arrest him. The second expedition, in 1593, that of Francisco Leyva de Bonilla and Antonio Gutiérrez de Humaña, even though it may have reached eastward into Kansas, had an even sorrier end. Leyva was killed during a vicious quarrel with Humaña, and the latter and most of his men were killed on the Plains by the Indians.

Meanwhile, New Spain had a new viceroy, the second Don Luis de Velasco. Still interested, Lomas petitioned a second, and a third time; but he failed to win royal approbation. Francisco de Urdiñola, son of the conqueror of Coahuila and in the early 1590s lieutenant-governor of Nueva Vizcaya, actually had the appointment. But, before he could move, he fell under suspicion, charged with having poisoned his wife, and royal approval was withdrawn. However, the royal desire to occupy New Mexico still persisted; but Velasco had no appointee.

At this juncture—it was now 1595—the ultimate winner of the New Mexico "sweepstakes" appeared, conferred with Velasco, impressed him favorably, and ended with the contract, which needed only to be ratified by the crown. The man was Juan de Oñate, son of Don Cristóbal. The father was a prominent and wealthy citizen of New Spain, having come to the province in 1524 and having posted an impressive record of long years of service before he became one of the so-called Big Four who opened the silver lodes of Zacatecas—Oñate, Juan de Tolosa, Diego de Ibarra, and Baltasar Treviño. Don Juan had followed in his father's footsteps of service to the crown. At the time he made his petition to Velasco he could point to two decades of experience against the Chichimeca and other troublesome folk on the early frontiers of the north, in Nueva Galicia and Nueva Vizcaya. In 1595 he seemed to be the best-fitted of the many candidates. Besides that, he was both wealthy and willing to invest heavily in the New Mexican project. The desire for fame, as well as fortune, was a powerful stimulant to many of the men of New Spain in that exciting sixteenth century, in which Cortés had been the pacesetter.

The terms of the contract which Oñate drew up with Velasco amply prove his interest and ambitions. He bargained to recruit at least 200 men, to be fully equipped and supplied with provisions. These soldiers would be paid by him, not by the royal treasury. Further, Oñate promised to take "1000 head of cattle, 1000 sheep for wool and another 1000 for mutton, 1000 goats, 100 head of black cattle, 150 colts, 150 mares, quantities of flour, corn, jerked beef, and sowing wheat," and also sizable quantities of other necessary and useful supplies. The crown, on its side, would commit itself to supply five priests and a lay brother, to be maintained at royal expense; also assured were several pieces of artillery, and a six-year loan of 6000 pesos. Oñate was to have the titles of governor and captain-general and, once in the land, that of *adelantado*. This last title, more honorific than anything else, would have put him in the class of such previous American greats as Balboa, Ponce de León, De Soto, and others. Oñate was to enjoy the right of *encomienda*, for three generations—having a large number of Indians assigned to him and his heirs; and he had the further right to grant *encomiendas* to his companions. This was one way in which the crown could and did recompense its devoted servants in those early days. Indians were "commended" to *benemeriti*, who had the right to collect from them the annual tribute owed to the crown; too often, when the natives could not pay this their labor was demanded in lieu thereof; the practice was open to serious abuses, of which one acquainted with the history of the conquest is more than aware.

There was one point in the original agreement which is of considerable interest in the light of future Borderlands history. Oñate was to be directly responsible to the Council of the Indies and thus would be relieved of having to proceed in his dealings with the crown through the intermediary of the viceroy. On this point the thinking seems to anticipate the legal and administrative position of the future *comandante-general* of the Provincias

Internas, who, in theory at least, enjoyed a large measure of independent action in governing the Borderlands in the last decades of the eighteenth century (see Chapter 10). The cause of efficiency might have been served, had this pattern held from the very beginning of the Borderlands development.

Unfortunately, before all the papers were in order and the contract properly formalized, there was a change of viceroys in New Spain. Luis de Velasco was shifted to Peru, and Don Gaspar de Zúñiga y Acevedo, Conde de Monterrey, arrived to replace him. Although Velasco strongly recommended Oñate to his successor, Monterrey, overwhelmed, perhaps, by his responsibility, felt it prudent to delay his final approval. Oñate was given tentative permission to proceed with his preparations, but his position now became somewhat precarious; the commission of conquest might or might not be his.

Then began a series of modifications of the original contract (one of which put Oñate and the enterprise back under the immediate control of the viceroy), misunderstandings, petty harassments by Monterrey, costly inspections, which delayed the expedition for close to three years and came very near to bankrupting Oñate even before he set forth. There was a time when Oñate even had a powerful rival, Don Pedro Ponce de León, who enjoyed strong support within the Council of the Indies. Only the king's lack of enthusiasm for Ponce prevented him from receiving the approval to carry through the enterprise for which Oñate had been preparing for many months past.

Finally, after months of frustration, the expedition left Santa Bárbara on January 26, 1598.[12] Some of the enthusiasm of an earlier date had definitely cooled. Oñate actually had trouble holding many of his enlistees. Even so, he had 129 soldiers in his company, some of them with families, when he reached the Conchos; there were 83 wagons and some 7000 head of stock. In March a band of 10 Franciscans, 8 priests and 2 lay brothers, headed by Fray Padre Alonso Martínez, moved up to join the larger company. It was early May before the party reached the ford on the Río Grande, El Paso del Norte. The subsequent advance up the valley was slow and painful. Progress was even slower when the pioneers came to the pueblos, for there was need to talk with the chiefs in each town in order to lay the groundwork for the establishment of Spanish authority. In mid-June Oñate chose the village of Caypa, far upriver, as his headquarters and rechristened it San Juan de los Caballeros. Sometime later, probably in 1600, Oñate transferred this capital to San Gabriel, to the west of the river. Under Oñate's successor, Peralta, there would be still another move, to Santa Fe.

The first months were busy ones. Oñate and his lieutenants explored; the first church was built and dedicated, at San Juan; there were threats of mutiny within the ranks of the Spaniards; and the friars were sent out to the nearby pueblos to begin what had been consistently proclaimed as one of the prime reasons for the occupation of the province, the spread of the gospel to the natives.

Days of trial lay ahead for Oñate and his men, and days of adventure as well. In the fall of 1598 Vicente de Zaldívar went off to the east, to see the "buffalo plains." He and his men failed in their attempt to bring back one of the animals alive and had to content themselves with the tales they could tell and with quantities of shaggy-cow meat from some of the beasts which they managed to fell with the aid of their firearms. A new day was dawning, and not a fortunate one, for the American bison; the white man's gunpowder and his horse would make life very precarious. There were expeditions to Ácoma, the first one friendly but the next quite the opposite, this last sent out to avenge the treachery which had brought death to Juan de Zaldívar and his little party. The Ácoma resisted stoutly, but Spanish resourcefulness and artillery finally broke them on the third day of the battle; two field pieces had been hoisted to the heights of the famous "sky city." Carnage was heavy; the pueblo was extensively damaged; and some five to six hundred Indians were carried off into harsh captivity. Vicente de Zaldívar, brother of the murdered Juan, was not a gentle conqueror, nor was Oñate an indulgent judge. The punishment meted out to the Acoma was meant as an object lesson for all Pueblo-land, and for the moment it worked. In the years to come there would be troubles with some of the peripheral nations, notably with the Jumano to the east; but it would be a good eighty

Ácoma. (Frederic Lewis)

years before the Spaniards had to battle a united foe. A Pueblo Revolt, such as the famous one of 1680, might well have developed early, had Oñate adopted less stern policies.

The agents of Oñate went off to Mexico City, in 1599, with reports of progress in the north and with urgent pleas for more soldiers and supplies. The country had proved very disappointing from the point of view of supporting the needs of the Spaniards; food was in short supply. The viceroy, still the Conde de Monterrey, was sympathetic, but even so, the whole business took time, for New Mexico was over a thousand miles beyond the established frontier. A small band of 7, with a friar along, left Santa Bárbara in June 1600; the main body of new people, numbering 73, did not set forth until the end of August and did not arrive at Oñate's capital until Christmas Eve. In the larger group were a half-dozen more Franciscans; their order was taking its commitment to the enterprise very seriously.

Within New Mexico increasing unrest and disillusionment among the colonists forced Oñate to broaden his horizons. He had originally planned explorations westward that might discover a link to the sea and had actually sent Vicente de Zaldívar on a reconnaissance in that direction in 1599. But rumors persisted of great wealth on the plains. To there he turned his attention.

In June (1601) a large expedition set out with the *adelantado* himself in command. Five months later the Spaniards returned to San Gabriel. They had pushed well into Kansas but had found nothing of promise; and they had had a rather stiff brush with the Quivira. Although they suffered no fatalities, many had wounds as reminders of the engagement. The situation awaiting them at San Gabriel did nothing to raise their spirits; it was, in fact, most disturbing.

While Oñate was on the plains, discouragement at home blossomed into revolt. Lieutenant-governor Francisco de Sosa y Peñalosa could not cope with the dissidents, who demanded nothing short of permission to abandon New Mexico altogether. There had been discussions, conferences, threats; the let's-go-home faction was decidedly in the ascendant, and some of the missionaries were standing with this majority. Hardly more than a dozen folk were loyal to Oñate when he and his tired men came back to San Gabriel in November. Some of the colonists had actually started back to Mexico. Hence, as 1601 went into its last weeks, there was a state of crisis. This was soon compounded by the charges which the deserters spread against Oñate and the highly uncomplimentary things they had to say about the province as they reached the older settlements and worked hard to justify themselves. In the Spanish order of things these defectors were technically deserters, having left their frontier without proper authorization, and as such were liable to punishment.

Oñate did what he could to counter the charges against himself and the criticisms of the colony; but little came of his efforts. New Mexico continued to have a "bad press"; and the black marks against the leader remained in viceregal and royal ledgers, to be brought up in his later *residencia,* the official accounting which every major royal officer had to face at the end of his term of appointment.

The manpower situation in New Mexico was hardly ameliorated during the next years, despite constant attempts by Oñate's friends at home to stir royal enthusiasm for the northern province. Charges against the *adelantado,* the title having been belatedly conferred in 1602, continued to pile up. Monterrey's report on the desertion episode and on the general straitened conditions in New Mexico cooled what spark of interest there may have remained within the Council of the Indies. Zaldívar went to Spain, in 1603, but won few concessions for his chief.

At this juncture Monterrey did make one decision which favored Oñate and his enterprise, when on his own authority he postponed the *residencia* which had been ordered by the home authorities. The viceroy feared that such an official inquiry might very well deal a death blow to the future of the province. Even though he was at the moment fairly well convinced that New Mexico had become a liability, he does not seem to have been willing to administer the *coup de grâce.* The viceroy was not securely certain that the crown should scuttle the venture, especially since there was the strong opinion of the theologians to the effect that the new converts in New Mexico could not, in conscience, be abandoned and left without spiritual help. In those days such an opinion had weight in Spanish policy-making. There was even some talk of solving this problem of conscience by removing the new Christians from their pagan surroundings and locating them closer to Spanish settlements in northern New Spain, in the event that New Mexico were to be abandoned.

Still nurturing an unflagging optimism that the province could be saved and his own fortune recouped, Oñate next tied his hopes on a successful expedition to the South Sea, which might turn up mines along the route. The party which set out from San Gabriel in October 1604 was small, just short of three dozen adventurers—30 soldiers, the *adelantado,* and 2 Franciscans. Their route took them first to the province of Zuñi, on to the Hopi, then after crossing several rivers to the Río Colorado, at or near the point later known as Bill Williams Fork. By slow stages the Spaniards moved downstream, past the Gila and on to the river's mouth at the head of the Gulf of California. They saw much new country, made contact with many new Indian nations, most of them rather friendly and some destined to figure in later chapters of the Borderlands story, but they encountered no consoling evidences of gold or silver. Later the viceroy summed up the expedition in a curt and cynical sentence: "Nothing but naked people, false bits of coral, and four pebbles." Padre Escobar picked up some fantastic stories about still more fantastic peoples. But even his gullible contemporaries were not quite ready to give credibility to the existence of folk with ears so large that they dragged on the ground, or to people, a whole tribe, who had but a single leg, or to humans who "sustained themselves solely by the odor of their food." On April 25, 1605, the explorers came back to San Gabriel, without loss of a man but still empty-handed.

Understandably, Oñate sought to magnify the importance of his discovery of a route to the sea. He talked of the great natural port which he had found. He was convinced that California was an island; hence, he thought himself justified in describing what was really the head of the Gulf as a port on the South Sea, which might be turned into a possible nothern harbor to figure in the Philippine trade, which by those early years of the seventeenth century, as will be seen presently, was developing.

Fray Padre Escobar went to Mexico City to report and to petition men and material aid. There was a new viceroy, the Conde de Montesclaros; he was unconvinced. In fact, he informed authorities in Spain that the north was a poor risk and that if the decision was to hold it, New Mexico could only be maintained at the price of a continual costly outlay of men and supplies. He further warned that the likelihood of finding as successor to Oñate another man willing to gamble his fortune was slim indeed.

The fate of New Mexico was the subject of much discussion on both sides of the Atlantic. In early 1606 the Council of the Indies, after reassessing the question, decided to try a policy of retrenchment, a sort of austerity program, in the hope of saving the province. The viceroy was to halt all further conquest of the province; Oñate was to be recalled; the next governor must be more interested in the Christianization effort (the friars were making their voices heard in high places); only the friars would be allowed to make further explorations, solely for missionary purposes, and these were to be carried out without a large and expensive complement of soldiery.

Midway through the next year (1607) Oñate tendered his resignation and forwarded the document to the viceroy. He and his family had spent upwards of 400,000 pesos on the New Mexican venture; he could go no further without royal aid. He added, in this letter, that, if no new governor had been appointed by mid-1608, he had agreed to give permission to the disheartened colonists that as many as wished might withdraw and return to New Spain, "for there will not be anyone to wait a day longer."

This letter came to the desk of a new viceroy, or rather to an old one. Luis de Velasco was back, the same Velasco who had encouraged Oñate almost a dozen years before. He, at least, was not willing to give up so easily. Oñate was ordered to remain, awaiting further instructions; eight soldiers were sent north with this directive; and all in New Mexico were to stay put and wait for a formal decision from the crown. Velasco did accept Oñate's suggestion that until a new governor arrived it might be well to put authority in the hands of another. Accordingly, one of the captains, Juan Martínez de Montoya, was named the governor pro tem; but he was ordered to work and consult with the *adelantado*, who was staying.

A full report went off to the king, as of March 7, 1608, based in large measure on the varied information supplied by Fray Lázaro Jiménez. The friar had come down from San Gabriel to push one or other of two alternatives: either the abandonment of New Mexico and permission for all Spaniards there to withdraw or firm assurance of the needed assistance in the event the province was to be retained. Regretfully, Velasco was inclining toward the first of the two.

The decision for abandonment was just about firm, when Jiménez came back to Mexico City with the news that his Franciscan brethren had begun to taste some success. The number of Christian neophytes had jumped from a previous four thousand to almost twice that figure within a matter of months. Informed of this new missionary harvest of souls, the king changed his attitude. As 1608 ended, the decision was made in Spain: New Mexico was to be held and turned into a royal province, with the crown footing the bills. Velasco, thereupon, in early 1609, appointed Don Pedro de Peralta as royal governor and sent him north.[13]

One of Peralta's early acts was to implement the recommendation in his instructions to relocate the capital. San Gabriel was too far north and too far from the center of the heaviest Indian population concentration. It had been well enough placed during an era of exploration, but now, by royal order, this age was to be ended. Peralta looked around and sought the counsel of the veterans of New Mexico. Finally, in 1609 he chose the site of Santa Fe, and the building of the familiar northern outpost was begun, to make Santa Fe the third oldest of the town foundations within the limits of the United States.[14] Saint Augustine was its senior by many decades (1565) and Jamestown by only a few years (1607).

The next decades saw slow but steady progress, in a relative sort of way. Governors followed one another every fourth year; some of them men of character and ability, others very ordinary, or even less so.[15] The number of Spaniards increased from a few hundred to a few thousand. They were never very prosperous; but they did lay the groundwork for future New Mexican agricultural and sheep-raising industries. They tended to cluster in a few centers on or near the Río Grande. Santa Fe long continued to be the only town, the Villa as it was called. In the 1630s it had a population of around 250 Spaniards, with about three times that many mestizos and civilized Indians. By that time there were two dozen or so friars, serving twenty-five missions and caring for the spiritual and temporal needs of about 50,000 Indians.

Thus New Mexico became the first of the western Borderlands. It began as a bright dream. Before it was ten years old, it had proved to be a mistake, but one which Spain decided she would have to live with for reasons of Christian conscience. In time this outpost province in the far north, set with its face toward the Great Plains, would to a degree justify its existence as a defense bastion against raiders, Indian and European. But in the overall picture of the Spanish empire in the Americas, New Mexico remained to the end more a monument to the crown's commitment to the spread of the Christian gospel in the lands which Columbus uncovered and which Pope Alexander VI portioned out to Isabella and her successors.

New Mexico was the first of the western Borderlands, but it had a companion, by several decades its senior, at the eastern edge of Spain's expansion into the North American continent: Florida or, as the Spaniards often said, "The Floridas." It too was a Spanish Borderland, even though its story does not always integrate too closely with that of the Spanish northward movement out of Mexico City. Florida is rather a Borderland of the island segment of Spain's American empire.

From beginning to end Florida was a defensive Borderland.[16] There was missionary effort in Florida, and for a century and a quarter a quite impressive and successful one; but this was regularly a secondary consideration. Again, there was some settlement; but this aspect of the Florida story also was incidental and largely subordinated to defense policies. Texas, occupied by Spain in the eighteenth century, would be the closest parallel to Florida in the Spanish Borderlands story. But Texas would have to defend against a less redoubtable enemy than Florida; France in the long run was a less dangerous foe than England.

By mid-sixteenth century Spaniards had failed four times at the southeastern corner of the continent—Ponce de León, Lucás de Ayllón, Pánfilo de Narváez, and Hernando de Soto. Yet they were not willing to give up. Dominican brethren of Fray Bartolomé de Las Casas' sought, in 1549, to apply his ideal of peaceful conquest, with the cross rather than with the sword—Spaniards in search of souls rather than of gold.[17] For their pains Fray Luis Cancer de Barbastro and his several companions won martyrdom at the hands of the Indians of Tampa Bay. The Florida natives made it very clear that they wanted no white men in their lands, no matter what their mission or intent. But the Spaniards remained unconvinced.

The next attempt to conquer and colonize Florida also stemmed, as its immediate predecessor, from New Spain. The second viceroy, Don Luis de Velasco, had his orders to see that the southeastern corner of the continent was occupied. In 1559 Tristán de Luna, a veteran of Coronado's quest, sailed out of Vera Cruz with an imposing armada of 13 ships, carrying 500 soldiers and twice as many colonists.[18] He was to found a settlement in the Alabama country and a second on the Atlantic side in the Carolina area, where Ayllón had failed over a quarter-century before. A first halt was made near the site of the future Pensacola. Hardly had he landed when one of the seasonal hurricanes roared up the Gulf Coast, hit and destroyed most of his ships and ruined his supplies. What winds had not scattered, human tempers soon wrecked as serious quarrels and deep dissatisfaction with the captain tore the band to bits. Ultimately, Luna had to yield the command to Angel de Villafañe, who sought to transplant the colony to Santa Elena, on the Carolina coast, only to have another hurricane deal a final blow to the enterprise. Florida might never have been colonized by the Spaniards had not the French made the next move.

Some years earlier Spain had begun to feel concern over the appearance in *its* Caribbean of French corsairs, carrying the raging Hapsburg-Valois feud of Europe into American waters.[19] Harassment of Spanish shipping was disconcerting enough, but when men like Jacques de Sores and François le Clerc attacked and held island towns for ransom, Spain recognized that action was in order. Spain worried, too, for the security of the homebound route of its galleons. When the Luna expedition had been organized, the European war was still in full swing. Spain knew that the pirates had bases in the Bahamas and it could not afford an unfriendly power on the strategic Florida peninsula, along whose coast the silver fleet out of Havana plied northward to pick up the trade winds off the Carolina coast. But, while Luna was failing in Florida, the two rival houses in Europe signed the Treaty of Cateau-Cambrésis to end their dynastic feuding. Philip II, for the moment, felt secure and this confidence, especially in the face of the Villafañe debacle at Santa Elena, led him, in 1561, to call off further enterprise in Florida. Very quickly, however, he learned that he had read the signs of the times badly.

Hardly was France out of its contest with the Hapsburgs when it found itself in an even more devastating internal conflict. France's Wars of Religion for the next several decades would pit its Catholic majority against a determined Huguenot minority. One of the chief Huguenot protectors, Gaspar de Coligny, Admiral of France and prince of the blood, planned a possible refuge for his prosecuted Calvinist fellows overseas. A few years earlier he had watched with interest Nicholas Durand, sieur de Villegagnon, try an ecumenical experiment in Brazil, when he brought both Catholics and Calvinists together on a distant shore. The Portuguese had done their full share to put an end to this trespass at Rio de Janeiro. By the 1560s it was evident that some other site of refuge would have to be found. Coligny thought of the vast Atlantic shoreline of North America to which France had staked paper claims, at least, since the voyage of Verrazano in the middle 1520s.

Accordingly, in 1562, Coligny sent out Jean Ribaut to find a suitable location, one, too, which might be close enough to allow the French to make life difficult for Catholic Spain.[20] Even though the two powers were at peace, a bit of highly motivated piracy might help to finance the refugee colony. Ribaut first looked at the mouth of the St. Johns River, on the north Florida coast—the French gave it the name of the River of May. Ribaut explored a bit inland, then sailed north to a spot on the Carolina coast, where on a broad harbor he laid out Port Royal. Leaving several dozen men to hold the "fort," Ribaut sailed back to France for more men and supplies.

His return was delayed, and this first French colony did not survive.

The French, however, were persistent. Coligny gathered another band, some three hundred settlers, and sent them off, in 1564, under René de Laudonnière; Ribaut at the moment was detained, a prisoner, in England. The new group, three hundred strong, came back to the River of May (St. Johns), the spot being known to Laudonnière, who had been with Ribaut on the previous reconnaissance. There they founded Fort Caroline, near the spot where Ribaut had set up his column of French possession two years before, to proclaim French ownership. The French did a bit of exploring inland and, according to the Spanish story, a bit of pirating along the Bahama sea-lane. When John Hawkins, returning in 1565 from his second bootleg venture to the Spanish Indies, looked in on the colony, he found a badly disheartened and disgruntled group of Frenchmen. Only the timely arrival of Ribaut with reinforcements and supplies saved the colony, at least for the moment.

The situation in Florida, however, was due to become very complicated, and immediately. Hardly had Ribaut arrived, when he and his fellows were challenged, there at the mouth of the St. Johns, by a formidable Spanish don. Pedro Menéndez de Avilés had built his reputation as Spain's hardest-hitting, most daring, and most resourceful sea captain, and this on both sides of the Atlantic.[21] Now he came, by Philip's appointment, as *adelantado*, governor and captain-general of La Florida, to sweep the Atlantic coast of corsairs and interlopers and to establish a Spanish base on the peninsula.

Menéndez had hurried off from Spain in late June 1565, even before his whole fleet was ready. He had paused for a brief few days in Puerto Rico. Then, apprized that the French were rushing to reinforce their position, he set out for the mainland with five ships, carrying 500 soldiers, 200 sailors, and 100 colonists. On August 25 he touched at Cape Canaveral. Three days later he put in at a pleasant little harbor, landed his company, and had one of his chaplains celebrate Mass on the site. Since it was the day of Saint Augustine of Hippo, this saint's name was given to the post that he founded there. Inquiries among the Indians brought the information that other white men were about twenty leagues up the coast.

At the mouth of the St. Johns he found the fleet of Ribaut already in the harbor. Undaunted, he sailed in to challenge them as trespassers. Ribaut gave orders to withdraw, and all but one of his ships escaped. The Spanish vessels, already somewhat damaged, were in no condition to pursue. Menéndez dropped back to establish formally and to fortify his little San Agustín, for the moment located on Anastasia Island. He unloaded two of his ships and sent them back to Santo Domingo for men and supplies. With the three remaining ships, he was in no position to repel Ribaut, who meanwhile had drawn up outside the bar. But then came a hurricane, in from the north, this time to favor the Spaniards. Ribaut had to run before it and seek shelter farther down the coast.

Don Pedro Menéndez de Avilés. (The Bancroft Library)

Menéndez was a gambler at heart, and his next move proved this amply. Taking as many of his men as he could spare, around five hundred of them, he pushed northward under the most difficult of climatic conditions and over rainsoaked and swampy terrain, hoping to catch the French, unsuspecting, at Fort Caroline; he knew that they would for the moment be undermanned. His daring move paid off. Fort Caroline was captured; its males were slain or scattered inland, but a few, along with the women and children, were spared; the spot, now desolate, was rechristened San Mateo; and the Spaniards hurried back to their base, leaving about half their number to garrison the former French post. Menéndez realized that the job was only half done, for Ribaut was still in the south.

Back at San Agustín, Menéndez pushed his men to strengthen the defenses and drew what information he could from friendly Indians. He learned that a group of shipwrecked white men was stranded a few leagues down the coast. He set out with as many men as he could spare, about fifty, found the Frenchmen, forced their surrender, and dispatched all but sixteen Catholic Breton sailors by the sword. Hardly finished with this forceful action at Matanzas Inlet, Menéndez returned to deal with the Ribaut party of about 300 survivors, who, friendly Indians informed him, had come up from farther south, where their ships, too, had been wrecked in the storm. Menéndez was as bold in confronting these 350 or so survivors as he had been in the previous instance. About half of them chose flight to surrender; the rest gave themselves up. These were dealt the same lot as their fellow men, death by the sword. Some time later Menéndez caught up with the rest, building a boat at Cape Canaveral. This time, having superiority in numbers, he spared their lives and ultimately sent them off, as prisoners, to the islands. The French threat was at an end. Their Dominique de Gourgues surprised San Mateo (St. Johns) in 1568, hanged the garrison in reprisal, but sailed off.

The events of 1565, by modern standards shocking to be sure, hardly open the Florida story on a pleasant note. The French and Spain's enemies of the day made much of them, using the actions of Menéndez to bulwark the Black Legend which was building against the first masters of the Americas. Philip II remarked of his *adelantado*, "He has done well." Time has allowed a somewhat more objective and decidedly less partisan evaluation. Menéndez does not emerge an unsullied hero; but he appears as less a monster, and very much a man of his times, when international rivalries were fierce and religious rivalries even fiercer. By Spanish standards the French were trespassers; more than that they were pirates, and as such merited no mercy; and most of all they were *"luteranos,"* the Spaniards' common designation for all those "new" Christians who had forsworn allegiance to the Mother Church of Rome, to which the men of Spain were passionately, even fanatically, devoted. Henry Bourbon's Edict of Nantes (1598), that first glimmer of religious toleration, was still thirty-odd years away. And later judgment also offers another point to explain the severity of Menéndez: he had too few men to guard so many prisoners and too little food to feed them for even as short a time as it might take to return them to their homeland or transport them to Spanish prisons.

The French threat successfully parried, the next job of Menéndez was to secure for Spain the land which he won. He explored the land, tried to make friends with the Indians, brought in Spanish colonists and encouraged them to tap the fertility of the Florida soil, built a line of small blockhouse forts from Tampa Bay around the tip of the peninsula and up the Atlantic coast to Santa Elena, near the Port Royal site of Ribaut's first little settlement. He was interested in obtaining missionaries for his Indians, for their conversion became one of his chief objectives. The Dominicans, two of them, came in 1566. He sent them north with a small detachment and an Indian convert, Don Luis, to found a mission in his land of Ajacán, along the Bay of Santa María (Chesapeake Bay). A storm prevented their reaching this goal. Before that year was out the first of the Jesuits came to Florida.[22] Their Padre Pedro Martínez was struck down by the Indians as he tried to land north of San Mateo (St. Johns); but his Black Robe brethren continued in the colony for the next half dozen years. They, in their turn, tried to bring the gospel to the folk of Ajacán; but their effort on the Rappahannock ended when their little band was wiped out in 1572.[23] Pressures on Jesuit superiors from insistent and powerful parties in New

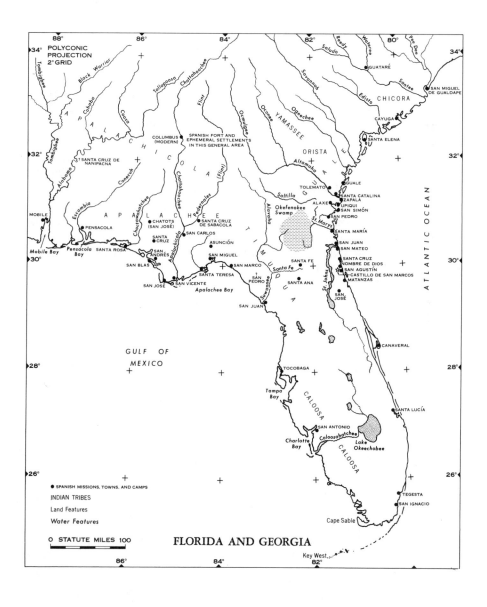

FLORIDA AND GEORGIA

Spain caused them to shift the few Florida survivors to the opening Mexican enterprise. But in the next year the Franciscans arrived in Florida.[24] During the next century their missions edged up the coast to Guale (Georgia) and Orista (South Carolina); they went into Timucua, west of San Agustín, and on to the land of Apalachee and still farther west to the Pensacola-Alabama country.

Menéndez was tireless in his efforts to build his colony. Seven times between 1565 and 1571 he crossed to Spain to win support and men, soldiers, missionaries, and colonists. Almost countless were his sailings into the nearby Caribbean, now for his colony but almost as often for the defense of this whole area, so exposed to the attacks of Spain's enemies. His last years King Philip held him in the mother country, for Spain's more immediate protection. He died there in 1574; but one of his last tasks was to scour his native Asturias for fifty families to send to Florida. He was in every sense the "father of Spanish Florida." He made it the one Spanish Borderland on the eastern end of the frontier ring.

Florida would never be tied closely to its sister provinces farther west; but it would share with them many common Borderland traits. It would be a defense outpost against Spanish enemies, protecting more valuable possessions nearer the heart of the Spanish Indies. For a time Florida would be a mission Borderland, and quite successfully so, until the day when aggressive Carolinians dealt a death blow to this Christianizing effort and later the Georgians would do a more thorough mop-up job. Florida could never attract much more than a skeleton Spanish population; but the few who came and stayed left a Spanish mark on the peninsula. More of this Florida story will find place in these pages as our historical time runs on.

◁ 4 ▷

First Steps on the Long Road to California, 1591-1711

*T*he year before Pedro Menéndez de Avilés headed toward the Florida coast to root out the Frenchmen at Fort Caroline, a little fleet, captained by Miguel López de Legazpi, with Fray Andrés de Urdaneta as chief navigator, cartographer, and sailing master, put out from Mexico's west coast. Its aim was to establish a base in those far western islands, which the men of Magellan had first seen in 1521 and which Villalobos had explored and named the Philippines in 1542. The successes of the Portuguese in terms of profit in their trade with the East had roused Spanish envy—Mexico was fine, so was Peru, but on the whole, Spanish luck in the Americas seemed to be running out. Charles and then son Philip schemed and plotted, trying to figure out a way for Spain to get its share of the profits. Direct belligerent competition along the sea route via Africa's Cape of Good Hope was ruled out by mutual agreement to respect each other's spheres of activity defined by the papal Line of Demarcation in 1493 and the Treaty of Tordesillas of the next year. The rich Indies of the East were in the Portuguese "half" of the globe. But this did not stop the Spaniards from hoping that around or through or beyond the North American continent they might find a north-

49

west passage, to match the southeast passage of their Iberian neighbors. Those "western islands" which Spain had discovered and claimed, without raising too vociferous objections from Portugal, seemed to offer a possibility. In 1564 the Spaniards set out to test just such a possibility.

The conquest of the Philippines began on arrival. Some resistance from the Portuguese on Cebu slowed the process temporarily, but by the time Legazpi died in 1572 the Spanish hold on the islands was secure, and Manila had been founded the year before. All this could have been to no avail, had not the Augustinian friar Urdaneta found a practicable way back to Mexico. Experimenting, navigationally, he took three of the ships of the original fleet northward from the Philippines, picked up the Japanese Current and the westerly tradewinds, and touched the American continent along the northern California coast. Soon he had the benefit of the Cabrillo-Ferrelo charts to guide him into the home port. The way was long, 129 days, but it avoided contrary winds and interception by the Portuguese. Within the next years the Spanish trans-Pacific trade was born, and Manila became the entrepôt to which the Orientals could be attracted. Year after year the volume increased as the so-called Manila Galleons sailed out of Acapulco with silver bullion and returned with the luxury goods of the fabulous East.[1] The silks and fine textiles, the precious stones and perfumes, the porcelains and the exquisitely carved chests, the spices and the rest found ready markets in Mexico and Peru, and there were some left for trans-shipment to the mother country.

Although trade boomed, it had its problems. Any possible opposition from the Portuguese was eliminated after 1580 when, on the death of the last scion of the House of Aviz, the two crowns were united in the hands of Philip II of Spain. But other problems remained; at first these were human in character, but after 1579 there were complicating international factors. The run from Acapulco to Manila took two to three months; the return required two to three times that long. But time was not the entire difficulty. More distressing was the toll which that dread scourge of sailing men, scurvy, took of human lives on the homebound voyage.[2] Mortality was high, and often the Galleon came into port with only a skeleton crew able or even alive. Officials began to think of the value of a way station on the western shore of the continent, a port for repairs to galleons and crews, where the water supply could be freshened and the food supply renewed. Long before the biochemists learned about vitamins, folk found that fresh fruit and vegetables were among the best antidotes for scurvy. California, which Spain had been inclined to write out of imperial plans after the Cabrillo-Ferrelo reports, might yet be turned to value.

The Spaniards were given more reasons for their interest in the west coast by trespassers in *their* Pacific.[3] First, there was Francis Drake, whose presence on the California coast in 1579 fired the imagination of his contemporaries.[4] Thomas Cavendish followed his lead and in 1586 raided the

Pacific coast of South America and off the tip of Baja California (the peninsula) caught the *Santa Ana*, returning from Manila, stripped it of its rich cargo and burned it to the water's edge. Others, like Richard Hawkins and the Dutchman Van Noort, came in his wake. Spain was seriously concerned. The trans-Pacific trade was too valuable to lose, and the pirates were threatening. A base on the California coast now had a dual purpose: a port of call for the Galleon and a station from which a coast guard might operate against the interlopers.

Even before Cavendish and his successors appeared, the Spaniards prepared to learn more about Alta California, at least about its coastline. Hoping to avoid a costly expedition precisely for that purpose, in 1584 Viceroy Pedro Moya de Contreras advised the veteran captain of the Galleon, Francisco de Gali, to sail in as close as he dared on his return trip in order to chart the California coast.[5] It was hoped that he might be able to furnish enough information to allow officials to formulate plans for the future. This method was next to useless. Moya's successor, the Marqués de Villamanrique, did nothing. But ten years later, in 1595, Viceroy Luis Velasco, Marqués de Salinas, returned to the original plan. Sebastián Rodríguez Cermenho had like orders.[6] He anchored the Galleon in Drake's Bay and with a party landed and pushed some little distance inland. During a sudden storm his *San Agustín* was caught in a crosswind, driven ashore, and shattered on the beach. The loss was total, ship and rich cargo. By good fortune, his carpenters had been assembling a prefabricated launch on the beach, intending to use it for closer shore inspection. Onto this *San Buenaventura* the men crowded and, almost miraculously, made their way back to the home port of Navidad. The Cermenho ill fortune had at least one salutary consequence: it marked the end of the peso-pinching policy.

Seven years later the job of gathering information on the California coast was done more sensibly, even though little came of the effort at the moment. Sebastián Vizcaíno, a veteran of several Pacific voyages, was assigned the exploration task. He had more recently (1596–1597) attempted a settlement at La Paz, on the California peninsula, and had been involved in pearl-fishing activities in the Gulf. Actually, he had strongly urged an expedition up the outer coast, in lighter boats and with a proper crew.

The Council of the Indies, somewhat reluctantly, agreed to underwrite the venture, largely because the current viceroy, the Conde de Monterrey, was interested. Not only did Monterrey put Vizcaíno in charge, but, acting on his own, authorized a slightly more elaborate fleet than the one ship provided for in the king's order. He put two small ships and a frigate at Vizcaíno's disposal.

In early May 1602, the little squadron was on its way, carrying upwards of 130 men, including three Carmelite friars, and only such cargo as was needed in the way of supplies and provisions.[7] Spain was learning a lesson, even though slowly. One of the friars, Fray Padre Antonio de la Ascensión, became chronicler of the expedition and provided posterity with one of the more interesting early descriptions of California and its peoples.

Sailing out of Acapulco, the ships headed along the Mexican coast until they turned westward toward the peninsula at Mazatlán. Headwinds stalled their progress in crossing the Gulf and along the outer side of the California peninsula, with the result that it was November before they reached San Diego Bay. It was this expedition which so christened that bay and port, and also a number of other California points. "On the twelfth day of the said month [November], which was the day of the glorious San Diego, the general, admiral, religious, captains, ensigns, and almost all of the men went ashore. A hut was built and mass said in celebration of the feast of Señor San Diego." With the priests on board it was possible frequently to celebrate the feast days of the saints commemorated in the calendar of November and December, and not infrequently their names were attached to sites where this took place. This accounts for Catalina Island being named for Santa Catalina, or Catherine of Alexandria (November 25), and the range of mountains, Santa Lucía, for the virgin Saint Lucy (December 13).

The Bay of Monterrey (in this instance the viceroy won the nod) was reached on December 14 and explored carefully during the next days. The reports were glowing:

> . . . we found ourselves to be in the best port that could be desired, for besides being sheltered from the winds, it has many pines for masts and yards, and live oaks and white oaks, and water in great quantity, all near the shore.

And after the landing party proceeded inland, the rhapsody continued:

> The land is fertile, with a climate and soil like those of Castile; there is much wild game, such as harts, like young bulls, deer, buffalo, very large bears, rabbits, hares, and many other animals, and many game birds, such as geese, partridges, quail, crane, ducks, vultures, and many kinds of birds. . . . The land is thickly populated with numberless Indians. . . . They appeared to be a gentle and peaceable people.[8]

The bay was named, as mentioned, for the viceroy. The familiar name of Carmel, attached to the little river of the southern headland, recalls the fact that three Carmelites were the chaplains of the expedition. Today this name does seem out of place in what most people think of quite exclusively as Franciscan-land.

There is little need for surprise that succeeding generations of Spaniards on reading such a glowing description should have dreamed of the Bay of Monterey as the ideal spot for the California settlement. Later parts of the Borderland story will show the impact of the Ascensión-Vizcaíno report.

By the time of the sojourn around Monterey the expedition had been out over seven months, and many of the men were sick. A council of the leadership decided to send one of the ships back with the invalids, along with a preliminary report; the other two would explore farther up the coast. This division was made early in January 1603.

Vizcaíno then headed north and managed to reach Cape Mendocino. At this point he felt that he had fulfilled his commission. The men were weak, the weather was consistently harsh, and the frigate, the smaller of the two boats, had become separated from the *San Diego* and was feared lost. The only sound decision seemed to be to turn back, lagging when possible in the hope that the little *Tres Reyes*, if not actually lost, might catch up. The party had little enthusiasm for further exploring on the homebound run. The *San Diego* made Acapulco on March 26. The frigate was already in Navidad, and had been there for almost a month; but its crew was so badly crippled that there was no attempt to sail the ship down coast to Acapulco. The Vizcaíno party, on arriving at the home port, was grieved to learn that very many of their companions on the "admiral's ship," which had preceded them, died before reaching Acapulco and medical assistance. And it was not until they had gone on to the viceregal capital in May that they received the heartening news of the safety of the men on the *Tres Reyes*.

The Vizcaíno expedition closes the first chapter in the Alta California story. As of 1603 the outer coast of the continent was fairly well mapped. Two ports had been thoroughly explored. That of San Diego had been known since the days of Cabrillo; that of Monterey was a new addition to the Spaniards' California geography. Once again the sailors had failed to uncover the real prize on the California coast, the Bay of San Francisco, *the* port and harbor. Vizcaíno had done a highly creditable job; the next move was up to the crown and its Council of the Indies. California was ready.

Fray Antonio de la Ascensión, in his *Brief Report*, written in 1620, strongly urged royal action; he also outlined an elaborate plan for the conversion of the Indians.[9] But long before that date the occupation of Alta California had become, temporarily at least, a dead issue. The pirate threat seemed to dissipate; and there was no wealthy private individual clamoring for permission to gamble his fortune on a California enterprise. The crown, already embarked on an austerity program, was not inclined to make the necessary outlay. During the next century and a half, the next 166 years to be more exact, the Spaniards knew that California was there, considered it theirs, but did nothing about it. In fact, no record has been found to show any Spanish vessel putting in to the California coast during those 166 years. The Manila Galleons continued to ply along the sea-lanes, homebound to Acapulco; but California interested them not at all.

Although they may not have realized it, the Spaniards were very effectively moving along the "long road to California" from 1591 onward. The connection between the west coast of Mexico and California was, probably, much less evident to the men of the seventeenth century than it is to later generations enjoying the advantage of hindsight and historical perspective.

From such a vantage point in time and against a background of forty-odd years of study and research in the history of the Spanish Borderlands, Herbert E. Bolton, toward the end of his long career (1947), described the Spanish northward movement as a three-pronged advance up as many corridors.[10] The middle arm went more or less directly north from New Spain's capital, first onto the Mesa Central and then, with a long jump forward, into New Mexico, whence the frontier looked out on the Plains and toward mid-continent. Progress on the right flank, in time, fanned into Texas. On the left, the frontier moved north along the western face of the Sierra Madre Occidental, up the "west coast corridor," through Sinaloa and Sonora, into Arizona, joined with another northward-moving line on the peninsula, and went on to California and the Golden Gate. The "long road to California" lay up this west-coast corridor.

By the last years of the sixteenth century the far northward thrust up the middle corridor had carried the outer edge of the frontier into New Mexico. There were still hundreds of untenanted miles between the mining frontier of north central Mexico and the distant outpost at Santa Fe, but in time some of that territory would be filled in. The advance on the left flank, up the western corridor, was more orderly and continuous.

The western slope of the Sierra Madre was not an unknown region in the last decade of the sixteenth century. Years before it had become something of a more or less well-traveled highway. The men of Cortés were at its southern end in the days immediately following the conquest—Cristóbal de Olid in Michoacan, in the land of the Tarascans, and Francisco Buenaventura into Jalisco. Next, Nuño de Guzmán and his ruffians went beyond Jalisco and into Sinaloa; they founded Culiacán in 1531 and explored farther north.

The next Spaniards in the west-coast corridor came down from the north—Cabeza de Vaca and his three travel-worn companions. Their stories, as has been noted, gave new life to the myth of the Seven Golden Cities. Fray Marcos went up the corridor and thought that he saw the cities from a distance. Coronado and his band hurried up with great expectations but returned disappointed (in 1542).

For the next several decades, from the late 1540s forward, Spanish energies shifted eastward. The day of the mining frontier dawned with the discovery and opening of the silver veins at Zacatecas. The eastern slope of the Sierra Madre and the Mesa Central were quickly pockmarked with the diggings. There was some prospecting on the western slope, but it was regularly unrewarding. By 1562 there were enough Spaniards and enough activity in the north to warrant the erection of a new province and the appointment of Francisco de Ibarra as its governor.[11] Nueva Vizcaya was cut off from Nueva Galicia, which was ceasing to be the frontier. In the middle corridor Durango became the northern capital.

Since his province was not bounded on the west by the Sierra, Ibarra crossed the mountains and spent several years in the later 1560s exploring and trying to develop the western slope. The Indians were troublesome— the Yaqui would continue that attitude. He found no mines; silver and gold were discovered in the west-coast corridor only at a later date. He brought in the Franciscans to establish missions, but they enjoyed slight success. Far beyond Guzmán's Culiacán, he built the outpost of San Juan, on the Río Fuerte. But it had to be relocated farther south, on the Río Petatlán or Sinaloa, and became San Felipe. By 1591 there was a question in the minds of many of the frontiersmen whether it and the area beyond Culiacán was worth holding or, even, could be held.

But that year, 1591, proved to be a turning point in the history of the western corridor. Two Jesuits, Gonzalo de Tapia and Martín Pérez, came up to the Villa de San Felipe, sent there by the new governor of Nueva Vizcaya, Rodrigo del Río y Losa, former lieutenant of Ibarra in the north. The Jesuits had arrived in New Spain in 1572. Though they came with the intent of working for the conversion of the Indians, their efforts were side-tracked for almost two decades, by official pressures, into educational and pastoral work primarily for the Spaniards.[12] As the years slipped by, many of the Black Robes, especially some of their young men, were chafing under these restrictions on their apostolic zeal and enthusiasm. They wanted a more dangerous brand of apostolic opportunities. Finally, their voices prevailed; Jesuit superiors negotiated with the viceroy, who left the choice of mission field to his governor of Nueva Vizcaya. Talk of New Mexico was rife on the northern frontier. Tapia would have jumped at that assignment; but Río y Losa, recently back from a tour of his province which had taken him across the Sierra, felt that Sinaloa needed help, and immediately. And so Tapia and Pérez went off to that land on the western slope.[13]

Beyond Culiacán, the land between the Sierra Madre and the Gulf of California was crossed by five rivers, tumbling down from the mountains and smoothing out as they reached the plain and ran toward the Gulf: the Petatlán or Sinaloa, the Fuerte, the Mayo, the Yaqui, and the Sonora. These rivers and the valleys they formed were to make possible a quite orderly advance of the frontier. One valley after another was opened, missionized, and readied for civilian occupation. The first three valleys (those of the Sinaloa, the Fuerte, and the Mayo) ran almost parallel to one another in a southwesterly direction. The fourth, that of the Yaqui, whose many tributaries created as many smaller valleys, was physiographically less orderly. And the fifth valley, that of the Sonora, ran from north to south rather than from east to west. In the last two valleys the frontier developed like so many fingers, pushed in between the spurs of the Sierra.

Beyond the lower Yaqui Valley the line of advance tended to pull the frontier inland and away from the Gulf coast.

Again, up to the lower Yaqui the padres generally chose a diffusion point in the valley and branched out upstream and down, until the Christian-

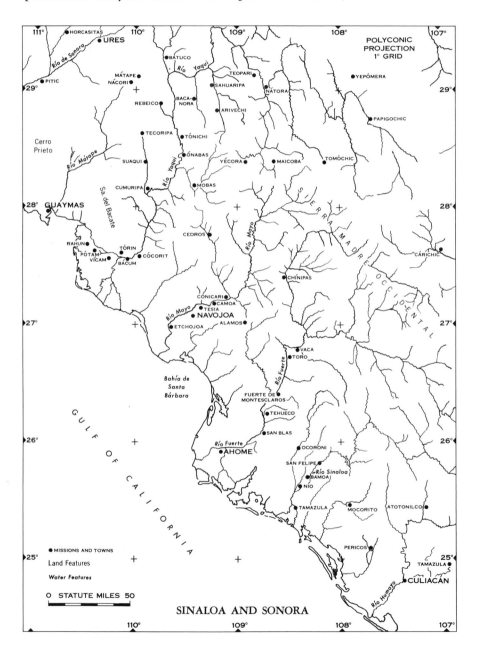

SINALOA AND SONORA

ization-civilization process was well under way. Then they went on to the next valley, whose Indians by that time were quite regularly disposed to receive the missionaries and ready to cooperate.

Tapia and Pérez, whose coming gave heart to the few Sinaloa pioneers, established their headquarters at the Villa de San Felipe, on the Río Sinaloa. From the Villa they began to branch out on their missionary excursions. Even though Tapia was brutally murdered (1594) by a native medicine man who saw his influence among his people threatened, the work did not stop.[14] Reinforcements were actually moving out of Culiacán when the distressing news reached the new padres. One of this second pair of Black Robes into the west coast corridor was the indefatigable Pedro Méndez, destined to pioneer on several of the rivers in the next decades.[15] And these two were only the first in a long line of missionary frontiersmen who came up to carry on the work of Christianization and civilization on the western slope.

By 1604 things were in readiness for the first forward advance, into the valley of the Río Fuerte. The viceroy's permission obtained, a *sine qua non* for each forward move on a Spanish frontier, Méndez, now with field experience of ten years behind him, pushed northward with a single young companion. In 1614 Méndez again was in the van as the line edged up to the Río Mayo.

The Indians of that Mayo valley had been well disposed for some years and were constantly urging the padres to move in among them. Frontier authorities had been reluctant to sanction this advance too quickly. The Yaqui from the fourth valley, whose elders had made trouble for Ibarra years before, had let it be known that they would not view any Spanish penetration among their neighbors to the south with tolerance. The frontier captain, Don Diego Martínez de Hurdaide, had more than a little trouble teaching these strong-minded Yaqui to respect Spanish power.[16] Three times between 1607 and 1609 he had faced them and each time he and his men were bested in battle and had to pull back to the new fort which was being erected on the Río Fuerte; it would carry the name of the current viceroy, Montesclaros.

As Hurdaide was preparing still another foray into Yaqui-land, circumstances played into his hands and he was astute enough to make the best of his chance good fortune. Since the explorations of Vizcaíno in the Gulf, prior to his reconnaissance of Alta California, the Spaniards had been much interested in the pearl fisheries which he had uncovered. There had been much activity in the southern areas of the Gulf, but in 1610 ships appeared along the Yaqui coast. Aware of Hurdaide's preparations for a new campaign and fearing that "El Capitán" was about to resort to two-dimensional warfare against them, the Yaqui concluded that it would be prudent to make friends with their white foes. They sent a delegation to the Río Fuerte to talk peace, to promise cooperation, and even to ask for missionaries. Hurdaide received them well but gave no long-term assurances. Instead, he bade them show by their subsequent actions that they meant what they said. However, he was sufficiently assured that he was willing to allow the padres to prepare for a move to the next river, the Mayo.

This Yaqui episode points up one significant aspect of the Spanish frontier, the importance of the presence of the military. The garrisons, in the seventeenth century, were never large, but the dozen or so soldiers were necessary. Obviously, there was the matter of defense; later, when the frontier had edged within striking distance of the Apache, this defense aspect was the prime consideration connected with the presidios. Not to be overlooked, however, is the police aspect of the frontier garrison. The presence of the presidials helped to hold malcontents in check, forcing them to think twice before stirring up trouble among their own people or among neighbors. The soldiers too were used as sort of truant officers, to track down fugitives from the missions who might go off to pagan tribes and rally them into an effective opposition. The initial brush with the Yaqui had come when Hurdaide went north in pursuit of runaways and found the Yaqui unwilling to surrender the refugees. The mission would never have been as effective and efficient a frontier institution without the assistance of the little garrisons, even though the missionaries were often at odds with the captain and his men over questions of jurisdiction and in the matter of morals.

The character of the frontier captain in many instances had much to do with determining the success of mission enterprise. The Jesuits were fortunate in a number of instances as they pushed northward along the western corridor; they had their fair share of outstanding men working with them. Hurdaide was both capable and cooperative. The same would be true of Juan Mateo Mange, friend and companion of Kino, at a later date. And in the eighteenth century the two Anzas, father and son, were remarkable individuals. All of these will come into this story in their own time.

A forceful captain could keep his men in line; a permissive leader could contribute significantly to their human lapses and aberrations and thus greatly weaken or even invalidate the Christianization effort by very unchristian example. In the early days on any frontier, besides the missionaries and a few prospectors or an even less frequent trader, the soldier was the only other Spaniard whom the Indians knew. The Indians were frequently conditioned in their response both to Christianity and the white man's civilization by the character and the actions of the presidial. His personal life and habits could be a powerful help or an equally potent hindrance to the whole frontier process. The Spanish image was regularly made or marred by him. The soldier on the Anglo-American frontier, at least in its earlier period, was a much less powerful factor in the success of the expansionist surge westward.

The advance to the Río Mayo came in 1614. Success was immediate among the Indians of that valley. So much so that three years later the line went northward into Yaqui-land. This time Padre Méndez was not the pioneer. One of the leaders was a younger man, Andrés Pérez de Ribas, destined to be the historian of the "Four Rivers"; later his frontier experience could be put to further good use when he became the Father Provincial for all New Spain. His *Historia de los triumphos de nuestra santa fee,* published in Madrid in 1645, is a delightful chronicle and one of the chief historical sources for those first Jesuit decades on the west-coast frontier.

Arrived at the Río Yaqui, the missionary frontiersmen had to face some new geographic problems as well as certain personal difficulties. In the first category was the fact that the Río Yaqui was not one of those pleasantly uncomplicated watercourses which rose in the Sierra and then flowed quietly and orderly westward and southwestward into the Gulf. Its lower reaches conformed to this pattern, but higher up it diverged therefrom in most disconcerting fashion. There a number of tributaries which made up the middle and upper Yaqui system rose in the Sierra but ran in almost helter-skelter lack of order to join the main stream. In the many little valleys thus created were settled two large Indian families, the Pima Bajo and the Opata. Geography, first, would make it difficult to reach them and, secondly, after doing so, to integrate them into the expanding missionary line of advance. Communications loomed as a major physical problem.

The same communications problem was bound to have other byproducts. Beyond the bend of the Yaqui, with the valleys running north to south, the future Pima and Opata missions might well become disastrously isolated and extremely difficult of access. Some of these might soon be more than a hundred leagues distant from Jesuit frontier headquarters at the Villa de San Felipe, back on the Río Sinaloa. Such a gap, it was foreseen, might well create serious administrative problems.

In a close-knit organization—and the Jesuit society was precisely that—it was essential to good government and general efficiency that superiors be in reasonably ready contact with the men in the field. These, in turn, must have easy access to superiors. That both of these things might soon be lost became painfully evident to all by 1620, and a source of great concern. The missions on the lower Yaqui were better than fifty leagues from San Felipe. The padres were already moving in among the Nebome, the first of the Pima nations; and invitations from other Pima nations and from the Opata farther up the Yaqui system were multiplying and could not be unanswered for long. And across the ranges, to the west, was Sonora and its Indians, a dream of the future.

In the year 1620 Jesuit superiors divided the expanding mission field and erected a new *rectorado* in the north, separating the Río Mayo and the Río Yaqui from the jurisdiction of the Padre Rector at San Felipe. Padre Cristóbal de Villalta was named the superior of this Rectorado de San Ignacio with headquarters at Tórin on the lower Yaqui. In time several more *rectorados* would be established as the frontier moved farther and farther northward. In 1620 there were 14 *partidos,* or mission districts, on the western slope, comprising 55 individual missions and serving some 80,000 baptized Indians. Figures for 1624 show 31 Jesuits west of the Sierra, 4 of them being lay brothers and the remainder priests.[17] Three years later there were 13 padres working on the Mayo and the Yaqui, the number amply justifying the division of 1620.[18]

One very definite advantage that flowed from this division was that it made possible the continuation of the semiannual gatherings of the missionaries at the headquarters station of their immediate superior. This practice, which had been in vogue since the Jesuits came to the western slope, had many advantages. These get-togethers gave the men in the field a chance to sit down with their brethren for a few days and to enjoy a companionship that was lacking farther afield. The padres were rarely numerous enough that they could be sent in pairs, with the result that loneliness became a severe problem. In this respect all frontiers had a common denominator; but it was even more pronounced in the case of celibate pioneers. These gatherings offered an opportunity to compare notes, to share experiences of success and failure, and to find a possible solution to universal difficulties. Regularly, they were the only occasions when the individual padre could confer with his superior. Like each of them, the superior had a mission of his own—the so-called *partido*; the main station, or *cabecera*, was his place of normal residence; in the vicinity were possibly two or more *visitas*, inchoate missions, which he visited every so often. He was ordinarily so busy with his own work that he had little, if any time, to make the rounds. Later, an official known as the *visitador de misiones* was added to the administrative hierarchy, who was left free to circulate. He was a veteran who could help to initiate the newcomers and could share with the older hands like himself. As is evident the mission frontier was no haphazard, hit-and-miss system; careful planning and constant supervision were universal notes of the northward movement, at all levels, ecclesiastical as well as civil.

The decade of the 1620s in the west-coast corridor saw considerable expansion and in many ways was historically quite eventful. Old figures passed from the frontier scene. Martín Pérez, of the original pioneer pair, and Captain Hurdaide were taken by death. Pérez de Ribas was called back to Mexico City to assume the burdens of administration as the Padre Provincial. The indomitable Padre Méndez, however, came back, after a short-lived retirement in the capital; the old "war horse" could not accommodate himself to the quiet life. He stayed for a time in one of the better-established missions on the lower Yaqui, then because this was not enough of a challenge, he went among the Sisibotari on the Río Sahuaripa, far up the Yaqui system. New men appeared in the north to become familiar figures in the Pimería Baja and the Opatería, both of them opening up in those years. To that mission field went Francisco Oliñano; Diego Vandersipe, a Fleming who slipped through the royal ban on foreigners; Michael Wading, who managed to hide his Irish origin under the name of Miguel Godínez; the colorful and scrappy Basque Martín Azpilcueta, and others.

Then came a period, through most of the 1630s, when the men in the field had all they could do to take care of their converts, new and old, and when superiors had no fresh recruits to send to the frontier. There was a slowdown in the pace of the advance. Such periods, while discouraging to the expansion-minded, did give the padres a chance to consolidate gains and to deepen the influence of the Christianization-civilization process. Only in the theological sense did baptism make Christians of the Indians.

In this second quarter of the seventeenth century the lower, or southern, end of the western corridor was experiencing its first real flow of settlers. This continued, slowly but steadily, through the "middle half" of the century. By 1678 Sinaloa had some 600 Spanish families and many mestizo folk, and the old Villa de San Felipe could boast of a population that topped 1200, by a few souls.[19] Here in Sinaloa the first phase of the frontier process had been completed: the explorers had mapped the country, and the missionaries had moved in to win and civilize the Indians. The final phase, civilian occupation, could now get under way. The trader, the rancher, the farmer found it safe to come up. The trader often had a ready-made market, for the padres had introduced the Indians to the white man's goods. Even more frequently, the rancher found that his industry had been pioneered by the missionaries. Many of the Indians had begun to learn techniques of animal care and breeding and were prepared to serve him as ranch hands; the missionaries, too, had acquainted their charges with European food and draft animals, so that the rancher had a ready-made market. The farmer could serve his fellows and the mestizos who were engaged in other economic pursuits. Some of the settlers or civilians were engaged in mining, though not a heavy proportion, since the mines on the western slope were neither many nor rich; these men, however, helped to furnish a market for the farmer and his products. Often on the farther edge of the frontier the Indians of the missions sold surplus foodstuffs to the miners.

Another aspect of the advance of settler-frontier civilization showed in the area of ecclesiastical organization. As the missionaries finished their preliminary Christianization work and moved on to a farther frontier, their places were taken by the diocesan clergy who established permanent parishes for the civilians and the "civilized" Indians. The erection of the first diocese on the western slope was still years into the future; but in the 1620s, in recognition of the expanding frontier, a new northern diocese, that of Guadiana or Durango, was cut off from the jurisdiction of Guadalajara. Toward the end of that decade Bishop Gonzalo de Hermosillo visited Sinaloa, was amazed and consoled by advances made, confirmed some 11,000 Indians, and had ample evidence that the nearer frontier was ready, or soon would be, for the coming of his own priests, so that the missionaries might be released for work farther north.[20]

The frontier which had edged up the Yaqui system took a swing slightly to the northwest when, in 1638, Padre Lorenzo de Cárdenas moved into the fifth valley, that of the Río Sonora.[21] In the next year Bartolomé

Castaño and Pedro Pantoja joined him in this new field. The Opatería and Pimería Alta were destined to be among the more successful of Jesuit enterprises in New Spain—in fact, their work there compared favorably with successes anywhere in the Americas.

The Opata, particularly, proved to be a most cooperative people. They did not equal the Pueblo tribes in their state of cultural achievement; but they were well ahead of most of the nations of the western slope. They were to a large degree a farmer folk, living in well-populated *rancherías*, making good use of the fertile soil of their little valleys, and quite skilled in the practice of irrigation. The pioneer missionary among them was thus relieved of the necessity of spending many of his first years trying to round them up and bring them into villages, as was so frequently the case with other peoples with whom his brethren had been working in decades past. The padres, almost immediately, were able to help them improve and diversify their crops, to teach them more effective irrigation techniques, to introduce livestock and new manual skills. Already collected and their food supply reasonably assured, they could be ready to receive instruction as Christians and potential citizens of the viceroyalty.

A report of Pantoja, in 1646, gives a rather complete picture of the Sonora missions toward the end of their first decade.[22] Pantoja, the *padre rector*, was in charge of Babiácora and Aconchi on the Río Sonora. Gerónimo de la Canal had just opened sites farther upstream, at Guépaca and Banámichi. Below the gorge of the river was Ures, the site or near the site of the Pueblo de los Corazones, mentioned by both Cabeza de Vaca and several of the chroniclers of the Coronado expedition. At this date the Black Robes were already edging to the west, at Nacámeri, and were making initial, though not too promising, contacts with the wild Seri along the Gulf coast, who would give the Spaniards so much trouble in a later day. In the first valley to the east of the Valle de Sonora, that of the Río Montezuma, the missions of Oposura and Cúmupas were already well established. Over one more ridge (Sonora's ranges presented something of a washboard effect, with valleys running parallel from north to south) a stray Fleming, who had changed his name from Van der Veken to Del Río, was getting ready to push up the Río Babispe from his mission at Guásabas. As Pantoja completed his swing through his *rectorado*—another new administrative division had been established in the farther north—he looked in on the two Batuc pueblos on the lower Montezuma, and then crossed the ridge to Mátape. He suggested that this last village might be an ideal spot for a Sonora presidio.

The next years saw further expansion. Sinoquipe, Arispe, and Chinapa were founded higher up the Valle de Sonora. The second of these, Arispe, was to play a rather important role in later Borderlands history: for a time it would be the headquarters of the Comandante of the Provincias Internas (see Chapter 10) and, in the middle 1770s, it was to be the staging ground for the settler group which founded San Francisco. The Jesuits also moved up the San Miguel Valley, to the west of the Valle de Sonora, pushing as far as Cucurpe. In the northeast, high in the Sierra, other Black Robes were opening missions among the Suma, at Babispe and Baceraca.

Another enlightening survey of this northwestern frontier was in the 1678 report of the Jesuit *visitador-general*, Padre Juan Órtiz Zapata.[23] Zapata came north as the representative of the Jesuit superior of New Spain, who, personally, was unable to visit his men and their works. Zapata was commissioned to visit and report on all the northern missions, on both sides of the Sierra Madre. On the eastern slope his Jesuit brethren had gone far beyond their earlier missions among the Tepehuan, to the north of Durango, and were already into the high country of western Chihuahua, among the Tarahumara. On the western slope there were two *rectorados* in Sonora comprising, in all, 50 villages and serving over 20,000 Indian converts. The recent decades, it was noted, had been primarily a time of consolidation. Existing missions had been strengthened, so that new forward thrusts might be possible when superiors could furnish added manpower.

The first trickle of non-Spanish Jesuits into New Spain toward the end of the seventeenth century was to make such new manpower available. Down to the 1660s the crown had been adamant in enforcing its prohibition

San Miguel de Oposura on the Río Montezuma. (Charles W. Polzer, S.J.)

against foreigners, even religious. But with the rapidly expanding mission frontiers and a marked decline in Spaniards available, the exclusion policy had to be revised. Toward the end of the third quarter of the century Jesuits from the northern countries of Europe, meaning generally the lands of the Holy Roman Empire, began to make their appearance on the mission rosters throughout the Indies.

Zapata also reported that the economic life of the missions had been greatly strengthened by the introduction of new cereals, such as wheat, which tended to flourish in Sonora's fertile soil, and also by the extension of the cattle industry to the north. This last development was one of the important by-products of the Spanish northward movement in general. Quite regularly the missionaries were the pioneer cattlemen of the frontier. As they sought to reduce their neophytes to a sedentary existence, which they considered an absolute prerequisite to successful Christianization, the padres recognized that they would have to provide a substitute for the meat which the Indians had formerly obtained by their hunting. The chase could be very disruptive in the routine of mission life, taking the men away for weeks, reacquainting them with their old freedom, exposing them, perhaps, to the baleful influences of nonmissionized neighbors. The introduction of European food animals, especially cattle, seemed to the missionaries the natural solution. From their early days on the western slope the Jesuits had bred large herds of cattle on the hacienda connected with their Sinaloa head-quarters, at San Felipe. Then it became standard procedure to portion out a number of the animals, for food and for breeding purposes, to each new mission as it was established. Sometimes old converts were sent north with the padre to help him develop his own herd and to teach his Indians the techniques of stock-raising. The padres, with proper modifications, worked on the old theory that "the way to a man's heart is through his stomach"; they substituted soul for "heart" and proceeded. They were gratified by the results and quickly learned that the well-fed mission Indian was both a cooperative convert and a highly persuasive advertising agent for Christianity among his not yet "reduced" fellows.

As the seventeenth century drew to a close, the padres and the presidials were not the only Spaniards on the northwestern frontier. There were some civilians in Sonora; exact numbers, however, are not available. The civilians left relatively few records behind them. They appear now and then in an official report, such as that of Don Gabriel de Isturiz, who, as *visitador* for the governor of Nueva Vizcaya, did a tour of inspection on the western slope, covering the "Provinces of Sinaloa, San Ildefonso de Ostimuri, and Sonora."[24]

Don Gabriel spent nine months on his tour out of his home base of Parral, in 1685–1686. In Sonora he visited the missions, looked in on the *estancias*, some of which to the south of the Río Yaqui were extensive and prosperous, and paid particular attention to the mining centers. He noted

Padre Eusebio Francisco Kino.
Statue by Julián Martínez.
(Charles W. Polzer, S.J.)

four of them. The Real de San Miguel, off the right bank of the Yaqui, in whose district four mines were being worked, was his first stop. Next he went far up the Río Sonora to the Real de Bacanuche, to record three mines in operation. Bacanuche had three *tiendas*, or stores. Thence he swung over to the valley of the Río Montezuma, to check the Real de Nacozari off its left bank and the Real de San Juan Bautista, farther downstream and toward the hills on the right bank. Nacozari could support five *tiendas*. And moving down the Río Montezuma and heading for the Real de San Ildefonso de Ostimuri, he noted several other smaller mining camps. He also noted the presence of at least a few African slaves in the north, most of them domestic servants or hands on the ranches, but some were workers in the mines. Although uncounted and most often nameless, civilians were beginning to find this far frontier safe for occupancy.

With the seventeenth century waning, the northwestern frontier was ready for the arrival of the great man who was to carry its outer edge beyond the Pimería and into a new Borderland, Arizona. Eusebio Francisco Kino was one of those occasional remarkable individuals who leave their indelible

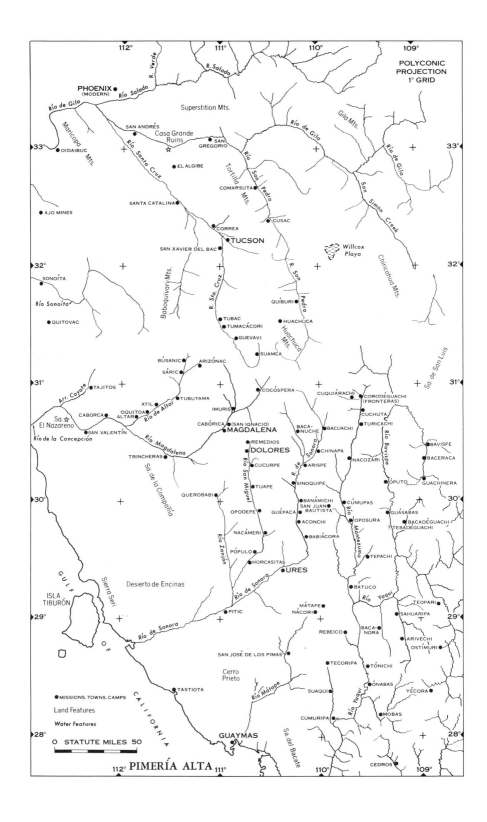

POLYCONIC
PROJECTION
1° GRID

112°   111°   110°   109°

PHOENIX ●
(MODERN)   Río Salado   R. Verde   R. Salado   Gila Mts.

Río de Gila   Superstition Mts.   Río de Gila   Río de Gila

33°   Maricopa Mts.   Río Santa Cruz   SAN ANDRÉS ●   Casa Grande Ruins ☆   ● SAN GREGORIO   33°

● OIDAIBUC   ● EL ALGIBE   San Pedro   San Simon Creek

● AJO MINES   SANTA CATALINA ●   COMARSUTA ●   Tortilla Mts.

SAN XAVIER DEL BAC ●   CORREA ●   ● CUSAC   Chiricahua Mts.

TUCSON ●   Willcox Playa

32°   SONOÍTA ●   R. Sta. Cruz   R. San Pedro   32°

Río Sonoíta   QUIBURI ●

● QUITOVAC   TUBAC ●   ● HUACHUCA   Sa. de San Luis

Baboquivari Mts.   TUMACÁCORI ●   GUEVAVI ●   SUAMCA ●   Huachuca Mts.

BÚSANIC ●   ARIZÓNAC ●

31°   Arr. Coyote   TAJITOS ●   SÁRIC ●   COCÓSPERA ●   CUQUIÁRACHI ●   CORODÉGUACHI ● (FRONTERAS)   31°

ATIL ●   TUBUTAMA ●   IMURIS ●   CUCHUTA ●

Sa.   OQUITOA ●   Río de Altar   BACA- NUCHE ●   BACUACHI ●   TURICACHI ●   Río Bavispe

El Nazareno ☆   CABORCA ●   ALTAR ●   CABÓRICA ● (SAN IGNACIO)   BAVISPE ●

● SAN VALENTÍN   MAGDALENA ●   CHINAPA ●   NACOZARI ●   BACERACA ●

Río de la Concepción   REMEDIOS ●   DOLORES ●   ● ARISPE   ● ÓPUTO   GUACHINERA ●

TRINCHERAS ●   CUCURPE ●   Río de Sonora

Sa. de la Compañía   Río San Miguel   TUAPE ●   SINOQUIPE ●

30°   QUEROBABI ●   BANÁMICHI ●   CÚMUPAS ●   30°

OPODEPE ●   GUÉPACA ●   SAN JUAN BAUTISTA ●   GUÁSABAS ●

NACÁMERI ●   ACONCHI ●   Río Moctezuma   OPOSURA ●   BACADÉGUACHI ●   ? TEBADÉGUACHI ●

Río Zanjón   PÓPULO ●   BABIÁCORA ●   TEPACHI ●

HORCASITAS ●   URES ●

Desierto de Encinas   BATUCO ●   TEOPARI ●

29°   ISLA TIBURÓN   Sierra Seri   Río de Sonora   ● PITIC   MÁTAPE ●   SAHUARIPA ●   29°

NÁCORI ●   BACA- NORA ●   ARIVECHI ●

REBEICO ●   OSTÍMURI ●

Cerro Prieto   SAN JOSÉ DE LOS PIMAS ●   TECORIPA ●   TÓNICHI ●

TASTIOTA ●   Río Mátape   SUAQUI ●   ● ÓNABAS   YÉCORA ●

● MISSIONS, TOWNS, CAMPS
Land Features
Water Features

28°   0   STATUTE MILES   50   CUMURIPA ●   Río Yaqui   MOBAS ●   28°

GUAYMAS   Sa. del Bacate   CEDROS ●

112° PIMERÍA ALTA 111°   110°   109°

stamp on the history of a nation or an area.[25] Foreigner though he was—a Tyrolese by birth, and a "German" by education among the German Jesuits of the Upper German Province—he became very much the prototype of the missionary frontiersman of New Spain.

Kino had been in America half a dozen years before his assignment to Sonora. Initially he had participated in Atondo's unsuccessful attempt (1683–1686) to establish Spaniards permanently on the California peninsula. His California experience left him with memories and unfulfilled apostolic ambitions that had an important bearing on much of his subsequent activity. With the California project suspended, temporarily at least for lack of royal financial support, Kino's provincial superior in the viceregal capital assigned him to the northwestern frontier, where he arrived early in 1687. The *padre visitador* at Oposura, Manuel Gonzales, opened to him the vast territory of Pimería Alta, which lay to the north and west of the then missionized frontier—the northwestern section of the present Mexican State of Sonora and the southwestern quarter of the State of Arizona. Here was the homeland of the upper Pima, the Pápago, the Sobaipuri, with the various Yuman peoples beyond, the Yuma, the Cocomaricopa, the Cocopa, and others. From his base, set about fifteen miles up the Río San Miguel from the mission outpost at Cucurpe and named Nuestra Señora de los Dolores, during the next quarter century he would range *his* valleys—the Santa Cruz and the San Pedro running into the Gila, the Gila itself heading toward the junction with the Colorado of the West, the Magdalena and the Altar moving westward toward the Gulf of California. In those twenty-odd years he spent almost as much time away from Dolores as he did there. But he was purposefully restless.

Within half a dozen years after arrival he had seen sizable sections of each of his valleys and founded a line of missions in the Altar and the Magdalena and farther up the San Miguel from Dolores. In 1695 the Pima, at least a few of them, went on the warpath, killed Padre Francisco Xavier Saeta at Caborca, and had the frontier trembling. After helping powerfully to restore peace, Kino went off, on a 1200-mile journey by horseback, to Mexico City to report to uneasy officials far away and to prevent a rumored shutdown in the Pimería. Such trips he took in his stride. A few years later, in 1700, he opened a mission station at San Xavier del Bac; next he set up Tumacácori and Guevavi as intermediate points in the Santa Cruz Valley; all three of these within the present limits of the United States, in southern Arizona.

Exploring and mapping the Pimería, the Papaguería, and beyond were among his great contributions. Even more important was his discovery after repeated expeditions to the Gila and down the Colorado that California could be reached by land, that it was in reality a peninsula, not an island, as the Spaniards had believed for more than a century. This discovery gave new meaning to the whole push up the western slope. Of a sudden the line

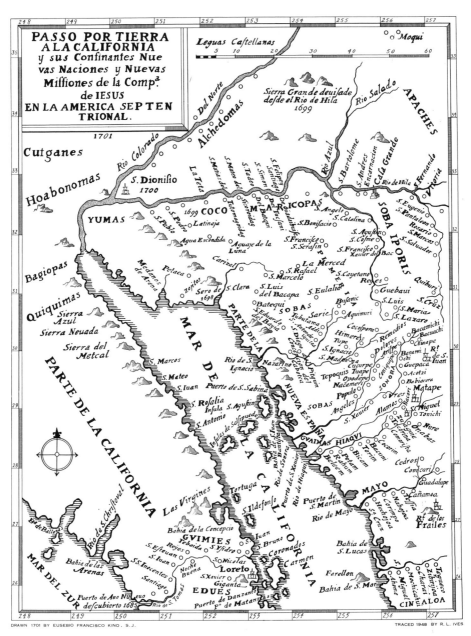

"Passo por Tierra," Kino's map of 1701.

of Jesuit missions through Sinaloa and Sonora and into the future Arizona was turned into so many hitherto unrecognized steps along the "long road to California."

Kino had come to Sonora believing that California was the large island which the men of his time held it to be. In the late 1690s he had encouraged Juan María Salvatierra to press for a reopening of the mission venture in Baja California, promising to make Sonora the supply base for the enterprise. He looked for a convenient port in the north and actually was assembling timber at Caborca for a supply boat. Then a seemingly small circumstance opened a new train of thought. On a trip to the lower Gila in 1699 Yuma friends had given him a gift of blue shells. Shells such as these—they were abalone shells—he had seen back in 1685 on his trip to the Pacific shore of Baja California. The like he had not found through any of his contacts with the Gulf coast. Inquiries told him that these shells had come from the west. He concluded that they could only have come from the shores of the Pacific and that Yuma-land must be connected with that coast. Several more trips to the Gila and down the Colorado to the head of the Gulf gave him ample evidence to claim a land passage between his Sonora and Salvatierra's California—"*California no es isla, sino penisla*" he wrote in triumph and then began to rectify the American map.

Padre Kino has become known as the "padre on horseback." A biographer (Bolton) gives the following tally of his journeyings in the north:

> Not to count the minor and unrecorded journeys among his widely separated missions he made at least fourteen expeditions across the line into what is now Arizona. Six of them took him as far as Tumacácori, Fairbank, San Xavier del Bac, or Tucson. Six carried him to the Gila over five different routes. Twice he reached that stream by way of the Santa Cruz, returning once via Casa Grande, Sonóita, the Gulf of California, and Caborca. Once he went by way of the San Pedro, once from El Sáric across to the Gila below the Big Bend, and three times by way of Sonóita and the Camino del Diablo, along the Gila Range. Two of these expeditions carried him to Yuma and down the Colorado. Once he crossed that stream into California and finally he reached its mouth.
>
> East and west, between Sonóita and the eastern missions, he crossed southern Arizona several times and by various trails. In what is now Sonora he made at least half a dozen recorded journeys from Dolores to Caborca and the coast, three to the Santa Clara Mountain [Sierra del Pinacate] to view the head of the California Gulf, and two to the coast by then unknown routes south of the Altar River. This enumeration does not include his journey to Mexico, nor the numerous other trips to distant points in what is now Sonora, to see the superior mission authorities, or to drive cattle and purchase supplies.[26]

As much as an average of thirty miles a day was normal, and there were occasions when he even bettered that record. It is small wonder that he was the great geographer of northwestern New Spain.

One must further marvel at the extraordinary courage and durability of this man in his exploration activities. He made his many forays into the northern "wilderness" with little aid and few companions. Frontier captain Juan Mateo Mange was often with him. But only once, his Gila trip of 1697, was there anything approximating a party; this time Mange was along, with 22 soldiers and another officer. Occasionally a fellow Jesuit, or two, accompanied him; Salvatierra, Antonio Leal, Francisco Gonsalvo, Adamo Gilg, Manuel Gonzales were companions at one time or another. He always had a small band of his faithful Indian friends—not infrequently some of his ranch hands from Dolores—to look after the stock that he took along as mounts and food.

He and his Indians at Dolores were remarkable ranchmen. There are records of his having sent 115 head of cattle and about the same number of sheep to stock a ranch at the infant mission of Caborca. After he had founded San Xavier del Bac, in 1700, 1400 head of cattle were soon on the trail thither. And in that same year he rounded up another 700 for shipment across the Gulf to Padre Salvatierra in Baja California. He also encouraged his Sonora Indians to cultivate their fertile valleys more intensively; he was largely responsible for the spread of wheat culture there. Later observers noted the high incidence of the wheat tortilla in those parts, substituting for the less easily digestible corn tortilla so common elsewhere in New Spain.

Though not successful in the long run, Kino did what he could to build the Indians of his Pimería into the guardians of the northwestern frontier against the increasing pressures of the hostile raiders from the northeast. The Apache menace was developing, and the Jocome and the Jano were learning fast, too fast. After he was gone, the folk of Sonora came to recognize his power and his influence.

Kino died at the age of sixty-six while on a visit to one of his foundations, Santa María Magdalena de Buquivaba, the modern Magdalena de Kino, to which he had ridden to participate in the consecration of a new chapel to be dedicated to his great missionary patron, Francis Xavier. Shortly after he had finished saying Mass, he passed away in the arms of a frontier companion of a dozen and a half years, Padre Agustín Campos. The year was 1711.[27]

For some twenty years following Kino's death, the mission frontier in the west-coast corridor remained static. His former companions did not have the manpower to permit the advances he had planned.[28] Replacements were few, when they came at all. During those years the Jesuit superiors were channeling all their available men to the missions in Baja California. (The story of this peninsular enterprise will be told in a later chapter.)

New life returned to the Sonora-Arizona frontier in the 1730s. The new crop of Jesuits, rather predominantly North Europeans, would pick up the Kino plans. By that time Alta California was only some hundred miles and thirty-odd years away. But much would have happened in the Borderlands before the Spaniards took the last steps along that "long road to California," to make the Pacific Coast the last Borderland.

The west corridor story is an excellent example, among many possible in the broader spectrum of Spanish experience in both the American continents, to assess the importance of the mission as a frontier institution.[29] The mission served a dual purpose in the Spanish scheme of expansion. Other American frontiers had their characteristic pioneer agents and institutions; the Spaniards relied heavily, though not exclusively, on the mission and the missionary. The primary function of the friar or the padre was the spread of the Christian gospel; but he also became a powerful promoter of the white man's ways and his civilization. He brought the faith, and many other things besides. Not only did he come with new agricultural products; he also introduced improved techniques by which the Indian could increase the yield of old and familiar ones. The missionary brought his own white man's food and draft animals, to work a revolution in Indian life, economy, and society. Personally or through helpers, often the lay brothers or well-trained "old Christians," he taught his neophytes new building and architectural techniques; most of the mission churches in the west corridor, as well as elsewhere, rose with the aid of newly trained Indian labor. The missionary came, too, with education, both the basics of the three R's and instruction in the manual trades. The mission schools were never pretentious, but they did offer the natives a fundamental acquaintance with learning. Sometimes the missionary could and did build on native skills, but more often what he gave was very new to the Indians. The missionary was a Christianizer and a civilizer. In the van of the expansionist thrust he opened each new frontier, tamed it, and readied it for incorporation into the Spanish empire of the Indies. He was the pioneer and the frontiersman par excellence.

Most, if not all, of the Borderlands were mission frontiers. The mission was, perhaps, the most significant of all Spanish frontier institutions, even though it was by no means the only one.

◁ 5 ◁

The Far Northern Frontier in Danger, 1680-1700

*T*he thrust of the Spaniards far up the "middle corridor" of their north-ward advance into the Borderlands, to New Mexico, added a certain number of problems to those already present on their sixteenth-century frontier. At first their northward movement out of Mexico City had been a fairly orderly sort of advance along a rather well-defined line running from Gulf to Gulf. The conquistadores and their immediate successors had incorporated the near-northern territory up to a line which ran roughly from Pánuco on the east to Compostela on the west. They were still rather predominantly in lands the Aztec had dominated. Then came the discovery of mines on the north-central plateau, beyond that line and in the heart of the land of the Chichimeca, whom the Aztec had never succeeded in bringing under their imperial control. The rush of prospectors, miners, and supporting civilians into the region of the precious-metal strikes brought Spain face to face with her first real frontier problems—distance, rugged country, and most of all, untamed Indians, who had known no previous Indian masters and were not minded to bow, without a struggle, to another conquest-minded group.

The Indians proved particularly troublesome and the challenge which they raised continually baffling. After a first flash of resistance the Indians of the old Aztec empire had capitulated, at least externally, and offered little consistent opposition to the Spanish take-over. Accustomed as they were to the idea of service to native overlords and also to tribute-paying, they submitted to the change of masters, to the *encomienda* and *repartimiento* systems which the conquerors brought with them from the Islands. When the Spaniards moved north, they felt that such devices for the control and exploitation of the natives had universal applicability and that they were destined for the same universal acceptance by all the Indians. The Chichimeca, not so conditioned to ready service, quickly shook Spanish complacency and self-assurance.[1] The *encomienda*, and much less the *repartimiento*, did not work.

The second half of the sixteenth century in the near-north was often a time of bitter warfare. But the yield of the mines was so tempting that the Spaniards refused to be countered. Still they sought a solution to their frontier problems other than warfare which would be less expensive in terms of blood and treasure and less burdensome to the Spanish conscience.[2] It is really on this near-northern frontier that they began to use the mission as an alternate frontier agency of control.[3]

The Franciscans who had gone north with the pioneer miners kept suggesting that perhaps the missionary rather than the soldier held the key to the solution. As the mining frontier edged into the future Mexican states of Durango, San Luis Potosí, and the western edge of Nuevo León, the Franciscans were given their chance. Working out of their missionary colleges (provincial manpower and training centers) of Jalisco and Zacatecas, the friars established themselves in most of the important little centers as far north as Saltillo. They often brought up to the frontier with them colonies of Christianized Indians, particularly Tlascalans, to aid them in the Christianization-civilization work. But the Franciscans needed more than Christian Indians in order to keep up with the demands of the expanding frontier; they needed co-workers.

As the new century dawned help came north with the assignment of the Jesuits, not only to the western slope of the Sierra Madre, but to the eastern slope as well.[4] The prospects of being able in time to close the gap between the mining frontier of north-central Mexico and New Mexico brightened. The Franciscans, who had recently agreed to man the new missions in Pueblo-land, were willing to yield the eastern slope. This would allow the friars to shift manpower a bit more to the east, to the valleys and plains of the Río Conchos system, and put them more into the heart of the middle corridor.

The Jesuit enterprise along the face of the eastern slope was, in a sense, marginal to the advance up the middle corridor. Yet it is important in that it secured the left flank and thereby helped to close the gap. The Jesuit line of missions ran through the mountainous country of northern Durango up into southwestern Chihuahua.

Converting the Indians. From Pablo Beaumont, *Crónica de Mechoacan*. (Rare Manuscript Division, New York Public Library)

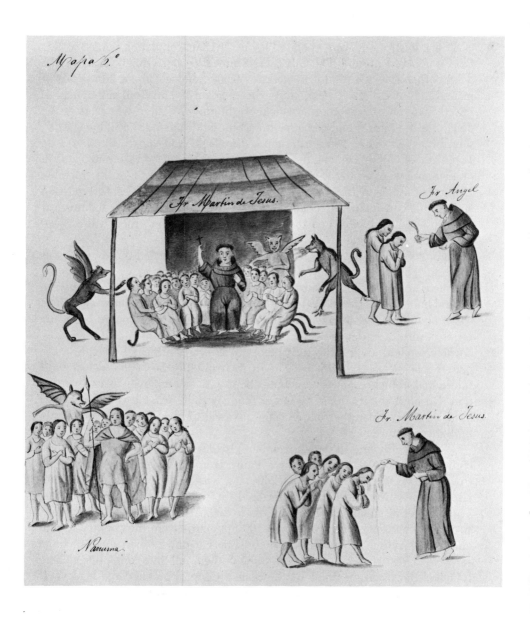

As early as 1593 a Jesuit had been sent to Durango in permanent residence; the little mining town, which at the time of its foundation thirty years before had been an outpost, had grown considerably. Within the next two years four priests and two lay brothers came north to join him. Their earliest ministrations were confined to the civilian population, which at this time numbered around 500; but there were also some thirty farms in the neighborhood, which produced close to 50,000 fanegas (about 2 bushels) of maize and wheat each year, and whose Spanish and Indian population raised that total by another two or more hundred.⁵ There was work to be done, but the padres had come to spread the faith among the Indians. They soon branched out to the north among the Tepehuan and to the Sierra de Topia and of Chínipa among the Acaxee and the Xixime.⁶ Padre Juan Agustín de Espinosa went off to the northeast to begin the conversion of the tractable Lagunero, living in the swampy country around Parras. The first mission among the Tepehuan was opened in 1598 by Padre Gerónimo Ramirez, at Papasquiaro. By 1616, when the Tepehuan Revolt flared, there were seven Black Robes operating in that area.

For several years before 1616 the padres had suspected that trouble was brewing; but their warnings to the governor at Durango went unheeded. The grievances of the Indians against the Spaniards, of whom there were several hundred scattered along the face of the Sierra in small mining camps, were mounting: high-handed treatment, forced labor in the mines or on the farms, exorbitant demands for supplies. The native medicine men, the *hechiceros*, had their grievances too; these were principally against the padres whose success with the natives was robbing the *hechiceros* of their traditional influence and threatening them with unemployment and extinction. On both counts the story had a familiar ring, or, at least, soon would have on every Spanish frontier. The advance of the European inevitably brought a culture clash.

The revolt came in mid-November (1616). Before the month was out, eight Jesuits had been struck down—Padre Hernando de Santarén, en route from his own mission of Topia to Durango, was the eighth victim.⁷ A Franciscan and a Dominican, also massacred, brought the clerical total to ten. The number of civilian deaths ran close to 200. At Papasquiaro, for example, two of the padres, along with about 100 Spaniards from the country roundabout, took refuge in the church, only to be cut down when the Tepehuan set fire to the thatched roof and forced them all into the open. There followed the usual manhunt by the Spaniards to apprehend the leaders. It was some years before other Jesuits could begin the work of reconstruction. This incident was typical, though perhaps a bit more bloody, of what occurred as the filling-in process continued.

There was a sputter of revolt in 1632 high up in the Sierra in the land of the Chínipa, during which two more Jesuits were killed. But also in that year a new silver strike took place in the neighborhood of Parral, which quickly brought a rush from the south. Before the year was gone Parral had a population of some 300 and soon there were as many as 400 claims staked and filed in the valley of the Río Florido, a tributary of the Conchos.[8] Parral became the new diffusion point. The Jesuits moved northwestward into the Tarahumara Baja; the Franciscans spread along the Río Conchos system; and the civilian frontiersmen followed in their wake.

Again, it was the same story. By 1644 the Indians were goaded to a state of exasperation, and the frontier flamed into revolt. In 1644 the Toboso led the movement, raiding isolated haciendas and ranches, supply caravans, and advanced mission stations. The Concho soon joined in, and the whole of southern Chihuahua was swept by destruction. At the end of that year (1644) the Spaniards were secure in only four towns on that far frontier: Indé, the Jesuit mission of San Miguel de las Bocas, the Franciscan outpost at Mapimí, and Parral. Before the revolt was quelled, other Indian nations from the east, the Salinero, the Julime, the Colorado, had added their numbers to the opposition. Then the revolt seemed to collapse almost as quickly as it had begun. But in 1646 the Tarahumara, up to that point peaceful, went on the warpath, killed forty Christian Indians and Spaniards at the Jesuit mission of San Francisco de Borja, and kept the northwestern sector of the frontier in turmoil for the next several years, until an energetic new governor, Diego Guajardo y Fajardo brought them to heel.

There were two more Tarahumar rebellions before these fierce mountain tribesmen were subdued.[9] In the first, Padre Cornelio Godínez lost his life at Papigochic and the Tarahumara were able to hold the Spanish troop sent against them at bay. Two years later, under the leadership of their quite capable Tepóraca, they rallied once more, murdered another padre, Antonio Basilio, at Papigochic, wiped out the Spanish settlement at Villa Aguilar nearby, and spread destruction eastward as far as Satevó and San Lorenzo, into lands where the Franciscans were laboring. Fajardo acted with all vigor possible, moved the bulk of his small force into the Tarahumara, at Tomóchic, ultimately captured and hanged the fierce Chief Tepóraca, and finally broke Tarahumar resistance. Even so, it was another twenty years before the Jesuits returned seriously to undertake the conversion of the Tarahumara Alta. Padres Francisco Barrionuevo and Juan Manuel Gamboa were the pioneers; but they were soon replaced by two of the giants in that mission story, José Tardá and Thomás de Guadalajara.

By the last quarter of the seventeenth century the southern and southwestern parts of Chihuahua were under control and filling with a small civilian population—miners, ranchers, farmers, Spaniards and mestizos, more or less tamed Indians, and a sprinkling of Africans, introduced for some of the heavier work in the mines. As the Jesuits went into the Tarahumara Alta, the Franciscans out in the flatter country to the east were pushing northward. Toward the end of the century, in 1697, they and a few civilians would lay the foundations of a farther outpost town; out of their Misión San Francisco

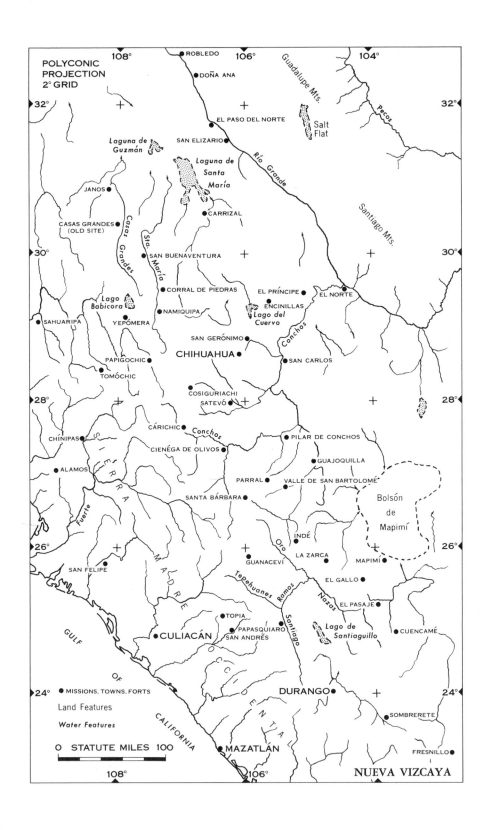

POLYCONIC
PROJECTION
2° GRID

108°   106°   104°

● ROBLEDO
● DOÑA ANA

Guadalupe Mts.

Pecos

32°   32°
+   +   +

● EL PASO DEL NORTE

Laguna de
Guzmán

Salt
Flat

● SAN ELIZARIO

Santiago Mts.

Laguna de
Santa
María

Río Grande

JANOS ●

● CARRIZAL

CASAS GRANDES ●
(OLD SITE)

Casas Grandes

Sta. María

30°   30°
● SAN BUENAVENTURA   +

Lago
Babicora

● CORRAL DE PIEDRAS   EL PRÍNCIPE ●   ● EL NORTE

SAHUARIPA ●   ● NAMIQUIPA   ENCINILLAS ●
Lago del
Cuervo

YEPÓMERA ●

SAN GERÓNIMO ●

Conchos

PAPIGOCHIC ●   CHIHUAHUA ●

TOMÓCHIC ●   ● SAN CARLOS

28°   28°
COSIGURIACHI ●   +
SATEVÓ ●

CÁRICHIC ●   Conchos   ● PILAR DE CONCHOS

CHÍNIPAS ●   CIENÉGA DE OLIVOS ●   ● GUAJOQUILLA

● ALAMOS   PARRAL ●   ● VALLE DE SAN BARTOLOMÉ

S I E R R A

SANTA BÁRBARA ●

Bolsón
de
Mapimí

Fuerte

M A D R E

26°   26°
+   +   INDÉ ●   +
● GUANACEVÍ   LA ZARCA ●
SAN FELIPE ●   Oro   MAPIMÍ ●

● EL GALLO

Tepehuanes   Ramos   Nazos   ● EL PASAJE

TOPIA ●
PAPASQUIARO ●   Santiago   Lago de
SAN ANDRÉS ●   Santiaguillo   ● CUENCAMÉ

● CULIACÁN

GULF

OF

O C C I D E N T A L

24°   24°
● MISSIONS, TOWNS, FORTS   +   DURANGO ●

CALIFORNIA

Land Features

Water Features

● SOMBRERETE

0   STATUTE MILES   100

● MAZATLÁN   ● FRESNILLO

108°   106°   NUEVA VIZCAYA

de Cuellar would grow Ciudad Chihuahua. In the new century this town of Chihuahua would do for the farther frontier what Parral had done for the "south" in the seventeenth century, namely serve as a supply and staging center for the north area and beyond. Actually, Chihuahua was to play an important role in the future history of New Mexico; but in the dozen or so years before its foundation the Spaniards had reason to wonder if there might be a New Mexico, for a crisis of major proportions had developed in the far north in those closing decades of the seventeenth century. For a time it looked as though Nueva Vizcaya might be Spain's farthest Borderland through the middle corridor.

The extension of royal authority over the New Mexico enterprise with the appointment of Peralta in 1609 brought a temporary solution to the immediate problems of the distant province, but by no means solved these permanently. The history of New Mexico through the first three quarters of the seventeenth century has little that is exciting.[10] The province had not lived up to the early hopes of Oñate and the pioneers in the matter of quick rewards. Royal orders and the Franciscans did more than anything else in keeping a civilian population in the far north. It must be remembered that the Spanish frontiersman did not have the same freedom to go and come which would be enjoyed by his Anglo-American counterpart in a later age; he was there by royal purpose and left only with royal permission. When the rewards were not proportionate, he became disappointed, discontented, disgruntled, and frustrated. Humans in such a frame of mind can often turn against fellow humans unfortunate enough to be less well advantaged than themselves. The Indians, at the bottom of the social scale, were to bear the brunt of Spanish frustration. Ultimately, Indian patience reached a breaking point.

By 1670 the Spanish population numbered around 2800 in the upper valley of the Río Grande. A sizable proportion of these were in the capital of Santa Fe or the immediate environs; there was no other center, as yet, which really deserved the name of town. The noncapital-dwellers were spread on haciendas northward from Socorro, sometimes in the proximity of the Indian pueblos but as often in isolated stretches. These Spaniards farmed or raised stock, with sheep culture predominant; there was a minimum of mining activity, although there was rather continual prospecting. A trade invoice of 1638 furnishes a key to New Mexican economy of that period, and it did not change greatly in the next decades. A shipment of goods to Parral showed some 2000 yards of coarse woolen cloth, 408 blankets, about 100 pieces of tailored clothing (wool), about the same number of drapes and hangings, buffalo and antelope skins, and 57 bushels of pine nuts, along with 900 candles.[11] Salt was another product which often went south from New Mexico. But, as is evident, no one of these items was likely to turn the New Mexicans into millionaires.

The economic problems of the New Mexicans in the seventeenth century were further complicated by the caravan trade by which the northern outposts were supplied. The New Mexicans, through their own labors and the too frequent requisitions laid on the Indians, were able to feed themselves and clothe themselves, roughly at least; but their other needs had to be filled from outside. In the early seventeenth-century decades this supply line, extending 1500 miles from viceregal capital to provincial capital, was maintained at royal expense. Later the Franciscans, the needs of whose missions accounted for a high proportion of the goods transported, actually took over the trade and operated it down to 1680. Trade via this Camino Real up the middle corridor had nothing of a fast-express character about it. The great wagons, not unlike the prairie schooners and the Murphy freighters on the Great Plains in another century, made the round trip, under normal conditions, on an eighteen-month schedule—six months up, six months at Santa Fe and intermediate stops, such as Parral, and six months back to the home base. The wagons generally carried about 4000 pounds each. This very long and precarious supply line, not to mention a very expensive one, contributed its share of hardships for the New Mexicans.

Another development of the seventeenth century contributed, indirectly at least, to the powder-keg situation of 1680. Through much of the "middle half" of the century there was a continuing church-state battle which divided the Spaniards and both mystified and heartened the Indians as the friars tangled with successive governors on a variety of counts.[12] Basically, this was a struggle for power. The friars, convinced that the prime reason for New Mexico was the Christianization of the Indians, seemed to feel that this fact should give them and their projects unquestioned priority. The governors had their own ideas about the supremacy of the civil power. Too often the battle was one of personalities as well as of issues. The divisions on top could not help but affect those underneath. And this type of friction did little to alleviate frustrations already present on all sides.

The result of this multiplication of tensions—the Pueblo Revolt of 1680—came as a shock to the Spaniards, but it hardly comes as a surprise to an observer of a later age.[13] Sooner or later something had to give. In the end it was the Indians' patience. The general poverty of the Spaniards made them testy and frequently much too demanding of the Indians. This nourished accumulating native discontent and bred strong desires for freedom from the constant exactions, from the too regular summonses to forced labor, from the sternly imposed routine of mission life, from the dozens of vexations that had entered their lives since the coming of the white man. Converts to Christianity though they were, old religious loyalties were far from dead; and the medicine men did all in their power to keep the sparks alive. The Revolt of 1680 was the end product of culture clash on all levels—material, personal, religious. There were others on the northern frontiers of New Spain, but this bloody confrontation in New Mexico was one of the more violent and for a time at least seemed to give promise of permanent success from the viewpoint of the native Americans.

As of mid-summer of 1680 the 2800 Spaniards in the upper valley of the Río Grande felt themselves reasonably secure. They certainly were not rich, nor were they precisely happy; but they were, so they thought, powerfully enough entrenched. New Mexico's peoples seemed fairly well under control—the Tano of the north, the Zuñi to the west, and the Keresan living on both sides of the river through the heart of the province. The Apache were beginning to threaten on the east; but they were considered to be beyond the pale and ultimately manageable with the assistance of the loyal Pueblo peoples. The Apache were not yet goaded to desperation by the pressures from their fierce Comanche neighbors; in the not too distant future this would be the case and would make the Apache a formidable problem on the far northern frontier. The year 1680 seemed like just another link in a long chain of years that was moving toward the centennial mark. There had been a little trouble in 1675, which had led Governor Juan Francisco Treviño to institute a cleanup drive against the native medicine men. From the beginning of Spanish occupation the Spaniards, friars and officials, had made a concerted effort to stamp out the traditional Indian beliefs and religious practices. At times when the governors were not as forceful as the friars thought they should be this fact contributed to the hard feelings between them. Understandably, these beliefs and practices were deeply ingrained. Further, the native priests, fighting to retain their position and influence in Pueblo society, worked ceaselessly, if surreptitiously and underground, to keep these older ways and loyalties alive. Their influence made the conversion of pagan Indians difficult and often threatened the constancy of the new converts. Religion became a rallying point for what should be styled Indian nationalism. The Spaniard of the seventeenth century was no champion of religious pluralism; tolerance was not part of his make-up; he was no ecumenist. Generally, the royal officials were willing enough to cooperate, in the name of their brand of nationalism.

In 1675 the governor received a tip that a number of the *hechiceros* were meeting at one of the northern pueblos. A well-planned raid netted forty-seven. Three of these were executed; the rest, before being released, were severely punished and sternly admonished to desist. Among the latter was one Popé of San Juan. Popé returned to his northern pueblo with new hate in his heart and plans for revenge in his mind.[14]

His anti-Spanish and anti-Christian propagandizing soon drew the unsympathetic attention of the authorities at San Juan, making it necessary for him to shift his base of operations. He went off to Taos, which for long had been a center of sullen acquiescence toward the new order. Here he built quite a following among the Indians, who were awed by his supernatural powers and increasingly convinced by his claims of intimate contact with the spirit world. Three powerful spirits, Caudi, Tilini, and Tieume, he

Native artist's Madonna. Painted on hide, *ca.* 1675. (Southwest Museum and American Heritage)

asserted, regularly visited and inspired him during long sessions in the estufa chamber. The plot began to take shape. Nothing short of the complete destruction of the Spaniards and the obliteration of every trace of their having been in Pueblo-land was the aim of the conspirators. Theirs was a bold scheme, and well planned.

The chiefs of the northern pueblos rallied, enthusiastically, behind Popé's scheme. Then, trusted chiefs from other towns were briefed and drawn into the plot. The strategy was to strike over the entire province simultaneously and to use the elements of surprise and ubiquity to prevent defense and possible retaliation by the white men. Further, the Indians would clean out the more isolated Spanish groups, prevent any escape to the Villa (Santa Fe), and then lay siege to the capital itself. After taking Santa Fe and killing all the Spaniards, they would sweep downriver and do a final mop-up in the Río Abajo towns and missions. No quarter was to be given to any Spaniard. Men, women, and children, and particularly the missionaries, were marked for destruction. The Pueblo were even prepared to call on their enemies, the Apache, to ensure the success of their plan.

As the designated day approached, Popé sent off messengers with knotted cords, each knot signifying one day of those remaining before the moment of attack. Each day one knot was to be untied. Two men, Catua and Omtua, went out from Tesuque, their cords having two knots; they were ordered to present them to the chiefs of the Tano, of San Marcos, and of La Ciénega. On August 9, 1680, the chiefs in this last pueblo sent word to Governor Otermín of the presence of the messengers in their towns. The governor immediately dispatched his *maestro de campo* to pick up the two Indians. Francisco Gómez Robledo, accordingly, brought the pair into Santa Fe that same evening. Questioned, the two frightened messengers told the fact of the projected revolt but disclaimed any further knowledge of the details, other than that it had been hatched in the north.

Word of the arrest of Catua and Omtua got back to Tesuque before nightfall. A council was summoned immediately, at which it was decided to begin the revolt that very night and to dispatch swift runners to the northern pueblos, suggesting instant action. It took some time for the messengers to reach the distant towns, but San Juan and Taos had word in time to open hostilities by daybreak of August 10. Word got to the other pueblos later in the day, and the whole province flamed into revolt (August 10).

Southward from Taos to Isleta and westward to Zuñi there was murder, pillage, devastation, desecration. Four hundred Spaniards were cut down. In a few of the outlying little towns the Spaniards were able to hold out for a few hours. In most instances, however, they were completely surprised, since the messengers from Otermín were unable to reach them in time to allow for defense measures. The few survivors in the north and the west made their way, as best they could, to Santa Fe, where preparations were in progress to sustain a state of siege. These activities were in full swing by August 15.

The advancing Indians offered the Spaniards a choice of signs; the red cross would mean intent to resist and the white one would signify a promise to withdraw completely from New Mexico. Otermín rejected both alternatives and did what he could to persuade the Indian envoy to use his influence to put an end to the rebellion. The Indian, named Juan, returned to his lines, and the siege of Santa Fe got under way. The Indians managed to cut the water supply into the city, and for two days the Spaniards suffered horribly—August is a warm summer month. Finally, on the morning of August 20 the Spaniards resorted to a desperate sally, caught the Indians off guard, for they had grown complacent and careless, feeling that they had already won the victory, scattered the besiegers, and gained enough time to start a long retreat downriver. The Spanish losses during the siege were only five; the Indian casualties were much higher, estimated at several hundred. Even so, the Spaniards recognized that it would be impossible to hold out. The trek southward began on August 21.

Meanwhile, Otermín's appointee, Alonso García, lieutenant-governor and captain-general of the Río Abajo settlements, had acted. By August 11 he had gathered as many of the settlers from his district as possible at Isleta. Just as Otermín was trying, unsuccessfully, to contact him, García was being foiled in his attempts to make connections with Santa Fe. Fearing that all in the north had been massacred, García called a council of his military and religious leaders to determine the immediate course of action. A preponderant majority counseled a retreat to El Paso, or at least to such a point where the group might meet up with the supply train, under the direction of Fray Padre Francisco de Ayeta, which they knew was moving northward toward New Mexico. A few of the men suggested that the fighters might split into two bands, one to defend the women and children against possible onslaught against Isleta and the second to push north to aid the Spaniards at Santa Fe, or wherever they might be gathered, and to ascertain the seriousness of the situation. These brave fellows were voted down. The order to move south was given by García on August 14.[15] In the north the siege of Santa Fe was about to open.

Ten days of hard travel brought the Río Abajo refugees as far as Socorro, into the land of the friendly Piros Indians, who had not gone over to the rebels. On the route thither, at a stopping place appropriately named El Alto, the southern band heard the first reports of the devastation in the north. Two of the survivors from Taos, Sebastián de Herrera and Fernando de Cháves, had in their flight approached Santa Fe and, finding it under siege and judging that all were or soon would be lost, skirted the capital and forged downstream.

At Socorro there was a second *junta de guerra*, or council, and again the overwhelming majority voted to continue the retreat southward. The weary band reached Fray Cristóbal in early September, and there, on September 13, the Otermín party, the survivors of Santa Fe, caught up with their fellows.

The southward flight of the governor's band had been eventful and trying, especially for the women, children, and older men. They had left Santa Fe on August 21. Progress was slow. All along the route they saw the disheartening signs of murder and destruction. At the end of a week on the road they arrived at Isleta and found the pueblo deserted. This was a new disappointment. At that moment Otermín was unaware of the sincere attempts of García to contact him and he was minded to censure his lieutenant for deserting. Even when the two men met at Alamillo, a short distance from Socorro, to where García had returned on hearing of the approach of his superior and the thousand or so refugees from Santa Fe, Otermín was still furious. However, on reading the records of the Río Abajo leader and his advisors, the governor relented and admitted that García had acted properly. It was at this point that Pedro de Leiva, rushing up from the wagon train which was still laboring northward through northern Chihuahua, met the refugees with badly needed supplies. Leiva also brought up several dozen men. But even with these reinforcements, it was felt that a return to the north at this time would be foolhardy. Otermín ordered the southward march to continue. On September 8 his band came into Socorro; five days later the two refugee groups were united at Fray Cristóbal.

There about 2400 Spaniards gathered in a spot which was not much more than a desert. Their plight was pitiable; they were weary, discouraged, and most of all hungry. Father Ayeta wrote to Otermín, suggesting that the refugees be brought down to El Paso with all possible haste, and knowing that this would take time, Father Ayeta loaded some of the wagons of his train with prime necessities and hurried upriver to their aid. He could not cross the river at the usual ford above El Paso and very nearly lost his life when he himself drove the lead wagon into the swollen waters farther upstream in an attempt to reach the west bank. Coming down in the nick of time, Otermín and his small advance party saved the situation. After much labor the precious cargo was carried across the river on the backs of the animals. Reformed and reloaded on the west bank, the wagon train pushed north with the greatest speed possible.

Otermín concurred with Father Ayeta that a removal of the whole refugee party to the neighborhood of El Paso was the only sensible solution to the current problem and sent such an order upriver with the train. Southward, to Mexico City, he dispatched messengers to report and to beg for every sort of assistance, soldiers, supplies, necessities. The arrival of the New Mexican survivors marked the beginnings of civilian settlement in the El Paso district, where, on the right bank of the river in modern Ciudad Juárez, the Franciscans had maintained their mission of Guadalupe since 1659.[16]

Officials in Mexico City were much disturbed by the reports of this serious defeat in the far north, and orders went up to Otermín to recover the province at the earliest possible moment. Spanish pride was involved. The governor found opposition among his own people, many of whom wanted to abandon the enterprise completely and to be allowed to return to safer provinces in New Spain. The result was that it was not until late 1681 that Otermín was able to attempt a reconquest, and then he had only a very small force—146 of his own men and 112 Indian allies.

As he pushed upriver, he found nothing but abandoned pueblos until he reached Isleta. There some 1500 Indians were gathered. These received the Spaniards, asked pardon, made their peace, and generously furnished the little army with badly needed food supplies. At the moment, it seems, these Indians were fearing raids from northern enemies and were much pleased to have Spanish assistance; it was a case of not being able to live with the Spaniards or to live without them. From Isleta Otermín sent Juan Domínguez de Mendoza to the more northerly pueblos, and he himself went to Sandía. There the governor took testimony from the Indians for the report which he meant for the viceroy. The northern Indians showed no inclination to submit. In a *junta de guerra* Otermín, since his present force was wholly inadequate, decided to return to El Paso to await reinforcements from Mexico. It was now early 1682. A sizable group of Isleta Indians accompanied the Spaniards back to the refugee camp. They and others were soon located in little towns downriver from El Paso, pueblos named for their former homes, Senecú, Socorro, and Isleta. But, in the broad view, the initial attempt at reconquest had failed.

Otermín was replaced as governor in mid-1683 by a veteran campaigner, General Domingo Jironza Petriz de Cruzate. During the next years Cruzate sought to strengthen the position in the El Paso district and ruled in kindly fashion, and well; but adequate assistance for the reconquest which had been ordered by the officials of the viceroyalty was not forthcoming. There was good reason for this; during the middle years of the 1680s the northern frontier was excited by rumors of a French intrusion into Texas. Officials seemed to feel that New Mexico could wait while they probed into Texas to ascertain precisely what the French were up to.

Cruzate was succeeded on the frontier in 1686 by Pedro Reneros de Posada; but two years later came back to his former command. In 1688 Cruzate led an expedition upriver and engaged the rebels at the Pueblo of Zía. Although six hundred Indians were killed, once again the Spaniards were without sufficient manpower and supplies to follow up the initial advantage. They had to retire to El Paso. To the people on the frontier it seemed that the crown was interested in reconquest only with words, decrees, and orders. This, however, was not the case, for even in 1688 Cruzate was being superseded in royal planning.

Despite the fact that Otermín had failed to reconquer the province of New Mexico and that Cruzate too had been unsuccessful, the crown was still determined that Spanish honor should be avenged in the north and that the province be restored to royal obedience and Christian practice. On June 18, 1688, Don Diego de Vargas, of noble lineage and with almost twenty years' experience in New Spain, was appointed governor and captain-general of New Mexico. Two years later the appointment was officially activated, and Vargas was able to plan for the task ahead. These preparations were delayed by the troubles besetting the El Paso district and the northern frontier in general during the early years of the 1690s. The year 1692 really marks the beginning of the *reconquista*.[17]

Although Vargas was willing to expend much of his personal fortune in the enterprise, he had considerable difficulty in assembling a sufficient force. Finally, in August 1692 the expedition set forth from El Paso (still located on the right bank of the Río Grande). By gradual stages the little army advanced into the heart of New Mexico, past the abandoned pueblos of Senecú, Socorro, and Isleta, to the former hacienda of Mejía, near the present Albuquerque.

Vargas, in September, pushed on toward Santa Fe with a force of 40 soldiers, 10 El Paso residents, 50 Indian allies, and three Franciscans. Along the way they found Cochití deserted and also Santo Domingo; their Indians were not yet ready for a confrontation with the Spaniards and had fled. On September 13 Vargas and his band stood before the walled city of Santa Fe and summoned the Indians to surrender and return to Spanish allegiance.

There followed several days of "skirmishing" in words. Then on the afternoon of September 16 Vargas and his party brazened their way into the Villa. The next morning Mass was celebrated on the plaza, and over a hundred children were baptized. The inhabitants had submitted, and chiefs from nearby pueblos began to filter in, in order to protest their loyalty. Vargas made a quick detour to Pecos and then turned north to win the allegiance of the upriver pueblos—Tesuque, the large settlement of San Ildefonso, Santa Clara, and San Juan. From temporary headquarters set up in San Juan, Vargas went on to Taos. This pueblo, which had spawned the revolt, also submitted without resistance.

Writing to the king from Santa Fe on October 15, Vargas reported that thirteen pueblos had returned to Spanish allegiance and the Christian faith, and that close to a thousand children, born since 1680, had been baptized by the friars. Vargas was already talking, in this letter, of plans for the recolonization of the province and requested the necessary permissions, along with supplies and financial support to implement his scheme.[18]

He next turned his attention to the pueblos west of Santa Fe. There he added four more to his trophy list, including the key town of Jémez. He returned to the valley, dropped down to Mejía, and then set out to win back the farther western pueblos. Ácoma was visited first; then Zuñi; next he went on to the Moqui (Hopi) towns. These last were the least receptive toward Spanish overtures, but finally agreed to renew their allegiance to Spain.

Back in El Paso in time for Christmas, Vargas had completed the first phase of the reconquest. Carlos Sigüenza y Góngora, the famous Mexican savant of the seventeenth century, writing about the events in the far north, rhapsodized:

> An entire realm was restored to the Majesty of our lord and king, Charles II, without wasting an ounce of powder, unsheathing a sword, or (what is most worthy of emphasis and appreciation) without costing the Royal Treasury a single maravedí.[19]

Vargas had proved himself a courageous leader, an expert diplomat, and a remarkable Indian psychologist. Often his personal courage bordered on the foolhardy. He took calculated personal risks in the hope of proving to the rebels that he came as a man of peace, not as the avenger of their past misdeeds and treason. For the moment, at least, the Pueblo seemed to believe him.

Enthusiastic and encouraged by his first successes, Vargas immediately set to work to ensure the permanence of the reconquest. The October (1692) report of the campaign, sent by Vargas while still at Santa Fe, had reached

Mexico City and the viceroy. Vargas was hardly back at El Paso when a congratulatory letter from the Conde de Galve arrived. He was lauded; his initial plan for the second phase of the reconquest was approved. Preparations, therefore, could proceed. Vargas was authorized to reestablish the presidio at Santa Fe and to man it with soldiers and recruits from Sombrerete, Zacatecas, Durango, Parral, and the surrounding areas. He could take back as many of the refugees who were gathered at El Paso as wished to accompany him. Those who returned would be "rewarded with the honors which belong to them as colonizers . . . declaring them noble settlers, and they shall be allotted lots and lands." Vargas was to receive 12,000 pesos from the Real Hacienda (royal treasury) immediately, to assist in defraying the initial expenses. Further, the frontier governors and royal officers were bid to assist him in every possible manner.

With the viceroy in this cooperative frame of mind, Vargas hurried other requests to the capital. His proposal of a permanent presidio at Santa Fe, to be manned by one hundred regulars, was specifically authorized. Twelve Franciscans were already at El Paso; ten more were promised. The viceroy also wrote that he, personally, would make himself responsible for enlisting more families to support the recolonization scheme.

The next months Vargas toured the north Mexican provinces, enlisting soldiers, gathering necessary supplies, and looking to all the details for the coming expedition. He ran into some opposition; but his own persuasiveness and optimism, plus the viceroy's strong support, broke down much of this.

In early October 1693 the expedition was ready. There were one hundred soldiers, some seventy-odd families, and eighteen friars. The company had about 900 head of livestock, over 2000 horses, and 1000 mules. Luis Granillo was second in command; Roque Madrid was in charge of the troops; Fray Padre Salvador was the superior of the Franciscan band. The party was further accompanied by a large number of Indian allies, some of whom were returning to their homeland in the north.

Progress up the valley was slow; provisions ran low; and the advancing season brought cold weather, to add to the general discomfort. Reports concerning a change of heart among the Pueblo, as the year 1693 ran along and the Spaniards did not return, reached the party and were, understandably, disconcerting. Faithful Pecos came out to meet the Spaniards and warned that many of the natives were threatening to resist the "invaders," as they now termed the reconquerors. Of this frame of mind were the Tewa, Tano, Picuris, Taos, Jémez, Zuñi, and Ácoma. This intelligence caused Vargas to regroup his forces, but all still forged on. Rumors multiplied. Delegations from some of the supposedly disaffected pueblos came to camp and left the Spaniards apprehensive: were their protestations of loyalty and friendship sincere or a cover for something truly insidious? In the midst of all this a small party of soldiers and settlers deserted and hurried back to El Paso and safety.

Vargas, still undaunted, used the whole range of his nonmilitary arsenal —bluff and courage, optimism and outward confidence in Pueblo promises, tact and diplomacy. By mid-December his band encamped, in the snow, before the walls of Santa Fe. On December 16 he was received on the plaza, and ceremonies of friendship were performed. Then the Spaniards withdrew to the nearby camp.

Hostilities were not long delayed. During the waning days of 1693 the so-called battle of Santa Fe was joined. The Spaniards won, and the new year (1694) opened with them in quite secure possession of their old capital. Twenty-two Spaniards had died of exposure during the days in the temporary camp; there had been but a single battle casualty. But victory in the province as a whole was far from decisive. Actually, only four of the twenty-odd pueblos could be reckoned definitely on their side. Folk from the rebel side had fled from their towns and, sometimes with neighbors, were entrenched on the strategic mesas or in the easily defensible canyons closer to their own homes. The task of reducing them to obedience loomed as one of considerable proportions.

Friendly Indians, used as emissaries to propose peace and obedience, were dispatched to the dissident nations, but their mission was regularly unsuccessful. Sometimes they were treated badly by the rebels and on one occasion at least the envoy was turned over to the Navaho to be slain.

Toward the end of February Vargas determined on an armed offensive. The mesa of San Ildefonso, the famous "Black Mesa," was his first objective. Here the powerful and numerous Tano were strongly entrenched and had attracted others to their company. The first siege was unsuccessful, and the Spaniards had to retire to Santa Fe. The Keres, on the mesa of Cieneguilla de Cochití, were attacked in April. In this campaign Vargas was moderately successful, but he had to interrupt it in order to hurry back to the capital to fend off a Tewa attack on Santa Fe itself.

The next months passed in fencing back and forth. The Indians raided, rustled cattle, stole horses and mules; the Spaniards retaliated to the extent that their slim forces allowed. Meanwhile, Vargas kept up constant attempts to win various rebel groups by persuasion and promises of complete amnesty, provided they would reaffirm their allegiance, return to their old pueblos, accept the missionaries, and live peaceably.

Vargas was ready for another offensive against the holdouts on the mesa of San Ildefonso by late June. But first he decided to test the temper of the peoples to the northeast, especially those of Picuris and Taos. He won a guarded pledge of cooperation from these. It was at this point that he made a foray into southern Colorado, hoping to overawe the non-Pueblo peoples on the New Mexican perimeter—the Navaho, the Ute, and the Apache of the north.

Back in Santa Fe in late July to pick up supplies and new forces, he then headed for the Tewa country and the forbidding mesa. Meanwhile, settler reinforcements, sent north by the viceroy, had arrived in Santa Fe under the leadership of Fray Francisco Farfán. It was now more imperative that the country be brought to peace so that these two hundred and more folk might be able to begin a normal and, most of all, a productive existence. Heartened by the very recent submission of the Jémez, the Spaniards set forth. Hostilities dragged through most of August, but ended with a Spanish victory.

Even though Taos and Picuris, along with the farther western pueblos, were still question marks, with the nearer countryside under control Vargas parceled out lands and ordered the reestablishment of missions in the valley towns. The new goal now was provincial self-sufficiency. Too long the Spaniards had allowed themselves to be primarily dependent on the Indians and on supplies brought up from Mexico. It was absolutely necessary that the colony begin to stand on its own feet, lest pre-1680 resentments be awakened. While Vargas was urging such an outlook on the settlers, new and old, his agent, Juan Páez Hurtado, was back in Mexico, looking for more colonists, more soldiers, and badly needed supplies of every sort.

A new settlement was founded by the families who had come up with Fray Francisco Farfán—the Villa Nueva de Santa Cruz de Españoles Mexicanos del Rey Nuestro Carlos Segundo. This town soon shortened its name to Santa Cruz, and later came to be known as La Cañada—an obvious boon to scribes, postal authorities, and letter writers. In May Hurtado returned from Mexico, triumphant; he brought forty-four new families with him. Many of these became the founders of the town of Bernalillo.

In 1696 the Indians sought to put on a repeat performance of 1680. June 4, this time, was their D-Day. Five friars, along with 21 Spaniards, settlers, and soldiers, fell victims to the new Indian fury. There was widespread burning and rapine. Only five of the pueblos remained completely

Walpi in Hopi land. (The American Museum of Natural History)

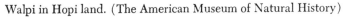

faithful and unaffected. Vargas acted quickly, however, and by the end of July a large measure of tranquility and security had been restored. Then, the governer faced the tedious and exasperating task of bringing the rebels back to order in their abandoned pueblos. This went on for some months more. Some of the rebels went off to live with the Apache and the Navaho, or with the Zuñi and the Hopi, neither of which nations had been brought back into the Spanish fold. The Zuñi would be reduced in time; but the Hopi continued to be holdouts far into the next century, always a challenge to the Spaniards, whether military or missionary.

By the end of 1696 Vargas could write with much truth that the final victory had been achieved, that New Mexico had been reconquered, that the Pueblo country was once again a province of the viceroyalty of New Spain. In a very few more years New Mexico, although needing periodic assistance from the royal government, was on the road to economic self-sufficiency. Its 2000 or so Spanish and mestizo inhabitants were turning it into a stable, though not necessarily affluent, area of the northern frontier. Farming and stockraising were the two foundations of its economy. Its time of crisis had been weathered.

In the eighteenth century this province would be an important link in Spain's northern line of defense and would in that measure fulfill one of the prime purposes of the Borderlands. New Mexico would be an advance bulwark against the pressures of the Plains Indians. Perhaps even more significantly, it would be an outpost against the western pretensions of the French, who, after establishing themselves in the lower Mississippi Valley and in the Illinois country from 1699 onward, looked westward with jealous and greedy eyes.

As the eighteenth century dawned, the Spanish northward-moving frontier was reasonably secure in the west-coast corridor and it had been anchored at the far end of the middle corridor. On the western side the line was destined to go much farther; through the middle it had reached its historical limit. The advance up the eastern corridor was lagging, but already circumstances were developing which rather quickly accelerated its forward pace.

◁ 6 ▷

The Borderlands Become International

*W*hile the Spaniards were suffering through their painful and humiliating late seventeenth-century years in New Mexico, in the Tarahumara, and in the Altar Valley of Sonora, European rivals were encroaching on the Borderlands. In the western Borderlands the French were making an appearance, to complicate by one the previous Indo-Hispanic cast of characters. On the far eastern flank of their extended frontier, in the Florida-Georgia area, the newest additions to the cast of characters were the English of the Carolinas. As the seventeenth century was coming to a close, the Spaniards, then, had to worry as much about Europeans as Indians. In the new century, particularly, the defensive role of the Borderlands became a dominant theme.

Seven years before Popé crystalized Pueblo dissatisfaction into open revolt along the upper Río Grande, the French were on another river that was to play its part in the Borderlands story. In 1673 a small party of Frenchmen had descended the Mississippi to the mouth of the Arkansas.[1] Père Jacques Marquette, on his return trip, stopped at Mission Saint-Ignace, on the Straits of Mackinac; Louis Jolliet went back to Quebec to report their findings to Governor Louis de Baude, Comte de Frontenac. They had not

Robert Cavelier, sieur de La Salle. Painting by G. P. A. Healy, 1882. (Chicago Historical Society)

descended to the mouth of "the great river of the west"; but they had seen enough and picked up supporting information from the Indians to determine that it flowed into the Gulf of Mexico, not into the Vermillion Sea (the Gulf of California), as all New France had so fondly hoped might be the geographic reality.

Untoward circumstances prevented both Jolliet and Marquette from following up their 1673 trip. Jolliet quickly had a more powerful rival for

Frontenac's favor and backing; Marquette, in 1675, had his career as missionary and explorer cut short by death as he was returning from a quick visit to the Illinois country. Robert Cavelier, sieur de La Salle, was to be the explorer successor to both; he would make France the rival to Spain in the western Borderlands.

La Salle was a Norman, born in Rouen in 1643. At the age of twenty-three he arrived in New France. During the next two decades he built the reputation of being one of the foremost, if not the foremost, of the French explorers of North America.[2]

His early activities kept him in the area of the Great Lakes and the Illinois country, but by 1681 he began to organize the expedition which was to follow the Mississippi to its mouth and to claim the whole valley of mid-continent for Louis XIV. The information that Jolliet and Marquette brought back and his own experience south of the Lakes convinced him that the English, perhaps not too far in the future, might lap over the ridges from their seaboard holdings to challenge France for control of the interior. He knew too that the Spaniards were poised at both corners of the continent—in Florida to the southeast and in northern New Spain to the southwest. If the Spanish closed their eastern and western frontiers and began to move up the Mississippi, France's position in the Valley might well be threatened from below. However, before any sound plan to prevent encirclement might be convincingly proposed to Versailles, full knowledge of the river was necessary. This was what he sought to gather in 1681–1682.

The La Salle party, moving down the Illinois, turned into the Mississippi in February 1682 and arrived at the delta in April. The possession ceremony was acted out formally on April 9. A wooden column was erected and at its base was buried a leaden plate, inscribed with the arms of France and bearing the Latin inscription, "Ludovicus Magnus, Nono Aprilis, MXDLXXXII." A formal declaration was read; the land was named Louisiana; and the company shouted *Vive le Roi!* and fired their muskets with enthusiasm. It was thus that France entered the Borderlands, claiming "the seas, harbors, ports, bays, adjacent straits, and all the nations, people, provinces, cities, towns, villages, mines, minerals, fisheries, streams, and rivers, within the extent of said Louisiana." In a word, France claimed the middle half of the continent and tried to leave no possible loophole.

La Salle went back to the Illinois country and as 1682 was ending started the construction of his Fort Saint-Louis, on Starved Rock. Then, leaving his lieutenant, Henri de Tonty, in charge, he proceeded to Quebec to lay his grandiose scheme before the governor. During his months in the interior his friend and patron, Frontenac, had been replaced by Lefèvre de la Barre. The official climate had changed notably. La Barre disliked La Salle, distrusted him, and gave no indication of sympathy for his great dream of running a line of forts and posts from the mouth of the Saint Lawrence through mid-continent to the mouth of the Mississippi—a cordon of protection against English intrusion. Thwarted at Quebec, La Salle, late in 1683, went to France to report his findings and to win royal approval for his plan to establish France at the mouth of the Mississippi.

At the court he found much more sympathy for his ideas. But there were complications. The renegade former governor of New Mexico, Diego Dionisio de Peñalosa, had preceded him, had won the ear of the influential Abbé Claude Bernou, and had already laid before Minister of Marine Seignelay, who was in effect minister for the colonies, an elaborate plan for the conquest of Teguayo and Gran Quivira, lands to the east and northeast of New Mexico and reportedly containing some of the world's richest gold and silver mines.[3] Peñalosa professed to have visited these lands some years before, prior to his run-in with the Inquisition, his imprisonment in New Spain, his failure to gain redress at the court of Spain, and his subsequent defection to France. Peñalosa had urged the establishment of a French base on the western side of the Gulf of Mexico, maybe even as far south as Pánuco. From such a base, he urged, France could move north, and he also dangled the rich silver provinces of northern New Spain before the greedy and inflamed imaginations of his hearers. The Frenchmen needed little briefing as regards these last prizes.

Seignelay was not nearly as enthusiastic about Peñalosa and his schemes as was Abbé Bernou. Still, he would admit that the plan had some merit and after hearing La Salle's proposal considered that both plans might be combined. Although La Salle was unhappy over this turn of events, he had to acquiesce. Any royal support for his own scheme seemed to be contingent on his willingness to go along with the other. But then the vagaries of international rivalries switched in La Salle's favor. In 1684 Louis XIV was showing signs of a willingness to make peace with Spain, in which event Spain would no longer be fair game. The monarch made La Salle commander of Louisiana and with this show of royal favor he was free to proceed with his own plan to occupy the Gulf Coast, starting with a settlement at or near the mouth of the Mississippi.

In late 1684 La Salle set forth from France, with four ships and some 300 colonists, men, women, and children.[4] The Sieur de Beaujeu, Seignelay's man, captained the fleet; he disliked La Salle and was mistrusted by the latter. One of the ships was lost to pirates before the party made port at Petit-Goave (Haiti). Historians are still at loggerheads as to why the expedition, when it came into the Gulf of Mexico, overshot the mouth of the Mississippi and ended on the Texas coast: was it through a mariner's error; or was the more westerly landing made, on orders from higher up, with the ultimate design of giving France a base from which to operate against the silver provinces of New Spain? In all events, the landing was made at Matagorda Bay. La Salle so decided, rather than attempting to backtrack toward the Mississippi.

Two of the ships discharged passengers and cargo without incident;

the other, trying to thread through the narrow channel affording entrance to the bay, ran aground and was wrecked. Crew and passengers were saved, but valuable supplies were lost. On the bay shore all hands set to work constructing temporary shelters. A short time later the contentious Beaujeu took one of the two remaining ships and sailed off to France, claiming that he had fulfilled his commission, having landed the party on the Gulf Coast. One hundred and eighty persons were thus practically marooned with La Salle, miles away from the original objective.

Cruel experience quickly proved that the site of the temporary settlement was far from ideal, and a search was undertaken to find a more suitable site. This was found on Garcitas Creek, and all moved there.[5] On that spot La Salle constructed another Fort Saint-Louis, destined to be no more fortunate than his first one in the Illinois country. Hard labor and privations, sickness and disease soon reduced the population by one-sixth.

La Salle began the first of his explorations in October (1685). The direction further confuses the question of the real objective of the expedition: the party set out on a northwesterly course and then turned west, ultimately reaching the lower Pecos and coming close enough to the junction of the Conchos with the Río Grande that those along feared a possible encounter with the Spaniards. Obviously, if they were looking for Teguayo and Gran Quivira, they did not reach their goal. Worn and weary, the explorers returned to Fort Saint-Louis, where Henri Joutel had been trying to hold the little company together.[6]

Back at the home base, La Salle's misfortunes still dogged him. Men sent down to check on his one remaining ship, *La Belle*, which had been anchored in the Bay, brought the sorry news that it had disappeared. Later they learned that it had been blown loose during a storm and wrecked on a sandbar. The French were now truly stranded. It was early 1686. There was no longer any way to send back to the islands for supplies, and these were desperately needed. Only one course remained: to get to the Mississippi in the hope of making connections with Tonty, whom La Salle had asked to come down from the Illinois to join him once he had arrived on the Gulf Coast.[7]

With a band of twenty men, which included his brother, the Sulpician Abbé Jean Cavelier, his nephew Morganet, and the Recollect Anastase de Douay, La Salle set out in April. The two priests left the record of the expedition. Along the way they found the Indians quite friendly; from them they heard reports of the Spaniards to the west, and saw a number of articles which had to be of Spanish origin. The party possibly reached as far east as the Sabine before new reverses forced them to turn back. La Salle was immobilized for several weeks with fever; ammunition and supplies were exhausted; and four of the party had deserted into the wilderness.

The situation at Fort Saint-Louis grew more and more desperate. The decision was finally made that the leader and a small band should try to reach his Fort Saint-Louis in the Illinois country and obtain help. Accordingly, in January 1687 La Salle set out with seventeen men. By March they had reached the country lying between the middle Brazos and the Trinity. Here tragedy struck. Morganet, La Salle's nephew, berated several of the men for their lack of cooperation and general insubordination. These men killed him and two others. When La Salle went out, with his own servant Saget, in search of Morganet and the Indian hunter Nika, the rebels shot him down from ambush. They then took charge, terrorized the rest for several days, and soon were quarreling among themselves. Soon only two of the rebels were left—Jean l'Archevêque and Hiens. The former, a lad of seventeen, was ultimately found by the Spaniards among the Caddo Indians. He later became a figure in New Mexican history. The second, Hiens, was a buccaneer who had joined up with La Salle; he also went off with the Indians, and at this point drops from history.

The survivors, now reduced to half a dozen—Henri Joutel, Abbé Cavelier, Father Douay, and three others—set off determinedly for the Illinois country with all haste.[8] On the Arkansas, some short distance from its mouth, they came upon two of Tonty's men, Jacques Cardinal and Jean Couture. These told of Tonty's attempt to contact La Salle, took them down to the little post that Tonty had founded—Poste des Arkansas—and then sent them on their way up the Mississippi. It was autumn by the time they reached Fort Saint-Louis des Illinois. Tonty was away; but the Sieur de Bellefontaine, left in charge, received them warmly. Here, too, Abbé Cavelier and the others made no mention of La Salle's death. They set out for Canada, but foul weather forced them back to the fort. Meanwhile, Tonty had come in; but again they kept their bad news to themselves. Only after arriving in France the following summer (1688) did they disclose the gruesome story of La Salle's murder.

They pleaded for help, but Louis XIV was much too preoccupied with European affairs to trouble himself with the survivors at Fort Saint-Louis in Texas. Actually, even had help been sent, it would have arrived too late, for Indians had already killed the Frenchmen and destroyed the little post. Alonso de León, governor of Coahuila, picked up this sad information in 1688 and the next year was an eyewitness on the site of the disaster. With the death of La Salle in 1687 the first phase of international rivalry in the western Borderlands came to an end; but it was only temporary cessation.

As a result of the presence of the French on the Gulf Coast in the later 1680s, Spain felt obliged to become considerably more interested in Texas than it had been for many decades past. There had been some mild concern previously,[9] just as there had been activity in the farther Mexican end of the "eastern corridor." Both were, perhaps unwittingly but nevertheless very truly, preparing the Spaniards for the next move in the Borderlands which the French were forcing on them.

Not one but two Texases shaped the Borderlands story, the western portion, lying close to the Río Grande and to New Mexico, and the vaster area of the modern state beyond, to the east. The nearer segment, or what we might designate as West Texas, did have some attraction, and had had such since the days of Oñate. Stories of the fabulous kingdoms of Gran Quivira and Gran Teguayo and of the even richer Kingdom of the Tejas became current on the frontier as early as the very first years of the seventeenth century and did spur some probings eastward. But none of these explorations turned up a reality to match the advertising.

Hope remained alive. As time went on, the New Mexicans had little to hold onto other than hope, since their own land was so disappointing. Fray Juan de Salas went east from Santa Fe in 1629 to the country of the Jumano. Five years later Alonso de Vaca pushed into the same country. The 1630 report of Fray Alonso Benavides indicated a continuing interest in the "kingdoms of Quivira and Aixaos" and suggested that some thought should be given to their conquest, lest the English and the Dutch get there first. The good friar's acquaintance with North American geography to the east of New Mexico was, quite obviously, a bit hazy; but he shared that lack of knowledge with most of his contemporaries in New Spain. In the second Benavides memorial, that of 1634, mention was again made of the kingdoms to the north and to the east.[10]

The relations of New Mexico, first, and then of Coahuila with the Jumano Indians actually readied the Spaniards for their ultimate expansion into Texas, although they may not have recognized this fact. Cabeza de Vaca had been the first European among them and had found them friendly. Nomads, they were encountered by later Spaniards in a variety of locations, but generally between the Río Grande and the Nueces. It was from them that the Spaniards first heard the stories of the "Lady in Blue." Her appearances among them and many of the other Texas tribes form one of the mysterious occurrences in the Borderlands of the seventeenth century.[11]

The "Lady in Blue" is identified with the Spanish nun Madre María de Agreda, who claimed to have been mystically transported to this section of the New World and to have prepared the folk there for Christianity. There is enough contemporary evidence among the Jumano and their neighbors to the east to cause the historian to be slow to discount the possibility of miraculous bilocation in the case of the saintly abbess. One might well expect the friars to be credulous; but they are far from being the only reporters.

Fray Juan de Salas, from Santa Fe, had been among the Jumano in 1629; and there were other missionary excursions from Isleta in subsequent years. An expedition captained by Hernando Martín and Diego del Castillo was in their country in the 1650s. Intrigued by the pearls which this group collected, Diego de Guadalajara went to investigate further in 1654. Thirty years later Juan Domínguez de Mendoza visited them, his party going out of El Paso.

During the latter part of the seventeenth century the northward-moving frontier in the "eastern corridor" edged into Nuevo León and Coahuila.[12] Beginnings actually date back to the last years of the previous century, when Francisco Urdiñola planted a colony of several hundred Tlascalans at Saltillo, to give stability to that frontier and to assist, principally by example, in the conversion of the northern tribes. In the seventeenth century the foundations of Coahuila were laid, largely by the friars of the Franciscan missionary colleges of Querétaro and Zacatecas. Beyond Saltillo the Franciscans had moved out to found an outpost at Santiago de Monclova, which in 1687 became, as well, a presidio and the capital city of the new province. The great missionary figure of this developing Coahuila frontier was Fray Juan Larios. And as he carried his contacts across the Río Grande, once again rumors of wealthy empires farther into Texas began to be heard. There are historians of Texas who feel that even though La Salle had never come to the western Gulf Coast, the Spaniards of Coahuila and Nuevo León had become sufficiently intrigued that there would have been expansion toward Texas—if not settlement, at very least full-scale exploration to satisfy themselves as to whether the earlier reports of the worthlessness of Texas were or were not justified.

As far back as 1678 intelligence came to the Spanish court from Paris telling of Peñalosa's presence in France and of the proposals he was making for a French settlement on the Gulf as a base for explorations to the north and operations westward against the "silver provinces." Charles II asked the viceroy of New Spain for a report on the geography of the area and also requested an opinion as to the feasibility of the suggestion made in the earlier Benavides Memorial that Spain occupy the Bay of Espíritu Santo. Actually, little came of this request at the moment. Very shortly, however, in the 1680s, the refugee town of El Paso became a focal point for interest in Texas.

In 1683 the Jumano chief Juan Sabeata came up from the La Junta area to request missionaries for his own people and those beyond. Answering this plea, Juan Domínguez de Mendoza and Fray Nicolás López took a small party and pushed eastward in the next year. They went as far as the Río Colorado, surveyed the country, checked the tribes and their dispositions, and returned with several thousand buffalo hides. They had promised their new-found friends that Spaniards would return within a year. Back at El Paso, the two leaders decided to go to Mexico City to present their views and petitions in person.

The pair encountered a certain reluctance on the part of authorities to furnish the men, soldiers, and Franciscans requested for the enterprise. Mendoza and López then prepared a lengthy memorial for the king, hoping to find more sympathy and assistance in that quarter. But before word could come back from Spain on this proposal, La Salle had sailed for the Gulf Coast. Authorities suddenly became very much interested in Texas—not so much as a field for missionary expansion, but rather to uncover the where-abouts of La Salle, and of his intent and that of France in dispatching him there.

In the later 1680s four expeditions went out of Vera Cruz and Florida by sea; five others were ordered out by land, from Monterrey in Nuevo León and Monclova in Coahuila.[13] Besides finding the French, these expeditions were also to find out something more definite about the much talked-of Bay of Espíritu Santo and to lay the groundwork for more extensive exploration of Texas. The Spaniards at this time seem to have considered that the Bay of Espíritu Santo was the body of water through which the waters of the Mississippi entered the Gulf.

In 1685 Martín de Echegaray sailed from Florida's east coast, around the tip of the peninsula and into the Gulf of Mexico. He wrote the king that the "Bay" should be occupied, but it is not clear whether he meant the mouth of the Mississippi or Mobile Bay. Juan Enríques Barroto sailed out of Vera Cruz in January 1686. He covered the Gulf Coast from Apalachee back to his home port and saw no signs of the French. The next year two ships went west from Apalachee and two others sailed from Vera Cruz. The latter found the wrecks of the La Salle ships at Matagorda Bay and concluded that the French intruders had perished. The other ships did a careful search of the coast from Mobile Bay to a point beyond the mouth of the Mississippi, but they found no signs of Frenchmen. The probings by sea ended in 1687; those by land would continue several years more.

The younger Alonso de León was the leader of the land expeditions which ran from 1686 into 1689.[14] These are significant in the Borderlands story, for they left the Spaniards with much exact information on Texas. On the first, in 1686, his party left Monterrey, reached the Río Grande, followed it to its mouth, and then skirted the coast eastward to Río de las Palmas before turning back. The following year Alonso de León headed out again, crossed the Río Grande, and got as far as the Río Solo. On his return he received news of his appointment as governor of Coahuila. Accordingly, he transferred his base to Monclova. Here he learned through Indian informants that a Frenchman was living with Indians beyond the Río Grande. He set out on his third expedition in late 1688, picked up the Frenchman, who turned out to be Jean Jarri, and brought him to Monclova for questioning before sending him off to Mexico City.

Jarri was unaware that La Salle had been killed and knew little of the colony which he had deserted several years previously; he did, however, furnish León with quite exact information about the site of Fort Saint-Louis. This led to the next land expedition, in 1689. On this occasion the governor was accompanied by Fray Damién Massanet, from whose letter to Don Carlos Sigüenza y Góngora comes very exact information on this foray. The friar, however, was much more interested in gathering data about the interior with a view to a possible follow-up of the contacts made by

Madre María Agreda among the Texas Indians than he was in finding the French. The governor's expedition, he felt, might well serve his purpose and afford him protection in the process. When León learned that Massanet had received reports on the French from Indian friends beyond the Río Grande, he was most willing to have the friar in his company.

This 1689 party left Monclova and proceeded almost due east. The farther along they went, the more they learned about the French, sometimes finding European clothes and books in the possession of the tribesmen. One day León heard of two Frenchmen who had been traveling with an Indian band; on another he found an elderly Frenchman who had been badly burned by a powder explosion and had been taken in by the natives. This Frenchman, hoping to protect the settlement, sought to divert the search party by informing the Spaniards that their Indian guides had them on a false lead. But Massanet had full confidence in the integrity of his two Indian friends who were along, and the Spaniards went on. The Frenchman, seeing that his story had failed to convince the Spaniards, then turned cooperative.

On April 22, 1689, León and his men reached the site of the settlement, about five miles up the Garcitas. A scene of complete destruction and death greeted them. The fort was in ruins; its former inhabitants dead or scattered. The León account is graphic:

> Having halted with the forces about an arquebus-shot away, we went to see it, and found all the houses sacked, all the chests, bottle-cases, and all the rest of the settlers' furniture broken; apparently more than two hundred books, torn apart and with rotten leaves scattered through the patios—all in French. We noted that the perpetrators of this massacre had pulled everything [the colonists] had out of their chests and divided the booty among themselves; and what they had not cared for they had torn to pieces, making a frightful sack of all the French possessed. . . . The Indians had done this damage not only to the furnishings, but also to the arms, for we found more than a hundred stocks of flintlock arquebuses, without locks or barrels. They must have carried these off, as was proved by an [arquebus] barrel found at some distance from the houses. We found three bodies scattered over the plain. One of these, from the dress that still clung to the bones, appeared to be that of a woman. We took the bodies up, chanted mass with the bodies present, and buried them. We looked for other dead bodies but could not find them; whence we supposed that they had been thrown into the creek and had been eaten by alligators, of which there were many. . . .

And the account of the destruction, pillage, and murder continued.

The Spaniards sent a party downstream to explore the bay. These men sighted the wrecks of the ships. A smaller band, including the governor and the friar, pushed up to the northeast as far as the middle reaches of the Río Colorado. They found two French lads living with the Indians, and from them received an account of the last days of the settlement. One of these young Frenchmen was Jean l'Archevêque; the other, unnamed in the record, was a native of La Rochelle. While in this area the Spaniards met the chief of the Nabedache, one of the westernmost branches of the Hasinai, or Texas, Indians. They gathered what information they could about the peoples farther east, and then headed back to the home base in Coahuila. Arrived there, León wrote a full account of this fourth expedition, to which he added a strong argument for occupying the lands recently explored, as well as those beyond, with both soldiers and missionaries.

León set out in 1690 with still another expedition, leaving Monclova on March 20. This time the Spaniards not only proposed to go beyond the point of their previous explorations but also to leave a settlement in eastern Texas. About a month after departure they were again on the site of the ill-starred French fort. From there, they pushed to the northeast. Near the Neches they set up two missions among the Texas Indians. These were the first Spanish establishments in what was to be the Spanish Province of Texas.[15]

Texas was officially created as a frontier province the following year (1691), and Domingo de Terán was named governor. He immediately made a trip to the Neches missions and pushed northeastward as far as the Red River. Little of interest or importance was encountered—certainly, no other French settlements, such as had been rumored by Indian informants. He found the farther Hasinai rather unfriendly. This fact and the absence of Frenchmen convinced officials of New Spain, when so apprized, that the Texas outpost might well be withdrawn because its maintenance was bound to be costly. Almost a hundred years had passed since New Mexico became a royal province, and it was now a poorer Spain that had to make a decision in the 1690s, not the relatively affluent Spain that had decreed a continuation of New Mexico largely from Christian considerations. The withdrawal order went out in 1693. The missions were abandoned, to the great regret of the Franciscans, and the few Spaniards in Texas were pulled back to the more prosperous frontier in Coahuila and Nuevo León.

But it was not the end. One of the friars, Francisco Hidalgo, was determined to keep alive the dream of missions among his recent Hasinai charges and in the course of time he was able to pass on to a number of his Coahuila brethren his zealous enthusiasm. These Franciscans were going to share at least some of the responsibility for the decision of the Spanish crown to reoccupy Texas in the second decade of the next century. The activities of the French, this time in Louisiana, were going to be the final force leading to this determination.

Far to the east at the other side of the Spanish Borderlands another group of Europeans were "internationalizing" the frontier in those last decades of the seventeenth century. In Texas the frontier would go out to meet the rivals; in the Floridas it had to pull back to protect the strategic area against the aggressive Carolinians. The day when Spain had North America much to itself was fast disappearing—at least its part of North America.

The early years of the 1570s were notable in Florida's history: the Jesuits, their manpower badly crippled by the disaster at their Virginia mission, were bid by their superiors to withdraw in order to concentrate forces in New Spain; in 1572 the "father of Florida," Pedro Menéndez de Avilés, went off to Spain, and to his death two years later; in 1573 the Franciscans came in to man the missions. The friars had something better than a century of hard, but often consoling, labor ahead of them, on this Florida-Georgia-Carolina frontier.[16] Many of them would give their lives and in the end their missions would one by one be destroyed. Until that happened, in the early eighteenth century, they proved their worth as frontiersmen. Actually, they and the soldiers were almost the only Spaniards on hand to hold this strategic Borderland province. Life was too difficult, dangerous, and unrewarding in La Florida to attract settlers. A few came, but the bulk of the nonmissionary and nonmilitary Spaniards were shopkeepers, catering to the military, and a few traders, battling the more aggressive English for the skins and other not-so-rich products which the Indians had for exchange.

Had it not been for the royal annual subsidy and the supplies from the Islands, Florida could not have survived. The missions of the Apalachee in time furnished some foodstuffs, corn and beans, but never in sufficient quantity to make the province economically self-sustaining. In the seventeenth century there were frequent plans to turn the province into a region for fruit-raising, fishing, even silk culture, and, of course, basic farming, but one and all came to naught. Florida, from first to last, had to be subsidized; but Spain considered the expenditure worth the price, which by 1700 had run as high as 100,000 pesos annually.[17]

The first interest of the Spaniards in Florida was to secure the coast against occupation by foreign rivals.[18] Menéndez de Avilés broke up the French settlements in 1565, but the line of posts established as far north as Santa Elena (South Carolina) was too poorly manned to prevent subsequent and frequent intrusions by French corsairs in the next years and into the next century. Their sassafras-gathering was disturbing enough; their intrigues with the Indians were the source of much of the early troubles, especially along the Georgia, or Guale, coast, and even inland in later years. Control of the Indians was the key to peace and security.

This goal the Spaniards sought to achieve through their missions. The Franciscans, after 1573, became the frontiersmen. They built sometimes on the mainland but more often on the little islands off the Georgia coast, and the Inland Passage became their highway. Fray Baltasar López and Fray Alonso Reynoso were important among the first founders. When Drake attacked San Agustín, in 1587, the small garrison at Santa Elena was pulled back to reinforce the presidio of San Marcos at the capital. The friars, too, withdrew to Santa Catalina, on Saint Catherine's Island, opposite the mouth of the Savannah River, and this for some years remained the northern outpost. In 1595 more manpower was available, and five friars, newly arrived, were detailed to Guale. And Indian revolt two years later practically wiped out the enterprise north of San Pedro Island. Three of the Franciscans were murdered at their missions and one was carried off a captive. Governor Méndez de Canzo took 150 men from his garrison at San Agustín and hurried north. This show of force awed the Indians and they scattered without putting up a fight. The governor destroyed their abandoned towns and crops. Taking advantage of the disturbed situation, French corsairs came back and pushed far inland. Restoration was imperative and, as soon as a complement of friars arrived, the new governor, Pedro de Ibarra, conducted seven of them to Guale. Old sites were reoccupied and new ones opened.

The next major event in this southeast corner of the continent was the foundation of Jamestown in 1607. Spain missed its chance to break up this English intrusion, as it might easily have done in those first difficult Virginia years. The English, in time, were to prove more determined and much more powerful and troublesome rivals than the French had ever been.

San Agustín, Florida. Copper engraving from Dapper's *America,* 1673. (Chicago Historical Society)

Knowledge of the English close by stirred the Spaniards to new activity in Guale. Fray Luis de Oro came over from the Islands in 1612 with two dozen co-workers. They strengthened the Guale missions, making possible a new push toward South Carolina, beyond the Savannah River. The next decades proved to be the "Golden Age of the Franciscans in the 'Old Southeast.' " [19]

The years prior to mid-century saw significant expansion on the Gulf side of the peninsula. Early in the days of Spanish occupation the Franciscans had edged westward from San Agustín and founded a chain of missions in the so-called Province of Timucua. Now with the growth of interest in the backcountry of Georgia, sparked by continuing rumors of white men present there, even though none were found when scouting expeditions pushed toward the interior, the Spaniards felt that action was necessary. Accordingly, they extended their mission frontier into the Province of Apalachee. By 1655 they had nine missions in the area, centered around San Luis, near the modern Tallahassee. And there was a port, San Marcos, on the Gulf Coast. Strategically this was a sound move, for it served as a check on the French pirates operating in the Gulf; it would be a springboard for future extension to Pensacola; and it put the Spaniards in a position to counter the activities of the English traders, which were soon to open, into interior Georgia. From Apalachee in the 1680s the Spaniards moved northward, up the Chattahoochee, in their attempt to outbid the English for the allegiance of the Apalachicola Confederacy (the Lower Creek).

The Spaniards moved none too soon, for the backcountry was becoming a bit "crowded." [20] South Carolina had been established on the seaboard, in 1670, and quickly the Carolinians, at first without a sound economic base for their colony, turned to trade with the Indians of the interior and to slave-hunting to fill the void. In the van was that interesting and well-nigh ubiquitous Englishman Dr. Henry Woodward, who had first appeared on the Carolina coast in the 1660s. Adopted by the cacique of Parris Island, when left there as a hostage by Robert Sandford, he set himself to learning as much about the interior and as many of the languages of the peoples living there as possible. He was picked up by the Spaniards and held for a time at San Agustín, which gave him an opportunity to measure his adversaries of the future. He escaped when Robert Searles attacked the Florida capital in 1668, and soon was back in Carolina, working out of the newly founded Charleston. First he probed the backwoods of South Carolina; next he crossed the middle Savannah and went on to the Westo Indians. A few years later, after these had been exterminated or scattered by the Carolinians, Woodward pushed out to the Apalachicola. The activity of Woodward and his fellows determined the Spaniards to counteraction on the Chattahoochee.

In 1685, on orders of Governor Juan Marqués Cabrera, Captain Antonio Matheos pushed north from Apalachee, intent on capturing Woodward and bringing the Apalachicola back to their recently professed allegiance to Spain. Apprized of their approach, Woodward and the Englishmen went into hiding, but not until he had penned a defiant note to his pursuer: "I am sorry that I came with so small a following that I cannot await your arrival. Be informed that I came to get acquainted with the country, its mountains, the seacoast and Apalache. I trust in God that I shall meet you gentlemen later when I have a larger following. September 2, 1685. *Vale.*" Matheos, in no mood for fun and games, destroyed a partially completed warehouse, left spies in the country, and returned to Apalachee.

In late December Matheos was again on his way north with a sizable force, moving overland rather than up the river, hoping thus to surprise the Englishmen. Cabrera had ordered that he command the Indians to turn over the English intruders. Chiefs of eight towns met with him at Caveta, asked pardon, and were restored to Spanish favor. The towns of the four holdouts were burned to the ground. The next year these made their submission. But, for all of that, they did not keep the English out—the trade prices of the Carolinians were too temptingly favorable. In 1689 the new governor, Rodrigo Quiroga y Losada, determined to hold the backcountry and had a fort built to the south of Caveta, near the village of Apalachicola. The next spring the chiefs from roundabout came thither to pledge allegiance to the Spaniards. For the moment it looked as though Spain had won. But time proved that this was only the first round in a long bout. By 1691 the fort was abandoned; the small garrison had to be recalled to strengthen that at San Agustín, again threatened by corsairs. And the Apalachicola had moved eastward to new homes on the Ocmulgee, closer to the English.

Meanwhile, the Spaniards had fared less well along the coast. Between the Carolinians and the pirates, especially Agramont in 1683, the Guale mission line shrank bit by bit. Santa Catalina was abandoned and then Zápala: the line was pulled back to Santa María. The Spaniards struck back. Thomás de León went north (1686) and destroyed the Scot settlement at Port Royal, established a few years before, sacked and burned Governor Joseph Morton's plantation on Edisto Island, and might have gone on to Charleston, had not a hurricane destroyed two of his vessels and forced the third to limp back to San Agustín.

In the first years of the new century the struggle in the backcountry for control of the Indians, particularly the Lower Creek, broke out anew. The English with their Indian allies planned to wipe out the Apalachee missions and then go down to the Province of Timucua. There was a battle on the Río Pedernales (Flint) in 1702; the Spanish were bested, and their Apalachee allies badly mangled.

These frontier skirmishes gained a new importance when Spain was drawn into the Anglo-French contest for North America. To match this reverse on the western frontier, now that Queen Anne's War (1702–1713) made full-dress hostilities legitimate, Governor James Moore came down from Charleston against San Agustín.[21] He took the town but was unable to capture the fortress of San Marcos, now built solidly with stone.[22] Although his reputation had suffered and he had been replaced as governor, Moore, in 1703, headed a campaign inland, which savagely destroyed the Apalachee missions.[23] Meanwhile, the seaboard mission line had been withdrawn from Santa María down to the St. Johns River. To maintain its hold on the peninsula at least, Spain had been forced to contract its frontier. Emboldened by their successes against the Spaniards, the English dreamed of taking Pensacola and even going beyond to challenge the French at Mobile and on the Alabama, who had been in those parts since the early years of the century. The Peace of Utrecht (1713) put an end to hostilities but did not settle the border conflict.

The Yamassee revolt against the English in 1715 shook Carolina complacency. These former friends of the English turned on their allies and, though scattered, ended on the Spanish side. The Creek, too, cooled in their loyalty and for a time went over to Spanish allegiance, going down to Pensacola to make peace. And their cousins, the Lower Creek, appeared at San Agustín for the same purpose. The Spaniards had not lost all, nor had they scored so heavily that they could be complacent. The struggle went on.

Thus the eastern Borderland, too, was "internationalized." In the southeast, Spain had to pull back in order to hold what was vital. Florida does not always fit the patterns of Spain's other frontier provinces. These may not always have been rich and prosperous; Florida never was. Florida never had any sizable civilian population. It was a defense outpost. The soldier was Florida's most important citizen. The missionary for a time shared this distinction, but with the constant pressures on the Indians, the natives would have had to be truly heroic to have stayed the sort of Christians the friars strove to make of them. In the other Borderlands pagan Indians could upset the Christian neophytes. On this southeastern frontier the friars were pitted against men much more insidious—Englishmen, who used the Indians to their personal and national advantage and seemed to care little for anything else.

⊲ **7** ⊳

Texas, a Defensive Borderland, 1685-1731

*I*n the eighteenth century the presence of the French in the Mississippi Valley, both in the Illinois country and in Louisiana, was a dominant force in shaping Spanish policy in the north. This could hardly have been foreseen in 1693. When the Spaniards pulled back from eastern Texas in that year, their policy-makers seem to have felt that French interest in the Gulf region had died with La Salle. However, as the seventeenth century was closing, intelligence reports out of France reawakened concern at the court of Spain. These reports told of preparations under way, and on a much larger scale than those of 1684, to make the Mississippi and its entire drainage basin exclusively French, in defiance of any counterclaims by Spain or other colonial rival.

Actually, French interest was not dead in the 1690s. It was simply dormant, made so by French involvement in European politics. France's attention was held on its side of the Atlantic by the conflict known variously as the War of the English Succession or the War of the League of Augsburg or in American terms as King William's War, which raged between 1689 and 1697. After the Treaty of Ryswick (1697) closed hostilities, the French became distinctly worried by the rumor from England that one Dr. Daniel Coxe, to whom some years previously Charles II had made an extensive western grant, was actually planning to begin a settlement to the west of the Carolinas and that he considered the Mississippi as his future outlet to the sea. Seignelay had been replaced in the colonial office by Louis Phélypeaux, Comte de Pontchartrain. The new minister was convinced that action should be taken, and quickly, to prevent an English take-over in the great middle valley. Pontchartrain saw France in America much more in line with La Salle's original plans than had his predecessor. Accordingly, Pierre LeMoyne, sieur d'Iberville, a Canadian of prominence and ability, was detailed to prepare and head the counterexpedition against the threatened English intrusion.[1]

Warnings went out from Madrid to the Spanish Indies. Spain, at the moment, was more concerned about Florida than it was about Mexico. The English were already pressuring that province from the north; Spain did not relish the idea of another rival to the northwest, on the Gulf Coast. Therefore late in 1698 Martín Zavala and Juan Jordán de Reina were dispatched from Havana with orders to occupy the nearest port on the Gulf Coast, namely Pensacola.[2] Andrés Arriola, on orders from the Conde de Montezuma, viceroy of New Spain, sailed out from Vera Cruz to Pensacola to assist in the construction of the presidio of Santa María. When Iberville came into the Gulf a few months later, he found the Spaniards strongly entrenched, and sailed on westward without pausing to challenge their position. The French established their first post at Biloxi; then a few years later they moved their center eastward to the more strategically defensible location on Mobile Bay (1702), and named the little town Saint Louis, honoring the patron of reigning Louis XIV.

The next years saw the French settlements in the lower valley expand somewhat haltingly.[3] France was deeply involved in a new war at home— the War of the Spanish Succession, and its counterpart in the Americas, Queen Anne's War, which kept France very busy elsewhere in North America. The crown had no funds to support the Gulf Coast enterprise; as a result, in 1712 Louisiana was turned over to a proprietor, the wealthy Antoine Crozat. He held the patent until 1717, when control passed back to the crown. During this Crozat period Antoine de La Mothe Cadillac was brought down from Detroit, recently founded, to be governor in the lower valley.[4] Exploration was pushed and trade activities with the Indians, especially those to the east of the Mississippi, were put on a sounder basis; the French were already strong with the Choctaw and were bidding for the friendship of the Creek.

It was during the governorship of Cadillac that the French, looking also to the Indians west of the river, set up a post—Natchitoches—on the Red River. The trade dreams of the French were not limited to the Indians east and west of the Mississippi; they even embraced the possibility of establishing a profitable traffic with the Spaniards, both those on the western shore of the Gulf of Mexico and those in the outpost province of New Mexico. Precisely how much the desire to capture the "silver provinces" of northern Mexico may have colored these western-oriented dreams is difficult to determine. Initially, at least, trade seems to have been the aim as the French looked westward.

In 1713 Cadillac sent his Canadian lieutenant, Louis Juchereau de Saint-Denis, to the Red River with several thousand dollars worth of trade goods and the commission to found a post at a strategic location upstream.[5] At the Natchitoches site Saint-Denis found what he was looking for, a sizable island in the middle of the stream, which made it easily defensible by a very few men.

In the next year Saint-Denis and a small band set out across Texas, with the Spanish establishments along the Río Grande as their objective. They meant to test the potential of the market for French trade goods, convinced that they could undersell Spanish competitors if once given the opportunity. Nor did French planning limit itself simply to the Río Grande towns; the French even thought of a possible contraband trade farther afield, in Coahuila, Nuevo León, and even into Nueva Vizcaya. The price differential was their incentive; the usual legitimate trade to the frontier was by the "long way round," via Vera Cruz, Mexico City, and the roads north. Further, much of the merchandise was not of Spanish origin in the first instance, having been imported into Spain before being transshipped to the Americas; therefore, by the time goods reached the frontier, when they did, they were outrageously expensive.

The appearance of the Saint-Denis party at San Juan Bautista, on the Río Grande, was a shock to the Spaniards, even though rumors of Frenchmen among the tribes to the east had been drifting in for several years past. In fact, in 1708 a small party under Captain Pedro de Aguirre, and including two Franciscans, Francisco Olivares and Isidro Felix Espinosa, had gone as far as the Colorado River of Texas, trying to make contact with the Texas, or Teja, Indians to warn them against doing business with the French working out of Louisiana.[6] From the very beginning both sides recognized that the friendship of the Indians would be a deciding factor in this game of frontier fencing which was getting under way along the western reaches of the Gulf Coast. Neither Spaniards nor Frenchmen were likely to have enough troops to engage each other in armed action in order to make good the claim to the territory in contest. The natives soon found themselves in the enviable position of being courted by both sides. The Indians, with their great sense of human cunning, would learn to make the most of their new advantage. And, very interestingly, in the process two very different approaches to the Indian would have a stern testing—the mission versus trade services: the first, the approach of the Spaniards, and the latter that of their French rivals. Saint-Denis at San Juan Bautista was a seemingly insignificant event, but it was to have far-reaching consequences in subsequent Borderlands history.

At San Juan, Captain Domingo Ramón was courteous to his uninvited French guests, but with the stern warning of 1713 from the viceroy to frontier captains before him, he had no other alternative but to arrest Saint-Denis and his three companions—Medar Jalot, Lergen, and Pénicault. They were not closely confined; but Ramón held them at San Juan until he could get word back from the viceroy with regard to what should be the next step in this international incident—for such it was. During this period of waiting Saint-Denis fell in love with the commandant's niece, Doña Emanuela, further to complicate the international situation by adding a new and very human dimension.

Word finally came from Mexico City in the early spring of 1715, along with a detail of soldiers from Monclova to accompany the Frenchmen to the viceregal capital for questioning. Saint-Denis and Jalot went off; their two companions were allowed to remain at San Juan Bautista.

In conversations with the viceroy Saint-Denis gave his version of the events of 1713–1714, a version which made much of a letter of a Spanish friar to the governor of Louisiana. In 1711 Fray Francisco Hidalgo had sent a letter to the French governor.[7] The good friar had been among the Hasinai Indians two decades before during the first Spanish venture into Texas and had waited impatiently in Coahuila for a chance to return to his neophytes. When he could get no firm promise from his own Spanish officials, he sent off a letter to the French governor, inquiring about the welfare of the Texas Indians, "his" Indians, and covertly asking for support in reopening the mission. This letter reached the hands of Cadillac in 1713, and at this point the governor acted, sending Saint-Denis up the Red River and ultimately across Texas to the Río Grande. Saint-Denis had a passport, which he had presented first at San Juan and now exhibited in Mexico City:

> The Sieur de Saint-Denis is to take twenty-four men and as many Indians as necessary and with them go in search of the mission of Fray Francisco Hildago, in response to his letter of January 17, 1711, and there to purchase horses and cattle for the province of Louisiana.

Saint-Denis went on to tell how he had proceeded up the Red River and then turned toward the Teja country. He had failed to find trace of the Hidalgo mission. At this point he sent most of his men back to Mobile, which was still the Louisiana capital, and then with three of his men went in search of the horses and cattle. Thus he had come to San Juan Bautista.

As a consummate diplomat, he told how the Indians of Texas were so very well disposed toward the Spaniards and how eagerly they desired to have the fathers return among them. He spoke as glowingly as possible of the beauty of the country and its fertility; and he commented most favorably on the character of the Teja Indians. He even offered the viceroy a map of the territory he had crossed and volunteered his services in the event that the Spaniards might wish him to guide missionaries to former posts in Texas. It should be noted that the wily Saint-Denis was prudently silent on such a matter as the length of time it took him to move from Natchitoches to San Juan Bautista; he had said nothing about the disposition of his trade goods; nor did he mention a quick trip from the Red River to Natchez, where he had conferred with Cadillac before pushing across Texas. The Spaniards may or may not have been suspicious. At any rate, they now knew something at least of the French moving westward from the Mississippi. The viceroy ordered his fiscal, the legal officer in his council, to make a full report for transmittal to the crown.

The report was ready quickly, and it was forceful. The viceroy convened his *junta general* to review his recommendations and to offer their advice. The ranking officials of New Spain counseled immediate action, even before word could come back from the crown, since they considered the situation serious. It was now late August 1715.

Agreeing with the view of his counselors, the viceroy ordered that preparations for an *entrada* be made immediately. Captain Ramón of San Juan Bautista was in the capital and drew up a long list of necessary items: arms, clothing, and supplies for the soldiers; gifts for the Indians; and a variety of things for the missions-to-be, such as tools, seeds, yoke for oxen. Ramón was made captain of the expedition; Saint-Denis, as *conductor de viveres*, or supply chief, was second in command.[8] The viceroy and the officials had, obviously, decided to take Saint-Denis' offer of assistance seriously. They were anxious to avail themselves of his knowledge of the country and what must have been his ability to get along with the Indians. On this latter count they were most perceptive; Saint-Denis did have a quite remarkable talent for mastering Indian languages, which gave him an equally remarkable ability to win their confidence.

Later historians have speculated as to the motives behind this seeming shift of allegiance by Saint-Denis.[9] The love affair which ultimately led him to marry into the Ramón family may have been a factor. Then, too, cunning Frenchman that he was, he may have been convinced that the maintenance of friendly relations with the Spaniards, even though they might advance into Texas, could be one of the surest ways to ensure the final success of his original mission, to establish trade relationships. There is evidence that during his months with the Spaniards in the capital, he was able to send at least two reports to Cadillac, informing his superior of his whereabouts and activities.

Ramón was not ready to leave Saltillo, his staging area, until mid-February 1716. The reoccupation of Texas was soon to be a reality.[10] A party of some seventy-odd Spaniards crossed the Río Grande at San Juan Bautista. There were 25 soldiers to man the projected presidio; there were 40 others—men, women, and children. Also in the company were 8 Franciscan priests and 3 lay brothers, from the missionary college of Querétaro,

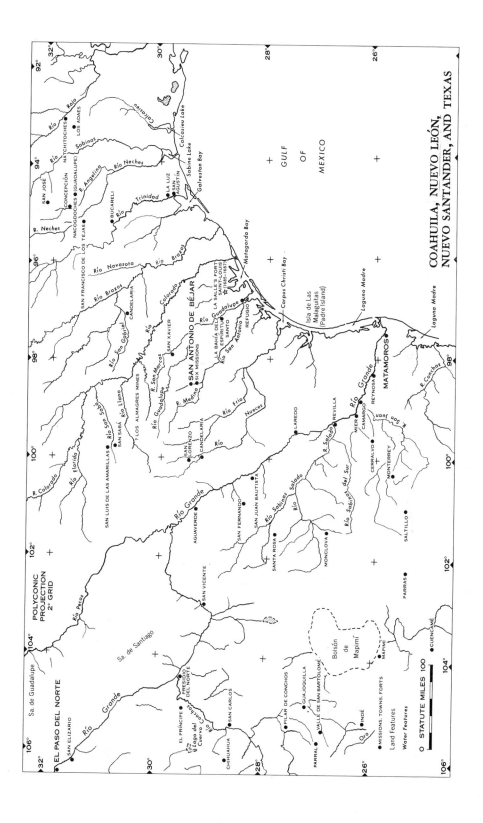

COAHUILA, NUEVO LEÓN,
NUEVO SANTANDER, AND TEXAS

MISSIONS, TOWNS, FORTS
Land Features
Water Features

0   STATUTE MILES 100

under Espinosa and Hidalgo, whose long years of waiting were now ending.[11] Other Franciscans, from the college of Zacatecas, joined the party a few weeks later; they had been delayed by the sickness of the one who was to become their most famous member—Fray Antonio Margil de Jesús.[12]

By slow stages the group advanced eastward, stopping often to rest or to explore or even to celebrate, as they did on May 5, when the mestiza Ana Guerra was married to Lorenzo Mercado, one of the soldiers. Along the way the Indians often came up to the Spaniards to express their joy at this return to their lands. As the company pushed into the country of the Teja and other folk of the Hasinai confederacy, the welcome became even warmer.[13] The Spaniards were heartened and hopeful.

On June 26, 1716, at a spot between the Trinity and the Neches rivers, there took place a frontier ceremony to match any of which records remain in the annals of colonial North America.[14] Saint-Denis had gone on ahead with the son of the captain, Diego Ramón, and had now returned. He was accompanied by more than 25 Indians, most of them chiefs. As they approached the Spaniards, those who came on horseback dismounted and advanced in a single line with Saint-Denis at their head. The Spaniards formed a double line, and then Captain Ramón and the friars filed out to meet the visitors and to conduct them to the council-ground, which had been spread with blankets. There was a great ceremony of welcome and mutual goodwill, speeches, rifle volleys, and finally a procession to the strains of a solemn *Te Deum*. The distribution of gifts followed; these included the best coat from Ramón's wardrobe which went to one of the young chiefs of the visitor group. The beginning, certainly, seemed auspicious.

Ramón and the friars spent the next weeks selecting sites for the presidio and the four missions that had been authorized. The captain set up the presidio in temporary quarters on the west side of the Neches. While construction was under way, the friars, with the aid of Saint-Denis and the even greater assistance of the Indian woman Angelina,[15] talked over possible mission locations with the Indians, trying to impress upon them the advantages of congregating in set locations. By July the four foundations had been made. San Francisco de los Tejas was set about a league from the temporary camp, beyond the Neches. Purísima Concepción was located half a dozen leagues to the northwest, beyond the Angelina. These two were left in charge of the Querétarans. Proceeding with the friars from the college at Zacatecas, Ramón went east-southeast a few more leagues and assisted in the erection of Nuestra Señora de Guadalupe, near the present Nacogdoches. This was to be the station of the saintly Fray Antonio Margil, superior of the Zacatecans. The fourth mission, San José, was established as a center for the Nazoni and Nadaco peoples, to the northeast of Purísima Concepción. Fray Isidro Espinosa, the Querétaran superior, made San José his headquarters.

Fray Antonio Margil de Jesús. From *Iconographia Colonial,* Museo Nacional, Mexico. (The Bancroft Library)

By the end of July 1715 the primary purpose of the expedition had been accomplished. There was a presidio in East Texas and four missions among the Hasinai. The foundations were far from the Río Grande. They were set in the country of those Indians who could make or break the Spanish effort in Texas. Further, they were very close to the French post on the Red River, which had been one of the purposes of Spanish officialdom in sanctioning the whole venture. Texas was to be an arena in which Spaniard and Frenchman were to struggle for the allegiance and friendship of the Indians. The French would use trade to this end; the Spaniards, while not completely rejecting trade possibilities, laid their initial hopes on the Christianization approach, which had been successful elsewhere on their frontiers.

East Texas had been occupied; but it was immediately evident that it could be held only if strong reinforcements, military and civilian, came up from Mexico, and quickly. The captain and the missionaries inaugurated their series of appeal letters to officials, both civil and ecclesiastical. Ramón had, as instructed, learned what he could of the strength of the French and of their influence. For this purpose he and Fray Antonio Margil, with a few companions, had gone east to look in on the Natchitoches post. They found two Frenchmen, who mentioned that they were momentarily expecting the arrival of ten or a dozen companions from Mobile. The Spaniards saw a well-built stockade and noted disturbing evidence of the quite warm feelings of the Indians roundabout toward the French. Largely as a result of this scouting expedition Fray Antonio laid the foundations of Misión San Miguel de Linares among the Adai in the fall of 1716, on or near the site of the modern Robeline. Still another mission was established, this one among the Ais and named Nuestra Señora de los Dolores. This sixth mission was located midway between Purísima Concepción and the new San Miguel.

The Franciscans set to work with vigor and enthusiasm, but progress was dishearteningly slow. The Indians were even slower to congregate at the mission sites; and this added to the feeling of pious frustration which took hold through 1717. In Texas the friars were face to face with a new breed of Indians, hunter nomads in the main. The north Mexican Indians had been less stable than the Aztec, but little by little they had been persuaded to settle down in the missions; here in Texas were natives who seemed on the move most of the time. Their villages were little more than bases from which they operated. Game was so abundant that they had never been forced to supplement the fruits of the chase with the produce of the soil. Semisedentary existence had never been part of their historic experience. Even at the end of the mission period in Texas, over a century away, the friars had distressingly little to show for their long years of unrelenting effort. The Franciscans in Texas were to be very much like the Jesuits and their fellows in New France, dealing with much the same sort of Indians and making relatively little headway. In these circumstances it is not wholly surprising that the mission failed to live up to its reputation as the Spanish frontier institution par excellence.[16]

As more months went by it became painfully clear that unless help came the 1715–1717 enterprise in Texas was likely to share the fate of the 1690–1693 effort. Back in the viceregal capital reports coming in from France of projected heavy reinforcements to the Louisiana colony did little to brighten prospects for the future of Texas.

But just as the reoccupation venture had its booster in Fray Francisco Hidalgo, the reinforcement scheme had its untiring promoter. This was Fray Padre Antonio de San Buenaventura Olivares. He had been in the Coahuila missions for some years and in 1709 had been with Espinosa and Captain Aguirre on the so-called San Marcos expedition to the Colorado River. Since that time Olivares had dreamed of a permanent mission on the Río San Antonio, having been greatly impressed both by the ideal location and even more by the character of the Indians of the region, seemingly more tractable than others whom the explorers had encountered to date. Olivares appeared in Mexico City in late 1716, intent on pushing his scheme. He came at a propitious moment, for authorities in the capital were studying and debating the first report of Ramón, who was insisting vigorously that East Texas must have immediate assistance. A way station, midway between the Río Grande and the Red, had its logic. Further, a mission upriver on the San Antonio might serve not only East Texas, but it could also be an inland base to support a possible, and desirable, presidio on the Bay of Espíritu Santo (the future La Bahía). The fiscal of the Hacienda (treasury department), always a powerful voice in the viceregal council, was much interested in this latter possible by-product of the Olivares proposal, for he felt that an establishment on the Gulf Coast proper might serve as a deterrent to French trade ambitions westward from Louisiana by sea.

Before 1716 was out, the viceroy acted. Don Martín de Alarcón, recently installed as governor of Coahuila, was named to head the San Antonio project and given the title of Captain-general and Governor of Texas.[17] Olivares was commissioned to found the mission, and orders were issued that he be furnished with the various supplies he had requested and also with the ten soldiers whom he had demanded as military protection.

Olivares left the capital immediately, dropped by his home college at Querétaro to pick up two missionary companions, and by early May 1717 he was back on the Río Grande. Alarcón tarried in the capital to obtain supplies but went north as quickly as he could. By June 1717 he was at Saltillo and in August had moved over to San Juan Bautista. Olivares was downriver, at Misión San José, ready and anxious to set forth. Then followed months of inaction. Olivares stormed; Alarcón blamed his delay on lack of specific instructions from the viceroy. An unfortunate rift developed between the two men.

Alarcón's instructions did not arrive until April 1718, but by that time the governor was already on his way. He had become impatient and set out on April 9. There were seventy-two persons with him as he crossed the Río Grande. Olivares may still have been pouting, for he and the other friars did not join the main body until several days later. Alarcón was less considerate of historians than was Ramón in telling about his company. In fact, the animals received more coverage than the humans in his account. The expedition had 7 droves of mules, 548 horses, and an undesignated number of cattle and goats.

Alarcón, possibly misreading his instructions, first did a quick turn downriver to scout the Bay of Espíritu Santo, before proceeding up the Río San Antonio. Olivares went on a more direct route and on May 1 laid the foundations of the Misión San Antonio de Valero. The Presidio de Béjar was not established until five days later. Perhaps, it was fitting that the friar, who was so largely responsible for the whole project, should have had the honor of being the founder of what was to develop into such a key town.[18]

Having fulfilled the first part of his instructions—the foundation of the mission and the presidio on the San Antonio—Alarcón next undertook his second order, which bade him to visit and report on the missions of East Texas. This tour took six months; he did not return to San Antonio until January 1719.

When he wrote his report on East Texas, it was neither rosy nor glowing. The enterprise had fallen on hard days some time before Alarcón appeared. Ramón had moved the presidio closer to Misión San Francisco de los Tejas; sickness had incapacitated the captain for several months and had taken several of his best men; desertions further reduced the complement; hence, the presidio was not a particularly strong defense against any belligerent opposition, whether it came from the Indians or from the nearly French. Sickness too had crippled a number of the friars and cut down their ministerial efficiency. Further, the Indians had not come to settle in the neighborhood of the missions, as had been planned, with the result that conversions were far from numerically impressive. There was a universal dearth of supplies, and in some of the missions even the wine for the celebration of Mass had run out. There was no real bright spot in this report on East Texas.

Alarcón detailed his progress to the east. Leaving Béjar in September he had first dropped down to the Bay of Espíritu Santo for a thorough inspection. Then his party pushed on to the presidio and mission of San Francisco, whose records showed only twenty baptisms to that date. Purísima Concepción on the Angelina was his next stop. Fray Espinosa had gone down to San Antonio to welcome the governor on his arrival in Texas and was back now to prepare the reception. Alarcón decided to make Concepción his headquarters during his stay in East Texas, and the Indians built him an interesting and serviceable governor's palace, a "round house" with walls of branches and a domed thatched roof. Indians from nearby nations came in for conferences and celebrations. At Concepción the baptism total had soared to 62. The next stops on the tour were San José, Dolores, and San Miguel.

From the last place the governor sent scouts forward to the Red River to gather information on the French at Natchitoches. These came back and reported that the little settlement seemed fairly prosperous and that twenty young Frenchmen were based there. Alarcón considered the possibility of routing them out by force, but he was dissuaded from such a course by wiser heads among the friars. They feared that a resort to arms might well upset the state of *entente cordiale* which then existed between the Spanish missionaries and the Gallic traders, even though the Franciscans were not exactly happy to have foreign competitors bidding for the loyalty of the same natives to whom the friars were appealing. The missionaries did not care to have a state-of-war situation added to their already sufficiently numerous problems.

Alarcón's tenure as governor ended in 1719. Actually, he had sent a letter of resignation to Mexico City after his return from the tour of East Texas. Officials in the capital did not press him to remain in the post, for by the time his resignation reached Mexico City reports from the frontier had been piling up, especially from the missionaries, and few of the reports had much good to say concerning Don Martín. His withdrawal from Texas would hardly be mourned. Besides, his expedition had been costly to the royal treasury and at very best its results had been minimal. The viceroy was already looking for a replacement.

In that year 1719 Texas was caught up in the web of international conflict which pitted Spain against France in Europe. As regularly happened, the belligerency of the mother country involved the American colony. France was challenging Spain's recent occupation of Sardinia and invasion of Sicily. It was the first clash between the two Bourbon crowns since the accession of Philippe d'Anjou, as Philip V, to the Spanish throne in 1700. Word of the conflict to nationals overseas was quicker out of France. Jean-Baptiste LeMoyne (Bienville), now governor of Louisiana, informed of the state of war in Europe, took instant action and surprised and captured Pensacola on May 14, 1719. At almost the same time Bienville gave orders that the Spaniards be dislodged from Texas.

Sometime between June 16 and June 22 the commandant at Natchitoches, one M. Blondel, appeared at San Miguel de los Adaes with a complement of seven men. This small force was wholly adequate to handle the one soldier and the solitary lay brother currently at the mission because the padre and the other soldier at the moment were off to Dolores on business. The lay brother managed to escape and on June 22 rushed, breathless, into Dolores with the news of the "attack." He announced further that the French had threatened to drive the Spaniards completely out of Texas and back to the Río Grande. He said that he had also learned that a hundred or more French soldiers were even then en route from Mobile to accomplish this objective.

Fray Antonio Margil decided that a withdrawal to Concepción was prudent. Arrived there, the little group from Dolores found that the news had traveled faster than they had. A state of near-panic prevailed at Concepción. The women were hysterical and professed themselves willing to brave the perils of the wilderness with just a pair of soldiers if allowed to leave immediately for San Antonio. Ramón did permit a retreat to San Francisco on the Neches. Still apprehensive, the Spaniards demanded that they be allowed to withdraw still farther, to the Trinity River. Again, Ramón had to accede to the pressures put upon him. Padres Espinosa and Margil, however, asked for and received permission to return to Concepción, in the hope of reassuring and holding the Indians until reinforcements would arrive and restore Spanish control. From the Angelina they dispatched a long and fervent, sometimes highly critical, letter to the viceroy, giving an account of recent developments and requesting immediate aid.

Things actually had been moving in the viceregal capital during the late months of 1719, even though the Spaniards in Texas felt that they had been forgotten. The messenger sent by Espinosa and Margil from the Angelina reached the viceroy in August. The Marqués de Valero had only recently been apprized of the state of war existing between Spain and France and later still learned of the capture of Pensacola. Now he had word of the reverses in Texas. Immediately, a major expedition was planned and word went north to Joseph Azlor Vitro de Vera, Marqués de Aguayo, then residing on his hacienda in Coahuila, asking him to accept the appointment as leader of the force to recover Texas.[19]

Besides being a wealthy man, Aguayo was a soldier of wide experience and a man of profound loyalty to the crown. He accepted and immediately enlisted and equipped 84 men and sent them off to reinforce the garrison at San Antonio. He next turned to the task of raising more men and gathering the necessary supplies to support a major expedition.

This was not a simple undertaking, and above all it was time consuming. Enlistees were not easy to find and commanders in the north Mexican presidios were reluctant to share their already slim manpower. Not until October 1720 was Aguayo ready to venture forth. By that time he had 500 men under his command, well equipped and well provisioned. Supplies had come up from Mexico City, but no small portion of the cost Aguayo bore from his own fortune.

Just before departure from Monclova, detailed instructions from Valero reached Aguayo. He was to reoccupy the province, restore the missionaries to their former posts, occupy and fortify the Bay of Espíritu Santo, and, if possible, erect a fort in the Cadodacho country as a bulwark for the protection of East Texas. He was to accomplish all this without engaging the French.

By April 10, 1721, the main body of the force marched into San Antonio. Some time before, young Captain José Domingo Ramón had been detailed with forty men to take possession of the Bay of Espíritu Santo and there lay the foundations for a fort. Word soon came up to San Antonio that Ramón had fulfilled his mission. The French had not put in an appearance, and the Bay was securely in Spanish hands. Before setting out for the east, Aguayo sent a long letter to the viceroy, suggesting that the supply service for Texas be established between Vera Cruz and the Bay by ship, since this would be more expeditious, and less costly, than the use of packtrains overland, and San Antonio could be used as a distributing center for the inland posts.

Aguayo and his little army pushed out of San Antonio in May. They crossed the Guadalupe River, the San Marcos, and the Colorado before the month was out. But then the summer rains came and the swollen streams greatly slowed their progress. The Spaniards were not able to clear the Brazos River until June 19; and it was July 8 before they reached the Trinity. This river was in flood, and the crossing was a long and tedious undertaking, which took several weeks. Beyond the Trinity River they were met by a delegation of Teja, who gave every evidence of being glad to welcome the Spaniards back into their country. Father Espinosa went on ahead and at his old mission of San Francisco sought to rally the Indians. He had a large number assembled when the army reached that point. The welcome on the Neches was equally cordial.

While at the Neches, Aguayo met Saint-Denis. The Frenchman reported that their two nations were once again at peace. (The French line of overseas communications continued to be more rapid.) Saint-Denis sought to dissuade the Spaniards from proceeding farther and he especially used all his persuasiveness to prevent the projected establishment at Los Adaes. Aguayo was courteous but firm. After the French commandant left, the Marqués ordered his force to continue eastward. He reestablished several missions along the way, sometimes shifting former sites to more favorable locations. This is one reason why the mission map of Texas can be very confusing; a single mission often existed in several spots through the eighteenth-century years.

Arrived at the old site of Misión San Miguel in late August, Aguayo began to look for the right spot on which to erect his presidio. The French lieutenant from Natchitoches, left in charge when Saint-Denis had hurried off for instructions to New Orleans, the Louisiana capital since 1718, sought to stall the Spaniards, but to no avail. Aguayo was a determined soul. September and October went by as the fort was being built. By November it was ready to be christened Presidio de Nuestra Señora del Pilar. Aguayo arranged to staff it with one hundred men and to leave six of his cannons as its armament. Natchitoches was hardly more than a dozen miles distant, on its island in the Red River. Don Joseph Benito de Arroyo was appointed commandant of the presidio. Meanwhile, Fray Antonio Margil, has relocated the mission, which now became San Miguel de los Adaes.

His job done, Aguayo headed back toward San Antonio. Before he left Los Adaes, however, the value of the fort at Bay of Espíritu Santo was very conclusively proved, for he received supplies which had come there by sea from Verà Cruz and then overland in about half the time it would have taken them to come up from Mexico City on the trails.

Winter had come—and it was severe—with the result that Aguayo's party did not reach San Antonio until late in January 1722. Arrived there, he made some changes and ordered the erection of the presidio, much too long delayed. While this work of construction was under way, he went south to strengthen the Spanish position at La Bahía, as the Bay of Espíritu Santo now came to be designated. A full-dress presidio was begun near the site of La Salle's fort, and the Misión del Espíritu Santo de Zúñiga was formally erected. Leaving enough men to raise the complement of the garrison to ninety, he pushed back upriver to San Antonio. Rains had slowed down the work on the presidio there. But with the governor back to drive the men, progress again was made.

Another winter was ending. Aguayo was completing a very strenuous three years of service; he was tired and his health was beginning to show signs of the strain under which he had been living. He was ready to retire once again to his lands in Coahuila. He left forty-four of his men at San Antonio and led the rest back to the Río Grande, where the party arrived in May 1722.

The best-informed student of the Aguayo expedition has made the following assessment, which is a well-considered judgment:

> The Aguayo Expedition, the last of its kind into Texas, exceeded all others in size and results. It was perhaps the most ably executed of all the expeditions which entered Texas, and in results it was doubtless the most important. It secured to Spain her hold on Texas for about one hundred and fifteen years. . . . When Aguayo retired from Texas he left ten missions where before the retreat there had been seven, four presidios where there had been two, two hundred and sixty-eight soldiers instead of some sixty or seventy before, and two presidios were for the first time erected at points where danger from foreign aggression was most feared—Los Adaes and Espíritu Santo.[20]

Viceroy Valero, recognizing Aguayo's signal services to the crown, was willing to accede to his petition to retire. The suggestion of the Marqués with respect to his successor was also accepted. The appointment went to Don Fernando Pérez de Almazán, who had been Aguayo's second in command. He had proved himself and, what was very important, he knew Texas well. The fact that on assuming his new charge Pérez de Almazán chose to make Los Adaes his place of residence, on the far eastern edge of his province, was highly indicative of the man's sensitivity to the problems of Texas and its role in the Borderlands strategy. At that point he would be in an excellent position not only to supervise and assist the vital mission effort in the east, but he could also keep close watch on the nearby French and check their activities among the Indians. He realized that the nation that controlled the Indians would control the province. During his years in office, Pérez de Almazán proved to be a capable and popular governor. He circulated from Los Adaes to La Bahía and to San Antonio, trying to hold his vast command together, to foster its internal growth, and to protect it against ever-present and ever-troublesome rivals on the borders, both French and Indian.[21]

Pérez de Almazán was succeeded in 1727 by Melchor de Mediavilla y Azcona. During the latter's administration two major developments occurred —one good and the other less so. A number of colonist families came into Texas, and in 1731 the civilian Villa de San Fernando de Béjar was added to the larger San Antonio complex. It had been Aguayo's suggestion that settlers might be found in the Canary Islands, and the king had approved the introduction of 400 families. Ultimately, only fifteen families could be persuaded to risk their future in Texas. Other settlers were recruited in the southern provinces of the viceroyalty.[22]

The second development was the tour of inspection by Brigadier General Don Pedro de Rivera in 1727. Rivera had been on the road since November 21, 1724, when he arrived in Texas in the spring of 1727.[23] In that former year he had been appointed by the new viceroy, Juan de Acuña, Marqués de Casafuerte, to visit the frontier presidios of the north in order to check on their operation, in the hope of reducing the rapidly rising expenditure of royal funds connected with their maintenance.[24] Rivera was given full power to look into the relations of presidial captains with their men, into the state of discipline prevailing, into the manner in which the presidios were armed and administered; he was to make a judgment about the advantageous location, or otherwise, of each presidio, also about its efficiency in serving the defense needs of the area in which it was located; he might suggest addition or reduction of personnel. Most of all he was to cut fruitless expenditure of funds, but still without jeopardizing the security of the frontiers, their forts, missions, and civilian settlements. His three-and-a-half-year tour took him to New Mexico in the north, over the Sierra to Sinaloa on the west, through the north Mexican provinces, and then to Texas on the east. It is estimated that he covered more than 3000 leagues.

In Texas his attention was concentrated on the four major areas of Los Adaes and the Presidio de Nuestra Señora de los Dolores de los Tejas, the Presidio de Nuestra Señora de Loreto de la Bahía del Espíritu Santo, and finally the San Antonio complex. In his report of 1728 to Casafuerte he made a series of recommendations, all of which were approved in the next year and their immediate execution ordered. In the case of Texas, however, the final dispositions were somewhat more radical than even Rivera had suggested, this principally in the number of soldiers left in the several garrisons.

Rivera did not feel that Los Adaes would prove particularly effective against a determined offensive by the French from Louisiana. He felt that the post should be retained, but that its garrison should be reduced from 100 men to 60. He saw no real justification for the continuance of the Presidio de los Tejas; it was discontinued. La Bahía, he felt, was over-manned; its force was reduced from 90 to 20. He would have reduced the garrison at San Antonio from 54 to 44; actually the final figure was 38. Rivera saw no need to retain the squad of twelve men at Saltillo, which had been established to escort the supply trains and personnel moving into Texas; this service was suppressed. Rivera was sincere and well intentioned, and his recommendations added up to an annual saving to the crown of some 60,000 pesos. But Texas was left as sort of a stepchild by a man who did not fully understand its problems. The outcries of the friars and the objections of the governor and responsible and informed Texas Indians went unheeded.

◁ 8 ▷

Borderland Irritants:
The French and the Indians,
1700-1763

*F*or long years the chief problem on the Borderlands frontier was the Indian. The Spaniard, after his experience with the Chichimeca on the central plateau, was conditioned to face this irritant. He sought to neutralize this vexation with what might be facetiously styled large and frequent applications of the mission formula. And he was reasonably successful despite periodic flare-ups. However, the farther north he pushed, the more virulent the irritation became. In the eighteenth century New Mexico and recently founded Texas had their Indian problems aplenty, especially as pioneers came into contact with the Plains Indians, who consistently resisted the Spanish attempt, be it military or missionary, to alter their way of life and/ or their religion. And in this resistance the Indians had assistance and encouragement from newcomers onto the Borderlands scene, namely the French after their occupation of the Mississippi Valley, beginning in 1699.

The appearance of the French in Louisiana and in the Illinois country added a new dimension to frontier irritation. Texas was added to the roster of the Spanish Borderlands as an antidote in one quarter; New Mexico geared itself for a new and a distinctly defensive role. Between them the

Indians hunting the bison. Charles Bodmer print from Maximilien Wied-Neuwied, *Travels in . . . North America*, 1843. (Library of Congress)

Indians and the French made life less than comfortable and secure for New Mexico and Texas during better than half of the eighteenth century. In 1762 the French irritant was removed; not so the Indians, however.

In the seventeenth century beyond New Mexico, through the Panhandles of Texas and Oklahoma and onto the Plains, there seems to have been a fair degree of stability among the Indians. They had their traditional intertribal squabbles; but few, if any of these, seriously disturbed the life of the Spaniards in Pueblo-land. Of course, in the last two decades of the century the Spaniards had troubles enough with the Pueblo peoples.

As the eighteenth century opened, the Indian lineup was something like this: closer in, on the eastern border of New Mexico, were the Apache, some of them mildly friendly, others rather consistently hostile. They were of many subtribes: the Faraon Apache were more or less due east; above them were the Jicarilla and the Carlana; and beyond them were the Cuartelejo and the Paloma. To the southeast were the Mescalero and the Lipan; they would be more troublesome to Texas and Coahuila. To the north of New Mexico, or better to the northwest, were the Navaho and north of them the Ute, who were enemies both of the Navaho and the white men. On the Plains, beyond the Apache, were the fierce Comanche, whose pressures, like the movement of the Huns in fourth-century Europe, would seriously upset Indian equilibrium on the lower half of the Great Plains in the new century. These Comanche would not have multiplied contacts with the Spaniards of the Borderlands until later in the century, but their presence and their subsequent loyalties would prove to be an important factor.

By the new century two of the white man's imports contributed very significantly to the restlessness of the Plains peoples, namely the horse and the gun.[1] The Spaniards were responsible for the first; the French, for the second. Of the two, strange as it may seem at first glance, the horse for long was the more important. The horse revolutionized the lives of the hunter Indians of the Plains. Initially their interest in the horse seems to have been largely as a new kind of meat in their diet; cattle and mules also fitted into that category. In time, however, the Indians learned to use the horse as a mount, and then things changed rapidly, and for the worse as far as the European was concerned. Much of the harassment to which the Borderlands were subjected grew out of the raids that the Indians made on the frontier ranches. The horse gave the Indian not only greater mobility, but also enlarged the range of his raiding potential. The gun became a factor, but during the eighteenth century no Indian group had a sufficient supply to make them formidable; in general, the possession of the gun simply made them more troublesome and worrisome.

Moreover, the appearance of the French in the trans-Mississippi greatly complicated the problems besetting New Mexico as the seventeenth century merged into the eighteenth. Prior to 1719 the record of the French to the west of the Mississippi is spotty and incomplete; but there is scattered evidence to prove they were there, at least on occasion. Either through actual contact or by lucky chance the Pawnee appear on a French map dating as far back as 1678, and this in the right location; no other records exist to substantiate French presence among them. Canadian *coureurs de bois,* unnamed, seem to have been along the lower reaches of the Missouri in the 1690s, and possibly even farther west onto the Plains.[2] Where they came from is not known, but the reports of white men to the northeast of New Mexico began to accumulate, and anxiety on that far frontier began to mount. Governor Don Diego de Vargas passed these rumors on to his superiors in Mexico City and at the same time suggested that several artillery pieces might be highly useful in New Mexico, at his presidio of Sante Fe, in the event of a French attack. Vargas had himself picked up some of these rumors when out to the northeast, in pursuit of some recalcitrant Pueblo, in 1696. Ten years later Juan de Ulibarri, on a similar "truant officer mission," reached out even farther onto the Plains and came back with more tales. In the second decade there were two campaigns against the Apache—one of Juan Páez Hurtado in 1714 and the second captained by Governor Antonio Valverde y Cosio himself.[3] By this time there was considerable raiding and counterraiding among the Indians on the Plains, and some of the action was disturbing the security of the charges and friends of the New Mexican Spaniards. Suspicion was growing that the French were behind much of this agitation.

Once the French had planted bases in the Middle Mississippi Valley, organized trading expeditions to the west became more frequent. In 1699 the Seminary Priests of Quebec established Mission de la Sainte Famille at

Cahokia (Illinois), opposite the site of the future Saint Louis, and opened their work with the Tamaroa of the neighborhood.[4] Several years later (1702) the Jesuits brought their converts down the Illinois and located them in new surroundings a few miles farther downstream at a spot to be known as Kaskaskia. Indian raiders from the east had been disrupting mission life on the upper Illinois, and the Black Robes, like their Spanish brethren of Paraguay, whose charges were being harassed by Portuguese *bandeirantes* out of São Paulo in the previous century, decided to relocate in the interests of peace and greater security. En route they had paused for almost two years at the mouth of River Des Peres, on the right bank and at the southern edge of the modern Saint Louis. Until the founding of Saint Louis, in 1764, Kaskaskia was the center of French population and activity in the middle valley. This Illinois country quickly attracted a small civilian population, both trader and farmer, some Canadian and some out of Louisiana.[5]

The potential trade markets to the west beckoned, and the Illinois Frenchmen were quick to answer the call; they did not, however, leave full records of their goings and comings.[6] Driblets of information have been gathered for these early eighteenth-century years. A *mémoire* of Pierre LeMoyne, sieur d'Iberville, first governor of the French enterprise on the Gulf Coast, mentions, as early as 1702, a number of the Missouri River tribes, such as the Missouri, the Kansa, the Oto, and several branches of the Pawnee, and locates them rather accurately. In 1705 a certain Laurain told Jean Baptiste LeMoyne, sieur de Bienville, brother and successor to Iberville, of an extended journey up the Missouri and onto the plains beyond. Another trader, Derbanne by name, claimed that in 1706 he had penetrated into the interior for a distance of four hundred leagues and had been very close to New Mexico, the Spaniards, and "their mines." There are other not too detailed reports of like nature in the French archives. Hazy geography makes them somewhat suspect; the *voyageurs* and the *coureurs de bois* may have been filling in such details as catered to hopes, rather than giving reports of actual observation or of personal experience. For example, the oft-repeated assertion that the Missouri River was the "natural" road to New Mexico and the reiterated report of the actuality of rich New Mexican mines would seem to back such a surmise; both bits of information would bring joy to the hearts of French officials and win a *carte blanche* for the reporters to continue their westward journeyings. Fully documented or not, it is certain that Frenchmen were "on the loose" in the trans-Mississippi early in the eighteenth century.

This disturbing news was reflected in many reports from New Mexican officials to their superiors in New Spain.[7] No Spaniard personally saw fellow Europeans, nor does any Frenchmen tell of having confronted a New Mexican Spaniard; but Indian friends of the Spanish did bring in evidence of French presence in the trans-Mississippi, such as objects of unquestioned French origin.

In 1719 the French record becomes more exact and helpful. In that year Paris-born Charles Claude du Tisné went overland to the Osage country, to the south of the Missouri River.[8] A few months earlier he had tried to ascend the Missouri by canoe, but the Missouri Indians had forced him back, unwilling to have him in the lands of their Osage enemies. This is an early instance of what the French encountered time and again among these trans-Mississippi Indians: a willingness to deal with the French themselves but an adamant unwillingness to allow them to proceed beyond the tribal sphere of influence, lest their enemies benefit by a French connection. Sometimes this was prompted by the Indian desire to become the middleman in a trade with tribes farther on; often the attitude grew out of a deep fear of traditional enemy neighbors, what might be called a sense, on a small scale, of "national security."

Back at Kaskaskia, Du Tisné picked up horses, loaded their packs, and set off for the Osage country. The Osage were initially friendly, but, when the Frenchman suggested that they guide him to the Pawnee, their cordiality changed to stubborn opposition. After he had consented to give them most of his guns, they allowed him to push on beyond.

A trek of four days brought him to the first of the Pawnee villages; this particular branch of the nation lived at the moment in northern Oklahoma. The Pawnee showed similar reluctance to allow him to go farther—to the Comanche, who were their mortal enemies. Du Tisné did not push his luck but turned back, with some furs, many buffalo skins, and a mule with Spanish branding. This bit of trading cost him his last gun.

Du Tisné had not been successful in the major intent of his expedition, to reach the Comanche, or the Padouca as the French called them; but he had made official contact with at least one branch of the Pawnee and laid some groundwork for cooperation between his people and these Indians. His expedition showed the French that there was a "Pawnee barrier," which had to be hurdled on the road to New Mexico. The French recognized that their next step would have to be to cement Pawnee friendship and then prevail upon these friends to allow trade with the Comanche. The French already knew that beyond the Comanche were the Apache and then Santa Fe.

Word traveled fast on the Plains. Du Tisné was hardly back in the Illinois country before New Mexican officials were apprized of his visit to the southern Pawnee. The Comanche, though no friends of the Spanish, leaked word that Frenchmen had recently been among their neighbors and, what was seriously disturbing to the Comanche, had left muskets among them. Governor Valverde saw all the frightening implications: guns in the hands of the Plains peoples could be literally as well as figuratively explosive for the future of his province. The Pawnee with guns would be a threat to the Comanche; the Comanche in terror might well push into the land of the Apache; and the Apache, in turn, with nowhere else to go and fearing the Comanche, would soon be pressing against New Mexico's borders. The prospect, to say the very least, was upsetting.

Disturbing reports had been reaching Mexico City from Texas. These, added to the recent information from New Mexico, convinced the officials of the viceroyalty that a threat was mounting which had to be countered, and quickly.[9] Viceroy Valero sent instructions to Valverde, ordering him to support the suggestion of the Franciscans who for some time past had been urging the foundation of a mission among the friendly Jicarilla Apache of northeastern New Mexico. Further, Valverde was to found a presidio at El Cuartelejo (in southeastern Colorado) and also to reconnoiter the Plains in search of the French.

Valverde acknowledged the communique but objected that the season was too far advanced for serious action on the Plains. It was August already and, more than that, all New Mexican manpower and resources were tied up in a projected punitive expedition about to set out against the Comanche, who had been particularly troublesome in late years and just the month before had raided both Taos and Cochití. Valverde felt that possibly, while in the Comanchería, he might pick up some news of the French. At the moment he did not want to shift plans and embark on a campaign which would take him much farther afield. He was probably justified in his thinking, for the expedition against the Comanche did not return until November. Its results were not too impressive, and little was learned of the French.

Back home at Santa Fe, Valverde called a council of war and submitted the viceroy's orders and recommendations to the members of the *junta*. The idea of a presidio at El Cuartelejo was voted down; it would be too far from the center of New Mexico and the expense of maintaining it might very quickly become prohibitive, to a greater degree than the viceroy could suspect. The advisors, however, were by no means opposed to a possible combination military post and mission among the Jicarilla. They all voted to proceed with preparations for an expedition onto the Plains.

For reasons undisclosed, Valverde chose to put this foray under the command of his lieutenant, Don Pedro de Villasur. The little band that set out from Santa Fe in late June 1720, consisted of 42 soldiers, most of them frontier veterans, 3 settlers, 60 Indian allies, Fray Padre Juan Mínguez as chaplain, Jean l'Archevêque, who had been with the Spaniards since the La Salle debacle in Texas, as interpreter, and the Indian Naranjo as chief scout.[10] By August the party was on the South Platte (Río de Jesús María). They followed it to the point where it joined with the other fork, the North Platte (Río San Lorenzo). Here they sighted a Pawnee village. A captive Pawnee who had been purchased by one of the Spanish captains was sent ahead and received a hostile reception. The Spaniards camped nearby and sought to open conversations with the tribesmen. Several of the Indians ventured into Villasur's camp and told of a white man in their midst. Villasur tried to communicate with this individual, sending a letter written in French by L'Archevêque. Whether the man could read or not, the effort was in vain. On August 14 the Pawnee slipped across the river and stampeded the horse herd of the Spaniards. Next, they fell on the party, now badly disorganized, and quickly killed the leaders and all but thirteen of the Spaniards; a dozen of the Indian allies were also slaughtered. The beleaguered Spaniards had inflicted heavy losses on their attackers, which was providential, for the Pawnee withdrew and did not follow the fleeing survivors. The remnants of the force reached Santa Fe on September 6, with their sorry tale of defeat on the Plains.

Informed of the Villasur disaster, the Spanish officials of New Spain were now seriously concerned. A state of war existed between their country and France; the French had recently been successful at Pensacola and also in East Texas,[11] and now on the Plains. They could not be sure whether this last defeat was connected with the other two setbacks, as part of an overall French plan of attack. Elaborate plans for the defense of New Mexico were drafted, orders were issued, but little effective assistance, in terms of men and material of war, was forthcoming. Word came of peace in Europe, and the Spanish officialdom relaxed.

The inspection of the frontier by Brigadier Don Pedro de Rivera, 1724–1728, was the next significant Borderlands happening.[12] In New Mexico, as in Texas, the inspector showed himself very budget-conscious. He ordered a cutback of the plans to extend New Mexican defenses by the establishment of a presidio among the Jicarilla. He suggested, instead, that these friendly Apache be encouraged to migrate to the neighborhood of Taos, where the missionaries could serve them without new military outlay. Later observers criticize this order, and it seems with much justification. The Jicarilla, as anyone acquainted with the frontier could have predicted, refused to leave their lands; they were eventually destroyed or absorbed by their Ute-Comanche enemies, and New Mexico's northeastern flank was left exposed. Few of Rivera's recommendations for New Mexico were practical. This illustrates a basic difference between the Spanish Borderlands frontier and its later Anglo-American counterparts. Anglo-American frontiersmen regularly made their own decisions; those of New Spain had decisions made for them, and frequently by men who had only the very slightest acquaintance with their day-to-day problems, pressures, and dangers.

The next governor of New Mexico, Juan Domingo de Bustamante, picked up rumors of Frenchmen as close as El Cuartelejo and he relayed these bits of intelligence to Mexico City, but the viceroy, the Marqués de Casafuerte, was not too alarmed. He professed to consider these Frenchmen simply as occasional traders, not as an armed threat to New Mexican security. The sequel did prove him correct. There was, however, one more major French thrust which, had there been a proper follow-up, might have made their European rivals, rather than the Ute-Comanche combination, New Mexico's prime problem in the second quarter of the century.

The first steps in this new westward push of the French came after the reports of Charles Claude du Tisné of 1719–1720 were carefully studied in the Illinois country and then sent downriver to officials at New Orleans. By this date Louisiana was administered by the Compagnie d'Occident, the brainchild of the famous John Law, financial advisor to the Regent Philippe d'Orléans, ruling in France during the minority of Louis XV. Bienville had replaced Cadillac as governor. To the men of the Illinois it was clearly evident that the next French move would have to be the winning of the Pawnee and then the Comanche. They did not anticipate great difficulty with the first; the second was very much in question-mark status. Bienville concurred in their analysis and began to look around for a man of the stamp of Saint-Denis, operating so successfully on the Texas frontier. His choice as the breakthrough agent was one of the more fascinating characters in the mid-continent story.

Etienne Véniard, sieur de Bourgmont, was of sturdy Norman stock, as were so many other of France's important North American figures.[13] He had been in America since the early years of the century. For some time he had served at Detroit, under Cadillac. In 1712 he was on hand when Detroit had to repulse another in a series of attacks by the Fox Indians. At this time a band of Missouri was present and assisted in the defense of the northern post. In the company, according to the contemporary reports, was an attractive Missouri maid, with whom Bourgmont fell madly in love. He followed her back to her own country and spent the next several years among her people. During these years in the Missouri country Bourgmont led an expedition up the great river highway to the Arikara and thence out the Platte as far as Wyoming. From all the peoples through whose lands he passed, Bourgmont probed for information concerning the farther tribes, especially the Comanche.

It is not too clear when Bourgmont left the Missouri country, but it is known that he shared his accumulated information with Bienville, who was much impressed with the young man. In fact, he recommended him for the Croix de Saint-Louis, when Bourgmont returned to France around 1718. He spent the next several years there, happily married to a wealthy widow. However, his American days were not over. He was back in Louisiana in 1722, with an appointment from the directors of the Compagnie d'Occident to carry out Bienville's plans for expansion up the Missouri Valley and onto the Plains.

Bourgmont went north to Kaskaskia in February 1723. One delay after another held him there until November; but in that month his party finally set out, rushing to beat the winter ice on the Missouri. He had three large boats and several canoes. Toward the end of the year the Frenchmen paused and chose a site for the fort which they had contracted to establish on the Missouri. It was on the Wakenda tributary and they called it Fort Orléans.[14] The party spent the rest of the winter building the post.

The following summer Bourgmont set out on the second half of his commission, to proceed to the land of the Comanche. Beyond the bend of the Missouri he made friends with the Kansa Indians, on the Kansas or the Kaw, and pushed beyond. Bourgmont, however, was taken sick and became so weak that he could not even ride a horse. They brought him back to the Kansa village and then floated him down to Fort Orléans. Before turning back, as a gesture of goodwill he sent off to the Comanche two Comanche captives, a woman and a boy, whom he had redeemed from his Kansa friends.

Rest at Fort Orléans restored the leader's strength. By September he was back on the Plains and heading toward the Comanchería. These fierce plainsmen pledged friendship and promised to make peace with the tribes allied to the French. Generous presents, such as Bourgmont's predecessors had furnished to their neighbors, did much to soften Comanche opposition. Convinced now that the way to New Mexico was open, Bourgmont headed back to Fort Orléans, having fulfilled the main stipulations of his commitment to the Compagnie.

Bourgmont still had one more job to do: to gather representative chiefs from the Plains peoples and take them on a goodwill tour to France. He assembled quite a delegation. The Indians charmed the French and had a memorable experience. All, save one who died en route, were in time returned to their tribes. Bourgmont seems never to have returned to America. But he had done his job well. In fact, men like himself—Saint Denis, Du Tisné, and others—were making life increasingly difficult for Spain in its Borderlands.

The presence of the French complicated the Indian problem. On hand with their goods and particularly with their guns, the French were in large measure responsible for upsetting the balance of power among the plainsmen. To a tribe supplied with this new kind of firepower, the temptation to prey on neighbors was overpowering. The neighbors had to run and in the process pressured their neighbors. The Spanish frontiers ultimately received the impact of the movement thus generated. Had the Spaniards supplied their friends with muskets, they might have saved themselves many anxious moments. But until it was too late, the Spaniards, at least on the official level, never quite realized that the Indians were going to get the gun and the horse.

The Spaniards had been resourceful in the latter part of the sixteenth and into the next century in adapting to the Indians of northern Mexico; the mission had served them well, and in the western corridor would continue to do so. The mission had worked well enough in Pueblo-land at the end of the middle corridor. Beyond that point and in Texas the system broke down. The eighteenth-century Spaniards seem to have lost the ability to adapt. The hunter nomads of the southern Plains both balked and baffled them, and this nowhere quite so completely as in Texas.

Aguayo secured Texas for the Spaniards to serve as a buffer against the

Misión San José de Aguayo, Texas. (Frederic Lewis)

aggressive French of Louisiana and against the troublesome Indians of the north. The province during the middle eighteenth century had to prove itself; it was, in the words of its best interpreter, "on trial."[15] Could it do the job? Could it and should it be retained? Was the heavy outlay of funds and manpower worth it all? The crown and the colonial officials hoped that the answer to such doubts might be affirmative. At all events, they were willing to try.

During the 1730s and into the 1740s the Spaniards sought to strengthen the major areas which Rivera had left them: San Antonio, East Texas, and the presidio-mission at La Bahía.[16] This last could hardly be dignified with the name of a population center, having no more than several dozen Spaniards, the soldiers and their families, and the Zacatecas Franciscans of the Misión de Nuestra Señora del Espíritu Santo de Zúñiga. However, within a few years the friars had their neophytes doing a bit of farming, and by 1737 the mission had a respectable herd of cattle. Conditions in East Texas, at the Presidio of Los Adaes, were deplorable, and the Misión de San Miguel was not much better off. East Texas had to depend largely on Natchitoches for its food and other supplies, and this situation was sanctioned by Spanish officials. The situation was improved slightly by the late 1730s, thanks in large measure to the development of the basic food crop, corn, at the mission.

The only area of Texas during these years of the second quarter of the century which gave much promise was the San Antonio complex. After the founding of the civilian unit, San Fernando de Béjar, in 1731, and in the same year, in accord with Rivera's orders, the transplanting there of three missions of the Querétaran friars from the Dolores district, on the Angelina, the San Antonio complex counted a presidio, a municipality, and five missions. The most interesting addition was the civilian settlement established by the ten families of Canary Islanders who had been brought over by the crown, landed at Vera Cruz, and then come overland to their new home. These Canary Islanders proved to be industrious settlers and quickly were raising their food and building their little herds, so engrossed in these necessary pursuits that it was some time before they had a church or any public buildings in their Villa.

With increasing harassment from the Apache threatening the supply lines on the road from San Juan Bautista to San Antonio and actually forcing a rerouting of the road from San Antonio to Los Adaes, the governors strove to increase the complement of the garrison, but with little support forthcoming from Mexico City. The two older missions, San Antonio de Valero (the Alamo) and San José y San Miguel de Aguayo, the only one belonging to and staffed by the Zacatecan friars, were functioning satisfactorily. So too were the three transplants of the Querétaran friars located downstream: San Juan Capistrano, San Francisco de la Espada, and Concepción.

In 1745 Fray Padre Francisco Xavier Órtiz made a thorough inspection

Instructing the Indians in *la doctrina*. Woodcut from *Cathecismo, En Lengua Castellana, y Timuquana*, Mexico, 1612. (The Granger Collection)

of the Querétaran missions and submitted a long report in which he described in detail the San Antonio de Valero mission.

> . . . the baptismal records of this, the oldest mission in San Antonio, showed that nine hundred and eighty-one Indians had been baptized up to 1745 and six hundred and eighty-five Christian burials had been performed. In the mission pueblo there were living at this time three hundred and eleven Indians of both sexes and all ages. Of these, two hundred and seventy-five were baptized Christians and thirty-six were being instructed in the *doctrina*. . . . The original church, which seems to have been an adobe structure, had fallen down and a new one was being built at this time. . . .
>
> The Indian pueblo, where the neophytes lived, consisted of two rows of small huts built on either side of an *acequia* (water ditch). These were built of adobe bricks and were generally roofed with straw. Along each row of houses there was a sort of street. The missionaries lived in their small friary, a two-story structure of stone and mortar, with three living cells on the second floor and offices and other rooms on the first. Next to the friary there was a large gallery where the Indian women worked at the looms to make the cloth for their dresses; then followed a granary for the mission corn and other grains, and beyond there were several rooms which were used as offices.
>
> The mission was well supplied with lands for the raising of crops and the pasturing of stock. . . . [The crops included corn and beans; also cotton; and watermelons, melons, and pumpkins.] All the land under cultivation was irrigated by a large ditch which brought an abundant supply of water from the river. All the products raised by the neophytes were used for their maintenance.
>
> To cultivate the fields and carry on the other work about the mission, San Antonio de Valero had twenty-three yoke of oxen, . . . a blacksmith shop, . . . a carpenter shop, . . . and all the necessary chisels and hammers for stone carving and masonry.
>
> In the room where the women and such men as were not capable of working in the fields were employed, there were three looms, six pairs of cards, eight combs, six shuttles, and twenty spinning wheels. To weave the various kinds of cloth the neophytes used the wool from the mission sheep and the cotton raised on the mission farms. . . .
>
> During the inspection, Father Ortiz ordered all the cattle and other stock belonging to the mission gathered and counted. It was found that there were at this time two thousand two head of cattle, not including about three hundred which could not be rounded up on account of the proximity of the Apaches. There were also one thousand three hundred and seventeen sheep, three hundred and four goats, and forty horses. . . . [17]

The other missions had relatively comparable records. With such a report before one, it is easy to lament that the Indians did not give the friars the opportunity to build many another mission like these of the San Antonio area. But the number of the natives of Texas willing to conform to the mission pattern of life was distressingly small. The Spaniards' traditional frontier institution just did not appeal to or work out with the native Texans.

Toward the end of the 1740s the Franciscans felt that the time had come to expand. True, there had been little success in East Texas, but those establishments in the San Antonio area were healthy and promising. To the northeast were various small groups of the Tonkawa nation, who gave some indications of a willingness to settle down to mission life. The friars of Querétaro were particularly anxious to reach out to them. The idea of several foundations between the Colorado and the Brazos was proposed. The reaction of officialdom was mixed—for example, former governor Juan Antonio Bustillo y Zevallos was adamantly opposed to expansion, whereas another former governor, Melchor de Mediavilla y Azcona, favored such a move. Finally, all permissions came and in 1748 Fray Mariano de los Dolores and his companions went out to open the San Xavier missions.[18] The first was named San Francisco Xavier; and in the next year two others were founded; the friars began to press immediately for the presidio which had been promised and also the civilian settlement. The governor of the day, Pedro del Barrio Junco y Espriella, was of the Bustillo school of thought on the enterprise and before long he and the friars were fighting; he liked neither the general idea of expansion nor the location of the missions. Barrio was overruled from higher up after Lieutenant José de Eça y Musquíz was sent to look over the situation. His report was favorable; he found 480 Indians resident in the three missions and could note that by 1750 there had been 266 baptisms. The presidio garrison arrived in the next year (1751).

Almost immediately the captain, Felipe Rábago y Terán, and the friars were at loggerheads. Rábago, within a month after his arrival, was suggesting a consolidation of the three missions and a withdrawal from the Río San Xavier to a location on the Río San Marcos, where he felt the proposed civilian colony might be more advantageously placed. The quarrel became bitter and acrimonious. Before it ended, the mission superior had been changed, the captain recalled, and one of the friars, José Ganzábal, and a civilian shot down at Candelaria in 1752. The captain was suspected of complicity in the murders, and a mission Indian had so stated; some years later, however, Rábago was cleared of this charge. He had been replaced by his brother Pedro, who got on somewhat better with the Franciscans; but, even so, the days of the San Xavier enterprise were numbered. The Apache raids were increasing, and mission growth was anything but promising. By 1755 all parties were convinced and there was a withdrawal to the San Marcos.

The next mission effort, the San Sabá venture with the Apache, was equally disappointing. In the decades following the settlement of the province the Apache loomed as a major problem.[19] Texas had to endure frequent raids from the Lipan branch of the nation. About the time that the Spaniards were beginning to despair, a shift in power politics among the red men seemed to play into their hands. The eastern Apache, particularly, by the 1740s were feeling the pressure of their dreaded enemies, the Comanche, and showed some signs of a willingness to be friendly; they seemed to foresee a time when they might need the Spaniards, not as unwilling suppliers of their needs or targets of their raiding, but as actual allies against the Comanche. Evidences of this changing attitude, slight though they may have been, offered the friars the opening for which they had been hoping and praying. The Franciscans had long been contending that the solution to the Apache problem lay with the cross and the gospel, not with the sword and the arquebus. Toward the middle of the century the time seemed ripe for action.

There was during the planning stage serious disagreement among the missionaries themselves on the approach to be adopted. Fray Mariano de los Dolores favored an establishment in the Apachería proper; Fray Benito Santa Ana, a man of equal prestige and experience, and at the moment in the viceregal capital, urged missions on the Guadalupe River, not too far from San Antonio, to which the Apache could be attracted. There was, in consequence, a period of delay and indecision. During this interim period a group of Natage Apache came down to San Juan Bautista and settled nearby on the Río Grande. Everyone was most interested, for this experiment might well prove the merit of the transplant theory. But within a year the Natage, rapidly tiring of the confining character of mission existence, packed up and went back to their former lands, leaving Fray Martín García heartbroken and the transplant party in a less strong position.

While the two proposals were still being debated at the official level, the one for missions in the Apachería got a strong boost from a revival of mining prospects to the north. Rumors of rich silver lodes in the Río Llano district drew several small prospecting expeditions there, to the mines which have been variously called the San Sabá, the Bowie, and the Los Almagres mines. On Spanish frontiers the precious metals had a way of "talking." Finally, the plan for a mission-presidio-colony project in Apache-land won official approval; it would be known as San Sabá. A not unimportant assist came from a generous promise of Don Pedro Romero de Terreros to support mission effort among the Apache to the extent of around 150,000 pesos. Don Pedro's Franciscan cousin, Fray Alonso Giraldo de Terreros, had awakened the interest of this quite remarkable eighteenth-century philanthropist.[20]

In the spring of 1757 Colonel Diego Ortiz Parrilla went north to the San Sabá River and laid the foundations of the Presidio de San Luis de las Amarillas, selected the site for the mission several miles downstream, and made ready for the arrival of the garrison and the hoped-for settlers.[21] Before many months were gone, Parrilla, it seems, developed marked skepticism in the enterprise and began to hint that the presidio, at least, might be more advantageously moved to the neighborhood of the mines on the Llano River. On this point he and the missionaries, who, understandably, did not wish to be deprived of military protection close at hand, disagreed. The friars in Texas had an uncanny knack for being at odds with their civil rulers, or perhaps it was vice versa. In the end the several establishments remained as founded, largely because the officials in the capital were pleased with the idea of a full-dress outpost in the north; that is, the complex of presidio, mission, and villa or civilian settlement.

Even with Spanish protection brought to them, the Apache were hesitant and did not congregate at San Sabá as it had been hoped; the Franciscans wanted more potential Christians, and the military would have welcomed them as allies. The Comanche swooped in for the first of a series of raids in March 1758. Their number was reported at around two thousand; they were mounted; and many were armed with guns.. The mission stores were plundered and the herd stampeded. Two of the friars, Terreros and Santiesteban, along with six persons were cut down, and also two soldiers sent from the presidio in an attempted rescue role.

News of this shook the frontier, as far away as Nuevo León and Coahuila. A squad of soldiers was hurried north from the San Antonio presidio, where there was real concern lest the mission Indians of that neighborhood might rebel; the mission of Guadalupe was abandoned; and cries for help went through the northern provinces and on to the viceroy.

The debate opened again, as to whether the San Sabá establishments should or should not be retained. The strong consensus was that they should be retained; to run would be a confession of weakness, and the Indians, friendly and otherwise, would be only too quick to sense this. A punitive expedition against the Comanche was ordered, and word sent to the frontier presidios to lend detachments from their garrison to build up this force.

Parrilla could not move out of San Antonio earlier than August 1759. In the meantime the Comanche and their allies had again descended on San Sabá, in March. On this raid they killed 19 persons and ran off some 750 head of stock. The Comanche, quite obviously, meant business, seeming to recognize that their own ascendancy on the southern plains was put in jeopardy by the existence of this Spanish outpost.

The company which put out from San Antonio in August was an imposing force. It numbered 380 soldiers from the northern presidios, 90 mission Indians, 30 Tlascalans, and 134 Apache allies, who must have known that their future was equally bound up with the defeat of their inveterate Comanche enemies. The way to San Sabá was clear and so too was the area immediately to the east. However, there was a skirmish in the upper Tonkawa country, in which 55 enemy Indians were killed and three times that many taken prisoner. Parrilla then pushed farther to the east, to the country of the Taovaya, on the Red River, thinking to overawe these farther peoples with a parade of Spanish might. This proved to be a mistake, for at one of the Taovaya villages, near the present Ringgold, the Spaniards encountered a large contingent waiting behind well-constructed palisades, flying a French flag, and armed with French guns. A four-hour siege ensued, during which the Spaniards lost some fifty men. Even with their small artillery pieces they could not breach the defenses. The call for retreat was sounded. The retreat turned into a rout; the next seventeen days, the time required to reach the presidio at San Sabá (on October 25), were harrowing and humiliating. The engagement was one of the worst Spanish setbacks on the northern frontier.

The Spaniards held on in the San Sabá district for a few more years. They sought to relocate the Apache in two missions on the upper Nueces, Candelaria and San Lorenzo at El Cañon; but this venture, too, met with scant success. By 1767 the Spaniards had withdrawn from San Sabá and within the next two years from the Nueces River locations. Efforts to Christianize the Apache had failed.

Not all Spanish activity in Texas during those middle decades of the eighteenth century was concentrated in central and eastern areas of the province. There was some attempt, after earlier exploration, to hold, missionize, and civilize the rugged area on both sides of the Río Grande southward from El Paso del Norte to San Juan Bautista. Out of this came the beginnings of the development of the La Junta country around the point of juncture of the Río Conchos with the Río Grande. The Presidio del Norte was established there to protect the missions on both sides of the Río Grande.[22]

More important was the expansion in the 1740s which led to the occupation of the lands along the lower reaches of the Río Grande and the establishment of the new Borderland of Nuevo Santander, through the modern Mexican State of Tamaulipas and embracing the southernmost triangle of modern Texas, as far east as the mouth of the Guadalupe-San Antonio.[23] Spanish attention to this hitherto largely unexplored and untenanted region was sparked by fears that rival powers in North America, in this case England, might take advantage of Spain's seeming disinterest and move in with trading stations and even more serious settlement attempts. In 1739 Spain became involved in war with England (The War of Jenkins' Ear) and there was concern lest English pressures on Florida might carry far to the west along the Gulf of Mexico shoreline beyond Louisiana, where England was also planning to harass the French.

The first royal order to choose a colonizer to conquer and occupy the so-called Seno Mexicano, the land from Tampico to the mouth of the San Antonio, came to Mexico as early as 1740. There were rivals, plans and counterplans, hearings, conferences, and debates. Not until 1746 did the viceroy and his Mexican officials choose their man. He was Don José de Escandón, "Corregidor of Querétaro, a man well known for his integrity, his great services rendered to the government on various occasions, and particularly for the pacification of La Sierra Gorda, which he carried out successfully in a very short time at his own expense."[24] At the time, Don José was forty-six years old but he had a wealth of American experience behind him, first in Yucatán and then in the Sierra Gorda, which was noted in the citation of his appointment. He knew the frontier, at least that frontier, was intelligent, perceptive, and above all energetic.

Escandón spent the next several years carefully exploring his new province and planning its settlement. In 1749 he was ready to move out of Querétaro with better than 3000 colonists, on what was one of the best-conceived and ultimately most successful of Spain's moves into the Borderlands. Within a short time he had twenty-odd little settlements, most of them on the south side of the Río Grande—towns which have endured to modern times, such as Reynoso, Camargo, Mier, Revilla, and others. On the left bank two of his more successful foundations were Laredo and Dolores. The lower Río Grande valley was fertile; his colonists turned to farming and stockraising. The land between the Río Grande and the Nueces soon became sort of a great ranch and one of the important birthplaces of the Texas cattle industry of the future. The province of Nuevo Santander was not without its Indian irritants, but these were much less troublesome and disturbing than the wild raiders farther north. And the French bothered the new province not at all.

The same cannot be said for East and Southeast Texas nor for New Mexico in those mid-century decades. The French came back into the picture most distressingly, and aggressively.

The area from the mouth of the Trinity eastward had drawn very little interest or attention from the Spaniards until rumors began to reach them that French traders from Louisiana were infiltrating the area.[25] Then, in 1745 news came to the effect that the French had actually founded a settlement at the mouth of the river. Joaquín Orobio Bazterra, captain at La Bahía, reported this intelligence to the viceroy, who in turn ordered him to investigate. The reconnaissance turned up no Frenchmen, but did confirm previous rumors that French traders had been among the tribes of the southeast. En route he made first Spanish contact with the Orcoquiza and the Bidai. During the next years Spanish traders, with goods purchased from the French at Natchitoches, moved in among these Indians. The goods thus obtained were purchased in direct violation of the law; but the governor, Jacinto de Barrios y Jáuregui, connived, and there was strong suspicion that he may have been the man masterminding the whole illegal operation. In 1754 one of the French merchants, Joseph Blancpain, was arrested and sent off to Mexico City. This arrest started action on the Trinity and elicited a strong protest from the governor of Louisiana, Louis de Kerlérec, who claimed that his man was in French territory. To anticipate a possible French move, in 1756 the Spaniards established a small presidio, San Agustín de Ahumada, near the mouth of the Trinity, and two of the Zacatecas Franciscans set up a mission, Nuestra Señora de la Luz, to win the Orcoquiza. Neither was particularly successful and both were abandoned in the next decade.

During the 1750s the boundary dispute over the line in East Texas was again reopened. Was the Texas boundary the Red River, in the Natchitoches district, as the Spaniards claimed, or was it to the west of that river, at Arroyo Hondo and La Gran Montaña, up to which natural line the French had advanced two decades before, after relocating Natchitoches on the west bank? Here, too, the French had become an irritant. The Spaniards were becoming touchy.

At still another point on the long Borderlands frontier the Spaniards had reason to revive their suspicions of the French. In New Mexico, when the French did not take advantage of Bourgmont's successes with the Comanche, the Spaniards tended to forget their European rivals and to concentrate on their ever-present Indian problem, which grew more and more serious as the years of the second quarter of the century rolled along. The Ute-Comanche alliance at first seemed to be the great threat to New Mexican security. But then there was a falling-out between the partners, followed by war, with the Comanche emerging victorious. Respite to the north was welcome. But almost as quickly as it came, pressures on the eastern side of the province built up. Flushed with their victory over the Ute, the Comanche next moved against the Apache. The Jicarilla, traditionally friendly to the Spaniards, were wiped out. Comanche pressure next forced the Faraon Apache against New Mexico's eastern flank and sent the Lipan Apache southward. New Mexicans had almost forgotten to worry about the French.

Then in 1739 the folk of Santa Fe received a shock, when a small party of Frenchmen appeared at their gates.[26] The French were now no longer shadowy rumors; they were there, in the flesh. With Bienville's blessing, two brothers, Pierre and Paul Mallet, had set out from the Illinois country with seven companions, intending to prove conclusively whether or not the Missouri River could be followed into Spanish territory. They went up the Missouri and reached the land of the Arikara, before they were convinced that this river was not the way to Santa Fe. Doubling back to the Platte, they followed its course overland to the forks, then down the south fork to the Rockies. The Frenchmen then pushed southward, along the face of the Rockies' Front Range, across Raton Pass into Taos, and on to Santa Fe. Perhaps simply because they were so taken aback by this daring trespass, the Spaniards received them with a measure of hospitality and ultimately allowed as many as wished to return to the French settlements in the Mississippi Valley. Two of the party chose to remain and married New Mexican señoritas. Three went back to the Illinois; the other four, including the two Mallet brothers, followed the Canadian River into the Arkansas and down the Mississippi to report to Bienville at New Orleans.

Their information gave Bienville the idea of trying to reach Santa Fe from New Orleans and even kindled the hope that from Santa Fe a route to the Pacific might be found. The French governor chose a naval man,

Fabry de la Bruyère, to implement this scheme. La Bruyère was furnished with letters to the governor of New Mexico, suggesting the opening of trade relations and asking the Spanish official to assist the Frenchmen in their quest westward. The governor of New Mexico did not have to play the diplomat, for La Bruyère did not reach New Mexico to deliver the letters. Low water on the Canadian, in that season of 1741, balked further advance, and the party returned to Louisiana. This failure, especially since it had been an expensive one, for a time at least cooled Louisiana enthusiasm to reach Santa Fe.

For a third time (in 1750) Santa Fe had French callers: four Frenchmen, headed by Pierre Mallet, who were intercepted at Pecos and arrested.[27] Ultimately, these four were sent to Spain in order that "His Majesty may decide what to do with them." Their appearance in his province very definitely upset the new governor, Tomás Vélez Capuchín, especially since the year before three other Frenchmen had been picked up at the Taos fair: Louis Fèbre, Joseph Raballo, and Pierre Satren had deserted from the Arkansas Post. They were not anxious to return to the Valley and asked to be allowed to remain in New Mexico. The fact that they brought certain skills with them—carpentry, tailoring, barbering, blood-letting—seems to have recommended them to the governor, who granted this permission.

Two more Frenchmen appeared in 1752. Jean Chapuis and Louis Feuilli had left the Illinois country with a string of nine packhorses well loaded. They had the bulk of their cargo when they arrived in Santa Fe and were ready to do business. Instead, they were arrested, their goods confiscated, and they were sent off to Mexico City for questioning. At Santa Fe, when challenged, they admitted that they knew that trade was strictly forbidden by the Spaniards. But they also knew that goods in New Mexico were quite regularly in short supply and always expensive. They gambled that Spanish legal scruples in this instance might be set aside because of the attractive prices they could offer. In this they simply confirmed common French thinking in the mid-continent.

These intrusions were the last French thrusts toward New Mexico. The French still had their dreams for the trans-Mississippi. Although the men of the 1750s did not know it, the time of the French in North America was rapidly running out. In a few years they would be forced to withdraw, making way for the victorious English to the east of the Mississippi and turning over the trans-Mississippi to the Spaniards—all this as a result of the French and Indian War which was under way as of 1754.

In 1762 New Mexico and Texas were rid of one of the Borderland irritants. The other remained. In fact, the Indians, if anything, stepped up their vexations, and Spain had to take drastic reform action in its Borderlands to calm the irritation. Spain would never be able to cure it.[28] The year 1762 was a watershed date in the eastern and the middle corridors; it was just another date in the story of the western corridor.

◁ 9 ▷

On to California, the Last Borderland, 1711-1784

*T*he advance of the frontier of New Spain up the west-coast corridor in the seventeenth century, even though the Spaniards of those years may not have realized it, was very truly the first stage on the long road to California's Golden Gate. Padre Eusebio Francisco Kino, some years before he died in 1711, had the vision of Alta California and its "great harbor of Monterey" in his dreams. This vision came into sharp focus after he had proved to himself that the California of his day, namely Baja California, was not an island but a peninsula, joined to the continent which stretched northward from his Pimería Alta. He had been to the Gila, over to its junction with the Río Colorado, and had picked up information on the vast lands and many nations beyond. He looked into the future and thought of the day when he, or more likely his successors, would win them for Both Majesties, God and King. On their western edge had to be that shoreline which Juan Rodríguez Cabrillo had uncovered, which Sebastián Vizcaíno had explored, and which year after year the Manila Galleon coasted on its homebound voyage to Acapulco.[1]

The most immediate result of his discovery of the peninsularity of California was the plan to link his rich Sonora with the much less favored

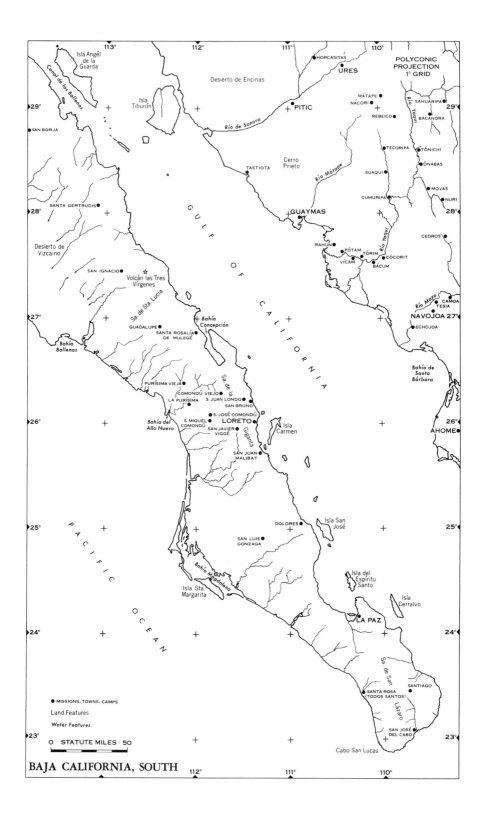

113°   112°   111°   110°

POLYCONIC
PROJECTION
1° GRID

Isla Angél
de la
Guarda

HORCASITAS

URES

Desierto de Encinas

MÁTAPE

Isla
Tiburón

NÁCORI

SAHUARIPA

29°

PITIC

29°

REBEICO

BACANORA

San Borja

Río de Sonora

SAN BORJA

TECORIPA

TÓNICHI

Cerro
Prieto

ÓNABAS

TASTIOTA

SUAQUI

MOVAS

SANTA GERTRUDIS

CUMURIPA

NURI

28°

GUAYMAS

28°

Desierto de
Vizcaino

RAHUN

CEDROS

SAN IGNACIO

PÓTAM

CÓCORIT

Volcán las Tres
Vírgenes

VÍCAM

TÓRIM

BÁCUM

CAMOA
TESIA

27°

Bahía
Concepción

NAVOJOA 27°

GUADALUPE

ECHOJOA

Bahía
Ballenas

SANTA ROSALÍA
DE MULEGÉ

Bahía de
Santa
Bárbara

PURÍSIMA VIEJA

COMONDÚ VIEJO
LA PURÍSIMA

S. JUAN LONDO

SAN BRUNO

S. JOSÉ COMONDÚ

26°

S. MIGUEL
COMONDÚ

LORETO

AHOME

26°

Bahía del
Año Nuevo

SAN JAVIER
VIGGÉ

Isla
Carmen

SAN JUAN
MALIBAT

DOLORES

Isla San
José

25°

25°

SAN LUIS
GONZAGA

Isla Sta.
Margarita

Isla del
Espíritu
Santo

Isla
Cerralvo

LA PAZ

24°

24°

SANTIAGO

MISSIONS, TOWNS, CAMPS

SANTA ROSA
(TODOS SANTOS)

Land Features

Water Features

SAN JOSÉ
DEL CABO

23°

STATUTE MILES 50

23°

Cabo San Lucas

BAJA CALIFORNIA, SOUTH

112°   111°   110°

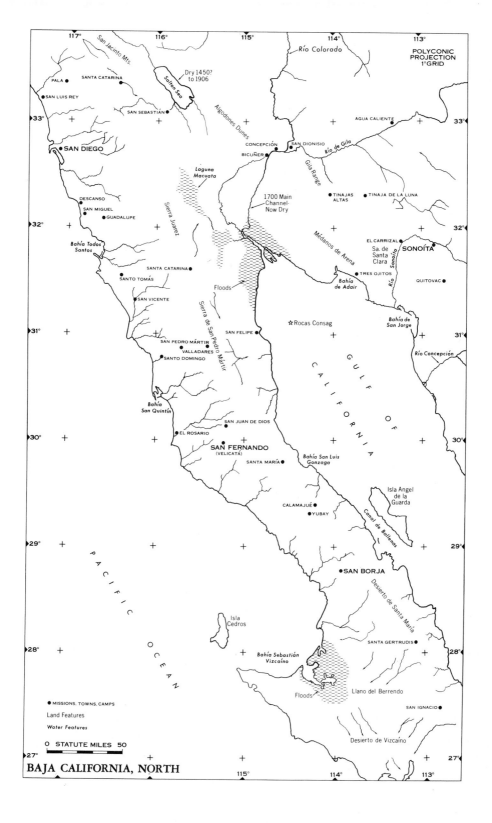

POLYCONIC
PROJECTION
1° GRID

117°
116°
115°
114°
113°

San Jacinto Mts.
Río Colorado

PALA
SANTA CATARINA
Salton Sea
Dry 1450?
to 1906

SAN LUIS REY

AGUA CALIENTE

33°
33°

SAN SEBASTIÁN
Algodones Dunes

CONCEPCIÓN
SAN DIONISIO

SAN DIEGO
BICUÑER
Río de Gila

Laguna
Macuata
Gila Range

DESCANSO
1700 Main
Channel-
Now Dry
TINAJAS
ALTAS
TINAJA DE LA LUNA

SAN MIGUEL
32°
32°

GUADALUPE
Sierra Juarez
Médanos de Arena
EL CARRIZAL
SONOÍTA
Sa. de
Santa
Clara

Bahía Todos
Santos
SANTA CATARINA
TRES OJITOS
QUITOVAC

SANTO TOMÁS
Floods
Bahía
de Adair

SAN VICENTE
Bahía de
San Jorge

Rocas Consag
Río Concepción

31°
SAN FELIPE
31°

SAN PEDRO MÁRTIR
VALLADARES
SANTO DOMINGO
Sierra de San Pedro Mártir
G
U
L
F

O
F

C
A
L
I
F
O
R
N
I
A

Bahía
San Quintín
SAN JUAN DE DIOS

EL ROSARIO
Bahía San Luis
Gonzaga
30°
30°

SAN FERNANDO
(VELICATÁ)
SANTA MARÍA

Isla Angel
de la
Guarda

CALAMAJUÉ
YUBAY
Canal de Ballenas

29°
29°

P
A
C
I
F
I
C

SAN BORJA
Desierto de Santa María

Isla
Cedros

SANTA GERTRUDIS
28°
28°

Bahía Sebastián
Vizcaíno

O
C
E
A
N
Floods
Llano del Berrendo

SAN IGNACIO

MISSIONS, TOWNS, CAMPS
Land Features
Water Features

Desierto de Vizcaíno

0   STATUTE MILES   50

27°
27°

BAJA CALIFORNIA, NORTH

115°
114°
113°

lands of Baja by an overland route. His Italian compadre, Juan María de Salvatierra, had been on the peninsula since 1697, laying the foundations for a chain of missions. Kino had almost gone with him in 1697 but had been held in the Pimería. Kino promised to help supply the California missions with the needed items which he knew from earlier experience the peninsula could not produce—most everything, actually, but first and foremost food. He had planned to do this by boat, from a Sonora port through which he would channel the necessities. The years that had elapsed proved that this method was possible but less than completely satisfactory, besides being expensive and dangerous. A land route would be much more practical.

In a letter to the viceroy (1703) Kino had talked of the possibility of a town of "some 300 or 400 families" which might be founded "on the banks of the bounteous and fertile Río Colorado, close to the head of the Sea of California."[2] This base could serve a number of purposes. From it California might be supplied; from it the frontier might be expanded "into the nearby country of the Moquis"; but he did not stop there, for he would also hope to see even farther expansion "along the northern coast on to regions known as the Gran Quivira and the Gran Teguayo, as far as Cape Mendocino and the land of Yeso, and following the northwestern and western coastline even as far as the territory close to Japan. . . ." To the northeast he envisioned expansion to the regions beyond New Mexico as far as the lands of New France. He was aware that Spain of 1703 had a Bourbon king (Philip V) and probably felt that the day of intense rivalry between Spain and France had passed.

Such was part of the legacy which the great Tyrolese Black Robe left to the northwestern frontier of his adopted New Spain—a bold dream. The land passage to Baja California would never become a reality. One such to a more northerly California in time would be something very real—a road from his Sonora to a new "outpost of empire"; but that was almost three quarters of a century into the future. However, for years after Kino, missions, settlements, presidios on the lower Gila and the lower Colorado were very much and very often in Spanish thinking, and so, too, the land connection with the mission chain slowly extending northward up the rocky California peninsula.

The Lower California story has a definite connection with the later "Superior California" thrust. The first two land expeditions into Alta California went northward in 1769, from a peninsula base. Salvatierra went to the peninsula in 1697 and before the first year was out had been joined by another Italian pioneer, Padre Francisco María Piccolo.[3] Soon the pair had three other missions centering around the headquarters foundation, Loreto, set strategically on a cove protected by Carmen Island, a little more than two hundred miles north of the peninsula's southern tip. In 1701 Honduras-born Juan de Ugarte joined them and until his death (1730) proved to be a giant in the difficult enterprise. Ugarte had been connected with the California project from the beginning, but as home-based fund raiser in Mexico; he, with Salvatierra, was one of the originators of the famous Pious Fund, the supplement from private sources which made possible the missions of the peninsula and later, too, of Alta California, the royal subsidy always being wholly inadequate.[4]

The work continued into the second quarter of the century. Progress was slow but steady. With great effort the padres were building some measure of economic sufficiency—in the garden patches, small fields, and on the even smaller ranches—but the mission was still largely dependent on the mainland. The king had recognized the value of the enterprise, both Christian and strategic, and had ordered some increase in the meager royal subsidy. The system of complete Jesuit control, not only in matters spiritual, but also civil, economic, and military, was periodically challenged but allowed to continue. In this respect California was a new frontier experiment. The padres wanted no civilian colonization; they were opposed to pearl-fishing in the Gulf, lest their Indians be dragooned into forced labor; they put up, grudgingly, with the soldiers of the presidio and the little garrisons, who even under control of the missionaries could still be a source of irritation to the natives, and possibly, too, of Christian disedification. In theory, the proposed temporary and complete isolation of their neophytes might be sound; in practice, the system was not always workable.

Things seemed to be going well as the 1730s rolled along. Then the first serious trouble broke. Troubles there had been from the beginning, but these were mainly of a physical and material nature—sustenance and survival. In 1734 the human factor sparked the blowup.

The Indians not only were of extremely low cultural achievement, but they also had a certain number of half-breeds among them, the children of occasional callers around the tip of the peninsula—English and Dutch pirates and crewmen of the annual Manila Galleon which may have paused there on its homebound route. Several mulattoes were among the leaders of the revolt which broke in 1734. During the uprising two missionaries, Lorenzo Carranco and Nicolás Tamaral, and several garrison soldiers were cut down. All four of the southern missions were destroyed. Padre William Gordon, a Scotsman, was absent from La Paz on business at Loreto and escaped; Padre Sigismundo Taraval of Todos Santos was forewarned in time to seek refuge, at Loreto. Forty-nine of his Christians—women and children—were killed when the rebels overran Todos Santos. This was not the end, for in January of the next year, by prearrangement with Tamaral, the Galleon put in at the San Bernabé anchorage to take on fresh water and whatever fresh food the mission Indians might supply. The landing party of thirteen was ambushed and killed; and the Indians even threatened the Galleon itself until repelled by gunfire, of which they had a mortal terror. The small military force from Loreto could not cope with the rebellion and it was not until late 1737 that peace was restored to the south.

One of the problems in reducing the rebels was the tardiness with which the viceroy, Archbishop Don Juan Antonio Vizarrón, took forceful action; at the time he was feuding with the Jesuits and seemed content to allow them to handle a situation which he felt was of their own making, the viceroy not being in favor of the royally sanctioned system of Jesuit control. Ultimately, Governor Manuel Bernardo Huidobro of Sinaloa was sent over with a small complement of troops and a number of Yaqui allies. However, Huidobro was not immediately successful and, cordially disliking the Jesuits, did a number of things which the padres felt were just plain stupid. To be sure, they did not help the tension between themselves and the governor by saying so.

By the time that peace had been restored to the peninsula the Black Robes had exactly thirty years and a few weeks before them in their California enterprise: they would be expelled from their missions there in January 1768 by the 1767 decree of Charles III.[5] During these years they rebuilt their southern missions and pushed their frontier northward. San Borja was founded in 1752, inland on the peninsula but in approximately the same latitude as the mouth of the Río Sonora; Santa María de Los Angeles was established some fifty miles farther on, in 1767, less than a year before the expulsion. Slowly but surely they were edging toward that possible union with the Pimería missions and the long-dreamed-of land passage.

Much of the work in the later Jesuit years of Lower California was carried on by non-Spaniards in Jesuit ranks, just as was the case on the other side of the Gulf, in Sonora and Arizona. After the mid-1660s the Spanish crown, as has been noted, relented and relaxed its previous ban against foreign missionaries working in the Indies. From the late seventeenth century onward a sizable number of Italians and Central Europeans (Germans, Poles, Hungarians, and other men from the Holy Roman Empire) began to appear on the mission rosters. Kino was an outstanding example, as were Salvatierra and Piccolo. Baja California had her share of these resourceful and enthusiastic newcomers. The California records of the mid-century decades show such names as Fernando Consag, Johann Bischoff, Franz Xavier Wagner, Joseph Gasteiger, Lambert Hostell, Georg Retz, Benno Ducrue, Franz Inama, Jakob Baegert, Anton Tempis, Wenceslaus Linck, and others.[6] Some of these men, besides being excellent missionaries, distinguished themselves otherwise. The Croatian Consag posted a record of exploration which put him in a class with Kino and the later Fray Francisco Garcés.[7] The Bohemian Linck, in the middle 1760s added even fuller information to the Spaniards' geographical knowledge of the northern reaches of the peninsula; he probably should receive some credit for conditioning Fernando de Rivera y Moncado, captain in the peninsula during the last Jesuit years, and preparing him for the big job ahead in Alta California, for Rivera was Linck's companion on the trail.[8]

On the other side of the Gulf of California, in the west-coast corridor proper, there was spasmodic activity in the post-Kino years.[9] The idea of advancing the northern edge of the frontier to the Gila and the Colorado persisted and at times seemed close to realization; yet each time some untoward situation or circumstance thwarted the plans. For the two decades after Kino's death, there was a serious shortage of Jesuit manpower in Sonora-Arizona. During those years a sizable percentage of the potential missionaries available was being channeled into the missions of Lower California. This lack of manpower was one reason why the Jesuits did not react with energy to the assignment of the Moqui field to them. A royal decree of 1719 officially transferred these northeastern Arizona Indians (the modern Hopi) to the Black Robes, removing them from the jurisdiction of New Mexico and the Franciscans. The manpower situation changed for the better in the 1730s with the arrival of a new contingent of non-Spanish Jesuits. Several of the abandoned mission sites in Arizona were reestablished, such as Santa María Suamca, Guevavi, Tumacácori, and San Xavier del Bac. And once again the Gila began to figure in the expansionist plans of the missionaries.

Then in 1736 Sonora rocketed briefly into the news, following the discovery of the quite astounding silver deposits at Arizonac (in the upper Altar Valley, just south of the present international boundary). The silver was in the form of balls rather than deposited in veins, giving rise to the name *Bolas de Plata* which was applied to the find; many of the nuggets were 500 pounds in weight, and one was even reported as weighing 3500 pounds. There was a rush of miners, away from Sonora's more normal and less immediately enriching lodes. Official attention, too, was drawn to the north. Some of this was occasioned by the dispute as to whether this Arizonac was a mine in the general sense, from whose output the king had the right to the usual one-fifth, or whether, because of the peculiar character of the silver uncovered, the king had rights to the whole treasure. The frontier captain of Fronteras, Juan Bautista de Anza, father of a later more famous son, claimed the Arizonac was a *criadero*, a growing-place of silver, and was, therefore, like a place of hidden treasure which traditionally went to the king in its entirety. The silver, however, soon ran out. But the interest in the farther north, which it had helped to spark, continued. Anza felt that the time was now right and pressed for immediate advance to the Gila and the Colorado. But again, the hopes were dashed.

The coastal Pima revolted in 1737 and for the moment distracted Captain Anza. Hardly had he calmed that disturbance, when he had to turn eastward to fend off the attacking Apache, who were becoming more and more troublesome along the northeastern frontier. In 1739 Anza lost his life in a campaign against them. Next the Mayo and the Yaqui grew restless. The interest in Sonora engendered by the *bolas* discovery and the Indian unrest led, in 1741, to the establishment of two new presidios. Pitiquín (or Pitic), founded on the site of the modern Hermosillo, was designed to serve as a base for the control of the Pima and an operating point against the fierce Seri along the Gulf coast; Terrenate, set somewhat nearer Arizonac, was meant as another outpost against the Apache.

The tempo of activity was stepped up in the 1740s. The crown urged the padres to move toward an attempted recovery of the Moqui; these Indians, the modern Hopi, had been part of the Franciscan mission family prior to the Pueblo Revolt of 1680. Following the reconquest by Vargas at the end of that century, which had not extended that far west, these Moqui had consistently refused Franciscan overtures. In 1742 a royal order came to Mexico, directing that an expedition be sent to the Moqui to look into the possibility of reopening missions among them. Padre Ignacio Keller was detailed by the Jesuit Provincial to go north from his mission at Suamca. En route the band was attacked by the Apache; their animals were stolen and one soldier was killed. The escort refused to continue. Subsequent attempts to reach the Moqui from Sonora also failed, and in 1745 the area was turned back to the Franciscans of New Mexico.

The Bavarian Jesuit Jacobo Sedelmayr, missionary at Tubutama and "father of the Pápago," became, in the 1740s, the great Arizona traveler and explorer.[10] Shortly after his arrival in the north (1736), he had done a turn in the Papaguería and persuaded a sizable number of these folk to come and settle in the neighborhood of Tubutama. In 1743 he went as far as the Gila. The next year Sedelmayr did his turn in the farther north which brought the first exact knowledge of the trans-Gila area onto the Spanish map. His route took him to the Casa Grande ruins, thence down the Salt River, which he called Río de la Asunción, to its junction with the Gila. Following the Gila, he was the first man on record to explore the Bend. His route next led him across the desert, through the lands of the Coco-maricopa, to the Colorado. He pushed northward along that important northwestern waterway as far as Bill Williams Fork before turning back. At his farthest point of advance he felt that he was fairly close to the lands of the Moqui and would have been willing to venture there, but could find no guides.

Much like Kino before him, Sedelmayr was not content to confide his apostolic dreams to letters. In the year after his Gila-Colorado trek (1745), he went down to Mexico City, personally to report to the viceroy, at the moment the Conde de Fuenclara. His arrival in the capital was timely. He was able to help Father Provincial, Cristóbal Escobar y Llamas, to draw up plans for the extension of the mission frontier to the Gila and the Colorado, an advance which had now been commanded by a royal cedula of the previous year. Officials were becoming serious about the move. The 1746 extensive exploration of Padre Consag to the north of the California peninsula was part of the interest which was triggered by the decree of 1744. The old Kino idea of a land route from Sonora to Baja California was far from dead.

The year 1746 brought a new king to the throne of Spain, Ferdinand VI, and a new viceroy to Mexico, the elder Conde de Revilla Gigedo. But the Council of the Indies, having received various reports from New Spain, kept the interest alive and prepared materials for the cedula of 1747. The land connection between Sonora and Lower California was to be a prime consideration; the occupation of the Gila-Colorado country was ordered, both to support and protect the land route and also to serve as base against the western Apache and also as a possible connecting link with New Mexico. The 1749 and 1750 trips of Sedelmayr to the Colorado were part of this larger scheme. On the second of these he pushed down the Colorado far enough that he was very near its mouth. Even though he found the Yuma Indians and those to the south somewhat less than friendly, plans for the northward extension of the frontier went ahead.

The royal decree of 1747 foresaw that the Seri along the Sonora coast would be likely to cause trouble and, therefore, it ordered that these Indians must be reduced. José Gallardo was sent up from the viceregal capital to survey the situation, since reports from Sonora seemed to indicate that Governor Agustín Vildosola had not given adequate attention to the Seri problem. Gallardo arrived in 1748, found that the presidio at Pitiquín had not been properly established and removed the garrison to San Miguel de Horcasitas as a more strategic location from which to operate a campaign against the Seri. Vildosola was replaced by Diego Parilla in 1749. The next year the new governor carried what was meant to be a war of extermination against the Seri strongholds of the Cerro Prieto and Tiburón Island. He was not nearly as successful as his reports would have indicated. The Seri continued to be a source of vexation and real danger in western Sonora. But, if as of 1751 the Spaniards felt that things were more or less in order for the projected advance, the Pima revolt caused a change in time schedule.

On November 20, 1751, the Pimería became an erupting trouble spot when Luis of Saric, governor of the northern Pima, led his tribesmen on the warpath.[11] A number of missions and mining camps in the northwest corner of Sonora were destroyed or badly damaged, two padres, Tomás Tello at Caborca and Enrique Ruhen at Sonóita, were cut down, and around a hundred Spaniards were killed. Padre Juan Nentvig of Saric, warned by Sedelmayr, escaped to Tubutama, where the two of them, with a few Spaniards and some of their Christian Indians were besieged in the church for two days. The rebels set fire to the roof of the building, hoping to flush them out. But darkness fell and the beleaguered little band was able to escape southward, regretfully leaving behind two soldiers so badly wounded that they could not be moved. The whole of Sonora reacted to the news; Parilla and the frontier captains moved up as quickly as possible. Within a few months the revolt died, almost as quickly as it had come. But the disorder further delayed the advance to the Gila-Colorado area.

Earlier in 1751 Fernando Sanchez Salvador, a captain with considerable background and experience on the west coast corridor, sent a series of five letters to officials in Spain and Mexico, offering a number of suggestions, some excellent and others less so, on the projected advance.[12] These Sánchez memorials received considerable attention. In the fourth, sent to the king, he advocated strong settlements on the Gila and the Colorado, with one or other new reason introduced for occupying the region immediately. This memorial raised the possibility of the French pushing past New Mexico and on to the Pacific Coast, it may be that Sánchez had heard on the frontier of the recent appearance in Santa Fe of several groups of Frenchmen. These Gila-Colorado settlements might serve as a base to prevent such westward penetration. They also, affirmed Sánchez, could be used as a staging area from which the Spaniards themselves might go on to Upper California. The Pima disturbances of that same year caused delay; but Spanish thoughts continued to be orientated northward.

On the Sonora frontier, as everywhere in human life, well-directed thoughts were not enough. The years of the 1750s and into the 1760s found the province in a precarious state.[13] The Seri continued to be a threat on the west and the Apache raided the northeast almost at will. After the Pima Revolt the missions were reestablished, but in many instances they had lost much of their influence. The padres worked hard, when they were not fighting with the authorities, but few new converts were made. There was a particularly acrimonious exchange with Governor Parilla over the responsibility for the Pima disturbance. Not until 1759 was the case declared officially closed by the Council of the Indies, and the Jesuits cleared. Parilla had blamed the harshness of the missionaries, and one or other in particular, as being the cause of Indian dissatisfaction; the Jesuits had claimed that Parilla himself was largely responsible, for having coddled Luis of Saric, the Pima instigator, turning him against the padres and unduly building his ego.

The greater number of "whites" in Sonora, scattered in the little mining towns and around its several presidios, numbering in the neighborhood of 1500, had their share in weakening the ties of the Indians to the missions. The natives were no longer as dependent on the mission centers as they had been at an earlier date; and this lack of dependence made them less ready to submit to the disciplined existence of mission life. The letters of the missionaries during the last Jesuit years were often punctuated with a note of discouragement. The report of Father Visitador Ignacio Lizasoain, of 1763, was most discouraging as regards Sonora. As a result, the projected secularization of the Sonora missions—that is, of turning them and the Indians over to the diocesan or parochial clergy—was pushed well into the future. Sonora was not as ready as was Sinaloa for this step: by mid-eighteenth century this latter province with its white-mixed blood population up to around 30,000 had pretty well passed beyond the frontier stage.

Sonora and the northwestern frontier, however, by the last years of the

1760s took on a whole new complexion. The area fitted into the immediate plans of the forceful and energetic José de Gálvez, who arrived in New Spain in 1765, with the broad powers of *visitador* and a number of commissions to fulfill for the entire viceroyalty.[14] On the ground, Gálvez saw other things which had to be done and, using his authority, set several projects in motion. Even before that of the occupation of Alta California reached the top of his agenda list, he had turned attention to the existing frontier provinces. As early as 1767 he and Viceroy Francisco de Croix outlined a proposal which, when refined and implemented in the next decade, turned the northern or Borderland provinces into a separate administrative jurisdiction, the Provincias Internas of 1776 (see Chapter 10). The Seri-Apache problem of Sonora, the Apache problem of Nueva Vizcaya, and the Apache-Comanche problem of Texas, each suggested new approaches as necessary. Peace in Sonora was at first an end in itself. Soon it became imperative for another reason, which was Alta California.

While Gálvez was in New Spain and busy with a number of tasks, one of which was to implement the decree of Charles III expelling the Jesuits from all Spanish domain,[15] the crown began to be seriously concerned about accumulating rumors of foreign interest in the Pacific Coast of the North American continent. In the 1740s England's George Anson had been in the Pacific and actually had touched briefly along the west coast of New Spain; a few years later two Dutch ships, with the aim of trading, had been on the Nueva Galicia coast. By the 1760s the possible French threat via New Mexico had been put to rest by the elimination of the French from North America—east of the Mississippi by the English victory in the French and Indian War, and west of the Mississippi by the French cession of claims to Spain in late 1762. But the English still could be troublesome, especially if they chose to push westward from Canada to their claims on the Pacific side of the continent. It was known in Spain that the Russians were operating in the North Pacific and writing openly of their exploits. The English, the Germans, and the French had translated these accounts and were giving them wide circulation.

A Spanish work that was circulating through Europe in the 1760s heightened apprehension. Entitled *Noticia de la California*, it was published in Spain in 1757 with all proper permissions, but anonymously.[16] The Jesuit Andrés Burriel had prepared it from an earlier and unpublished manuscript of Padre Miguel Venegas and other materials. Although the book was a defense of the Jesuits and their work in Lower California, it went much further. Aiming to show the importance of the Jesuits in the whole frontier enterprise of New Spain, continental and peninsular, Burriel spoke of possible future mission projects in the north for which their cooperation would be vital. Later he became even more specific, to indicate how important Spanish strength on the peninsula should be both as protection for the homebound route of the Manila Galleon and in relationship to a possible extension of the Spanish frontier to the coast of that other California: San Diego, Monterey, Mendocino. A first English translation of this Burriel-Venegas work appeared in London in 1759. In short order there were Dutch, French, and German translations. All of this flurry of non-Spanish interest in the Californias roused Spanish apprehension. The Gila-Colorado project seemed to gain new pertinence. But there were the troubles in Sonora, with the Seri and the Apache, to cool Spanish ardor for a quick advance. The remote preparations for what became in the 1770s the Elizondo campaigns against the Seri in Sonora were ordered by Gálvez in this connection.

In order to be in a position to supply, by sea, the Elizondo anti-Seri drive, with both men and matériel, in late 1767 Gálvez had given orders for the founding of the port of San Blas.[17] Early in the next year the viceroy, Croix, seconded these plans and indicated that the new coastal base might also be used to secure the Californias, first the defense of the peninsula and next the possible exploration of the northern coastline. Gálvez was probably already thinking in those terms, for there are bits of evidence which seem to show that at least some exploration, by sea, toward Monterey was in his plans. En route to San Blas, to supervise the establishment of the port and the building of ships, Gálvez received news from Spain that word had reached the Minister of State to the effect that the Russians were planning settlements on the North American coast. The governor of California was warned to be on the lookout. Spain was definitely worrying. So was Gálvez, and he determined to take action. He informed the viceroy of his intentions; Croix approved and passed on the plan to Julián de Arriaga, then minister-general for the Indies. By October 1768, word came back that Charles III favored the scheme. Alta California was to be occupied.

Gálvez, meanwhile, crossed over to the peninsula to survey the conditions there, arriving in July. He did not find the situation particularly encouraging and quickly recognized that the Alta California enterprise could never count heavily on Baja for much in the way of support during its infant years. The land was poor, the Indians backward, and the missions, despite the earnest efforts of the Jesuits during their seventy-year tenure, were hardly thriving. The last of the Black Robes had sailed off to New Spain and exile earlier in that year (1768). Only recently Franciscans, fourteen of them from the missionary college of San Fernando in Mexico City, had come over to replace them. Fray Padre Junípero Serra was their superior, or father-president.[18] At Loreto there was a presidio; its garrison of three dozen men was commanded by a Baja California veteran, Fernando Rivera y Moncada. The governor, Captain Gaspar de Portolá, like the friars, was a recent arrival. Gálvez may not have realized at the moment how important these three men were to be in his project.

As the weeks went by, the plans of Gálvez took more definite form.[19] Alta California would not simply be explored and scouted; it would be occupied, for only thus would the Spaniards be able to fend off a trespass by the Russians or any other intruders who might appear. San Diego would serve as an anchor in the south. Monterey, "the great harbor" which had been in Spanish thinking and dreaming since the days of Vizcaíno, would be the principal center: a base for defense and expansion, and a port of call for the Manila Galleon, where it might replenish its stores. And since no Spanish frontier was complete without the mission, Gálvez also thought of men to staff these vital agencies. In time missionaries would be supplied from Sonora, once Elizondo had restored that province to peace and a land route had been established. Right now missionaries would have to be drawn from the Franciscan complement on the peninsula. Accordingly, Gálvez talked with Serra and found him enthusiastic; Fray Junípero gladly accepted the role as *Padre Presidente* of this newest Franciscan adventure.

Gálvez then sent orders to San Blas for the two little ships which were being readied there to load and proceed to La Paz as quickly as possible. Meanwhile, Serra did a turn through the southern missions, to see what they could spare in the way of supplies, altar furnishings, and anything else for the projected new establishments in the north. The peninsula began to hum with activity. Rivera y Moncada likewise did his turn through the missions, gathering horses, mules, and whatever surplus supplies were available.

The first of the two little ships, the *San Carlos*, was able to clear the La Paz harbor in early January 1769.[20] It was commanded by Vicente Vila and carried a total of sixty-two persons. There was the engineer Miguel Costansó, to "mark and map the ports and lands that might be discovered" and to lay out the plan for the presidio at Monterey; there was the physician and surgeon Don Pedro Prat and a Franciscan chaplain; also on board were Don Pedro Fages and his company of 25 infantrymen, Catalans recently arrived from Spain. The second ship, with its crew of 26 and two more Franciscans, checked into La Paz and on February 15 sailed forth. The *San Antonio* had a rather uneventful voyage and put into San Diego Bay a full three weeks before its sister ship arrived. The *San Carlos* had a difficult and trying run, beset by storms and, worse still, plagued by scurvy and sickness, which took a number of those on board. Besides, her pilot misread the charts, missed San Diego, and was as far as the Channel Islands off the Santa Barbara coast before realizing that he was too far north. On the 111th day out of La Paz the *San Carlos* put into the harbor at San Diego, with most men aboard in sorry condition—it was April 29.

The land expedition was divided into two companies. The first, under Rivera y Moncada and with Fray Juan Crespi as chaplain and historian, left Velicatá, the newest of the mission chain, on March 24.[21] For some distance, although there was no road, Rivera was on ground somewhat familiar to him and one or other of his men. Three years before they had gone up to a spot called La Cieneguilla with the Jesuit Wenceslaus Linck. At this point

Fray Junípero Serra. Painting in Santa Barbara Mission. (The Bancroft Library)

that exploring party had turned eastward toward the head of the Gulf of California. Beyond La Cieneguilla the advance party was moving through unknown territory, as far as the Spaniards were concerned. As they skirted the foothills of the San Pedro Martir Range, the country began to show green and rich and watered by occasional small streams, one of which they called the River of Roses, where there were "so many rose bushes in flower that a purveyor of perfume could easily make a fortune." And there were wild grapes too. Beyond Ensenada they held rather close to the shoreline. On May 14 this Rivera-Crespi party reached San Diego.

Governor Gaspar de Portolá commanded the second party, with Serra in the company. It started from Loreto, followed the trail that had been blazed by the Jesuits as far as Santa María and then beyond that point had to rely on the paths marked by the other expedition.[22] Serra was often severely handicapped by his sore leg, which the hundreds of miles in the saddle, on muleback, aggravated to a worrisome degree. Six weeks after the pathfinders made San Diego, Portolá and Serra and their party, which had dwindled to several dozen "whites" and Indian allies, came in on the first day of July.

The situation at San Diego was critical.[23] All of the crew of the *San Carlos*, save one sailor and the cook, were dead. Eight men from the *San Antonio*, including three of the Catalans, were also gone, and almost all the rest were deathly sick. With as many as could attend added to his own companions, on July 3 Serra raised a cross on Presidio Hill and gave a formal beginning to the first mission of Alta California.

Despite conditions at San Diego, Portolá felt that he must follow instructions and go on to Monterey. Personnel was apportioned: Serra, two of the other Franciscans, Juan Vizcaíno and Fernando Parrón, a few of the soldiers and most of the workmen were to stay at San Diego with the sick and to start to build. Portolá took Fages and the majority of the surviving Catalans, Sergeant José de Ortega and 26 of the "leather-jackets," 7 muleteers, a pair of orderlies, Rivera y Moncada, Fray Juan Crespi, and a second Franciscan, Francisco Gómez. The Monterey party set out on July 14.

Working slowly northward, noting as they went possible sites for future missions and settlements, they finally reached their destination in early October but failed to recognize it as anything other than a very beautiful bay, hardly the potentially great harbor and port which had been in Spanish dreams since the days of Sebastián Vizcaíno. Feeling that their objective must be still farther north, Portolá pushed on. He came to Half Moon Bay and from there, the day being clear, he could recognize in the distance landmarks long charted by the pilots of the Galleon: Point Reyes and the Farallon Islands. These they knew were far north of where Vizcaíno had located Monterey; hence, Portolá realized that he had missed the "great harbor." His men were in dire straits and he hesitated to continue the search, at least for the moment. Before turning back, however, he sent a few men under Sergeant Ortega to scout the surrounding country to the east. Ortega and his band were the first to see the Bay of San Francisco, a possible port so great, as Crespi noted, that "not only all the navy of our Most Catholic Majesty but those of all Europe could take shelter there." Exciting though this new discovery might be, it was not Monterey. Portolá felt that he had failed and by the standards of Spanish officialdom, which was most often very literalist, this was true. There was a Monterey; Monterey was to be occupied; Portolá had not uncovered it; Portolá had failed; and it made little difference what else he might have found, provided it was not a fabulous gold mine or silver lode. Portolá ordered a return to San Diego.

Back at the home base, in late January 1770, Portolá had major decisions to make. First, the situation at San Diego had not improved; the bulk of the men, his own included, were sick and badly provisioned, and the neighboring Indians were restless and threatening. Rivera hurried back to Velicatá on the peninsula, to round up what supplies he could. Portolá determined to make one more attempt. Before he left, however, the *San Antonio* came back from San Blas. Spirits rose; the food and medicines brought up worked magic.

By late March of 1770 Portolá and Crespi with their party were back at the high cross which they had raised some months before on what they had called the "Bay of Pines," and which on more careful exploration proved to be Vizcaíno's Monterey. They had found it after all, but the disparity between the reality and the fantastic billing of Vizcaíno had misled them. On May 31 the *San Antonio,* with Serra aboard, anchored in the bay. There were formal ceremonies two days later—Mass, the *Te Deum,* and the royal proclamation of possession. The mission and the presidio of San Carlos Borromeo came into being.

Here was the last of the Borderlands, much like New Mexico in its early days, miles and miles away from the nearest frontier. The new land was held by only a handful of men, soldiers and clerics, and guarded by two very small presidios, San Diego at the southern end and now Monterey in the north, with several hundred miles in between. Any determined enemy arriving in force could have broken the tenuous Spanish hold on Alta California in a matter of days, if not hours. Obviously, much still had to be done to make California an effective Borderland.

Having fulfilled the terms of his commission—the establishment of Spaniards at San Diego and more particularly at Monterey—Portolá returned to Mexico. Pedro Fages was left in charge. Authorities in the viceregal capital were pleased and immediately took action to secure this newest outpost. The *San Antonio* was back at Monterey in May 1771; on board were ten friars to make possible the five missions which Gálvez and Croix had projected. Serra was overjoyed to receive the new hands and immediately prepared to carry out the plans of his civilian superiors.

In July (1771) Serra went off with Fray Manuel Pieras and Fray Buenaventura Sitjar to lay the foundations of Misión San Antonio de Padua, inland from Monterey.[24] Returned to his base, he and Crespi decided to move the Monterey mission to a site on the Carmel River, in order to be a bit farther away from the presidio and the not unlikely bad example of the soldiery to their hoped-for neophytes. All the missionaries had learned long ago that much as they needed the presidials for protection they very often had to regret the necessary proximity of the military. The soldiers were not always paragons of Christian virtue and morality; they could and did cause trouble and give scandal to the new Christians. The frontier presidials were often *castas,* mixed-bloods, a socially unstable and morally restless breed of men who could and did upset a young society. More than one missionary was confronted with the question from his neophytes as to whether there were two brands of Christian practice, the one which he was teaching and demanding of them, and the other which the Spaniards themselves followed.

Fray Angel Somera and Fray Pedro Benito Gambón went north from San Diego in August to lay the foundations of San Gabriel; the actual foundation date was September 8. Due to the restlessness of the Indians at San Gabriel, Fages determined to postpone the establishment of the fifth mission, which was to be at San Buenaventura. He did not feel that he could get away and he felt that he should accompany the friars and assist in any new foundation.

Another spring came and Fages, on orders from the viceroy, set out from Monterey with Crespi and a band of fourteen to explore the Bay of San Francisco and to spy out a site for a future mission along its shore. Since something was known of the territory along the ocean side of the Bay, the future "Peninsula," from the days of Portolá, Fages sought to reach Point Reyes via the eastern edge. In the process his party explored much of the future Santa Clara, Alameda, and Contra Costa counties, but, blocked by the Sacramento River, they were unable to complete the circle. They returned to Monterey by a route beyond the bay shoreline and thus they

California Indians, Misión San José de Guadalupe. Engraved after a painting by Wilhelm von Tilenau, 1806. (Library of Congress)

first saw the northern section of California's great interior valley, the San Joaquin.

In late summer of this year (1772) Fages and Serra went south to secure supplies. En route Serra founded Misión San Luis Obispo de Tolosa and left Fray José Cavaller in charge. Arrived at San Diego and with the supplies sent on the way to the north, Serra then reopened the question of a foundation at San Buenaventura. He had been much impressed both by the Indians of the neighborhood and by the promise of the site as he had come southward. Fages was less excited on both counts. Unable to supply a guard to protect the missionaries at what he considered a rather isolated location, Fages refused to second the apostolic wishes of the Father President (Serra). The quarrel which ensued was one of the less edifying episodes of those early California years. Unfortunately, it was not to be the last serious altercation between the civil officials and the friars.

Serra ultimately decided to take the matter to Mexico City. Besides lodging his complaints against Fages (and this dispute was only one of several), Serra felt that this trip would give him a chance to report in person on the missions and also to meet the man who had replaced Francisco de Croix as viceroy, Don Antonio María Bucareli y Ursua.[25] The friar spent most of 1773 in Mexico City. He found Bucareli fully as cooperative and interested as Gálvez and Croix had been. California and its future loomed large in official thinking and planning: the missions and their support, the military, the problems of supply, the question of civilian settlers, and the matter of a possible overland route from Sonora which would relieve such great dependence on the service by sea out of San Blas. Serra was able to do much business for California and got most of his requests, including a replacement for Fages. Ortega would have been his choice as governor. He had to settle for Rivera y Moncada.

Back in California, this year 1773 had been equally important. The Dominicans had taken over most of the Lower California missions, releasing the Franciscans stationed there. Fray Francisco Palóu, superior in Baja, was able to bring most of his men northward to strengthen and expand the Franciscan establishment in Alta California. Palóu settled at Monterey, to await Serra's return.

The year 1773 was also notable as the first in which a full report on the Alta California enterprise was published, summarizing the accomplishments of the first five years. The record showed just short of 500 baptisms, a large proportion of them coming in the last months of the period. The work was slow, but Christianity was beginning to have an appeal, and the hopes for the future were rosy. Nineteen friars were at work in the five missions; the military force numbered 60, garrisoned in the two presidios and parceled out in smaller squads at each of the missions. There were a few civilians, craftsmen and servants, but as yet no settlers or colonists proper.

One of the developments which came as a result of the official interest in California and the conversations with Serra during his 1773 visit to Mexico City was the first trip of Juan Bautista de Anza from Sonora to San Gabriel and Monterey in 1774. Since the occupation of California the problem of supply had been a prime concern to all involved, whether at the viceregal capital or on the far frontier. The barren peninsula could not possibly feed the new establishments; in fact, the Spaniards and the Indians of Baja could hardly care for their own needs consistently; help very regularly had to come from the mainland to keep the peninsular establishment alive. As a result, one of the ordinary Spanish frontier patterns had to be revamped. Regularly the older missions had given the newer ventures their start in more ways than manpower. For instance, the west-coast story of New Spain, that of Sinaloa and Sonora, had been an excellent example of the functioning of this step-by-step mode of advance: the new missionary went north with many things of a material nature furnished from an older establishment. The provisioning of California in the first years had been done almost exclusively by sea, which was a slow process besides being precarious and expensive. Officials, and very particularly Serra, hoped that a land route from "food wealthy" Sonora might be developed to solve the provisioning problem, until California became economically self-sufficient.

Viceregal orders went north, late in 1773, to the frontier captain at Tubac, the Arizona presidio, commanding him to test the possibility. This captain, Juan Bautista de Anza, was a third-generation frontiersman in the north.[26] His grandfather and father before him had served in Sonora. He was, besides, the ideal man for the assignment—intelligent, rugged, experienced, and highly knowledgeable as regards the Indians. And he had two magnificent companions, Fray Francisco Garcés and Sebastián, a San Gabriel Indian who had recently deserted from California and wandered beyond the Río Colorado. Garcés, pastor-at-large in the north country, was officially the missionary at San Xavier del Bac since 1768.[27] However, he had been away from his mission almost as much time as he spent there. He was even more restless than Padre Kino in his explorations and his probings into the far reaches of heathendom beyond his own mission territory. He was a great frontiersman in his own right and as such was an invaluable companion to Anza.

With Garcés and another Franciscan, Juan Díaz, the Indian Sebastián, and 30 men, Anza set out early in January 1774. The band had 165 horses and was also driving 65 head of cattle for food on the way. At the junction of the Gila and the Colorado they met the famous chief Palma and won his friendship and a pledge of cooperation. March 22 saw the party at Misión San Gabriel. Anza went on to Monterey and then returned to Tubac, having been on the road close to five months.

From Tubac Anza continued on to Mexico City to report his findings. There he received his next assignment, to lead another expedition to California. This time he was to take a body of settlers, and his goal was to be a foundation on the Bay of San Francisco. Viceroy Bucareli, who was most interested in and sympathetic toward the California enterprise, authorized Anza to recruit and outfit twenty settler families at royal expense. Further, he could enlist ten veteran presidial soldiers as guards for his overland party; and he was given broad permissions to gather the animals necessary to support his expedition. He returned to Sonora to get things in readiness.

The years 1774 and 1775 were not exclusively "Anza years" in the California story. The first of these saw the beginnings of an important development which would extend into the future. Being established in California was not enough; Spain felt that this was only the first step in securing its priority claims to the entire Pacific Coast of North America. In 1773 Juan Pérez, commanding the new California ship, the *Santiago*, went north to explore and to establish, so to speak, Spain's presence. In the next years several other Spanish voyages were made beyond California. Pérez had sailed to 55 degrees latitude; Bruno de Hezeta reached the mouth of the Columbia; Juan de la Bodega y Cuadra got to 58 degrees north and on another voyage was in Alaskan waters. None of these Spanish captains saw Russians. But since the reports of the voyage of England's Captain James Cook to the North American coast in 1778, Spain had also begun to worry about the English. And well Spain might, for Cook had discovered the fur resources of the north country. Soon other Englishmen followed in his wake. The day of paper claims as insurance of possession against foreigners was fast waning. Actually Spain had occupied California none too soon.

Anticipating some of the later problems may have contributed to the new importance which the occupation of some key point on the Bay of San Francisco assumed in Spanish plans of 1775. Word came up to California from Mexico that the bay should be explored thoroughly. Accordingly, Rivera and Serra went north from Monterey, one of their tasks being to pick a place for a presidio and mission somewhere on the tip of land guarding the south side of the Golden Gate.

Anza, meanwhile, was back in Sonora readying the projected land expedition to open the land route and to bring settlers to this post on the bay. About the time the day of departure was nearing, disaster hit. The Apache raided Tubac and ran off the entire horse herd which had been gathered, some five hundred head. Despite this setback the settler party set out from Horcasitas on September 28, 1775. At Tubac 63 more persons joined the group, raising the company to 240. As they left that last place they had 695 horses and mules and were driving 355 head of cattle.

At the first night's camp beyond Tubac the company sustained its sole casualty, but in the process gained a replacement—a young mother died in giving birth to a son. The child survived the 1500-mile journey and thus kept the human complement at the initial 240 figure. From Tubac the party moved north to the Gila; Anza wisely avoided taking that many people over the somewhat shorter but more desolate Camino del Diablo approach

Don Juan Bautista de Anza. Portrait at Tumacacori National Monument. (National Park Service)

to the junction of the Gila and the Colorado. At the junction Yuma Chief Palma proved as good as his word and received the Spaniards with all hospitality. Negotiating the Colorado was a challenge. The crossing was made without serious mishap, although there was one close call: a little girl, riding in front of the horseman, was swept off, but soldiers downstream scooped her up to safety, frightened but only slightly waterlogged.

An overly exuberant Christmas Eve party drew stern words from Padre Pedro Font, the strict and humorless chaplain, in the sermon at the Christmas Mass. But the travelers felt that they had good reason for celebration, since that Christmas Eve night they knew that they were safely coming close to the end of the first leg of their trip. On the second day of the new year (1776) they were at San Gabriel.

This band of pioneers was still a good 500 miles from its destination, but those miles would be over what was becoming a well-known Camino Real. By March the party was at Monterey. Anza and Font went north to select sites for the presidio, the mission, and the pueblo. This had not yet been done previously because Rivera did not favor the occupation of the San Francisco site. However, a letter from Bucareli, ordering the settlement of that point of land, arrived in time to settle a possible altercation between Rivera and Anza. Anza then turned his people over to Lieutenant José Moraga, on his return to Monterey, and headed back to Sonora. Moraga, with Fathers Palóu and Gambón, led the settlers to the tip of the peninsula and within sight of the Golden Gate founded the city of San Francisco. The date was September 17, 1776. Mission Dolores was laid out a few weeks later. Here was Spain's "outpost of empire" on the Western Ocean.

A few months later an important change was made along the Pacific. In 1777 the governor of California, Felipe de Neve, up to that time based at Loreto in the peninsula, came north to set the capital at Monterey, indicating that Alta California was now the senior partner in the combination. Rivera y Moncada went south to Loreto, as lieutenant-governor. During the Neve administration, the first two real settler pueblos were formally founded: San José in 1777, with fourteen families gathered from Monterey and San Francisco, and Nuestra Señora la Reina de Los Angeles de Porciúncula in 1781, with eleven families which Rivera had sent up from Baja California. It devolved on Neve to set up the first "civil constitution" for the province, which he did in his *Reglamento* of 1779. Under Neve the economic life of the province was rethought and expanded. The basis for several more missions was laid, although the actual foundations came after his term—San Buenaventura in 1782, Santa Barbara in 1786, and Purísima Concepción in 1787.

Neve went off, in 1781, to punish the perpetrators of the Yuma massacre and never returned to his province. Instead he was promoted to the rank of Inspector General of the recently established Provincias Internas. Pedro Fages was Neve's replacement in California, arriving in 1782. His second term in command was less stormy and much more productive than his earlier "governorship."

In a sense the first period of Alta California history may be said to end on August 28, 1784, with the death of Junípero Serra. This remarkable and tenacious Mallorcan, in New Spain since 1749 and veteran there of two difficult mission fields—Sierra Gorda in Nuevo Santander and Baja California—had come north with Portolá and had been, if not *the* strong man, at least one of the strong men in the California enterprise during its first fifteen years. As the father-president, or superior, he had been the founder of the mission system as a whole and of many of the missions personally. He was seventy-one at the time of his death. During all of his California years he had been handicapped by a leg that gave him much trouble and no little pain. Yet the infirmity did not slow his driving pace; it may, how-

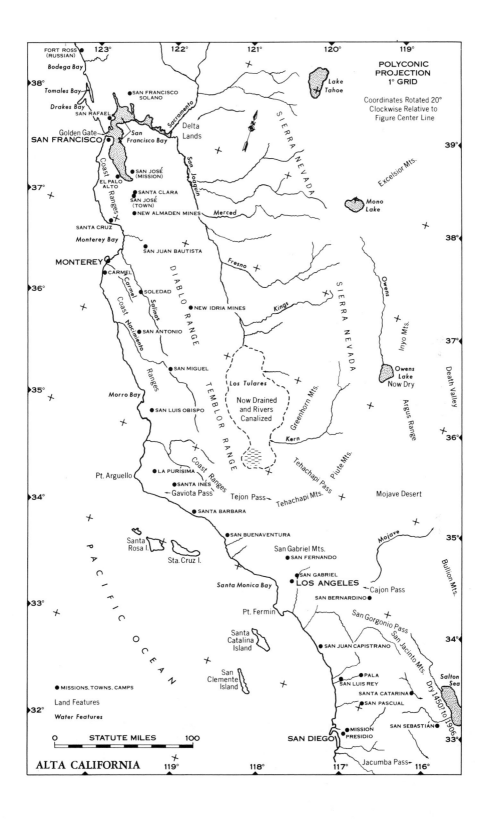

FORT ROSS
(RUSSIAN)
Bodega Bay
123°   122°   121°   120°   119°

POLYCONIC
PROJECTION
1° GRID

Coordinates Rotated 20°
Clockwise Relative to
Figure Center Line

Lake
Tahoe

38°
Tomales Bay
Drakes Bay
SAN FRANCISCO
SOLANO
SAN RAFAEL
Golden Gate
SAN FRANCISCO
San
Francisco Bay
Delta
Lands
Sacramento

39°

SAN JOSÉ
(MISSION)
37°   EL PALO
ALTO
SANTA CLARA
SAN JOSÉ
(TOWN)
NEW ALMADEN MINES
Merced

San Joaquin

Excelsior Mts.

Mono
Lake

SANTA CRUZ
Monterey Bay
SAN JUAN BAUTISTA
Fresno
38°

MONTEREY
CARMEL
36°   Carmel
SOLEDAD
NEW IDRIA MINES
Kings

SIERRA NEVADA

Owens

SAN ANTONIO
Inyo Mts.
37°

35°   SAN MIGUEL
Morro Bay
Los Tulares
Now Drained
and Rivers
Canalized
Owens
Lake
Now Dry
Death Valley

SAN LUIS OBISPO
Greenhorn Mts.
Argus Range
36°

Pt. Arguello
LA PURISIMA
SANTA INÉS
Gaviota Pass
Tejon Pass
Kern
Tehachapi Pass
Piute Mts.
Mojave Desert

34°
SANTA BARBARA
SAN BUENAVENTURA
Tehachapi Mts.

Santa
Rosa I.
Sta. Cruz I.
San Gabriel Mts.
SAN FERNANDO
Mojave
35°

Bullion Mts.

Santa Monica Bay
SAN GABRIEL
LOS ANGELES
Cajon Pass
SAN BERNARDINO

Pt. Fermin
San Gorgonio Pass
34°

33°
Santa
Catalina
Island
SAN JUAN CAPISTRANO
San Jacinto Mts.
Salton
Sea

San
Clemente
Island
PALA
SAN LUIS REY
SANTA CATARINA
SAN PASCUAL
Dry 1450? to 1906
SAN SEBASTIAN
33°

MISSIONS, TOWNS, CAMPS
Land Features
Water Features
32°

MISSION
PRESIDIO
SAN DIEGO

0   STATUTE MILES   100

ALTA CALIFORNIA   119°   118°   117°   Jacumba Pass   116°

Coast Ranges
DIABLO RANGE
Salinas
Nacimiento
Ranges
TEMBLOR RANGE
Coast Ranges
PACIFIC OCEAN

ever, have contributed on occasion to his irascibility, especially toward the military commanders and the civil officials. Without question, he was a great American figure. He had one fine stroke of fortune in having a first-rate biographer—his contemporary, warm admirer, and close associate, Fray Francisco Palóu. Palóu was his immediate successor as superior but held the post of father-president only one year and then passed on the spiritual leadership of California to the very capable Fray Fermín de Lasuén.

Lasuén was superior for eighteen years, from 1785 to 1803. Without neglecting the spiritual side of his position, during those years he did much to develop the material side of the mission system. With his encouragement and often under his personal direction the basis was laid for two very important California industries, agriculture and stock raising, both of which got their start in the shadow of the missions. Serra passed on a going enterprise; Lasuén accelerated the progress.

By the middle 1780s Spain was reasonably secure in this last of its Borderlands. California was Spain's farthest northward penetration into the North American continent. The new province was established just in time to become part of the reorganization scheme which, beginning in 1776, turned Spain's northern frontier into the administrative jurisdiction to be known as the Provincias Internas. Somewhat belatedly, perhaps, Spain recognized that these frontier possessions had their own special kinds of problems and acted to give them their own special kinds of solutions. In the end Spain lost them all to Mexico, and in time Mexico lost most of them to its aggressive northern neighbor. But 1821 and 1848 were still far into the future. Significant years were ahead for all of the western Borderlands, from New Mexico, the oldest, to California, the youngest.

◁ 10 ▷

Borderland Reorganization: The Provincias Internas

*E*ven before there was an Alta California with its problems, the Spaniards had begun to recognize that their far-flung frontiers in North America were beset with a whole range of problems peculiar to themselves and often with slight relationship to those of the rest of the viceroyalty of New Spain. Successive viceroys were becoming less and less well equipped to deal with these problems intelligently and effectively. This was not necessarily a reflection on the ability or even the energetic goodwill of the officials. For one thing the element of distance contributed its full share to the situation. No administrator based hundreds of miles away from the trouble centers could be expected to be at his best in all his decisions—and even if these were good, they arrived on the frontier with paralyzing slowness. And it would be a remarkable viceroy who could, so to speak, get the feel of the frontier without having known it firsthand. Many things in New Spain needed reforming in the latter half of the decade of the 1760s. The move into Alta California was not the only defensive action required. The occupation of that province added new cogency to an already existing need. On the frontier there was another enemy more immediate and almost as powerful as the Russian. The northern Indian, and specifically the Apache, had to be controlled. The reorganization of the frontier and the erection of a new administrative jurisdiction belong in this frame of reference.

From the first days of the Spanish conquest of North America the native Americans, very understandably, resented and, to the best of their ability, opposed the intruding Europeans. The folk of Tlascala bitterly contested the advance of the men of Cortés. When bested, they joined forces with the invaders, but only because they hated the Aztec more. The Aztec used all their might to save their empire and their way of life, but it proved not enough. In time they learned to live with the conquistadores, being realists enough to recognize, at least after 1521, that they had no other choice. As the Spaniards pushed north, they had, in a sense, to fight each step of the way. Gradually they developed techniques to aid and then to secure their conquests; but each new frontier had its anxious and precarious days, even years. Not infrequently the Spanish frontiers knew setbacks, temporary in most instances, but setbacks nonetheless.

Before the sixteenth century was out the successors of the conquistadores had learned to lean heavily on the missionary as one of their foremost agents of expansion.[1] The padre or the friar was regularly flanked by the presidial soldier, but very much of the responsibility for readying the frontier for settler occupation rested on the shoulders of the missionary. The mission system worked tolerably well into the eighteenth century, and the Spaniard, as he branched out into new American areas, saw no reason why the well-tested methods of the past would not apply universally. His experience in Texas, however, had caused him to reassess his hitherto certain convictions.

True, the Pueblo Revolt in New Mexico for a dozen or so years after 1680 threatened to shake the Spaniard's previous faith in the mission approach. But following the reconquest of New Mexico, the old system of mission-presidio seemed to regain its former validity. It was working in Chihuahua, Coahuila, and Nuevo León, with the Franciscans in charge. On the western slope, in Sinaloa and Sonora, the Jesuits had been remarkably successful, with an assist from the presidials. The Black Robes had been equally successful among the Tepehuan, after an early flare-up of Indian resentment, and also among the more difficult folk of the mountainous Tarahumara as the seventeenth century merged into the eighteenth. But the Texas Indians turned out to be a new kind of challenge, and some new approach to the problem of securing the frontier was in order.

In Texas the Spaniards for the first time began to encounter Indians who showed little willingness to subject themselves to the necessarily disciplined existence of the mission life and routine. Quite apart from the natural human resistance to regimentation, there were other considerations which can help account for the lack of missionary success in Texas.

Food, largely in the form of game meat, was plentiful enough that the Indians were not tempted, as in other areas, to trade their freedom for the dietary security which the mission offered. Again, in the absence of strong military protection from the Spaniards, these Texas Indians seem to have felt that they could do better on their own in small groupings, rather than congregated in missions where they might be more easily attacked by enemy neighbors, who were often distressingly too many. Understandably, these Texas Indians had a very human distaste for turning themselves into "sitting ducks."

The spread of the horse among the Indians of southwestern North America was a factor which greatly revolutionized the life of the Americans of the Great Plains and gave some of the tribes a power to strike quite out of proportion to their numbers.[2] This fact was bound to upset traditional balances between the Indian nations.

At first the horse and the mule were primarily elements in the Indian diet, a new kind of protein which had a great taste appeal. Before long, however, the natives learned to use the animals as mounts and thus gained a new and unwonted mobility, first as hunters and then as warriors and raiders. The horse, for example, radically changed the age-old methods of the buffalo hunt, making the task of food-gathering less tedious and less hit-and-miss—much more effective and efficient.

Little need be said of the contribution of the horse in the area of warfare. To be sure, not all the old military techniques of infantry days were abandoned. The terrain very often did not lend itself to cavalry maneuvering. But there is no doubt that the horse added a new dimension to Indian potential for resisting the encroachments of the white man. One thing that should not be overlooked is that the horse gave the Indian great mobility as a raider and thus weakened the security of the white man's hold on a frontier, even after he had been able to establish his outpost position. The Indian could swoop in, raid, pillage, and kill, and then make off. Then, if and when firearms were added to the Indian offensive arsenal, the native American became the match for the European, who saw his early advantages neutralized. And it should be noted that the mounted and armed Indian was also in a favored position against enemy tribesmen.

With the Indian threat increasing on northern frontiers, Spain had to begin to rethink frontier policies. The farther northern edge of Spain's North American empire had to be secured. The Borderlands became a defensive buffer, or so many defensive buffers, whose strength and vitality were necessary protection for the valuable "silver provinces" of northern Mexico. Nueva Galicia, parts of Nueva Vizcaya, and areas of Nuevo León were vital to the economy and prosperity of New Spain and Spain itself. From their mines came the treasure which sustained not only New Spain locally, but also made it possible for the viceroyalty to pay the increasing imperial tax requisitions. It must also be remembered that the output of the American mines, both north and south, was about all that was keeping Spain in a condition of near-solvency. Therefore, Borderlands reform was an absolute necessity in that third quarter of the eighteenth century.

Even areas of northern New Spain which had not been financially productive needed the buffer type of protection which the Borderlands could afford. Sinaloa, for example, by the third quarter of the eighteenth century had become a settled province, adapted to the institutions and ways of the white man. Its capital, San Felipe, around 1760 had a population of 3500.[3] This province had to be protected by a strong and orderly Sonora to its north. An equally strong and orderly Texas would have to perform a similar function for Coahuila and Nuevo León.

When one thinks defense, the inclination is to look for European rivals. The French in the Mississippi Valley fit the pattern, and the Russian threat, real or imagined, along the Pacific coast also influenced Spanish thinking. But in the 1760s and 1770s the real and the immediate enemy in the Borderlands was the unfriendly Indian, often mounted, sometimes armed with

Raider Indians of the Plains, the Comanche. Photo by Will Soule, 1873. (Library of Congress)

guns, regularly intractable. Most frequently this frontier troublemaker was an Apache, of one brand or other.[4] Fortunately for Spain, these numerous members of the Southern Athapascan family were not a united nation. They were not even the sort of close-knit confederacy that the Iroquois had been in the northeast against the French. But, united or not, the Apache were there, and at times seemed almost to partake of the supernatural gift of omnipresence. They were along the upper reaches of the Río Gila, beyond the northeastern edge of Sonora; these the Spaniards called the Gileño. In southwestern New Mexico were the Chiricahua; to the northeast the Jicarilla; down the Río Grande and extending into the valley of the Río Pecos were other branches of the Apache family, notably the Natage, the Mescalero, the Lipan. Filling in the area around El Paso, north, west, and south, were non-Apache tribesmen—Manso, Jocome, Jumano, and other relatively small groupings. Most of these, having become "horse Indians," to some degree at least, had turned into troublesome neighbors. They still had not learned the techniques of stockbreeding and were, in consequence, dependent on the Spaniards for their mounts. These they obtained by raiding and stealing.

But the Apache were not the only worrisome folk in the Borderlands. To the northwest of New Mexico were the Navaho and behind them the Ute. Farther east and beyond the Apache ring were other nations, pressing southward and in their turn seeking to become "horse Indians."[5] Fiercest and closest in were the Comanche; and on their flank the Wichita—the Quivira of Coronado and post-Coronado days, and latterly called the Taovaya. One and all were pushing relentlessly southward, unsettling, threatening the security of the Borderlands.

Had it not been for the Apache and their fellows, the years 1762–1763 might have brought some peace on the Borderlands frontier, even though temporary. The French rivals beyond Texas were gone, since Spain had inherited the western half of Louisiana. New Mexico, too, would not have had to worry about French intrusions across the Plains from the Illinois country. Quickly enough the British might have become almost as bothersome; but at that moment England was simply worrisome. Still, Spain knew that its northern frontiers had to be secured against any future threat from a rival colonial power. Spain might have had a short respite, but it could not allow itself the luxury of complacency, as the whole California incident was to prove very quickly. But, even with European rivals gone, or at least quiescent, there were the Indians, and the Indians were to get their full share of official attention in the later eighteenth century.

Shortly after 1763 the Spanish empire overseas, and New Spain in particular, drew much reform-oriented attention from the young monarch Charles III. His predecessors in the Bourbon Century had directed most of their energies to affairs in Europe, and the Indies had been left rather much to shift for themselves, at least to the small extent that Spain was ever willing for this state of affairs to prevail. The "neglect" was not precisely "salutary," at least as far as the Borderlands were concerned, for the Apache problem was moving toward a state of crisis.

In 1765 Charles III made two appointments, each in its own way designed to step up the reform program in New Spain. José de Gálvez, as has already been noted, crossed the Atlantic with the title of *visitador-general* and orders to direct a thorough overhaul of the administrative and economic machinery of the viceroyalty.[6] Involvement in the California venture and in the expulsion of the Jesuits from New Spain were not originally included in his commission. He was to have been a sort of general "troubleshooter."

The second appointee was Cayetano María Pignatelli Rubí Corbera y San Climent. He is more conveniently known as the Marqués de Rubí. He came with a commission bearing on the Borderlands. He was to conduct a careful inspection of the military organization and the state of defenses on the far northern frontiers. His tour is an integral part of the Borderlands story.

Rubí spent the better part of the two years 1766 and 1767 on the frontier, gathering the materials for his extensive report and his subsequent recommendations. In the process he visited the northern provinces of Nueva Vizcaya and Sonora, Coahuila, New Mexico, and Texas, and finished with a quick swing over to the western province of Nayarit, before returning through Nueva Galicia. In all, he and his party covered upwards of 7500 miles, almost 3000 Spanish leagues. His report was largely the work of his constant companion, the highly intelligent and keenly observant Nicolás de Lafora, Captain of the Royal Engineers.[7]

Rubí's inspection of the frontier was not wholly unique. Forty years before, between 1724 and 1728, Pedro Rivera had gone north on a similar mission. Rubí's report, however, was particularly valuable, since it came at a time when the Spanish frontier had reached its limits into the Borderlands in all areas save California, whose occupation was still several years into the future.

The Marqués arrived in Mexico City in December 1765, reported to the viceroy, the Marqués de Cruillas, and stood by to await specific instructions. Meanwhile, he devoted much time to the study of maps, documents, previous reports, and such other materials as might prepare him for the fulfillment of his mission. When no word from the viceroy was forthcoming by mid-February, Rubí, anxious to be on his way, wrote him, to jog his memory. Cruillas, finally, drew up the instructions, and the party set forth on March 10, 1766.

The principal task of Rubí was to examine the entire presidial system of the north. He was to review the internal administration of the forts, the

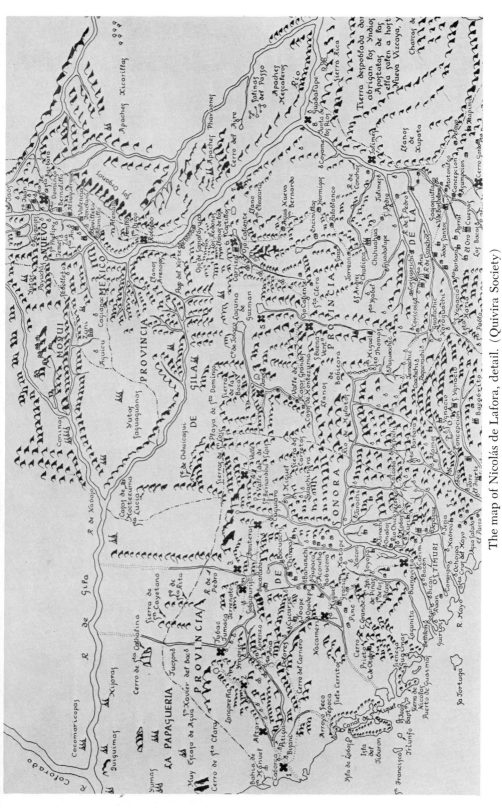

The map of Nicolás de Lafora, detail. (Quivira Society)

relations of the captain with the soldiers, the character of the men and their fitness for their assignments, the state of finances and also of equipment and matériel, and the management of royal funds. In this last category it was hoped that he might be able to effect notable economies, for the royal outlay was becoming a matter of serious concern. More than that, Rubí would be expected to give a considered judgment as to the retention, relocation, or abandonment of each post. Further, he was ordered to send back detailed and frequent reports, by special courier and at royal expense, and also to accompany these with sectional maps, showing the general terrain of the particular area covered, its boundaries, and the routes available. Although not specified in his instructions, Rubí recognized the great importance of this matter of routes and followed, whenever possible, alternates going and returning. The map of Nicolás de Lafora which came out of this tour of frontier inspection was one of the most comprehensive surveys of northern New Spain in colonial times. Lafora completed and submitted it in 1771.

Santa Fe was Rubí's first objective. He set out on March 14; Lafora trailed him four days later. The road to Durango was through well-settled country: Querétaro was a town of over 14,000; Celaya was almost as large, "more agreeable because of the many olive trees"; Salamanca and Silao were the next stops on the route; many of the 3000 houses of León, it was noted, were "built of stone"; Lagos was less prepossessing; Aguas Calientes was surrounded by several large haciendas and many smaller farms which produced wheat, maize, and chili, and there were rather good pasture lands in the area; Zacatecas of 1766 was suffering from the decline of the mining boom and its population was dwindling; Sombrerete, too, reflected the mining depression. Durango, capital of Nueva Vizcaya, was the residence of the governor and also of the bishop. Its population was just short of 10,000, counting its "Spaniards, mulattoes, and mestizos" and the ninety-five Indian families living in the nearby village of Analco, "which is close by and may be considered as a suburb." The plain roundabout was beautiful, but uncultivated for lack of water. Water, even for drinking purposes, was in short supply in the whole Durango area.

El Pasaje was the first presidio visited. Here Rubí experimented with what was to develop as his regular method of procedure. First he inspected the garrison and the horses; next he looked into the administrative procedures and checked all equipment, interviewing each soldier on the matter of pay, of prices charged for provisions by the captain, of tasks imposed by him beyond those of a strictly military nature. At Pasaje Rubí found discrepancies in the books of the captain, and always to the officer's own personal advantage. The equipment was inferior and in bad condition.

Guajoquilla was the next stop. To reach this point the party passed through the attractive Valle de San Bartolomé. It was there that they saw for the first time evidence of Indian depredations. Despite the dangers from Indian raiders, the town of San Bartolomé had a population of 4751 and was quite prosperous. Lafora noted that grapes were grown in the region "from which they make a passable brandy." Guajoquilla was one of the newer presidios, founded in 1752 in the days of Viceroy Revilla Gigedo. Its original complement of 66 men had been reduced to 40; the others had been taken off the previous year (1765) to help garrison the recently established presidio of San Buenaventura.

As the party moved toward Chihuahua, there were increasing signs of the passage of the Apache. The presidio at Conchos had been abandoned; the little village of Guadalupe was in pitiable condition; Chancaple had nothing to show but its ruins. Chihuahua, once thriving because of the mining activity in the neighborhood, had sunk into a state of depression and fear because of the almost constant Apache raiding. Even before Rubí got to his first intended stop on this leg of the inspection, the presidio at the junction of the Conchos with the Río Grande, he was informed by messenger that the fort had been abandoned and the garrison transferred to Julimes. He noted in his report to the viceroy that he thought this move a mistake.

The party had been on the road over four months when the visitors arrived at El Paso—Nuestra Señora del Pilar del Paso del Río del Norte. It was July 19 and they were now within the jurisdiction of New Mexico, and beyond Nueva Vizcaya. The El Paso complex consisted of the presidio, its pueblo de Guadalupe, and the five mission towns downriver. The population was around 5000, of every color and complexion. El Paso had been the anchor for the reconquest of New Mexico at the end of the previous century, following the Pueblo Revolt, and it was considered by Rubí as the key to the defense of the entire region, both to the east and to the immediate west. However, the town was sufficiently populous that its defense could be entrusted to a well-organized militia company. Accordingly, he suggested that its existing garrison might be more advantageously located to the south, at Carrizal, where it might plug a hole in the defense line and be more effective in repulsing the Apache and turning them back from northern Nueva Vizcaya.

To the north of El Paso and while traveling along the left bank, on the fourth day out the party sustained its first attack by the Apache. The Indians tried to steal the horses, but, failing this, they were able to run off most of the sheep which were being driven along as food for the little company. The Spaniards gave chase, were able to recover most of their animals, and held the raiders at a comfortable distance. As they continued north, the Spaniards saw grim reminders of the days of the Pueblo Revolt. There were familiar New Mexican names for sites no longer inhabited, such as Perrillo and Fray Cristóbal. Then came the series of Pueblo towns of the

Río Abajo, the Villa de Albuquerque, and finally the New Mexican capital, historic Santa Fe. Tomás Vélez Capuchín was the governor; the town counted a population of 2324 persons; the garrison was a company of 80 soldiers, including a lieutenant, an ensign, and two sergeants. Lafora was not impressed with the presidio—"incapable of being defended." The very knowledgeable engineer felt that a smaller well-constructed fort would be a greater assurance of protection.

Recalling his recommendation concerning the removal of the garrison from El Paso and its relocation at Carrizal, Rubí discussed with Governor Capuchín the advisability of establishing a presidio-settlement at some point upriver from El Paso, in order to protect the caravans moving north, since El Paso would no longer have soldiers, other than militiamen, to fulfill such an assignment. The citizen soldiers would not be likely to undertake such convoy duty willingly. Rubí suggested that the site known as Robledo might be the most advantageous spot for this possible new foundation. His recommendation to this effect subsequently went to the crown, but nothing was done to implement it, and that long stretch of New Mexico's *Camino Real* remair ›d unprotected.

Completing his New Mexican tour, Rubí retraced his steps to El Paso; in this instance he was unable to choose an alternate return route. From El Paso, in October 1766, he headed west for Sonora. The new presidio of San Buenaventura was poorly placed to do its supposed job of protecting Chihuahua and the surrounding countryside and he recommended relocation in the valley of Ruiz. From San Buenaventura a long and hard fifteen-day journey, past Las Casas Grandes de Montezuma and through treacherous Ramos Pass, brought Rubí to the Presidio de Janos, westernmost of those of Nueva Vizcaya. Although the condition of the folk there, about 450 persons, was anything but prosperous, Rubí felt that the presidio was very advantageously located and strongly urged that it be both reinforced and generously provisioned. Janos had already more than once proved its worth.

The two northern presidios in Sonora were next visited, Fronteras and Terrenate. The first, Rubí felt, was poorly located—too far from Janos and in a spot from which quick movement against Apache raiders was next to impossible. Terrenate too was badly placed. The few settlers on the site had to go much too far afield to find fertile patches on which to plant their small crops, on which they and the soldiers depended heavily. To confirm his opinion of these two presidios and their respective locations, the Marqués noted that in proceeding from Fronteras to Terrenate his party had passed four pueblos that had been abandoned because of constant Apache raids.

West of Terrenate the Rubí party moved into Pimería Alta, the land which the famous Jesuit Kino had opened in the later years of the previous century. Following the great man's death, in 1711, there had been a temporary decline on this northwestern frontier, but two decades later there was a mission renaissance. However, the mine strike at Arizonac, in the upper Altar Valley, had brought many unscrupulous fortune hunters into the area and their coming had precipitated unrest and revolt among the Pima in the early 1750s, which had exacted a toll of over 100 Spanish lives, including two Jesuit padres. The foundation of the presidio of Pitiquín just before the troubles did not prevent them and did not effectively control them once they had erupted. Subsequent to the Pima Revolt two new presidios had been founded: one at Altar, in the valley of that name, and the second at Tubac, to the south of San Xavier del Bac. Tubac was strategically located and, further, was well administered by the younger Juan Bautista de Anza. The little settlement at Tubac might be sufficiently strong to protect itself and, accordingly, Rubí suggested that the garrison might be more advantageously moved to a site somewhat farther southwest. He made a similar recommendation for the presidio at Altar. This one should be transferred downstream to a spot on or near the coast of the Gulf of California, where it might be of greater service in protecting the province from the incursions of the Seri. These tribesmen from the Gulf and Tiburón Island had become worthy rivals of the Apache as the prime troublemakers for Sonora.

San Miguel de Horcasitas, at the moment the capital of Sonora and the place of residence of the governor, impressed Rubí not at all. Its presidio was another of those which he marked for extinction. Dropping southward to the upper Yaqui, he visited Buenavista. The garrison there might be used more profitably elsewhere, although he did not specify precisely at what point.

From Buenavista Rubí headed back over the Sierra Madre, by roads which were next to nonexistent. Until the party had cleared the Tarahumara, on the eastern side, the going was rough; then they were again on the Chihuahua road. Toward the end of May 1767, the travelers put in at El Pasaje, their frontier starting point of a little more than a year before. But the job was not yet done. The third leg of this remarkable tour still lay ahead—the visit to Texas.

On May 27 Rubí set out once again from El Pasaje. He skirted the southern edge of the Bolsón de Mapimí, which had become the hangout of the Mescalero and Natage who preyed on Nueva Vizcaya and Coahuila. In passing he visited the interesting Tlascalan town of Alamo, one of several such in the north. These Indians, friends of the Spaniards since 1519, when Cortés had bested them as he moved on to Tenochtitlán, were among some of Spain's best native colonizers. Beyond was Parras and then Saltillo, with its own Tlascalan Pueblo de San Esteban nearby. Saltillo's foundation dated back to the last years of the sixteenth century; it had quickly become an important center in the north, of settlement, farming, and supply. In the course of time it had sent out small colonies to establish other towns in the north, in Nuevo León and Coahuila; and it had been one of the staging areas for Texas. Rubí's next major stop was one of these towns, Monclova, which was one of the key presidio-settlements of this middle frontier. Monclova had been founded some eighty years before, in 1687. Santa Rosa was inspected and then the party crossed the Río Grande into the country of the Lipan Apache, the branch which was particularly troublesome in western Texas.

They decided to move toward San Sabá first and, therefore, headed northeastward from the river. They passed the missions of La Candelaria and of El Cañon, where the discouraged Franciscans had seen their hopes of converting the Lipan Apache dashed. The Indians had refused, and not always politely, to cooperate with the zealous friars. Lafora noted that the little pueblo of San Lorenzo de la Santa Cruz, known more commonly as Misión del Cañon, tied up a detachment of thirty men and an officer who could be much better used at San Sabá. The two missionaries were without neophytes to care for; all they had was apostolic optimism. Lafora did admit that the pueblo-mission served as a provisioning point for the packtrains moving to San Sabá, but he was still dubious about its value to the frontier. There were two small cannon there, but no balls to fit their particular bore (interesting decorations for the little town, but hardly of much protective value). In general, the first impressions of Texas were not exactly favorable. Later ones were not much more so.

The road to San Sabá for a considerable distance was next to impossible. Four times it crossed the Río Nueces, went through very rough country, and finally opened into rather lush meadows which attracted large herds of buffalo, but also Indian hunters. Many of the natives who gravitated toward this hunting ground were Comanche, as well as Apache, neither of them friends of the Spaniards.

Rubí reached San Sabá on July 26, 1767. Great hopes had been put in this venture, this far outpost designed to attract the Comanche. It was hoped that they might be converted or at least rendered friendly; then they might be enlisted in the Spanish war on the Apache, who were their age-old enemies. However, this presidio-mission complex had been a disappointment almost from the beginning. The inspectors recorded the number of casualties suffered there in the relatively few years of the post's existence, considering the deaths entirely disproportionate; they also noted that the Franciscans had withdrawn. The presidio was still retained for some time thereafter; but the days of San Sabá were numbered. It was closed in the year following the Rubí visitation, in 1768.

Five days southward from San Sabá brought the party to San Antonio de Béjar, with its pueblo or Villa de San Fernando and its cluster of missions, five of them strung along the Río San Antonio. Despite almost continual harassment, this San Antonio complex had been able to survive and, in a moderate sense, also to prosper. Even though San Antonio, along with Santa Fe, was to be left beyond the ring of presidios which Rubí recommended as the outlying line of defense, he still felt that every effort should be made to retain this Texas center.

From San Antonio his tour led him to visit the establishments in East Texas. En route he looked in on the stations at Nacogdoches and Los Ais. He found them, as the Franciscans already had, disappointing from the viewpoint of missionary results. Farther east, Los Adaes had had some reason for existence when France was in control of nearby Natchitoches. But now that Louisiana had been ceded to Spain, Rubí could see no compelling reason for this former capital of the province. Accordingly, he recommended its abandonment, along with the other posts of East Texas. These were all very expensive, difficult to provision and maintain, and now quite useless.

Moving southwestward, the party visited San Luis de Ahumado, or Orcoquizac, and its nearby mission. Conditions there matched those previously observed in so many of the Texas posts. Both mission and presidio were labeled useless. Not so, however, the presidio of Nuestra Señora de Loreto and its mission on Bahía del Espíritu Santo. The way there had been difficult from Orcoquizac, involving the crossing of the Trinity, the San Jacinto, the Brazos, the Colorado, the Guadalupe, and San Antonio; Rubí was thus exposed to one of the major problems of travel in Texas, the grid pattern of rivers running toward the Gulf which in flood times made communications and transportation slow and difficult. La Bahía was close to the Gulf and could serve as an outpost against possible British attempts to intrude from the coast. Besides, the post was so situated that it might be a point of control against the intractable Karankawa, always potential troublemakers. Rubí not only voted its retention but suggested it as the easternmost anchor of his presidio chain.

From La Bahía, Rubí proceeded to San Juan Bautista on the Río Grande. His only recommendation for this old, old establishment was that it might be located a bit nearer to the river; otherwise, it was to be retained at all costs. From there the route led to Monterrey, capital of Nuevo León; its presidio was judged unnecessary.

Rubí then set off for a look at the relatively new province of Nayarit. En route he again visited Saltillo and Zacatecas and, on the return from Nayarit, once more passed through Querétaro. He was back in the viceregal capital in late February 1768. His had been a fantastic tour. The report which he drafted is a most valuable historical document for the Borderlands record, giving as it does an overall view of the northern frontier at a time when the advance almost everywhere had reached its farthest limits. On April 3, 1768, his report was submitted and a week later his *Dictamen*, or list of recommendations, was ready. Both went off immediately to the minister of the Indies, Don Julián de Arriaga.

Rubí's *Dictamen* suggested a line of presidios extending from the mouth of the Río Concepción in Sonora to the mouth of the Río Guadalupe in Texas. Along this line presidios were to be spotted at intervals of about forty leagues. Some of the existing presidios were to be suppressed, others were to be more strategically located, and six new ones were proposed, these to be built between El Paso and San Juan Bautista along the Río Grande in order to close the gap through which Indian enemies were wont to penetrate. Horcasitas and Buenavista in Sonora were marked for elimination; likewise El Pasaje in Nueva Vizcaya, Monterrey in Nuevo León, and Los Adaes and San Luis Ahumado in Texas. Only Janos, San Juan Bautista, and Bahía del Espíritu Santo were to remain undisturbed in their actual locations. The others were to be kept in their general areas but moved to sites more advantageous to overall frontier defense and mutual assistance in times of attack. Rubí suggested that each presidio have a garrison of 50 men and be properly equipped and provisioned. He recognized that he had left both Santa Fe and San Antonio beyond his proposed line of defense; yet he strongly urged not only that hold on them be retained, but that their garrisons be more adequately manned, to the extent of 160 men. Rubí would put the defense of the frontier in the hands of just under 1000 men; but these he wanted to be well trained and so cared for that they would be a loyal and enthusiastic force. Besides the military considerations behind his plan, he also pointed out that his proposals would reduce the defense budget in the north by some 80,000 pesos.

Back in Spain his *Dictamen* was given close, but not necessarily quick, study. The royal order, the so-called *Reglamento*, or New Regulations of Presidios, was not formulated and promulgated until 1772, after a lag of almost four years.[8] But when it did come, a new frontier office, that of inspector-commander, was created to implement the *Reglamento*. Out of this provision came the next step in the organization of the Borderlands. They soon were to become the Provincias Internas.

Viceroy Bucareli had the task of putting the *Reglamento* into effect. For the post of inspector-general—with unified military authority over all the frontier provinces, from Texas to California—he appointed a favorite of his, Don Hugo O'Connor, who was at the moment in Texas and knew that segment of the Borderlands rather well.[9] The red-headed Irishman, who ultimately changed his Gaelic patronymic down to the more manageable Oconór, had been in New Spain and on the frontier for a dozen years. With the Apache as one of the main problems, he was well acquainted with this adversary and was therefore a good choice. He had two jobs to do: to relocate the presidios in keeping with the Rubí recommendations and to organize an all-out campaign against the Apache.

During the next years Oconór admirably lived up to his reputation. It has been estimated that he covered upward of 10,000 miles in moving back and forth through the Southwest; his activities did not take him to California. He was quite in accord with Rubí in most instances with regard to the relocation of the presidios in order to set up a more sensible and manageable line of defense. Some of the older sites were abandoned, such as those in East Texas; several of the forts were moved to better positions, both that they might be more easily defended and that they might be close enough to their immediate neighbors to be of assistance. A good example of relocation was the transfer of Tubac to Tucson, where the garrison could be better placed to protect the much-talked-of route to the Gila-Colorado junction. In Chihuahua, San Buenaventura was established and Carrizal was shifted; in Coahuila the line was more tightly drawn in the hope of closing what had been a too convenient and unguarded gateway along the Río Grande into the interior.

While Oconór was revising the cordon of presidios, he kept a close watch on the Apache, and speedily carried the war against them. In 1773 he attacked the Mescalero in the Bolsón de Mapimí. Next he sought to organize a pincer-entrapment of the Lipan. Jacobo Ugarte y Loyola, governor of Coahuila, was to move into the San Sabá region, while Governor Mendinueta of New Mexico was moving down the Río Pecos; then Pacheco from San Juan Bautista was to set out upriver while Manuel Múñoz edged over to close a possible escape gap to the south. The full effect of the planned campaign was lost when Mendinueta could not fulfill his assignment because the horse herd for the New Mexico contingent had been run off. However, a number of the Lipan were flushed out and their casualties, in dead and captured, ran close to 250. The campaign of 1776, also, failed to reach full strength. During these years 1773–1776 Oconór had to work without help from Sonora; Bucareli had Anza and many of his men tied up in the overland move to California. Oconór had done a much more than passable job by the time he left the northern frontier in 1776 to become governor of Guatemala. He might have been even more successful, had he been better able to curb his Irish temper and his glib and biting tongue; he was much too quick to criticize his provincial governors and other key men such as Athanase de Mézières.

This year 1776 brought a new and important development in the Borderlands. The unified military command under Oconór had proved the value of considering the northern provinces of New Spain as something of a distinctive entity in the viceroyalty. There were still problems, and big ones; but a new orientation had come to official thinking. In a sense this was not completely new, for in the days of José de Gálvez in New Spain he and some of his advisors had had exchanges on this point. Since 1771 Gálvez was back in Spain in the important post of Minister-General of the Indies. By

1776 he felt that the time had come to realize his old scheme for the frontier more fully. After extensive study and discussion in the royal council, the king, in May, gave the order. The northern provinces were taken out from under the direct jurisdiction of the viceroy and erected into a separate administrative unit, the Comandancia General de las Provincias Internas, with an official of quasi-viceregal authority in charge. To the post of comandante-general Charles III named Don Teodoro de Croix.[10]

Nephew of the immediate past viceroy of New Spain (Francisco de Croix), Don Teodoro was of French descent but had served Spain in Europe since 1747, and in 1756 had been decorated with the Cross of the Teutonic Order. This last circumstance accounts for his frequent designation as *Caballero*, or knight. In 1766 he had first come to New Spain with his uncle and had served in several important posts during his term of rule. When his uncle was relieved in 1771, to be replaced by Bucareli, Don Teodoro returned to Spain with him. The result was that when Don Teodoro came back in 1776, he was no stranger.

Three days before Christmas, 1776, Croix presented himself to Bucareli in the viceregal capital. Well into the next year Croix busied himself in Mexico City, working in the archives in order to familiarize himself with all possible details concerning his new command: the maps of his provinces; data on the presidios, missions, and settlements; the reports of Oconór and other frontier governors and officials; and information on the personnel at the moment on the frontier. During these months he kept a constant stream of letters going back to Gálvez, submitting his thoughts and plans, asking for advice and counsel from the very knowledgeable colonial minister. In the meantime, there developed certain petty frictions between himself and the viceroy. Croix did not have too high an opinion of Bucareli, who seems to have resented both Croix and the new arrangement he represented, which unquestionably added up to a diminution of the viceroy's power and might even be taken as a slur on the viceroy's ability. Bucareli seems to have been particularly irked by the fact that, in theory at least, Croix was to have the supervision of the California enterprise.

By the time Croix left México City, on August 4, 1777, he had his plans well formalized and approved, in general, by Gálvez. He paused in Querétaro and there received news from Anza concerning the revolt of the Seri and of growing unrest among the Opata in Sonora. This confirmed his previous conviction that many more troops would be needed in the north to bring the frontier defenses to a state of efficiency than the number called for in Rubí's recommendations, which for the moment were set up as his guidelines. It was this early that Croix began to press for a complement of at least 2000 men in the presidios—something that he would never see. Bucareli, frightened, perhaps, by the prospect of a rocketing military budget, sought to convince Croix that, once on the ground, he would see that the reports were exaggerated. Croix, far from convinced, replied with detailed figures for a five-year period which he had recently received from Governor Barri of Nueva Vizcaya.

The Barri figures gave a rather good indication of what Croix was going to have to face. They covered the years 1771–1776 and were as follows: persons murdered, 1674; persons captured, 154; haciendas and ranches abandoned, 116; livestock stolen, 68,256; not included in these statistics were presidial losses in men and animals, nor persons killed as they traveled the roads to Nueva Vizcaya. Croix tended to feel that his request for 2000 soldiers was conservative.

Pushing north, Croix came to Monclova and there assembled the first of a series of councils of war (*juntas de guerra*). Governor Jacobo Ugarte y Loyola of Coahuila was present with his captains for this conference on problems and strategy.[11] Many questions were probed: How long had the Apache been seriously harassing the Spaniards? What was their probable strength in numbers? What was known about the "Nations of the North" (the Plains tribes)? With whom should the Spaniards seek to ally themselves, with the Comanche against the Lipan, or vice versa? The majority consensus was that the Apache were the prime enemies and that an alliance with the Comanche, if at all possible, would best serve the interests of the eastern half of the frontier. It was decided that a campaign against the eastern Apache (Natage, Mescalero, Lipan) be readied as quickly as possible. For this projected offensive a force of 3000 men should be gathered, to include regulars, militiamen, and friendly Indians.

Croix held a second *junta de guerra* at San Antonio, in January 1778, when he arrived there on his first tour of the north. At San Antonio his informants were fulsome in their praise of the work of Athanase de Mézières among the northern Indians.[12] This very capable Frenchman, in Spanish service since the transfer of Louisiana, had been highly successful with the tribes formerly in the French sphere of influence. To De Mézières and Governor Juan María Vicencio de Riperdá of Texas was entrusted the not inconsiderable task of working out a plan to win the Comanche to Spanish allegiance so that their assistance might be used against their traditional Apache enemies.

By all odds, the most significant of these councils of war was the one held at Chihuahua, in June and July 1778. In attendance were the key frontier figures of the day: Anza of Sonora; Mendinueta of New Mexico; Barri of Nueva Vizcaya; Ugarte of Coahuila; Croix's second in command, José de Rubio, who had the title of inspector-general; most of the presidio captains of Nueva Vizcaya; and a number of prominent citizens of the province. All present approved the projected Comanche alliance. They did suggest that possibly the Mescalero might be courted and won over to the Spanish side, which maneuver would leave the troublesome Lipan at the mercy of the Spaniards. But it was noted that the presidial complement would have to be increased by some 1800 or more men, in order that a sufficient force might be left in the home presidios to protect against a possible counterattack by the Apache while the main body was in the field. The Apache often resorted to such a strategic maneuver. All the conferees called for closer cooperation among the frontier garrisons and for improved communications so as to ensure united action.

Croix's next task was to implement the recommendations of these several councils. Accordingly, Croix and his associates set to work with vigor. Then, in February 1779 came the bombshell. A royal order reached the comandante-general directing him to adopt a policy of making friends with Indian enemies and of attempting to convince them to settle peaceably in the environs of the missions and the presidios. Again, decisions for the frontier were coming out of Spain. Disappointed, Croix made ready to obey; but he still bedeviled Gálvez to approve the request for 2000 men.

Then, word reached the north that Spain had entered the war against England (the American Revolutionary War) and Croix was realist enough to recognize that his hopes for more troops were thereby dashed, at least temporarily; manpower and funds would be funneled into the war effort. Therefore, Croix went off to Sonora, where he established his headquarters at Arispe, as had been originally envisioned. At Arispe, Croix had to revise and revamp his thinking. Knowing that he could never take offensive action with the existing manpower, he must abandon the projected aggressive type of warfare and go back to a defensive pattern. Accordingly, he planned to rework the line of presidios, as outlined by Rubí and established by Oconór prior to his arrival.

Sonora now assumed new importance, since it had become the land link with Alta California, in 1776. In this setting the Seri problem took on great significance, and the question of the presidio-mission settlement at the Gila-Colorado junction was back to the fore.[13] Croix, however, felt that he had to make choices. His first inclination, for example, was to consider the recent move of the garrison at Tubac to Tucson ill advised, since in the more northerly location that presidio garrison was poorly placed to be of quick assistance against the Seri. Yet Tucson was a necessary link on the route to the Gila, to the junction, and to California. Croix, finally, decided to allow the garrison to remain at Tucson. Then he had to strengthen Altar as his advance post against the Seri and also as a possible block to forestall any union of the Gila Apache and these same Seri. And he had to make adjustments elsewhere, in an attempt to spread his too few men as effectively as possible.

In Sonora he did one thing which had some promise. He established the idea of the *presidio volante*, a mobile troubleshooting force. Captain Joseph Vildosola was furnished with 476 men on whom he could call for defense or offense according to his judgment. Croix set up two new presidios in Sonora: one in the high country at Babispe, which was to be largely staffed by Opata, and a second at Las Nutrias, on the road which he hoped Anza, now governor of New Mexico, might be able to open between his province and Sonora.

To the east, in Nueva Vizcaya and Coahuila, Croix made similar adaptations. In the former province, Janos, San Buenaventura, and Carrizal—this last with a *presidio volante* force—were formed into a western defensive combination; the second, or eastern, division was based at El Paso. In a number of the smaller towns Croix worked to establish a local militia for defense, and envisioned its use for wider assistance when needed. Much of this new strength he managed to develop with local, rather than royal, funds. Had the Borderlands been able to attract more settlers, some of their defense problems might have been lightened. The number of civilians on the farther frontiers were regularly too few.

One presidial reform which Croix sought to introduce was the idea of stabling the horses, rather than having them pastured at some distance from the fort where they were liable to be stampeded and stolen by Indian raiders. But on this point he met some vested-interest opposition. The frontier suppliers worked on the theory that the more horses stolen, the better the market to the military; the hay farmers were less well organized.

The year 1781 was one of cruel disappointment for Croix. The Gila-Colorado junction had at long last been occupied in the previous year, but was poorly staffed and defended. On July 17 the Yuma revolted, killed the two friars and most of the male settlers at San Pedro y San Pablo, and took the women and children captive. The next day another Yuma band moved against Purísima Concepción and killed Rivera and his detachment. On the following day they murdered the other two missionaries: the peerless Francisco Garcés and Barraneche, his companion. Rivera y Moncada had a few weeks before brought an expedition of 40 recruits and their families up from Baja California en route to found Los Angeles and had fortunately sent them on their way while he and a dozen or so of his men remained at the junction to refresh their animals before proceeding. Before they got under way the Yuma struck. This massacre was a shock to the frontier. It spelled the end of the Gila-Colorado experiment and, for that matter, of the overland trail to California.[14]

Croix sent out a punitive expedition in the fall of 1781, under Pedro Fages. He was able to ransom some of the captives. In the next year Romeu of Sonora moved into Yuma territory with a larger expedition. This 1782 campaign killed about 200 of the rebellious tribesmen and recovered over 1000 horses. But that closed the Yuma chapter of the story for many decades to come.

In 1782 Croix was dealt another blow. Juan Ugalde, governor of Coahuila, sustained a severe humiliation at the hands of the Apache. Campaigning against the Mescalero into the Bolsón de Mapimí, where results were minimal, he left several of the settlements exposed to Apache raids. His failure to protect the towns angered Croix, who replaced him with Don Pedro de Tueros.

Croix's service in the north was coming to an end. In 1783 Charles III, very evidently appreciative of his accomplishments on the frontier, rewarded him with one of the real plums of the Indies, the viceroyship of Peru. His half-dozen years in the Provincias Internas, despite setbacks, had seen solid achievement in dealing with the prime frontier problem, the Indian. He had not beaten the native Americans, but his policies had, temporarily at least, halted them on most fronts. He had set a pattern for a second line of defense with such organizations as the Provincial Militia Corps of Nueva Vizcaya. His versatile *presidio volante* provided a mobile striking force, for defense or offense, as the situation warranted. His relocated presidios and the several new ones added in highly strategic areas of Nueva Vizcaya and Coahuila pulled the cordon of defense more tightly and plugged a number of the gaps through which the raiders had been wont to penetrate almost without opposition. His dealings with California—or perhaps lack of them—have caused some California historians to be less than enthusiastic in evaluating his accomplishments. And his censures of two Borderlands favorites, Garcés and Anza, in connection with the Yuma massacre have angered others.

Croix was not on hand in the north to share the exhilaration of seeing one of his goals achieved in 1786. After his California exploits Juan Bautista de Anza had been named governor of New Mexico, in 1777.[15] The problems of Sonora held him in that province for a time after the appointment. By 1779, however, he was operating out of his capital at Santa Fe. Many were his successes of the next years—campaigns against the Moqui (Hopi) to the west, the breaking of the Navaho-Gila Apache alliance, cowing the Ute. But his greatest achievement was the defeat of and the peace he won with the western Comanche. Anza brought these troublesome plainsmen to terms and into an alliance with the Spaniards which lasted for several decades, almost to the end of Spain's regime in the Borderlands. Had there been more men of his stamp in the Provincias Internas, the idea that had suggested their formation might well have paid off most handsomely.

However, this was not to be. Croix's immediate successor as comandante-general was Felipe de Neve, a man who had proved himself in California and might have been even more successful than Croix, had not death taken him while en route to his new command, in 1783. Joseph Antonio Rengel was named comandante ad interim, and during the time he held the office the Provincias Internas were put back under the direct control of the viceroy. In 1785 Jacobo Ugarte y Loyola, a veteran in the north, received the appointment, and Rengel resumed his post as second in command, inspector-general. There were a few short, too short, months between 1785 and the fall of 1786, when Bernardo de Gálvez, nephew of José and with broad American experience, having been governor of Spanish Louisiana, held the viceroyship of New Spain. He understood the problems of the Provincias Internas as few of his predecessors, or successors, had. His instructions of 1786 to Ugarte de Loyola show him a master of frontier know-how and Indian psychology.[16] His days of leadership were too few. Following his untimely death, in 1786, Manuel Antonio Flores succeeded to the viceroyship. Flores implemented one of Croix's parting recommendations and divided the northern frontier into an eastern and a western command, but deprived the northern commanders of much of their autonomy, which was hardly a Croix suggestion. Juan de Ugalde, back in favor, was placed in charge of the first district, which comprised Texas, Coahuila, Nuevo León, and Nuevo Santander. Ugarte, by far the more capable of the two, was retained as commander in the west, with jurisdiction over New Mexico, Nueva Vizcaya, Sonora, and, in theory at least, the Californias. Both men were responsible to the viceroy in most matters.

During the next several years Ugarte proved to be the strong man in the

New Mexican neighbors, the Navaho. Lithograph after a drawing by H. B. Mollhausen. (Library of Congress)

north and turned the major part of his attention to the Apache problem in his district. By the end of 1790, when he was removed from his command and sent to a post farther south, at Guadalajara, he had in large measure brought a measure of stability to the frontier. From long experience he knew the Apache and their ways. He was often at odds with Flores because of his willingness to accept truces and what he well knew might be only temporary periods of friendship; these he considered preferable to constant warfare and devastation. With the instructions of Gálvez as his guide, he sought to win a more lasting peace by the system of gifts and goods and recognition, on the part of the Apache, of a necessary dependence on the friendship of the Spaniards as a guard against traditional enemies, notably the Comanche. Ugarte could be and was tough when occasion demanded. He often turned Apache against Apache, using the friendly nations against the trouble-makers, and even the tractable groups within a single nation against the dissidents. He also used traditionally pro-Spanish Indians against Apache marauders—the Opata and the Pima of Sonora, the Pueblo, Navaho, and Ute of New Mexico, and the southern Comanche.

Ugarte was one of the more capable of the later northern frontiersmen.[17] In late 1790 he was succeeded by Pedro de Nava, who was commander in the west and, like Ugarte in his last months in the north, held an ad interim appointment over the other half. In 1793 the Provincias Internas were again united and once more withdrawn from the authority of the viceroy, as the unit had been initially conceived. However, several of the provinces—Nuevo León, Nuevo Santander, and the Californias—were pulled out of the complex and reserved for viceregal supervision. So the arrangement remained until Spain lost its North American possessions in 1821, when Mexico won its independence.

This story of the Provincias Internas contradicts the statement some-times made that Spain was little interested in the farther reaches of its North American empire. Spain was vitally interested, even though at times this interest did not turn out to be completely rewarding. This story shows how varied were Spain's imperial problems, not only in the overall picture of its American Indies, but even as regards individual areas. These northern provinces of New Spain brought the mother country little tangible return on its considerable investment, in the form of precious-metal wealth, although they often contributed rewards of a spiritual sort in terms of the Indian converts made by the missionaries. These loomed larger in Spain's seventeenth-century thinking than they did in the next century, which was not nearly as apostolically oriented and was much more materialistically minded. But even to the pragmatists of that century, the Provincias Internas had an importance as defense bastions against threatening European rivals. Spain's north Mexican "silver provinces" had to be protected; the defense line of buffer areas had to be maintained at all costs. Of course, Spain hoped that these costs could be held to a minimum. This last consideration is one that prompted much of the reforming urge so notable in the days of Charles III, and out of which the reorganization of the frontier came.

The withdrawal of the French in 1762 and the cession of their trans-Mississippi claims to Spain relieved some of the pressures. But this very fact raised up another colonial rival—more formidable, potentially, than France had ever been or than Russia was or would ever become. With Britain just across the Mississippi and after the Treaty of Paris of 1763 in Florida, Spain had some serious rethinking to do. Whether Spain liked it or not, it had to turn its newly acquired *Luisiana* into another Borderland.

Spain's "headaches" came at twenty-year intervals. In 1763 Spain acquired the British as neighbors; in 1783 the even more worrisome and aggressive Americans replaced them; and in 1803 these Americans ceased to be somewhat remote neighbors and became neighbors who felt that their lands extended far, too far, westward, especially in Texas and through the Plains.

◁ 11 ▷

Luisiana, a Quasi-Borderland 1762-1800

*I*n November 1762 the Spanish Borderlands picture changed significantly. France, decisively beaten in North America in the French and Indian War by Britain and heading toward the Paris Peace Conference (February 10, 1763) sought to salvage a possible future foothold on the continent by antecedently deeding to Spain (November 1762) its claims to New Orleans and the western half of the Mississippi Valley. Spain, under the terms of the Second Bourbon Family Compact, had entered the war against England in 1761 and had fared badly. Since 1700, with a Bourbon prince occupying the throne of Spain as well as that of France, relationships between the two nations had generally been friendly. France, hard pressed in the Americas as elsewhere in the colonial world during the contest, had finally persuaded Spain to join it, by arguing that New Spain might be the next target for victorious Britain in the Americas. Reluctantly but realistically, the Spaniards became belligerently involved, in the hope of keeping England a manageable rival.[1]

Soon Spain regretted this step, for among other minor setbacks Spain sustained a major defeat when it lost Cuba. The peace preliminaries indicated that Spain might have to yield its Florida territory to England, in order to redeem Cuba, the "key to the Caribbean."[2] Spain might be fortunate, if the victor did not demand both. The cession of Florida would be a blow to Spanish pride and might weaken Spain's position at the southeast corner of the continent, on what was still the homebound route of Spain's ships from the Indies. Spain could not afford to lose Cuba, especially with England already in possession of Jamaica, and of some of the smaller of the Caribbean Islands. France recognized Spain's predicament and, besides harboring some ulterior motives, felt that half of Louisiana might help to assuage the pain of loss for its ally. In all events, in late 1762 the trans-Mississippi became Spanish by a stroke of the pen and *La Louisiane* began to be spelled *Luisiana*. This state of affairs was destined to prevail through the rest of the eighteenth century.

Spain was not happy over this turn of international chess playing. It did recognize that the sizable buffer of the trans-Mississippi between New Spain and the westward-moving Briton might have advantages. But Spain's newest acquisition also meant that its Borderlands frontier would be stretched far beyond the breaking point, at least in terms of manpower and in economic terms. As of 1762–1763, it must be remembered, Spain still had its own Borderlands problems to solve closer to home; the concept of the erection of the Provincias Internas was only then forming in the minds of a few perceptive frontiersmen. José de Gálvez was not yet in New Spain, to share these ideas and to give them some workable form and direction; and he was still almost ten years away from the desk of the Colonial Minister back at the court. *Luisiana* was destined to be a quasi-Borderland. It would never be part of the future Provincias Internas; from the beginning it formed part of the captaincy-general of Cuba and was never under the viceroy of New Spain or the comandante-general. Still, Luisiana was to be called upon to play a Borderlands role, at least on the score of being a defensive buffer.

Spain was slow to pick up its "prize."[3] When word reached the French of Louisiana of the change of sovereignty, feelings were mixed. Most of them felt that they had been betrayed by France and were minded to oppose any take-over by the Spaniards. Besides, Spain's choice of its first governor was unfortunate. Don Antonio de Ulloa was no diplomat, nor was he a good psychologist. The French sought to block him at every turn and ultimately went into open revolt and practically drove him from the colony. In 1769 Charles III next sent Don Alejando O'Reilly as governor. O'Reilly, Irish born, had been in the service of Spain in Europe for some years, and also had campaigned for France and Austria. He had been in Havana and more recently was credited with having saved the monarch's life during the Madrid insurrection of 1765. He was a soldier-minded administrator, rough and tough when the situation warranted. Within six months he had established Spanish rule in Louisiana, executed five Frenchmen who had been involved in the revolt against Ulloa, and won from the Creoles the uncomplimentary title of "Bloody O'Reilly." His successor, Luis de Unzaga y Amezaga, had no further difficulty with Spain's new subjects, who may not always have liked the Spanish regime but had the good sense to hold their tongues and to keep their heads.

By 1770 Spain was, theoretically, in control of its newest Borderland. Louisiana offered imperial administrators many of the same problems with which they had had to wrestle for almost two centuries, but also some new ones. The acquisition of the trans-Mississippi forced Spain to revise its thinking about boundaries. For example, Spain no longer shared the Gulf of Mexico coastline with France, whom it had, so to speak, boxed in by Florida on the east and Texas on the west. England was now the next-door neighbor, and the division of the Gulf coastline had drastically altered. Now that England held Florida, the eastern half was definitely England's and England was in a position to make trouble for Spain. Spain's claims stretched westward from the mouth of the Mississippi, along a strand of Texas shoreline which was poorly known and even more inadequately held until one reached the Bay of Espíritu Santo. Spain knew that it was vulnerable and had already responded to rumors of British infiltration by increasing its watchfulness over the coastal area to the east of La Bahía.

A major problem that Spain inherited with Louisiana was a new brand of Indian challenge. Spain had already run into this to some degree in eastern and northern Texas, where nomadic hunter tribes defied the traditional methods of pacification used in Mexico and the northwest; but now Spain had it magnified and extended far to the north, to the still undetermined Canadian border. Spain already knew that the mission was not the answer, much as imperial policy and apostolic hopes might wish it otherwise. The French up the Red River and beyond the Mississippi had tried to control the Indians through trade and presents and had accustomed the Indians to think in those terms and to live by them. Spain would have to revise its whole approach. The only consoling thought was that even though French sovereignty had been withdrawn the Frenchmen, skilled in Indian relations, were still on the ground. Spain would have to ensure their services and win their loyalty.

In instances, Spain was highly successful in enlisting some of these very knowledgeable Frenchmen. The case of Athanase de Mézières was one in point.[4] De Mézières, Paris-born, had served France in Louisiana for thirty years prior to his taking service under Spain. During many of those years he had worked out of Natchitoches and had enjoyed quite remarkable success with the Indians of the Red River country. After 1763 he worked tirelessly and efficiently for his new masters, even though some of his Spanish superiors did not always trust him—at least in the earlier years. In time, however, his achievements won their confidence. Don Teodoro de Croix was one who recognized his worth, treasured his advice, leaned on his experience, and ultimately was influential in having him named governor of

Texas. He did not live to assume that post, dying at San Antonio in November 1779. His biographer notes that "the chief service of De Mézières to the Spanish government was to win to Spanish allegiance the Nations of the North, which, though friendly to the French, had been hostile to the Spanish, and to maintain their allegiance both in Texas and Louisiana."

In its new Borderland Spain also inherited still another new and, at first, baffling problem. Spain found itself with a sizable number of Frenchmen on its hands. Spain's first experiences with these new subjects in New Orleans and environs were less than pleasant. In time, there and elsewhere in the trans-Mississippi the Frenchmen became reasonably loyal subjects, but there were moments when they showed themselves a bit contentious, and they always needed careful handling.

As of November 1762, the French had few settlements to the west of the Mississippi in the middle and Upper Valley, north of Louisiana proper.[5] There was the Poste des Arkansas, at the mouth of the river of that name, founded in the previous century by Henri de Tonty; in the future State of Missouri there was Sainte Genevieve and a few mining camps in the lead belt; and there were several more lead mining operations in the future Iowa. Most of the French mid-valley settlement had been on the left bank, on the Wabash to the east, beyond the western of the Great Lakes to the north, and in the Illinois country. Within a few months (in 1763), these Frenchmen seemed destined to become British subjects. Few of them relished the prospect.

A development was in the making very soon which would give these Frenchmen an alternative and which was also destined to have a marked influence on the future of the Spanish Borderlands. In August 1763, before word of the secret treaty of 1762 or, for that matter, of the Peace of Paris of 1763 reached New Orleans, the French commandant, Charles Phélipe Aubry, gave permission to the firm of Maxent, Laclède et Compagnie to found a post at or near the mouth of the Missouri and to open trade in that river valley. Before the year was out, Pierre Laclède Liguest, one of the partners, was headed upriver with a small party. After looking over the lands near the confluence of the Missouri and the Mississippi and finding them unsuitable for Company purposes, Laclède dropped back downstream and chose a site on a low bluff fifteen miles to the south of the junction. He then headed back to Fort de Chartres, where he had stored his trade goods, in order to wait for better weather. In February 1764 he sent young Auguste Chouteau and a few men to the designated spot to ready things for occupation. A few weeks later Laclède came up with the rest of the group to what was to be called Saint Louis des Illinois.[6]

Soon the first Saint Louisans became aware of the international dispositions concerning themselves and their land. They were not precisely pleased to find themselves subjects of His Most Catholic Majesty of Spain; but they were consoled, at least, that they were not under Protestant England. Within a few months many of the Frenchmen from the left bank—in process of being taken over by the British, choosing what they considered to be the lesser of two evils—crossed the river into Spain's *Luisiana.* As a result, almost overnight there was a population explosion, which turned little Saint Louis into a post boasting several hundred inhabitants.

In 1767 Governor Ulloa sent Francisco Ríu upriver from New Orleans to report on the situation in the middle valley. Three years later, in 1770, O'Reilly commissioned Don Pedro Piernas as the first lieutenant-governor of Upper Louisiana, and Spanish authority was formally established at Saint Louis.

Spain quickly learned that the passing of the French and the cession of the trans-Mississippi to Spain, instead of solving one of its major rivalry problems in North America really presented it with another problem—not only of the same character, but even potentially more worrisome. The French had been troublesome on the Texas frontier, and mildly so against New Mexico. Now Spain had England as a neighbor—and an aggressive one—just

across its Mississippi River boundary. Farther to the north, Spain had inherited some of the French as its subjects, but England got the bulk of them—the French Canadians. These last as British subjects were potential troublemakers.

As early as 1773 word came into Saint Louis that a certain Jean Marie Ducharme, armed with an English license, was operating among the Little Osage Indians of middle Missouri.[7] Piernas dispatched Laclède to expel him. Ducharme escaped but left his goods behind; some of his men were taken. He and his kind would be back. Ducharme seems to have been but one of the advancing horde of fur traders who soon made Prairie du Chien, at the mouth of the Wisconsin River, their springboard outpost for the penetration of Spain's trans-Mississippi lands. These men, most of them in the employ of the newly founded and definitely aggressive North West Company of Montreal, soon were filtering into Iowa, Minnesota, and beyond. Before the 1770s had run their course British traders were reported among the Sioux, who at the moment were located to the east of the upper Missouri River; in the next decade the traders had gone on to the Mandan on the Upper Missouri, in the territory of the future South and North Dakota. They came well-stocked with trade goods, cheap enough to make competition difficult for possible rivals. These Britishers also had another advantage, that of freedom from stringent governmental regulations, which allowed them great mobility. Spain recognized that these foreigners might very well develop into another threat to New Mexico, the defense buffer for its valuable North Mexican "silver provinces." A further worry was the knowledge that the Indians of the middle and northern trans-Mississippi were trade minded and not at all mission minded. Spain would have to put its new Indian policy—trade and presents—to work.[8]

Almost from its inception, in 1764, the new post of Saint Louis des Illinois assumed great strategic importance on Spain's far-flung frontier. Saint Louisans might not be enthusiastic Spanish subjects, but Spain knew that it could count on them to dislike the English. For some years they were not numerous enough nor strong enough to contest the British in the Upper Mississippi Valley, but they could, and did, serve as a bulwark against the English in the Illinois country and thus could secure the approaches to Santa Fe via the Missouri and the Arkansas. In 1780–1781 they had done more than that, when they were able to fend off a British-inspired Indian attack and to mount a counterattack on English positions at the south end of Lake Michigan—this as a part of the Anglo-American Revolution, in which Spain had become involved as an ally of France. Had Spain been able to reinforce the Saint Louisans at this time, they might very well have secured ascendancy in the Upper Mississippi Valley. But it was the same old story of restricted means and an inadequate realization of the opportunity of the moment. However, Spain should not be blamed too severely, for in the mid-continent it was dealing with a very new kind of frontier. Miners and

Worship of the Sun. Drawing by Captain Eastman, in Henry Schoolcraft, *Information Respecting . . . Indian Tribes of the U.S.*, 1853. (Library of Congress)

ranchers Spain could handle; traders, their psychology and needs and ways of operating, were little known.

In the early 1780s Spain found an even more fearsome neighbor across the Mississippi—the young, aggressive, self-confident United States, whose boundaries ran to the east bank. Immediately, Spanish officials learned to distrust these Americans even more than the British. In the later 1780s official pressures from New Orleans urged the establishment of forts at the mouth of the Des Moines and the Minnesota rivers; but neither funds nor men were forthcoming. Spain did, for a time, try to maintain a gunboat patrol on the Mississippi; but it was never particularly effective, since the flow of Americans and Britishers continued westward.

In the last decade of the century Spain's attention turned very definitely to the Missouri River country.[9] Much of this was sparked by a faulty geographical concept. Until the Americans' Lewis and Clark had made their trip to the Pacific (1804–1806), the conviction was general that the Missouri had its source in the Rocky Mountains, not too far above the Platte River. If this was true, then New Mexico might be vulnerable to enemies who could ascend that river to its headwaters, then by southern tributaries work their way up those streams to a point where the headwaters of the Río Grande would not be too far removed. The Spaniards still remembered that the Mallet brothers, in 1739, made it to Santa Fe overland from the Platte. Spain concluded that sound defense strategy demanded that its subjects be the first to the sources of the Missouri. Then they would line the banks of that stream with trading posts and/or forts, win the Indians over, and turn them against any rival trespassers, be they British or American.

Between 1790 and 1792 the elusive trader-explorer Jacques d'Église, whose goings and comings in the Missouri River country are so difficult to catalog, was definitely in the Mandan country, as he reported to Lieutenant-Governor Zénon Trudeau at Saint Louis, in late 1792. This fact made him the first Spanish subject that far up the Missouri.[10] His information was both enlightening and more than a little upsetting. Among the Mandan he found evidences of English intrusions and learned that these tribesmen were quite regularly in contact with British traders, whom, they said, were a fifteen-days' journey to the north; while there he saw New Mexican leather goods and also ran into a Frenchmen, Ménard by name, who claimed to have been living in those parts and with those Indians for about a dozen years. Trudeau, in turn, reported this information to the governor at New Orléans, François Louis Hector, Baron de Carondelet. The governor, in reply, requested more information, for he already had plans churning.

Earlier in 1792 Carondelet had decreed that all Spanish subjects might engage in the Missouri River trade; all they needed was proof of their Spanish allegiance and a license from the lieutenant-governor.[11] This decree had drawn strong protests from some of the Saint Louis merchants who objected to so completely open a policy of licensing. As a result Carondelet revised his directive and set down a series of regulatory restrictions. These Trudeau submitted to the merchant-trader group, the Corps de Commerce of Spanish Illinois. In October of the next year that body of Saint Louisans approved the regulations in the main, offered a few possible revisions, in the direction of greater strictness, and prepared to take advantage of the new state of affairs. Spain was learning, on this frontier at least, that there was merit in allowing some measure of individual enterprise; the currents of the Enlightenment were, obviously, reaching to the Borderlands.

In that same month of October 1793 the first "Missouri Company" came into being—"Company of Explorers of the Upper Missouri."[12] Despite their official title, the men involved were traders; exploration would be incidental to this first interest. Jacques Clamorgan, one of the more enterprising and forward-looking of the Saint Louis group, and a man most interested in challenging the British in the upper Missouri country, was the chief promoter.

Even though the Company was not formalized until the spring of 1794, the partners were already assembling an expedition. By June 20 they had prepared a list of instructions for Jean Baptiste Truteau, whom they had selected to head a nine-man party. The objective was the Mandan country, the establishment of Spanish control in the north, and profits, to be sure, for the directors. Truteau was also to learn, if possible, something of the distance separating the Mandan villages from New Mexico.

Truteau and his party were up to the mouth of the Platte by August. They went into winter quarters below the Sioux country, having been blocked by the Teton Sioux. Truteau had hoped to be able to contact the Arikara, whose help he wanted to enlist in breaking through the Sioux barrier. The party did some trading during the winter and with the opening of the river, at the coming of spring, Truteau sent his largest boat, loaded with furs, back to Saint Louis, and he and several men pushed upstream. He moved through the Ponca, who were along the lower reaches of the White River; two of his companions had previously traded with these Ponca. Arrived among the Arikara, on the Missouri in middle South Dakota, Truteau found that D'Église, operating on his own, had already skimmed off the best furs of their winter catch. Truteau was stranded among the Arikara until the following spring—at least this is what seems to come from the records. Meanwhile, he sent messengers and tobacco gifts to Ménard and René Jusseaume for distribution among the Mandan and the Grosventre; both of these men had been with those tribes for some years past. Truteau also asked these men to assure the chiefs that he was expecting new supplies from Saint Louis and that he himself would be coming north presently. Actually, the Company expedition of 1795, sent out under Lecuyer, failed to make contact, and Truteau never reached the Mandan country. During that summer, however, he did make friendly contacts with the Cheyenne, then living in middle South Dakota, on the river to which they gave their name. The next spring (1796) Truteau returned to Saint Louis. In a sense, his mission had failed; still, important Spanish contacts had been established with the upper Missouri River tribes and evidence of interest had been shown.

Neither the Missouri Company nor the Spanish officials were minded to give up. James Mackay, a Scotsman with wide experience in the north country during his years of service with the North West Company and who had recently come down to the Spaniards, was the next hope of the Company and of Spain. He was appointed to succeed Truteau in 1795 and went off in August of that year with four boats, each well provisioned but the cargo of each very definitely earmarked. The trade goods and presents in one were for the Arikara; the second was similarly provisioned, but its goods were meant to be bribes for the Sioux, in order to ensure passage northward unimpeded; the third was loaded with goods for the Mandan trade; and the fourth had a cargo of presents, largely to be used as needed to facilitate passage beyond the Mandan to the Rocky Mountains. By the time that autumn was waning Mackay was only a short distance above the mouth of the Platte. There he constructed a temporary post, among the Oto, left several of his party, and himself went off to the Omaha. He ultimately decided to spend the winter with them, at the invitation of their Chief Black

Bird. From this point, named "Fort Charles," Mackay dispatched John Evans overland to the Arikara.

John Evans was another foreigner appearing on the frontier during those years in the service of Spain.[13] The Spanish antiforeigner prejudices, along with other traditional aspects of Spanish policy, were being set aside in the trans-Mississippi. Evans was a Welshman who had come to America in search of "Welsh Indians," purported to be found in the upper Missouri River country. He gravitated west from Philadelphia, came to Saint Louis, made friends with the patriarch of that town, Auguste Chouteau (Laclède was long dead), entered the service of the Missouri Company, and was with Mackay on this 1795 trip up the Missouri.

Evans, then, set out to contact the Arikara. Before his little party had progressed very far, they encountered a not too friendly band of Sioux hunters and thought it prudent to return to the fort. Soon, however, they were on their way again, with detailed instructions from Mackay to discover the sources of the Missouri, if possible, and to proceed thence to the Pacific Ocean. Notions of the geography of the Upper Missouri River country were still very hazy.

Mackay went up to the Arikara and, while stopping, met with some chiefs of the tribes to the west, notably the Cheyenne. He did not reach the Mandan villages until December. There he took possession of the British "fort," enjoined the Indians to trade no more with the English, and raised the Spanish flag at the post. Soon several Britishers came up; but neither group was in sufficient force to contest the presence of the other. Mackay contented himself with sending letters by these men to the officials of the North West Company and the Hudson's Bay Company, warning the English that in their dealings with the Mandan they were trespassing on Spanish territory. Mackay's presence among the Mandan did reinforce Spain's claims. But this confrontation, while a victory for Spain in theory, did not prevent the English from returning. When Lewis and Clark wintered with the Mandan during the season 1804–1805, they reported Britishers in the country; the American message was like that of Mackay, "Keep out!"

Both Mackay and Evans were back in Missouri by the end of 1797. Other "Spaniards" probably went upriver after that date, but the records are very sketchy. It is known that in 1802 François Marie Perrin du Lac was in the north; and the next season Jean Vallé, of Sainte Genevieve, was on the Cheyenne River and went on toward the Black Hills. Clamorgan entered into a new partnership in 1800, with François Régis Loisel. He sent Hugh Henry to the Upper Missouri; and Loisel himself was out in the field. But in those early nineteenth-century years Spain was no longer owner of the trans-Mississippi, Louisiana having been retroceded to France, by the demand of Napoleon. The shadow of France fell across the lower Mississippi Valley, but it did not extend very far up that river. The year 1804 was the changeover one in the trans-Mississippi.

While Spain was still in control, Saint Louis had a connection, if only very temporary, with the Borderlands proper. Interestingly, it was a Frenchman, one Pierre or Pedro Vial of Lyon, who was the link. In a certain sense he became in a way a successor to Athanase de Mézières in the list of Frenchmen rendering important services to Spain in the trans-Mississippi. He was explorer and trailbreaker, rather than diplomat to the Indians; but his contribution has its measure of Borderlands significance. And, had Spain had more years in its period of Louisiana tenure, Vial might well have been responsible for drawing Missouri more closely into the complex of the Provincias Internas.[14]

Vial's trek from Santa Fe to Saint Louis and back, in 1792–1793, is really part of a development in the Borderlands dating back to the middle 1770s (in a facetious sense the whole might be termed "Operation Tying-Together-Loose-Ends"). This story begins with the Spanish occupation of Alta California and recognition in the early 1770s that this outpost province should be linked with New Spain by a more secure and less expensive connection than the sea route from San Blas to Monterey. This conviction sparked the interest in the overland route from Sonora and led to the work of Juan Bautista de Anza and Fray Francisco Garcés in the middle 1770s.[15]

Plaza, San Antonio de Béjar. Engraving by J. Smillie after a drawing by A. Schott. (Charles Phelps Cushing)

About the same time that San Francisco was becoming the "outpost of empire," there was another Spanish expedition in the field, probing a possible connection between Santa Fe and Monterey.[16] In late July 1776, Fray Silvestre Vélez de Escalante set off from Santa Fe with a party of nine, which included Fray Francisco Atanasio Domínguez, his religious superior, three other Spaniards, and half a dozen mestizos and Indians. Moving northwest from Santa Fe, they cut through the southwest corner of Colorado, near Mesa Verde, and then pushed on into Utah, going northward to the neighborhood of Spanish Fork and Utah Lake. When no likely route to Monterey appeared, they gave up that quest, dropped down to the Colorado, crossed it, finally, after thirteen days of looking for a ford, then went back to the home base via Zuñi. The expedition had not opened the desired connection with California, but it left the Spaniards with their first sound knowledge of the Utah section of the Great Basin country.

The next interest in establishing connections between outposts came in the 1780s and was eastward oriented; these trailbreaking efforts involved Pedro Vial. It will be remembered that the *Reglamento de los Presidios*, which had come out of the Rubí recommendations, in 1772, left two key Borderlands settlements outside the defensive cordon established. Santa Fe and San Antonio were isolated, although there was never thought of abandoning them. Jacobo Ugarte y Loyola, comandante of the Provincias Internas in the middle 1780s, was concerned and decided that the two should be joined by some line of communications. The job of tracing the San Antonio-Santa Fe link was assigned to Pedro Vial.

Vial had been on the frontier for some years and, it seems, had been living among the Indians and plying his trade as gunsmith—the arquebus was still much of a mystery to the tribesmen, at least when it failed to function. Vial was evidently not only known to the tribes of central and northern Texas but was also respected by them, for he was able to make his first trek in safety with only a single companion.

He and his companion left San Antonio de Béjar on October 4, 1786. They were on the road until the end of May 1787, for they made several extended stops, one of six weeks among the Tawakoni and another of five weeks among the Comanche. Vial found the latter particularly friendly. The Comanche even asked for a Spanish post in the north in order that they might be relieved of having to go to San Antonio to do their business, a trip which took them through the country of their sworn enemies. It is interesting to note how dependent these Plains people were becoming on the white man's goods. Contacts with the French had begun the process; now, with the French gone, they were willing to do business with any suppliers. This was precisely the situation which Bernardo de Gálvez wished to create and exploit, as he outlined the strategy in his *Instrucciones* of 1786.[17]

Governor Fernando de la Concha of New Mexico received Vial most cordially. At Santa Fe, Vial completed his diary and his map and, at

Concha's urging, drew another showing the areas of the trans-Mississippi with which he was familiar. Vial's route had not been very direct. Concha hoped to straighten it out and sent José Mares and two companions from Santa Fe on such an errand. They left on the last day of July 1787 and were in San Antonio on October 8. Their time was better, but the mileage was no great improvement. Mares' return route to Santa Fe was considerably more direct. Both he and Vial had improved on the old right-angle connection between the two points—from San Antonio to the Río Grande, through Nuevo León and Coahuila to Chihuahua, thence up the long hard trail to the New Mexican capital. They had showed the practicability of the hypotenuse, even though it did become a bit elliptical.

Vial's trailblazing days were far from over. In 1788–1789 he went from Santa Fe to Natchitoches, thence to San Antonio, and back to Santa Fe, covering a distance of some 2500 miles and proving very conclusively that these Borderlands outposts could be tied together.

The Spaniards next used his experience in breaking a trail which was in time to have greater and more enduring significance. Growing concern over activities of the Americans in the trans-Mississippi, real and imagined, led to his new assignment. In this instance, when Governor Concha sent him from Santa Fe to Saint Louis, he was acting not simply on his own authority, as in the previous instances, but at the urging of the new viceroy, the Conde de Revillagigedo. Officials not only wanted a trail opened, but they seem to have been even more interested in having more exact knowledge of the distance which separated their New Mexican outpost from that other in the far-off Mississippi Valley. Missouri was becoming more and more of a Borderland in their thinking.

With detailed instructions from Concha, a letter to the commandant at Saint Louis, and two young companions, Vicente Villanueva and Vicente Espinosa, Vial set out from Santa Fe on May 21, 1792. The trio spent their first night at the pueblo of Pecos, then moved on to the Canadian and then on to the Arkansas. Along this latter river they encountered their only definitely inhospitable reception, when, taken captive by a band of Kansa Indians who were minded to kill them, they were rescued by some old friends of Vial's French-trader days who happened on the scene at the right time. Released, the travelers pushed up to the Kansas, or Kaw, River and followed that stream to its confluence with the Missouri. On the Kaw they met a trader out of Saint Louis, who welcomed them, gave them a share of his goods, and sent them off with many helpful suggestions for the rest of their trip. Along the lower Missouri Vial recorded meetings with bands of Osage and Missouri. On the evening of October 3, 1792, the trio arrived in Saint Louis. Zénon Trudeau, the lieutenant-governor, gave the three a warm reception.

Vial wintered in Saint Louis and the following June (1793) headed back to his home base at Santa Fe, this time traveling the trail in the direction more familiar to later Anglo-Americans. Trudeau sent him and his companions up the Missouri in a pirogue, accompanied by four young Saint Louisans who were heading up the Missouri to trade. Vial stayed with them as far as the Little Nemaha, a point in southeastern Nebraska where the four paddlers intended to trade with the Pawnee. Leaving them there, Vial and his two young men set out for the Arkansas, went on to the upper Canadian, and were back in Santa Fe on November 25. The information he brought back was interesting but not always reassuring to the Spaniards of New Mexico. Saint Louis was really not too, too far away; and the Americans, the Kentuckians as they were coming to be known, were certainly not far from Saint Louis. Spanish officials began to think that perhaps they might take an interest in the middle segment of their *Luisiana* not wholly unlike that which they were actually promoting in the upper Missouri River country. They could well use a "Missouri-Kansas-Nebraska" Athanase de Mézières.

Unhappily, Spain inherited few Frenchmen with skills such as those possessed by the traders and explorers of the Texas-Louisiana border or the middle trans-Mississippi or the upper Missouri River country to help it face the problems of Lower Louisiana. Downriver the challenges to Spain's "quasi-Borderland" were of a quite different character. The Indians and men who could get on with them played a very minor role. The Anglo-American "westerners" were a completely different breed of rivals: they were determined, aggressive, and with each passing year more ominously numerous. They were not men of passage, as were the traders; they were settlers, greedy for land and seemingly insatiable in their hunger for more and more territory. From the confluence of the Ohio with the Mississippi southward these *Americanos* made Spain's Louisiana years, at least from 1783 on, quite unpleasant.[18] After that date Spain owned Florida again, and it, too, had to play a Borderland role.

Almost as soon as the United States became a recognized independent nation, the matter of a southern boundary rose to a level of high importance. In the diplomatic maneuverings which had led to the Treaty of Paris (1783), Spain made it unmistakably clear that it would be thoroughly unhappy with the 31st parallel boundary favored by the United States. Spain hoped to get all the lands from the Gulf of Mexico northward to the Ohio River, with the watershed of the Appalachian Highland as the boundary on the east. Only thus, Spain felt, would *Luisiana* and Florida be properly protected against the land-hungry Americans. Spain had most reluctantly assisted them in their drive for independence—it was an ally of France during the war, but never in fact an ally of the upstart colonials. Foiled at the peace table, where the 31st parallel was made the divider, Spain determined to make life difficult for the much-detested Americans by holding onto the several posts it had acquired during the war to the east of the Mississippi and north of the 31st parallel.

The Americans, understandably, were vexed and, when diplomatic remonstrances proved unavailing, began to be downright angry. The situation was soon aggravated by the question of American rights and claims as regards navigation on the Mississippi. The Treaty of Paris had assured the Americans free use of the great mid-continent waterway which, on paper at least, was the western boundary of the United States from its source to the 31st parallel; beyond that latter point to the sea, American use was to be unimpeded, in accord with the principles of international practice. As the Old Northwest and the Old Southwest began to fill with farmer folk from beyond the Appalachians, these Mississippi River rights assumed a vital importance to the economic well-being of these "westerners." Their products were bulky and the roads to markets on the Atlantic seaboard were almost nonexistent or, at best, very bad. To the frontier farmers of the trans-Allegheny the river network of mid-continent, even granting that it would be the long way round, seemed to offer the only natural and obvious alternative route to markets until more direct connections were developed. Despite the treaty stipulations, the Spaniards of the lower Mississippi adamantly refused to allow Kentucky-Tennessee-Ohio goods to clear through New Orleans without payment of prohibitive customs duties. Here, then, was another source of friction.

For a dozen years after 1783 Spain turned a deaf ear to American protests and refused to be overawed by the threats and rumored conspiracies of the westerners. Then to Madrid came word that England had agreed to some of the American demands and had drafted a compromise document (known in United States history as Jay's Treaty). Even though Spain knew that this agreement was not wholly satisfactory to the United States, it did ease the tension between those two powers. Spain had reason to fear that the Americans might now be free to turn their full and undivided enmity against it. Spain at last decided to deal with Thomas Pinckney, who was in Madrid to press American claims. The resulting accommodation was the Treaty of San Lorenzo, or Pinckney's Treaty, of 1795.[19]

By the terms of the Pinckney Treaty the United States was assured its boundary in the south, as Spain agreed to withdraw from its posts to the north of the 31st parallel. Further, Spain granted the "right of deposit" at New Orleans, which would allow the westerners to float their produce downriver and to store it there, under bond and without penalty, until an ocean-going vessel could pick it up and carry it around to the Atlantic seaboard or to foreign markets, in the West Indies or overseas. Actually, the concession looked better on paper than it proved to be in practice, since there regularly developed a seasonal glut at the port, which put the producers at the mercy of the brokers and the shippers. However, for the moment the Americans of the West were placated.

With the westerners quiet, Spain slyly planned to thwart the other terms of the San Lorenzo agreement and to hold onto the posts to the east of the Mississippi.[20] But the Americans were not to be denied; they wanted everything that was rightly theirs, and more. Conspiracies were hatched, and the scope of their goals disquieted the Spaniards. One, that of Senator William Blount of Tennessee, planned a three-pronged attack on Spanish Louisiana-Florida. One force was to cross the Mississippi against New Madrid (Missouri), a second column would strike at New Orleans, and the third set the capture of Pensacola as its objective. Spain decided that it would be prudent to withdraw. In 1797 the Spaniards pulled back from Fort Confederation on the Tombigbee and from Fort San Fernando at Chickasaw Bluffs. The new governor of Louisiana, Manuel Gayoso de Lemos, in 1798, gave orders to pull back from Natchez and Nogales, at the mouth of the Yazoo.

The Spaniards did not have time to see what these moves might have meant in the way of bettering relations with the United States in the mid-continent.[21] Soon news of the retrocession of Louisiana to France came to New Orleans. With another stroke of the pen Spain lost its quasi-Borderland, and *Luisiana* once again had to be spelled *Louisiana*. The Spanish officials remained for the next years, implementing French decrees, which quickly aroused the westerners once more.[22] However, if Spain allowed itself to feel that its other Borderlands might be protected by a French buffer, it was quickly shaken from such complacency by another bit of international trading. Napoleon's deal of 1803 with the United States—the Louisiana Purchase—gave Spain most unwelcome neighbors, along the entire length of its older Borderlands frontier. *Luisiana* had given Spain's Provincias Internas some sense of security. As of 1803 that was gone and Spain was back where it had been in 1762.

No one of the events of the next years was reassuring. Almost immediately the American President Jefferson began to argue about the southwestern boundary of the territory his nation had purchased. Texas came back into prominence in the area of Borderlands defense. In 1804 Lewis and Clark were on their way to the headwaters of the Missouri; and during the winter of 1805–1806 they were at the mouth of the Columbia in territory which Spain claimed on the continent's Pacific side. Saint Louis traders were showing up in Santa Fe. In 1807 Zebulon Montgomery Pike was intercepted and arrested on the headwaters of the Río Grande. Other Americans were being turned back on the Red. Spain's deep-seated and long-harbored fears of the *Americanos* were quickly being proved fully justified.

◁ 12 ▷

Spain's Last Years in the Borderlands, 1783-1821

*T*he year 1821 was to close the story of Spain in North America. Events far from the Borderlands rather abruptly effected a change of political sovereignty on the frontiers, as an independent Mexico took charge of the former viceroyalty of New Spain, with all its problems, responsibilities, and challenges. The Spanish Borderlands became the Mexican Borderlands. Changes would not be profound; but 1821 marked the end of an era. In a sense, Spain may not have been too unhappy to be relieved of the burden of a long extended North American frontier, for the last several decades had been troubled and aggravating, almost to a greater degree than the previous three centuries. France in mid-continent had been vexatious; England to the east of the Mississippi, after 1763, had been worrisome; Spain's latest neighbors, the Americans, had quickly become not only worrisome but aggressive.

The year 1783 had, on paper at least, brought the Americans up to the Mississippi from its source down to the 31st parallel. The same Treaty of Paris returned the Floridas to Spanish control, the peninsula, which Spain had held just short of two centuries (1565–1763) before being forced to yield it to England, and the strip westward along the Gulf of Mexico to the Mississippi, which Spain obtained for the first time with a clear title. Spain had its troubles with peninsular Florida. But it was in the territory westward from Pensacola, the area known as West Florida, that Spain found itself with something of a new Borderlands situation. Here the Spaniards met the Americans head on, as they tried to keep them as far as possible removed from their Gulf of Mexico, ringed for the moment with Spanish-held lands.[1]

In West Florida Spain fought a losing battle. During the years of British occupation, 1763–1783, some settlers and traders had come into the area; therefore, in 1783 Spain inherited a number of Protestant foreigners. This in itself was a new experience for Spain in the Americas. Indians the Spaniards had learned to handle. Even with the relatively few French of Louisiana Spain had, after the first years, managed to live reasonably peaceably—their mutual Catholicism at least was something of a common bond. Now Spain had a new breed of subject, the Protestant Anglo-Saxon. But in the next years these Anglo-Saxons of West Florida proved not nearly as worrisome as their American cousins, the Kentuckians and the Tennesseans and other brands of westerners.

During the last years of the War of the American Revolution, when Spain was joined with France in the battle against England, Spain had allowed American agents to establish bases in New Orleans. They became the forerunners of many of their countrymen.[2] Some came without invitation; others arrived, like Bryan Bruin, with passport from Don Diego Gardoqui, Spanish chargé d'affaires at Philadelphia, to ask for land grants for himself and other Americans. For a time Spain nurtured the dream of Americans, Catholics preferably but as many others as would swear allegiance to His Catholic Majesty, settled in West Florida on generous land grants as agents of defense against the aggressions of their former countrymen. Spain's Louisiana officials, such as Governor Estevan Rodríguez Miró, hoped that unrest in the West and the periodic distrust of the westerners toward the new federal government of the United States might redound to Spain's advantage. Miró was inclined to solicit American immigrants for West Florida and Louisiana. In the early 1790s, during the governorship of the Baron de Carondelet, the policy shifted and Spain began to fear the Americans once again. The intrigues of Citizen Edmond Genêt among the westerners caused Spain to feel that West Florida was not safe from enemy French and land-hungry anti-Spanish Americans.

After the Treaty of San Lorenzo (Pinckney's Treaty), in 1795, Spain thought that it might be able to live at peace with the "Kentuckians."[3] Spain allowed them free navigation on the Mississippi and the right of deposit at New Orleans; but, when it was tardy in pulling back from several of the posts to the north of the 31st parallel, Spain found them testy and contentious.[4] But then (1789–1790) came the fear of war with Britain and a possible invasion from Canada.[5] American immigration was once more allowed, even encouraged. Some Americans came into Spanish Illinois (Missouri); more arrived in West Florida; others were even allowed to settle to the west of the Mississippi, in Lower Louisiana. Spain was destined to know trouble with the last two groups; but this came after the shadow of Napoleon had fallen across the Mississippi Valley.

In 1800 word came to America that Napoleon had demanded and received the retrocession of the territory, which had been since late 1762 Spanish Louisiana. Spain was forced to rethink its frontier policies. Already Spain's position in the West Florida province was becoming less secure since the Americans there were proving anything but enthusiastic Spanish subjects. Ultimately, in 1810 they would take West Florida by force and parcel out the land to the Territories of Louisiana, Mississippi, and Alabama.[6]

Spain was also under pressure in East Florida.[7] It was on the British side in the War of 1812 and "its Indians," primarily the Creek, seriously vexed the Americans. At Fort Mims, near the junction of the Alabama and the Tombigbee, on August 30, 1813, these Western Creek massacred 547 settlers and soldiers. The tribesmen seem to have had their own grievances, but Spain was blamed by the frontier folk. Andrew Jackson of Tennessee was on the road to becoming a national hero, even before the Battle of New Orleans, by his forceful campaign which ended in a vindication of American power at the battle of Horseshoe Bend, in 1814.[8] After the war frictions between the Spaniards in East Florida and the Americans increased. They ended only with the complete withdrawal of Spain following the mutual ratification of the Adams-Onís Treaty.[9] The negotiations began in 1819 between John Quincy Adams, secretary of state under President James Monroe, and the Spanish ambassador to Washington, Don Luis de Onís. The United States was interested in acquiring East Florida, by purchase. Spain was willing to listen to this overture, but desired to tie into any such agreement a settlement of the western boundary question which had been causing friction between the two nations since the days of the Louisiana Purchase, and on one or other occasion had very nearly led to hostilities along the Louisiana-Texas frontier. This aspect of the conversations delayed final ratification of the treaty until 1821. The United States acquired East Florida, and the line of the Sabine to the Red to the Arkansas to the Rockies became the Louisiana boundary. Thus, it can be said that Spain's last years on its northeastern frontier were anything but calm and peaceful. The easternmost of Spain's Borderlands went to foreigners who almost from the beginning, whether they were French or English or Americans, had made Florida the most atypical of the Spanish Borderlands.

Before Spain had been able fully to assess the return of France to the trans-Mississippi, it was jolted by a new turn of international bargaining which it saw immediately could have an important, not to say a dire, impact, at least on the Spanish "middle" Borderlands, Texas and New Mexico. The

Louisiana Purchase of 1803 gave the Spaniards the worrisome Americans as neighbors much too close for comfort.

Even before the Purchase Spain had allowed some Americans into lands west of the Lower Mississippi.[10] For example, in 1804 fifteen Americans were living in the Nacogdoches district of East Texas; others were on the Red and the Ouachita rivers. There had been some Americans trading not only in Louisiana, but into Texas, and talk of the good lands beyond the Red River, of well-watered river valleys and lush prairies, of wild cattle and wilder mustangs, fired American imaginations and built dreams, more often of settlement but not infrequently of possible conquest. The case of Philip Nolan is indicative of what was facing Spain in its last decades in Texas.[11]

Philip Nolan was born in Belfast, Ireland, in 1771. Not much is known of him until he appeared in Spanish Louisiana in the late 1780s and through the 1790s. There was some connection with James Wilkinson of Kentucky, himself one of the mysterious characters in the history of the Lower Mississippi Valley—trader, land speculator, promoter, master of intrigue, conniver, on the payroll of the Spaniards, general in the United States Army, and territorial governor—a man of many facets, and not all of them admirable or even honorable.[12] During the 1790s Nolan made several trips into Texas, and with proper passports, since he was friend of several of the Spanish governors; he collected wild mustangs and also a mistress, the wife of one Antonio Leal of Nacogdoches, probably did his full share of contraband trading, lived for a time at San Antonio, then managed to arouse official suspicion that he was an agent for the British and later for the Americans. His career was as complex and complicated as any fictional thriller—with all the elements of daring, intrigue, love interest, and conspiracy.

Ultimately, in 1800 Nolan led a band of two dozen adventurers like himself into Texas. Ostensibly, they went there to gather mustangs; but it is highly probable—and so the Spaniards thought—that he and his fellows went as advance agents for American conquest, not only of Texas but also of the north of Mexico. Nolan knew the country well and had co-workers and confederates among the Spaniards in Texas. Lieutenant Miguel Francisco Músquiz, commandant at Nacogdoches, had been alerted to be on the lookout for Nolan as early as the summer of 1800. In March 1801, tipped off by some of his Indian scouts as to the location of the Americans' camp, Músquiz moved toward the Brazos with a detail of some seventy regulars and fifty militiamen, surprised the Nolan band, and demanded their surrender. The adventurers (filibusters may be the more correct term) at first sought to resist. In the ensuing exchange Nolan was killed, and the resistance wilted. Some of the men escaped; the rest were taken prisoners to Chihuahua. Only one, Ellis Bean, survived and returned to tell the tale. The Nolan affair came to an inglorious end. But the Spaniards were now definitely on the alert for American infiltrators.

The transfer of Louisiana, which gave the Americans New Orleans as a base, immediately accentuated the problem for Spain in Texas. Texas became overnight a defensive Borderland. One point of friction was the boundary question, which President Thomas Jefferson pressed from the very beginning. He had hoped that Napoleon might solve this problem by indicating what France considered to be the Louisiana-Texas dividing line. In this Jefferson was disappointed, for Talleyrand, French minister of state, met all suggestions with the well-known quip that the Americans had struck a good bargain and that he was sure they would make the most of it. In any event, Jefferson proposed to do precisely that. He claimed the Río Grande as Louisiana's boundary on the southwest and he even included West Florida on the east, at least up to the Río Perdido. Spain objected on both counts but was more immediately concerned over the Louisiana-Texas boundary; it did not want Americans too close to its North Mexican provinces. Spain countered with its claim, which set the dividing line a few miles west of Natchitoches. Thus, Texas became debatable land.[13]

Early in 1806 Spain reestablished the old East Texas post of Los Adaes, as the Americans seemed to be strengthening Natchitoches, a few miles away on the Red River. Spain next concentrated over a thousand regulars at Nacogdoches, gathered from various presidios throughout the eastern Provincias Internas and put under the command of Don Simón Herrera, governor of Nuevo León, and Don Antonio Cordero y Bustamante, recently appointed governor of Texas. Spain further strengthened the garrison at San Antonio.[14] Now it was the turn of the Americans to be concerned. Governor William C. C. Claiborne of Louisiana reinforced Natchitoches and General James Wilkinson soon arrived to take command there. He moved up to the east bank of the Sabine; Herrera faced him across that stream. The confrontation led to a state of international tension. But bloodshed was avoided when the two commanders prudently agreed, on November 6, 1806, to leave the settlement of the dispute to the boundary commission which had been appointed by their governments.

At this point the Aaron Burr conspiracy, whatever precisely it was, was intruding into the Louisiana-Texas picture; but just how importantly it is difficult to say.[15] There seems little doubt but that the conquest of Spain's northern provinces, at the very least, was one of the aims of Burr and his associates. It is known that some of Burr's emissaries made contact with Wilkinson at Natchitoches in October 1806, prior to the confrontation across the Sabine. Further, about this time Wilkinson sent Major Walter Burling, his aide-de-camp, to Governor Cordero of Texas; his job was to arouse the anxieties of the Spaniards and to suggest that their best hope of protection was in a deal with Wilkinson, for a monetary consideration, to be sure. Wilkinson at this time seems to have decided to break with Burr and turn patriotic; but he could not pass up an opportunity to have this resolve pay off in more tangible coin than the honor of being a loyal United States citizen. Some of this may have been background for the agreement between himself and Herrera, on the Sabine, in November. At any rate, the border dispute cooled for the moment.

It was fortunate for Spain that the dispute had cooled, for within a few years the Spaniards had other worries in Texas. These were internal problems. On the night of September 15, 1810, the pastor of the little town of Dolores, Padre Cura Miguel Hidalgo, raised the standard of revolt. Elsewhere in the Spanish Indies, the year 1810 (*"el año de diez"*) saw colonial unrest reflect the troubled conditions in the mother country, precipitated by the French occupation of the Iberian Peninsula. The movement for independence of Spanish colonies in the Americas was under way. The Hidalgo revolt brought to the fore many colonial grievances, especially on the Indian-mestizo levels of Mexican society, sparked a similar revolt in the south led by another priest, José María Morelos, and enjoyed a number of signal, but rather frightening, early successes. Word of the Hidalgo movement reached Texas by January 1811.[16] Juan Bautista Casas, militia captain, rallied the folk of San Antonio, proclaimed for Hidalgo, imprisoned Governor Manuel María de Salcedo and other royal officers, and declared himself governor. His excesses and those of his appointees quickly estranged many of the folk in the Texas capital, among them the *padre cura*, Juan Manuel Zambrano. The padre engineered a plot to return things to the old order. By March he and his fellows were in control. At this juncture, Juan Aldama, one of Hidalgo's key lieutenants, arrived in San Antonio en route to the United States for assistance. He was arrested by the Zambrano party and sent to Monclova, where he was subsequently tried for treason against the crown of Spain, condemned, and executed. As 1811 closed, Texas was securely under royal control, but Spain's troubles were just beginning. More filibusters were on the way.

First came the Gutiérrez-Magee invasion in 1812.[17] Bernardo Gutiérrez de Lara had espoused the Hidalgo cause early. After the capture and execution of the priest, in 1811, Gutiérrez vowed to carry on the fight. On his way to New Orleans, he fell in with a young American army lieutenant, Augustus Magee. This young man had been stationed at Natchitoches. Like many others along that troubled border in those early nineteenth-century years, Magee, dreamed of the possible conquest of Texas. He resigned his army commission so that he might devote full time to preparations to realize this hope. He and his followers were approached by Gutiérrez and they agreed to join forces with him.

The filibusters first moved against La Bahía, on the Gulf Coast, took the fort with relative ease, but soon found themselves besieged in their own stronghold. During the siege Magee died, but his companions voted to carry on. In 1813 they succeeded in raising the siege and drove off Governor Salcedo and the royal force. With the Spaniards in retreat, the invaders pushed up the river to San Antonio, which surrendered to Gutiérrez on April 1. There followed a period of highly arbitrary rule by the Mexican caudillo, climaxed by the brutal slaughter of the Spanish prisoners—Governor Salcedo, General Herrera, and fifteen others. Shocked by this unwarranted act of treachery and cruelty, most of the Americans abandoned the Gutiérrez faction but still continued their fight against the royalists. However, when José Alvarez de Toledo took charge of the "republican" army, the Americans again joined the Mexicans in common cause.

A new comandante-general of the eastern Provincias Internas, Don Joaquín de Arredondo, determined to secure the province. He moved east from Laredo with a force of about two thousand men. Toledo and his conglomerate band left San Antonio to challenge the royalists. Arredondo proved the superior strategist, drew the republicans into an impossible position on the Medina, and cut them to bits. He then moved on to San Antonio without opposition, took the capital, and then fanned his men out to sweep the country clear as far as Nacogdoches. Once again Texas was under royalist control.

Many of the "Mexicans," as the republicans came to be designated, and not a few of the Americans who had been in Texas withdrew to safety beyond the Texas-Louisiana border. These refugees found a good deal of sympathy in the United States. Enough, in fact, that President James Madison felt constrained to issue stiff warnings to Americans not to allow themselves to become involved in hostile acts against Spain, which was still a friendly power. This did not prevent a fair measure of private American aid from supporting Mexicans, under José Manuel de Herrera, who set up their own government on the Gulf Coast, in 1816.

The next years continued to be haunted by the specter of the aggressive Americans so close at hand. Even the negotiations carried on with the United States by the Spanish ambassador, Don Luis de Onís, concerning the boundary question did not allay Spanish anxiety in Texas. The Spaniards were acutely aware that many Americans were thoroughly provoked by what they interpreted as their government's willingness to sacrifice Texas as part of the price for the acquisition of Florida. The Texas-oriented Yankees along the southern frontier, when the terms of this so-called Adams-Onís treaty became known and it was definite that the United States would withdraw claims to the area beyond the Sabine and the Red rivers, refused to acquiesce. Their discontent found expression in still another filibustering group. This time, in 1819, a band of several dozen led by James Long of Natchez[18] surprised Nacogdoches, declared Texas a free and independent republic, then, when a sufficient number of American recruits failed to show, they appealed to the French freebooter Jean Lafitte, at Galveston, for men and assistance. The wily pirate refused to be involved even when Long came south in an attempt to persuade him to reconsider. During Long's absence Spanish troops appeared at Nacogdoches and put an end to his Republic of Texas.

A new government in Spain in 1820 moved quickly to lessen pressures on Texas. In that year a revolution, the so-called Riego Revolt, broke out, which put the Spanish Liberals in power. Before the year was out, the Spanish Cortes passed a measure which, it was hoped, might ensure Spain's secure possession of Texas. Harking back to Roman practice in dealing with the worrisome Germans beyond the Rhine-Danube frontier of the fourth century, the Spanish Liberals determined to revive a technique of their imperial mentors. Authorities in New Spain were empowered to encourage Americans to come into Texas by the offer of generous land grants. To qualify for such largess there was a sole condition, that the colonists become Spanish citizens. The Liberals hoped for better success than their predecessors of the 1780s and 1790s had enjoyed in building up West Florida and Upper Louisiana; they did not reenact the earlier stipulation that these colonists, besides accepting Spanish citizenship also embrace the Roman Catholic faith.

Curiously enough, at the time such a policy was being debated and adopted in the Spanish Cortes, an American was on his way from Missouri to San Antonio to make a similar colonization proposal to the Texas governor. The American was Moses Austin.[19] Connecticut born, Austin had lived and worked in Philadelphia and then in Richmond, before coming to the lead-mining area of eastern Missouri at the end of the Spanish period. Reverses of fortune led him to think of other fields and he came up with a colonization scheme for Texas. Governor Antonio Martínez, still not aware of the policy adopted by the Spanish Cortes, was cold to Austin's proposal to settle three hundred families in Texas on generous land grants to be made to the colonists. Had it not been for the intercession of the Prussian soldier of fortune Baron de Bastrop with the governor, Austin might have failed.[20] Even the fact that Austin was a Catholic and that he had been for a short time a Spanish subject during his first Missouri years did not impress Martínez.[21] However, out of deference to Bastrop he agreed to forward Austin's request to the comandante-general of the Provincias Internas at Monterrey. On January 17, 1821, Arredondo approved, and the message went off to Austin. But meanwhile he had returned to Missouri.

The long trip had undermined his already impaired health. Moses Austin received the news of the grant on his deathbed. He left the grant as a legacy to his son Stephen, as he passed on, in June 1821. By the time Stephen could fulfill his father's dying commission, Spain's days in North America had been ended by the successful drive of Mexico for independence. Texas had become a Mexican Borderland and Austin's subsequent dealings had to be with the successive governments of the new nation.

While Moses Austin was negotiating, and Martínez was seeking the advice of his superior, and Austin was passing from the scene and willing his grant to his son Stephen, events in the heart of the viceroyalty of New Spain had been moving at a rapid pace, in late 1820 and into 1821. The

Riego Revolt in Spain in 1820 had forced King Ferdinand VII to accept the liberal and anticlerical Constitution of 1812 as the law of the land. Word of these developments was upsetting to the upper classes in Mexico, the *criollo* (American-born Spaniards) aristocracy and the churchmen, who began to fear for their age-old position and privileges. When the viceroy, Juan Ruíz de Apodaca, showed no great unwillingness to impose and enforce the Constitution of 1812 in New Spain, talk of opposition began to mount. Agustín de Iturbide, who earlier had been one of the major military men in putting down the Hidalgo-Morelos bids for independence—which movements had rallied relatively little sympathy from the "white" classes—rose to a position of leadership.[22] With the support of Vicente Guerrero and a number of the surviving chiefs of the earlier revolution, Iturbide issued a platform known as the Plan de Iguala. Its three guarantees—protection for the Catholic religion, independence for Mexico, and equality for Mexican and Spaniard alike—quickly won universal acceptance throughout New Spain. When the Spanish Cortes sent over a new viceroy, Juan Odonojú, to enforce its Liberal policies, Iturbide met him in force at Vera Cruz. Odonojú, recognizing that he was in no solid position to resist and that the Mexicans were in overwhelming agreement with the Plan de Iguala, signed the Treaty of Córdoba, on August 21, 1821, and withdrew. The disavowal of his action by the Cortes made no difference. Mexico had already embarked on its career as an independent nation. It was the end of an era for Spain in North America, for the viceroyalty of New Spain, and for the Spanish Borderlands.

On paper, in the Treaty of San Ildefonso, Spain's days in Upper Louisiana, or the Spanish Illinois, came to an end in 1800. However, as in the Lower Valley, France was slow to take possession, and Spanish officials continued to function until the next turn of the international pinwheel which put all Louisiana into the hands of the Americans: the purchase treaty of 1803 and the formal cession at Saint Louis in March 1804. As with Texas, the Louisiana Purchase, practically speaking, turned New Mexico overnight into a Borderland once again. This first of the western Borderlands had enjoyed a few decades of relative peace and security after the French bowed off the American scene in 1762. The great expanse of Spanish territory stretching to the far-off Mississippi served as a defensive buffer for New Mexico. True, there was an anxiety in those last decades of the eighteenth century, lest the British fur men and traders come down from the Upper Plains. But, again, Spanish subjects, most of them Frenchmen it was true, working out of Spanish Illinois and up the Missouri River were trying to forestall a British trespass from the north. New Mexico continued to have Indian problems, but harassment from Europeans dropped back to second place in its worries. The Americans, however, were going to make Spain's last years in the New Mexican Borderland something less than pleasant.

Word of the purchase reached American Illinois some time before the formal cession took place at Saint Louis. The Americans in the trans-Mississippi, who were relatively few as of 1803, and the many across the river began to let their trader dreams run wild almost immediately. Some saw greater freedom in the fur trade up the Missouri opening to them; others had trader ambitions with a definite southwestward orientation.[23] Santa Fe had a certain compulsive lure for men of the middle Mississippi Valley; it was a magnet which had attracted them for several generations past.

William Morrison, a wealthy businessman of Kaskaskia, could no longer resist. In the summer of 1804 he equipped a pair of agents, Baptiste Lalande and Jeannot Metoyer, and sent them off to Santa Fe. Spanish records show them in Santa Fe in the next year. How long they had been there is not clear. The same 1805 records indicate the presence of one Lorenzo Durocher, who had been in the upper Missouri River country with Jacques d'Église. We know that D'Église came down to New Mexico in 1805 or 1806, for he was murdered there in the latter year.[24] About the same time there were "two Frenchmen and one American" in Santa Fe—Jean Baptiste la Croix and André Terien, both known to be associates of Regis Loisel of Saint Louis; the "one American" was a James Purcell or Pursley of Baird's Town, Kentucky. The records are very sketchy and exasperatingly incomplete, but these traces of Americans, with French names, were indicative of what was to come. The Spaniards girded themselves for the worst.

That the Americans were to be quite a universal problem was evidenced by the concern in Spanish official circles over the reports of the expedition of Meriwether Lewis and William Clark.[25] As early as December 1803, the Spanish commandant at Saint Louis, Lieutenant-governor Charles du Hault de Lassus, had tipped off the Marquis of Casa Calvo, the former governor of Louisiana, concerning the American expedition which was being readied across the Mississippi from Saint Louis. Little or nothing definite was known of its intent or goals. This intelligence touched off a veritable explosion of correspondence among ranking Spanish officials; each fretted, but no one made a firm decision to take forceful action. In the meantime, Lewis and Clark and their men pushed determinedly up the Missouri, through what was now American territory. While the Spaniards continued to debate as to who should do something to block the Americans, Lewis and Clark were actually in Spanish territory, once they had crossed the Rockies. They wintered (1805–1806) at the mouth of the Columbia. Their Fort Clatsop was built on land still claimed by His Catholic Majesty of Spain. However, this act of trespass was too far away to affect New Mexico, at least not directly. Spain's *Californios* could have had more cause for concern.

Even so, this successful American exploration venture triggered a number of developments in the trans-Mississippi West, and some of these very soon began to touch the Spaniards in New Mexico. Lewis and Clark had seen some of the rich potential of the Louisiana Purchase territory in its northern half. The immediate consequence was a great upsurge of interest in the fur-trade potential of the whole Missouri River system, from the river westward up its tributaries to the mountains. In a few years the fur men were probing into the southern reaches of the purchase territory. There, too, the Americans had an exploring expedition to open their eyes.

Before Lewis and Clark returned to Saint Louis, in September 1806, Governor James Wilkinson had been in Upper Louisiana. He is as much a man of mystery in that area as he was in Lower Louisiana and on the Texas frontier. One is never quite sure for whom he was working, other than his own interests. (For example, we know that Burr visited him near Saint Louis in the fall of 1805 before proceeding downriver to New Orleans.)[26] Following his arrival in Saint Louis, Wilkinson set things in motion. Zebulon Montgomery Pike was sent north from Saint Louis to seek the Mississippi's source and to spy out the fur potential of the region. Wilkinson's son, Lieutenant James B. Wilkinson, went up the Missouri to found a post at the mouth of the Platte. Lieutenant George Peter, with Auguste Chouteau of Saint Louis, was dispatched to the Osage country, to check on the possibility of a river route to Santa Fe which would make use of the Missouri, the Osage, and the Arkansas rivers.

Then came the Pike expedition to the west.[27] What Pike's orders precisely were when Wilkinson sent him out in July 1806 after Pike's return from the Upper Mississippi Valley has never become clear. Was his a military reconnaissance, preliminary to a possible future invasion of Mexico via Santa Fe and the Chihuahua Trail? Or did Wilkinson simply have in mind possible future trade with New Mexico, largely for his own personal benefit? Or was Pike really, as he himself later affirmed, sent only to find the headwaters of rivers, such as the Red, which might figure in the resolution of the boundary dispute between the United States and Spain? Whatever the purpose, honest or otherwise, the Pike expedition to the west turned American attention toward New Mexico and the lands and opportunities of Spain's Provincias Internas.

Spanish intelligence through the Borderlands in those years immediately following the Louisiana Purchase was efficient and effective: much information was furnished by some of the Indian friends whom Spain had won along its far frontiers since 1762. In the summer of 1806 the Spaniards learned that some sort of an expedition was being prepared in Saint Louis and was destined for the west. They surmised that this expedition might be directly pointed toward their Provincias Internas. Already, in April of that year, Francisco Viana had turned back a party of Americans which had advanced some two hundred miles up the Red River from Natchitoches, under command of Lieutenant Thomas Freeman.[28] In this instance, the Americans, badly outnumbered, had not challenged the Spanish border patrol but had retired. This new story of activity at Saint Louis was another straw in the wind sweeping the Borderlands.

Orders went up to Santa Fe, where Lieutenant Facundo Melgares had recently arrived with a force to strengthen New Mexico. Governor Joaquín del Real Alencaster sent Melgares out with his 105 men, some 400 militia, and about 100 Indians. The party was furnished with supplies enough for half a year. Melgares first headed for the Red, went down that river a distance, but saw no Americans—Viana had already forced the Freeman party to turn round. Melgares next proceeded northward into the lands of the Pawnee, as far as the Republican River; but, again, he neither saw nor picked up word of an American party. He then returned to Santa Fe, in October (1806). Actually, the Spaniards were in Kansas ahead of the Pike party by about a month.

Pike left Saint Louis in mid-July 1806. In his band was Wilkinson's son, James, Dr. John H. Robinson, one sergeant, two corporals, sixteen privates, an interpreter, and a party of fifty-one Osage Indians, whom he was to return to their own people as he passed by.[29]

Well out on the Plains, Pike's party was split into several small groups. Young Wilkinson, at odds with the commander, turned down the Arkansas with several men; others were left near the present Larned (Kansas); Pike went on to Pueblo (Colorado), where a small fort was built. Then he took the remaining few men, crossed the Front Range of the Rockies and on the west bank of Conejos Creek, at a point near its junction with the Río Grande, constructed another "fort." Here, in late February 1807, a Spanish detachment arrested him as a trespasser on Spanish soil.

Taken to Santa Fe, Pike professed innocence of deliberate trespass, claiming that he thought that he was on or near the headwaters of the Red River and feigning surprise when Governor Alencaster informed him that his fort was very near to the source of the Río Grande or Río del Norte. Actually the Americans had camped hardly more than 75 miles north of Taos. Pike and his companions, all of whom had been rounded up by the Spaniards, were held for a time at Santa Fe and then sent to Chihuahua. There Pike was further questioned by Nemesio Salcedo, then comandante-general of the Provincias Internas. Most of Pike's papers were confiscated by the Spaniards. He did manage to secrete his journal in the gun barrels of his men. When released, he was thus able to reconstruct his story with considerable exactitude.[30] Its publication contributed still further to the growing American interest in Spain's Borderlands.

In the wake of Pike a number of small trading expeditions went out from Saint Louis and, by a variety of paths, made their way into Santa Fe, further to worry and vex the Spaniards of New Mexico. For example, Manuel Lisa, or at least some of his men, reached Santa Fe in 1806 or 1807. Jacques Clamorgan, despite his seventy-odd years, appeared in the New Mexican capital in December 1807, was sent down to Chihuahua, where he was allowed to sell his goods, and then was permitted to return to Saint Louis via Texas and Natchitoches.[31] The fact that he had been a cooperative

Spanish subject during Spain's Luisiana days may have contributed to the consideration shown him.

By 1810 Americans were no longer a novelty in Santa Fe; but this does not mean that the Spaniards were becoming more permissive.[32] Actually, by that date, they were becoming sufficiently concerned that they were stiffening. When a party which had set out from Sainte Genevieve (Missouri) in late 1809 arrived in Santa Fe, the interim governor, José Manrrique, promptly clapped them into jail. This was the Joseph McLanahan, Reuben Smith, James Patterson, and Manuel Blanco band. The word of their detention caused a stir in some quarters of the United States, and there were even plans for an armed party to go out and force their release. Actually, these Americans, although detained, were not badly treated; they were released and returned home in 1812.

In that same year (1812) Robert McKnight, Samuel Chambers, and James Baird arrived in Santa Fe with six mule-loads of goods.[33] They came at an unfortunate moment, for themselves. Spanish officials on the frontier, now fully informed of the events in the viceroyalty connected with the revolutionary movement which Father Hidalgo had sparked in September 1810, and aware that although it had been broken Hidalgo and his chief associates had tried to reach asylum in the United States, decided to strike a blow for Spain. These Americans, the latest to venture into Santa Fe, were arrested, their goods were confiscated, and they themselves were sent off to prison at Chihuahua. There they were accused of complicity in the attempted Hidalgo escape, tried, "convicted," and sentenced. Several of these unfortunates, even after the charges against them were proved groundless, did not regain their liberty until 1820.

The climate officially as regards Americans in New Mexico kept changing. The treatment of the Jules de Mun-Auguste Pierre Chouteau party was an example.[34] This band reached New Mexico in 1815 to find an acting governor, Alberto Máynez, who was friendly. He allowed them considerable liberty to trade and trap while he waited for an official ruling in their regard from his superiors. De Mun was even permitted to make a trip back to Saint Louis in the interim. By the time he returned, the order had come in from the comandante-general that they were to withdraw. Trusting in the friendliness of Máynez, they were slow in complying, since their activities had become so highly profitable. This delay proved a mistake, for Máynez was replaced by Pedro María Allande, who quickly showed himself anything but cordial or permissive. The Americans were arrested and imprisoned, and their goods confiscated. They were detained in jail for six weeks, then released and ordered out of the province.

Spain's days in New Mexico were fast coming to an end.[35] The quite rapid turnabout as regards the American traders which followed almost immediately on the Mexican take-over in 1821 calls for some explanation. New Mexico had never been one of Spain's wealthier Borderlands. Life for the New Mexicans from the very beginning had been a struggle, and the situation did not improve with the passing years. With hard and persistent work they managed to grow the basics of their food needs—corn, wheat, beans—on their not too fertile valley lands, and this in most instances thanks only to skillful use of irrigation. They had developed sheep-growing into their major pastoral activity. But they needed more than their supplies of raw wool and the live animals which they shipped south to maintain anything even approaching a sound balance of trade with the Chihuahua merchants, who were their chief suppliers of other necessities.[36] Their few craftsmen and manufacturers never had a surplus of products for exchange; even so, the domestic market was rarely adequately supplied. A report of 1804 showed the serious state of economic imbalance under which New Mexico had to operate. The province, whose population was moving toward the 30,000 mark, with about 10,000 Pueblo Indians, imported goods to a total of $112,000 but only had exports to the extent of $60,000. And this would not seem to have been an unusual year. Spain's strict trade regulations put the New Mexicans at a distinct and consistent disadvantage. Small wonder, then, that when New Mexicans came into control, after 1821, they relaxed trade policies in favor of the Americans and to their own advantage. American goods were already well known in the province and demand for them, especially at American prices, was growing.

During the last Spanish years the Americans were much more worrisome than New Mexico's traditional irritants, the Indians. There was some problem with the Navaho, who had gone into Arizona's Cañon de Chelly, until the Spaniards during the days of Alencaster's governorship went in to reduce them and bring them to friendship. The Comanche and the Apache, wooed into a sort of *entente cordiale* by Spain's new policy of treaties and presents, were quiet and at times even cooperative in keeping the Spaniards posted on American movements on the Plains.

Toward the end of the Spanish regime, in 1810, the New Mexicans had a very unique experience, for them, when they were bid to elect a delegate to the Spanish Cortes, during the days when the Junta Central was ruling in the mother country through the period of French occupation of the home peninsula and the detention of King Ferdinand VII. Native-born Pedro Bautista Pino was the choice.[37] His report of November 1812 to the Cortes has greater importance as a window on life on the frontier than it had effect in winning fulsome support for the needs of the province which Pino presented. He asked, among other things, for a reorganization of military personnel on the frontier, the addition of several new presidios, a separate bishopric for New Mexico, still under the authority of the bishop of Durango, an audiencia for Chihuahua in order to bring judicial authority closer than Guadalajara, and also support for the establishment of a school system.

Geography helped to protect the next Borderland, Sonora-Arizona,

Misión San Xavier del Bac, Arizona. (Library of Congress)

from the *Americanos* who were contributing so much toward making Spain's last years in the north so uncomfortable. However, the Spaniards were hardly out, when some of the early American adventurers, such as James Ohio Pattie, Ewing Young, David Jackson, and young Kit Carson, were trapping and trailing through the Gila River country later in the decade of the 1820s. But even so, Spain had its troubles during its last decades on that frontier.[38]

The mid-eighteenth-century years, following the Pima Revolt of 1751, saw a sharp decline in the effectiveness of the mission. Obstreperous Seri, raiding Apache, and Yuma on the warpath not only threatened the province from without, but also engendered a spirit of unhealthy restiveness among the Christian natives—the Pima, Opata, and Pápago. The expulsion of the Jesuits in 1767 stripped the province of a strong and regularly loyal royalist support. The Franciscans, who filled in for the exiled Black Robes, were not less loyal, but their numbers were never adequate.

During the later eighteenth-century and the early nineteenth-century years there was some measure of mining activity; but nothing to match the brief boom of Arizonac. For the several decades following 1790 Sonora-Arizona knew an unwonted blessing, a period of peace with the western Apache. Some of these tribesmen even came in and settled in the neighborhood of such far northern centers as the presidios of Tubac and Tucson and the great Franciscan mission center at Bac. There was a time when the Franciscans had hopes of wholesale conversions among them. In this area and among these western Apache the Spaniards, before they were forced off the North American scene in 1821, had a chance to see their newest approach to the Indian problem working encouragingly well.

Back in 1786 the dynamic and highly knowledgeable, but much too short-lived viceroy of New Spain, Bernardo de Gálvez, had sent a set of "instructions for governing the Interior Provinces" to his commandant on the frontier, Jacobo Ugarte y Loyola.[39] Generally, old solutions to the Indian problem were discarded. Admittedly the mission had worked well until the frontier of the friar and the padre encountered the Apache and his equally intractible neighbors. The presidio, even when multiplied and more strategically located, was not a completely adequate substitute. Gálvez was convinced that the trade-and-presents policies of the French, especially as Hispanicized by Athanase de Mézières on the Louisiana-Texas frontier, held the key to a peaceable future. But he had very interesting adaptations to go along with the adoptions.

The key idea which Gálvez proposed was that the Indians should be made so completely dependent on the Spanish trader that their very lives would be in his hands, both economically and defensively. Wean them from their bows and arrows, was his advice; these they can supply themselves. Instead, give them guns; but make sure that the guns were not top quality so that their newly acquired firearms might quickly need repairs and parts which only the Spaniard would be able to supply. He was gambling; but he felt that it would be many years before the Indians could become efficient and effective enough with these guns to match the age-old skill of the Spaniards with weapons. And, in the new approach, Gálvez very shrewdly noted that there would always be the matter of ammunition; this the Spaniards could control. Again, he was gambling, first, that the Indians would be short on lead, and, next, that they would be slow to master the techniques of shot and bullet manufacture.

Again, Gálvez counseled, since the Indians had developed a taste for the meat of Old World domesticated animals, furnish them with their own herds and thus remove the constant temptation to raid and rustle those of the Spaniards. Further, give them convenient outlets for bartering the goods which they grew, gathered, or produced.

He went on, and in a tone reminiscent of Roman practice of centuries before and which had worked well with distant ancestors of the Spaniards, to suggest the policy of "divide and conquer." Thus, they might be kept off balance. The trader could become something of a practitioner of a scheming brand of diplomacy, a manipulator.

Some, even much, of this pragmatic advice was put to use on the Sonora-Arizona frontier during the last years of Spanish control there. When the Mexican successors failed to follow through, the Apache once again became a major problem.

During the Spaniards' last decades in America, they fared better in many respects in California than elsewhere in the Borderlands; at least those years were often more constructive and much less harried.[40] The Indians were tractable and the Americans pleasantly far away. The Russians were in northern California, but in small numbers and not particularly worrisome.

The death of Father Serra, in 1784, did mark the end of an era in the Alta California story, its opening chapter.[41] He had been one of the chief founders of this "Last Borderland." The idea of occupation was not his; it had been in Spanish planning for almost two centuries prior to 1769. Nor was the decision to move toward Monterey his. He was on the peninsula after the expulsion of the Jesuits in 1767 in a sense by accident. But once his superiors involved him in the new enterprise, the strength of his character, the force of his personality, and the importance of the position as father-president of the Franciscan force, all these turned him into a key figure among the founders. During the fifteen formative years (1769–1784) he was a power, perhaps even *the* power, in California. At his death he left the province with the strong tradition of Franciscan influence and service, with nine links of the ultimate chain of twenty-one missions founded and functioning, with new life breathed into the mission as a frontier institution at a moment when this traditional solution to the Indian problem was losing its vitality and effectiveness elsewhere in the north. Serra well deserves the honor which came to him much, much later as one of California's two allotted representatives in the National Statuary Hall of the United States capitol.

Serra's immediate successor was his long-time friend, his companion and biographer, Fray Francisco Palóu. But in less than a year Palóu begged his way out of the superiorship, and in 1785 Fray Padre Fermín de Lasuén assumed the role of father-president.[42] This proved an excellent choice, for Lasuén was a remarkable administrator, builder, planner, and also much more of a diplomat than was the fiery and forthright Serra. The new father-president got on much better with the civil officials and the military. Everything was not the proverbial sweetness and light, but the frictions were reduced. In California, as elsewhere in the Borderlands, the first Franciscans quarreled often with, and quite regularly censured, the soldiery, admittedly not always of highest caliber or of outstanding moral character.

Without neglecting the spiritual and apostolic aspects of the friars' enterprise in California, Lasuén turned his attention to the development of the material side of the mission system. He gave great encouragement and much attention to farming and stock raising at the missions, in an attempt to make them as self-sufficient as possible. In this work Lasuén should be credited with laying the foundations for what were to become the two principal economic activities of the Californios—Spanish first and then Mexican—down to the day when, for a time, mining overshadowed all others.

Crops new to the province were introduced; in fact, most everything which the Spaniards brought was new, for the Indians previously had little, doing much food-gathering and a little hunting and fishing for their subsistence. The prime American agricultural staples of maize and beans came in, as did wheat and other cereals. Various fruits were introduced, along with vine culture. The friars brought in the cow and the horse, both destined to play a large role in the California economy of the Mexican decades, when ranching and the hides-and-tallow industry were so vital.

Into the early years of the nineteenth century the missions furnished much of the food for California, for the presidios and even the several civilian settlements. Things which the missions could not grow or make were supplied via the sea lanes, out of San Blas and other west Mexican ports. After the Yuma Massacre of 1781 the overland route from Sonora ceased to be used with any regularity. The precariousness of this supply-by-sea and the consequent periodic scarcities were among the reasons why in time the Yankee traders en route to the Chinese markets found that the Californios were willing to exchange food for some of the manufactured goods which they, the Americans, could bring.

The closing of the overland route from Sonora-Arizona had another far-reaching result after 1781. It slowed the process of peopling California. In the first years, the 1770s, few civilians other than the military, were in the province. A new day seemed to be dawning when Juan Bautista de Anza led his party of 240 to California in 1776. In the next year (1777) the first civilian community, other than the little clusters which gathered around the presidios or the missions, came into existence at San José. Four years later the party of civilians who founded Los Angeles came overland and were lucky to have cleared the Gila-Colorado junction only a few weeks before the Yuma Massacre. A large segment of their military escort, and their leader to that point, Fernando Rivera y Moncada, were less fortunate, when they tarried to rest; they were killed by the rampaging Yuma. These first Angelenos were the last of the major settler bands to come overland, at least for many years. The third civilian *pueblo*, founded in 1797 near the present Santa Cruz and named Branciforte for the ruling viceroy, failed quickly largely because of the character of its pioneer population. Officials in Mexico had rounded up a number of convicts and shipped them up by sea. Through the last Spanish years there was a dribble of settlers, many of whom were not the most desirable type of colonists. By the end of the Spanish regime the non-Indian population of California, counting all the Spaniards and the *castas* (crossbreeds) of varying complexion, was estimated at around 3700 only.

Lasuén was father-president for eighteen years (1785–1803). During his term he matched Serra with the number of his foundations—nine. Only three more missions would be added to the existing eighteen; in the last Spanish years Santa Inéz (1804) and San Rafael (1817) were established, leaving only San Francisco de Solano at Sonoma (1823) for the Mexican period. The Lasuén presidency was the boom time of the missions; the number of converts was estimated at somewhat better than 50,000 Christian Indians, through his years. The missions had become not only producers of the cereals, meat, and fruits; but the introduction of craftsmen and artisans from Mexico, sometimes at Franciscan and more regularly at royal expense —a development which Lasuén greatly encouraged—made the missions centers of early California manufacturing and training schools for the "building trades."

In 1786 California had its first foreign visitors of record when Jean François de la Pérouse and his fellow scientists during their world cruise paused at Monterey for a ten-day visit.[43] The Frenchmen were received cordially by orders of the Spanish crown; Spain and France at the time were on friendly terms at home. The Frenchman left in his journal impressions of this Spanish outpost, and his men, at least the geologists and botanists among them, collected data and specimens. La Pérouse had reason to be laudatory in some of his observations on California's simple economy, for when his ships sailed off, they were splendidly provisioned with meat, vegetables, fruit, and poultry (chickens). He was not impressed with the Indians and somewhat dubious about the long-term value of the efforts of the friars in their regard.

A few years later, in 1791, a Spanish scientific expedition was on the California coast, captained by the Italian Alessandro Malaspina.[44] He and his men not only reported on the Spaniards and the Indians of the province, but also produced some of the best of the early maps of the California coast.

The Englishman George Vancouver was California's next distinguished visitor.[45] On his first visit, in November 1792, he was well received at San Francisco and at Monterey. He was even allowed to penetrate far enough inland to visit the mission at Santa Clara. There were exchanges of courtesies at San Francisco; but he was rather royally feted at Monterey and Carmel. On a return visit the next year (1793) his reception was less cordial, and his report reflects his pique and irritation. Possibly by the time of the second visit the Spaniards of California may have been better informed on the reasons for Vancouver's presence on the Pacific Coast.

Vancouver had initially come out as Britain's commissioner in the discussions between England and Spain which sought to settle the rival claims to the Northwest occasioned by the Nootka Sound incident of 1789.[46] The visit of Captain James Cook, in 1778, and the rather wide publicity it subsequently received seriously worried the Spaniards, who in the years previous were evincing interest in the coast to the north of California. In 1788–1789 Spain sent two more expeditions northward to reinforce its long-standing claims to the area.[47] Captain Estevan José Martínez, on arriving at Nootka, found several English vessels anchored in the sound. These he seized, with their crews, alleging trespass on Spanish territory. The act very nearly led to war between the two countries. Meanwhile, two American ships came into the area, Robert Grey's *Columbia* and John Kendrick's *Lady Washington;* but the Americans did not involve themselves. Negotiations between the Spaniards and the English were carried on, with Vancouver as the English agent. Ultimately, the rival claims were adjudicated at a higher level and in 1794 the so-called Nootka Convention was signed at Madrid. By its terms Spain was forced to yield its earlier exclusive claims to the Northwest Coast. In the intervening years the Spaniards had maintained a post at Nootka, which was provisioned out of California. By 1795 the Spaniards had withdrawn, and this California "outpost" ceased

Misión San Carlos Borromeo de Carmel, California. (DeYoung Museum)

to be, although Spain would continue to claim rights in the Northwest for another twenty-odd years.

Captain Cook had been looking for the fabled northwest passage, in 1778. He had failed to find the western outlet of a strait, but he had uncovered a somewhat unexpected source of wealth, which soon turned foreign attention to the Pacific Coast, much to the discomfiture of the Spaniards. Some of his men traded trinkets with the Oregon Indians for sea-otter pelts. Sailing over to China, Cook found that these pelts brought $100 apiece. When he reported his experience, the sea-otter trade was born.[48] British traders soon followed in his wake; and Yankee seamen were not far behind. Captain Gray was one of the New England pioneers. Before long the Russians became interested, and Alexander Baranov, head of the Alaska-based Russian-Amedican Fur Company, began to look southward. For a time, at least, these traders did not disturb the Spaniards of California. If they landed, it was only in passing, and then were off with their catch. However, as they discovered rich hunting fields along the California coast, especially in the Santa Barbara area and on the islands in the Channel, it was only a matter of time until contacts would be made.[49]

An American ship touched at Monterey as early as 1796 to pick up food and water, and dumped ten men and a woman on the beach at Carmel as it went off, much to the dismay of Governor Diego de Borica, who ultimately sent the unwelcome foreigners off to Spain. The Spanish prohibition against foreigners in the Indies was still in force, and for the next few years California officials were ordered to enforce it strictly. However, in time it came to be honored more often in the breach than in the observance. In 1799 an American ship put into San Francisco Bay, again for food and water; the next year San Diego had another American visitor. Stiffened by viceregal prodding, the shore battery at San Diego opened fire on the *Lelia Byrd,* in March 1803. In the next several years at least two sea-otter hunting parties which had landed, one around San Quentin in San Francisco Bay and another to the north of Santa Barbara, were tracked down and ordered on their way. The Yankee clipper ships were bringing the worrisome Americans to this far-off Spanish Borderland. Officials were disturbed, but the Californios were often happy enough to engage in a contraband trade with the Yankees, which was beneficial to both parties. Especially after 1810, when troubles in the viceroyalty cut the legitimate supply lines from Mexico to California, the people of the province had to rely more and more on the seaborne fur traders for many necessities. These contacts during the last Spanish years laid the basis for the profitable commerce with the whalers during the Mexican period and for the even more important hide-and-tallow trade.

In the early years of the nineteenth century Spain's problems with foreigners in California were compounded by the southward push of the Russians.[50] Nikolai Petrovich Rezanov came to San Francisco in 1805 for food for his starving fellow countrymen who were operating along the Northwest Coast, at Sitka and southward. The story of his falling in love with the young daughter of the commandant, the reportedly beautiful Concepción Arguëllo, his departure, her long wait, unaware that the prince had died in Siberia on his way to Saint Petersburg, is a bit of charming early California romance. Rezanov did not return, but soon other Russians, under Ivan Kushov, came to California to found a post and a settlement which might grow into a food supplier for their fellow countrymen in the north. Fort Ross never lived up to expectations and the Russians had to rely on the Californios for vital food supplies. Spanish governors, José Joaquín de Arrellaga first and then Pablo Vicente Solá, recognizing that the Russians were not likely to develop into a serious threat, contrived to wink at the commerce which developed between them and San Francisco. Nor were these governors overzealous in enforcing prohibitions against the Englishmen and the Americans. At the official level in the last Spanish years, it was realized that the regular system of supply had rather completely broken down and that some substitute, even though illegitimate, had to be accepted.

Unlike Texas, which had felt the ripples of the periodic revolutionary waves that had upset the heart of the viceroyalty of New Spain, from the Hidalgo revolution of 1810, California was spared contacts with the independence movement until 1818. In that year Monterey, Refugio, Santa Barbara, and San Juan Capistrano were visited by Hippolyte de Bouchard,[51]

The Presidio of San Francisco. Lithograph by V. Adam after Louis Choris. (Library of Congress)

who was working in the patriot cause during the Latin-American wars for independence after 1810. He and his gang of roughnecks appeared in two privateer ships off Monterey; he was working out of Buenos Aires, had been to the Hawaiian Islands, and was en route back to his home port. Bouchard landed and peremptorily ordered the surrender of the king's properties in the name of the American patriots. Rebuffed, he and his ruffians pillaged the California capital, fired it, and sailed off to wreak havoc at other points down the coast. If this was a sample of what independence promised, the Californios quickly decided that they wanted none of it. The Bouchard visit, if anything, reinforced royalist loyalties in the province, at least temporarily.

Word of this Bouchard raid got to Mexico City. The next year (1819) the viceroy dispatched two hundred troops to California in order to strengthen the presidios—half from Mazatlán under Pablo de Portillo and the others from San Blas under José Antonio de Navarrete. Solá and the Californios would have been much more grateful for this show of royal interest had the troops been of better character as individuals, particularly the men out of San Blas, who were convicts or little better. In the later Spanish years too often did Mexican officials seek to solve the population and defense problems of California by using the province as a dumping ground for undesirables.

Spring of 1822 brought word of the developments in Mexico of the year before: New Spain's decision to defy the Spanish Cortes, the Plan de Iguala, Agustín Iturbide, and the proclamation of independence. Solá, in April, convened an assembly at Monterey which voted to swear allegiance to the new government in Mexico. The day of Spanish rule in the farthest of Spain's Borderlands came to an end. The Spanish Borderlands became the Mexican Borderlands, and the story closed after three centuries. Much has happened since Juan Ponce de León first attempted settlement in Florida in 1521.

◁ **13** ▷

The Borderlands in North American History

~~~~~~

*T*he decade of the 1520s opened the history of the Spanish Borderlands. Three centuries later, in the 1820s, that story closed, at least as far as Spain was concerned. By 1821 Spain had withdrawn from Florida, leaving the land to the United States by terms of the Adams-Onís agreement. In that same year, or its immediate successor, to the west of the Sabine and below the Red River, Spain reluctantly yielded its sovereignty to rebellious Mexican colonials.

On the western half of Spain's former broadly extended frontier there opened in 1821 an interlude during which those provinces became the Mexican Borderlands. This interlude lasted for fifteen years in Texas; westward it ran for a dozen more—in New Mexico, Arizona, and California. During all those years, 1821–1846, the Anglo-American pressures, already building at several points in 1821, became progressively greater, until the Americans broke through during the belligerency period of 1846–1848. Early in that latter year, by the treaty of Guadalupe-Hidalgo between Mexico and the United States, the Borderlands changed sovereignty once again, and title too, to become "the American Southwest and California."

The Anglo-Americans who came into Texas with Stephen F. Austin were not in the true sense pioneers; they found not a wilderness, but a society already in existence, and a foreign power in possession. Neither were the traders who came across the Great Plains to traffic at Santa Fe and southward into Chihuahua. Folk of European origin were already well established and had a society ready to do business. The forefathers of not a few had been established there some years before there was a Jamestown, quite a few more than that 1620 date which saw the Pilgrims arrive, and so, too, of other proud Anglo-American centers. The few hardy souls, trappers generally, who slipped beyond the Divide and wandered southward, to become acquainted with Arizona, also found European men before them—not many, perhaps, save those around Tucson and Tubac. Along the Pacific coast Yankees from their clipper ships, then mountain men, and later settlers coming overland found a flourishing society in California. Nowhere in the Borderlands was the Anglo-American a pioneer. His frontier in these parts ran head-on into another and older one. The collision of the two was not always peaceful and the fusion, such as it was, of the two was rarely painless. However, that is part of the post-Spanish Borderlands story.

Spain's frontier movement in North America, stemming out of Cuba and the islands on the eastern or right flank of the advance and out of Mexico City in the west, planted Spain's brand of Western civilization in considerable areas of the future United States. The roster of states with some trace of Hispanic background is impressive. The Spaniards were briefly in Virginia, on the Rappahannock, with a mission enterprise which did not last long. They were not much longer in South Carolina, at Santa Elena, in the late sixteenth and early seventeenth century. They were stronger and stayed longer in Georgia, through most of the seventeenth century. Florida was Spanish from 1565 to 1821, save for a brief interlude of English sovereignty from 1763 to 1783. Between 1783, and the Treaty of Paris of that year, and 1810, when the United States seized West Florida, Spain held the Gulf strip of Alabama and Mississippi, and for a time extended even farther inland. Between 1762 and 1800 the Spaniards were the lords of the entire trans-Mississippi up to the Rockies. However, their sovereignty was established only along the river—in Louisiana, to some degree in Missouri, but almost not at all in Arkansas and Iowa. These states were touched by Spain working out of Caribbean bases. It should be recalled that Spanish Louisiana was administered from Havana.

More significant was the influence of Spain's northward movement out of the capital, Mexico City, of its viceroyalty of New Spain. The future states of Texas, New Mexico, Arizona, and California were Spanish long before they became Mexican or American. Spanish explorers and on occasion military parties were in Kansas early; one band in 1720 was massacred on Nebraska's Platte River; later expeditions took the Spaniards into Colorado and into Utah. Spanish seamen were often along the Oregon coast and also the coast of Washington; in the latter area, in late eighteenth century, an incident developed at Nootka Sound which very nearly precipitated a war with England.

The tally of states with some trace of Hispanic background shows an impressive figure, running, if one stretches a point, very close to twenty. Spanish influence, however, was hardly profound in other than five states (Florida, Texas, New Mexico, Arizona, California). In these, the Spanish Borderlands, Spain established a society, planted its institutions, and passed on its language, its traditions, its religion. Into these areas Spain pushed its frontier.

When the Anglo-American frontier edged into the Borderlands, the westward-moving pioneers found the Hispanic-Americans and the society which they had built very different and strange, at least at first glance. At first the Anglo-Americans were anything but sympathetic.

The Borderlanders were foreigners, and the Anglo-American frontiersman was a particularly chauvinistic soul. More than that, the Borderlanders were, ethnically, a curious breed of men, in many instances the product of a racial intermingling with the native Americans, whom the Anglos disliked and distrusted and whom they never took the trouble to understand. It might have been no better for the Borderlanders had their blood line been pure Spanish. However, the life and opportunities on the Borderlands frontier had rarely been sufficiently attractive to lure the so-called better classes of New Spain's society to the north. Pure-blood Spaniards, apart from the top officials, were relatively few in the Borderlands—in the 3000 or so Texans who were ranged in the category of *gente de razon* ("rational" and civilized), or the 3500 Californians, or the less than 1000 Arizonans, or even the 30,000 of "populous" New Mexico.

Mixed in with the "Spanish" Borderlanders were some thousands of Christianized Indians—an overall figure of any exactness is quite impossible to give, but it would hardly run beyond 75,000, and probably should hardly be half that. To the newcomers, however, Christian or not, these Borderlanders were just Indians. Even the brand of Christianity to which they had been exposed rendered them suspect, for the Anglo-American frontiersman, in general, considered Roman Catholicism as something non-American. The universal Catholicism of the "white" Borderlanders, also, served to set them apart.

The Borderlanders, save the farmers, who were most everywhere a minority, made their living in pursuits which were in a sense new to the Anglo-American. Many Borderlanders were stockmen and ranchers, some of them with impressive herds. Some of them were miners.

Again, the Anglo-American found Borderland home construction puzzling. Adobe to the Anglo was just plain mud—his frontier had not yet tried to settle the treeless plains and the sod house was several decades into the future.

In time Anglo-American intolerance softened and the newcomers to the Borderlands discovered some of the fine qualities of the firstcomers. They came to recognize that the northward-moving pioneers had faced many problems similar to those which challenged westward-moving frontiersmen, and sometimes problems even more difficult to surmount. They even got to the point where they wanted to know more about the Spanish past and took steps to preserve its traces—the "cult" for example of the California missions, and even a Spanish monument or two in Texas and in Florida, the Alamo and the Castillo de San Marcos. A sympathetic curiosity begot a certain admiration, and an interest in the Spanish Borderlands was born. Out of it came recognition that there were frontiers in North America other than the more familiar Anglo-American frontier, which land-hungry men and women from the United States—impelled by a strong belief that it was the "manifest destiny" of their nation to expand to the Pacific Ocean— pushed westward. In short, Anglo-Americans became acutely aware that there was a frontier of Spanish culture.

Spain may not have had a "manifest destiny," but it had its reasons for reaching out so far from its Mexico City and its comfortable ring of civilized provinces—hoped-for wealth, pagan souls for Christianity, and strategic defense.

The Anglo-Americans changed much in the Borderlands and yet kept much too. They turned Texas into a giant, but its first prosperity due to the cattle industry had Spanish roots. New Mexico became "the land of enchantment," but basic to this charm were the Indians whom the friars had tried to turn into Spaniards and into Christians. In Arizona, to the south of its mountains and canyons, miners probed more deeply and cattlemen ranged more widely over the cactus-mesquite desert lands and through the little valleys which run northward to the Gila—areas that the Spaniards had seen and worked years and years before. The lazy, easy-going, romantic California of the padres and the rancheros they transformed most profoundly, uncovering and developing its riches, publicizing its beneficient climate and turning it to advantage for a legion of modern industries. The Anglos, however, were mindful of the Spanish past. The place names and those of avenues and boulevards, a distinctive architectural style and furnishings to match, commemorative fiestas, and the chain of missions—many of them were restored and proudly kept. Without always admitting it to themselves the Anglo Borderlanders built upon a Spanish past.

Had they had the population, the Spaniards might have conquered the Borderlands economically as well as politically. In their far northern provinces the population rarely numbered in the tens of thousands. Civilians, other than the military men connected with the presidios and their families, never bulked large. There were miners, some ranchers, not too many farmers, and not many more merchants. Even at the end of the Spanish regime population clusters that merited the name of towns were few. In

Texas there was San Antonio, La Bahía on the coast, and Nacogdoches in the northeast; Los Adaes, once the frontier capital, had dwindled to almost nothing. New Mexico had its capital, Santa Fe; Albuquerque hardly qualified; but there was El Paso (which then was subject to the jurisdiction of New Mexico rather than to that of Texas), which, with its surrounding missions, almost qualified as a "metropolitan" district. Arizona could boast only of Tucson and Tubac. California had three official pueblos, San Diego, Los Angeles, and San Jose; San Francisco was more presidio and mission than pueblo; the attempt to establish a fourth town, Branciforte, near the Mission Santa Cruz, was unsuccessful.

Again, had the Spaniards been as fortunate as the latercomers in enjoying the advantages of a land that had already been opened up, they might well have been successful. As it was, the Spaniards had to lay the foundations, had to pioneer against a not too friendly Nature and the regularly less than friendly aborigines.

Nature in the north was rugged, arid, and often sterile. True, the Spaniards were not, by national heritage, great farmers, since their homeland's soils had never been too rewarding. Sugar in the Islands was the most important product of their Indies; but the climate of the Borderlands was not adapted to cane culture. They brought their cereals with them, but none really flourished in the Borderlands. There was some wheat-growing in Sonora and elsewhere, but crops were hardly abundant enough to serve even local needs. The Borderlands had to rely principally on the hardy maize, borrowed from the Indians. From them, too, the Spaniards borrowed beans and chili, along with the varieties of gourds and melons. The Spaniards did contribute better methods of tilling the soil, more efficient tools, and more ingenious techniques of irrigation. The missionaries were largely responsible for introducing these and training in their use; from mission fields and gardens often came much of the food supply for the civilians of an area. In California the land was better, and the missions became "agricultural experimental stations"—for grains and fruits and grapes. Of course, this more intensive agricultural interest was a practical necessity, since the original Californians had little know-how and less practice in such matters, and the Spaniards would not have survived long on a meager diet of roots and nuts and berries. Until the missions were well established, the problem of food supply to California was one of major concern and imperial expense.

The Spaniards were better stockmen and laid the basis for the range industries in all their western Borderlands—sheep in New Mexico, cattle in Texas, in Sonora and Arizona, and in California. Horses, too, and mules they brought to the north. The introduction and spread of the Spanish horse is one of the fascinating tales of post-Columbian America. The military, particularly, had great need for horses and gave the breeders a ready and constant market. These northern breeders were not too resentful of Indian raiders, provided they confined their rustling activities to the presidio's *caballada* and left their own untouched. The mule was the great draft animal of the north. These sturdy beasts furnished much of the motive power for the wagons and carts and packtrains which supplied the Borderlands, on roads that were often so in name only and that needed the mule's surefootedness and strength.

The missionaries were regularly the pioneer stockmen of the Borderlands. Among the Jesuits, for example, each missionary who pushed out to a new area along the western slope of the Sierra Madre went with a few Indian Christians from the older mission and a small herd of cattle and, perhaps, a horse and a mule or two; if particularly blessed, he might have a Black Robe companion to share his labors and some military protection. But the animals were the constants in his necessary equipment. The Franciscans who went to New Mexico and Texas went similarly stocked. Civilians, too, brought small herds and/or flocks.

Through central and into northern Mexico the Spaniards wrung much precious-metal wealth, especially silver, from Nature's subsoil. As they approached the Borderlands, however, the rich veins seemed to peter out. Mining, which the Spaniards did best of all among their economic activities, was but a minor enterprise in the Borderlands. Sonora and Chihuahua had some rewarding lodes, but not to compare with those closer to the capital, in Nueva Galicia or southern Nueva Vizcaya. New Mexico was consistently disappointing and so, too, was Texas, save for the Los Almagres area on the dangerously exposed Río Llano. Arizona got its name from the too quickly exhausted *bolas de plata* at the Arizonac site. The "black gold" of Texas went undiscovered; perhaps just as well, since the Spaniards had no use for petroleum. Even the Texas ranchers of a later day were none too happy about the oil seepage which poisoned the streams at which their cattle watered. Ironically, the Spaniards never ventured far enough into California's interior to uncover the riches of the Mother Lode.

Besides Nature, the Spanish pioneers in the Borderlands had to face the challenge of the original owners of those vast lands. The Spanish record in this department was considerably more successful, though not entirely so. It was better from New Mexico westward and southwestward than in Texas. The Indians were the reasons behind the two most typical Borderland institutions, the mission and the presidio.

After the middle of the sixteenth century, when the frontier began to move beyond the effective limits of the Aztec empire and into the lands of those still unsubdued Indians whom the Spaniards first lumped together under the name Chichimeca, the successors to the conquistadores found to their dismay that traditional Indian-control practices, the *encomienda* and the *repartimiento*, would no longer work. After several proposed solutions, one as drastic as war-to-the-death, the Franciscans convinced officials that the mission approach should be tried. As a result, in the last years of the sixteenth century the "mission as a frontier institution" came into its own.

In 1591 the Jesuits went off to the western slope, to Sinaloa, to put the new approach to the test. Seven years later the Franciscans accompanied Oñate to New Mexico's Pueblo-land with the same aim in view.

In New Mexico the friars found the Indians already gathered in villages and could begin to catechize and convert immediately. On the western slope the Black Robes had first to convince the Indians to gather at mission sites. Later, in Texas, the Franciscans were faced with a similar problem; but they had less success, for their Indians were less tractable and, perhaps, less hungry. In this latter connection it might be noted that the security offered the neophytes was often an inducement to submit to the mission routine and discipline. With the Indian congregated, the varied tasks of the missionary were somewhat simplified. Regularly these went far beyond instruction in the tenets of the Christian faith. The mission was an agency for the transmittal of the white man's civilization as well, his crafts and skills, his political, economic, and social patterns. It was designed to put the Indian on the road to becoming an integral part of the Spanish society.

When the Indian had been, so to speak, brought under control and rendered reasonably friendly, it became possible for the civilian frontier to move forward. The missionaries, meanwhile, had also advanced, to ready another frontier for occupation. The mission was not always a sure-fire answer, for "civilized" Indians could and did revolt—the Pueblo Revolt in New Mexico of 1680, the Pima uprising of 1751 in Sonora, and there were others. Often, too, there were Indians whom the missionaries failed to win, like the Apache of Texas or the Seri of Sonora or the Yuma at the strategic junction of the Gila and the Colorado rivers, and after the Pueblo Revolt the Moqui (the modern Hopi) of northeastern Arizona. But, by and large, the mission was a successful institution and the missionaries quite remarkable frontiersmen—without regular counterpart on Anglo-American frontiers. The presence of the missionaries is a very distinctive characteristic of both Spanish and French frontiers in North America.

The mission Indian was exposed to the Spaniard's Christianity and to the Spaniard's ways. Sometimes the Spanish way of life "took" and again it did not. In all events, the native became part of the Spanish society, even though often only a junior member. The Anglo-American, with vastly different attitude and outlook toward the American native, found it difficult to accommodate to this other approach, when he took over the Borderlands. This contributed in no small way to later frictions.

At first the presidio was quite closely tied to the mission. One of its main functions was to make the task of the missionary easier and his life safer. The presidial captain was a combination policeman, truant officer, and only incidentally a guardian of the frontier. Such a man, for example, was Diego de Hurdaide of Sinaloa or Juan Mateo Mange of Pimería Alta. In time the presidio became a defensive agency, to secure the frontier against marauder Indians and, on occasion, against rival Europeans. Contact with the seemingly omnipresent Apache in very large measure effected the change, from the Gila Valley to Texas. Try though they did, the missionaries knew no lasting success with these fierce tribesmen. And the Comanche and equally warlike people behind the Apache further complicated the situation, especially when some of these were abetted by French rivals of the Spaniards. The intrusion of the French on the coast of the Gulf of Mexico and their establishment in the Mississippi Valley, just as did the expansion of the English into the Carolinas, added a new dimension to frontier defense, one of an international character. Florida was more ex-

Monterey soldier and his wife. Drawings by José Cardero, 1791. (The Bancroft Library)

posed than were the Borderlands of the west; but East Texas had a new role, and its Los Adaes acquired particular importance, at least for some decades, and so did La Bahía del Espíritu Santo.

Defense of one brand or other became a prime concern in Borderlands thinking and planning by the third quarter of the eighteenth century. For example, it prompted the extended inspection tour of the Marqués de Rubí, in the 1760s, and was the basis for the recommendations which he submitted for the reorganization and tightening of the Borderlands cordon of presidios.

The presidio may not have been the most efficient of defense bastions. Equipment frequently was inadequate, outmoded, and in bad repair; the Rubí inspection showed this in too many instances. The garrison soldiers were not always the professionals they should have been. Recruitment was difficult, regulars were never numerous enough to go around, and royal resources were not too generous. The life of constant danger too often lacked the glory of achievement which could have made it attractive and appealing to the courageous and the nobleminded youth of the viceroyalty. Presidio captains on too many occasions were unscrupulous grafters and dishonest paymasters. Morale was often low and discipline lax. The missionaries complained about the loose morals of many of the presidials, were at odds with the captains, and yet knew that they could hardly have existed without them. The arrangement in Baja California, where the padres for a time had complete control of the military, did not work to mutual satisfaction. As noted, the presidio was not always the most efficient frontier institution, but, even in its inefficiency, it did a quite remarkable job of holding the advanced line of occupation.

On more than one occasion in the preceding narration, note has been made of what is possibly the most distinctive and different characteristic of the Spanish frontier in comparison with that of the Anglo-American westward movement; namely the personal situation of the Borderlander. From first to last he was a subject of a strong and for long an absolute monarch, rather than the citizen of a republic, as was the Anglo-American. This fact had great influence on his life and his achievements. The frontiersman in the Spanish Borderlands was never his own boss, the master of his own fate. He went to the frontier with permission, sometimes was even sent there, even though he was a civilian. The Borderlander went by royal order or was recruited by royal officials or by an individual who had been given permission to open a new area. Once on the frontier, he had neither the freedom to go where he would nor the option to withdraw if things did not measure up to his dreams. He was part of a royal plan and almost every aspect of his life on the frontier was governed thereby. Self-determination was not part of his small list of rights—small, at least, by Anglo-American standards. He was much like the Virginia "planters" during the first dozen years of that colony, before the London Company gave them their own land and privilege of naming burgesses to represent them and to legislate for local conditions. Perhaps the Borderlander enjoyed a slightly greater measure of freedom than might have been his in a more settled province, but he still was not a free man. The note of rugged individualism, so often associated with the Anglo-American westward movement and so often, too, contributing to its astounding success, was foreign to the Borderlands. Of course, rigid regimentation in the life of the Borderlander was, subjectively at least, not so oppressive as one might imagine; he had never known anything else.

Despite his handicaps and the challenges which he had to face, the Spaniard in the Borderlands proved to be a remarkable frontiersman, worthy to rank with most any whom North America saw. His story has an intrinsic interest as an example of human pioneering. Further, it formed an integral and significant chapter in the history of the United States and of North America generally. Again, it has value as a basis for comparison of two national approaches to human problems—the comparative method is often so very rewarding in the acquisition of knowledge, understanding, and appreciation. Furthermore, the Borderlands story is a fundamental starting point for the comprehension of the problem of one of the nation's contemporary minority groups, the Mexican-Americans, the descendants of those sturdy Borderlanders of yesteryear who made real contributions to that real but somewhat nebulous thing called American civilization. The two American frontiers—the Spanish frontier and the Anglo-American frontier—may not have the monopoly on having made America what it is, but they had their full share in developing important aspects of its distinctiveness in the world family.

NOTES

Chapter 1: The Spanish Borderlands, Another Kind of Frontier

[1] Chronicles of America, *The Spanish Borderlands: A Chronicle of Old Florida and the Southwest*, Vol. 23 (New-Haven: Yale University Press). This study was not originally envisioned by the planners; Bolton convinced them that the Spaniards needed more notice in American history beyond that given by Irving B. Richman in the *Spanish Conquerors* volume, excellent though this contribution was.

[2] See the exchanges between Bolton and Allen Johnson, editor of the Chronicles of America series, in the Bolton Correspondence, Bancroft Library, University of California at Berkeley, *passim*, 1916–1917; especially Bolton to Johnson, November 26, 1917. One of Bolton's editors may deserve the credit for having originated the term; be that as it may, Bolton certainly was its greatest popularizer, he and the many students whom he inspired to study this important segment of American history.

[3] R. Stafford Poole wrote on this Third Provincial Council in his doctoral dissertation, The Indian Problem in the Third Provincial Council of Mexico (1585), Saint Louis University, 1961, unpublished.

[4] The presidio is beginning to attract research studies. See, as examples, Sidney R. Brinckerhoff and Odie B. Faulk, *Lancers for the King* (Phoenix, Ariz., 1965); Faulk, "The Presidio: Fortress or Farce?" *Journal of the West*, VIII (January, 1969), 21–28; Paige W. Christiansen, "The Presidio and the Borderlands: A Case Study," *ibid.*, 29–37.

[5] See Max L. Moorhead, "The Presidio Supply Problem in New Mexico in the Eighteenth Century," *New Mexico Historical Review*, XXXVI (July, 1961), 201–229; and the same author's "The Private Contract System of Presidio Supply in Northern New Spain," *Hispanic-American Historical Review*, XLI (February, 1961), 107–122.

[6] Herbert E. Bolton, "The Mission as a Frontier Institution in the Spanish-American Colonies," *American Historical Review*, XXIII (October, 1917), 42–61.

[7] Herbert E. Bolton, "Defensive Spanish Expansion and the Significance of the Spanish Borderlands," in *The Trans-Mississippi West*, ed. by James F. Willard and Colin B. Goodykoontz (Boulder, Colo., 1930), pp. 1–42. This piece, the previously cited study, and others have been reprinted in John Francis Bannon, ed., *Bolton and the Spanish Borderlands* (Norman, Okla., 1964).

Chapter 2: The Conquistador Explorers, 1513–1543

[1] A recent study is Carl O. Sauer, *The Early Spanish Main* (Berkeley, Calif., 1966).

[2] Literature on the conquest and on Cortés is extensive and need not be detailed here; suffice it to recall the classic account of the conquest, Bernal Díaz del Castillo, *Historia Verdadera de la Conquista de México*, which has appeared in several editions in the original and in even more English translations and editions.

[3] A short sketch of this northward movement in its early phase is Carl O. Sauer, *The Road to Cíbola* (Berkeley, Calif., 1932); see also Volume I of Hubert Howe Bancroft, *History of Mexico* (6 vols.; San Francisco, 1880–1888).

[4] Donald E. Chipman, *Nuño Guzmán and the Province of Pánuco, 1518–1533* (Norman Okla., 1966).

[5] There have been several translations and editions of the Cabeza de Vaca account: Fanny Bandelier, *The Journey of Cabeza de Vaca from Florida to the Pacific, 1528–1536* (New York, 1922); Frederick W. Hodge, *The Narrative of Alvar Núñez Cabeza de Vaca*, in Hodge and T. H. Lewis, *Spanish Explorers in Southern United States, 1528–1543* (New York, 1907); Cyclone Covey, *Cabeza de Vaca's Adventures in the Unknown In-*

terior of America (New York, 1961). See also Cleve Hallenbeck, *Alvar Núñez Cabeza de Vaca: The Journey and Route of the First European to Cross the Continent of North America* (Glendale, Calif., 1940); Morris Bishop, *The Odyssey of Cabeza de Vaca* (New York, 1933); an early attempt to map the route is Bethel Coopwood, "Route of Cabeza de Vaca in Texas," Texas State Historical Association *Quarterly*, III (July, 1899), 54–65; (October, 1899), 108–141; (January, 1900), 177–209; (April, 1900), 229–265; IV (July, 1900), 1–33.

⁶ Arthur Scott Aiton, *Antonio de Mendoza* (Durham, N. C., 1927).

⁷ For the account of Fray Marcos see Percy M. Baldwin, "Fray Marcos de Niza's *Relación*," *New Mexico Historical Review*, I (April, 1926), 193–223; see also the documents in George P. Hammond and Agapito Rey, *Narratives of the Coronado Expedition* (Albuquerque, 1940); and Bonaventure Oblasser's translation, *Fray Marcos' Own Personal Narrative* (privately printed). There has been much written about Fray Marcos and the credibility of his claims: George J. Undreiner, "Fray Marcos de Niza and His Journey to Cíbola," *The Americas*, III (April, 1947), 415–486, in a lengthy study supports Fray Marcos; Henry R. Wagner, "Fray Marcos de Niza," *New Mexico Historical Review*, IX (April, 1934), 184–227, is less sympathetic, as is Carl O. Sauer in *Road to Cíbola* (Berkeley, Calif., 1932), and "The Discovery of New Mexico Reconsidered," *New Mexico Historical Review*, XII (July, 1937), 270–287, and "The Credibility of the Fray Marcos Account," *ibid.*, XVI, (April, 1941), 233–243; Lansing Bloom, "Who Discovered New Mexico?" *ibid.*, XV (April, 1940), 101–132, disagrees with Sauer on a number of points. Fray Marcos is studied in Cleve Hallenbeck, *The Journey of Fray Marcos de Niza* (Dallas, 1949); Mabel Farnum, *The Seven Golden Cities* (Milwaukee, 1943); Bonaventure Oblasser, "The Franciscans in the Spanish Southwest," *Franciscan Educational Conference Report*, XVIII (1936).

⁸ Interest in Coronado and his expedition has been considerable; many of the contemporary accounts have been translated and edited, among these the most recent and most complete is George P. Hammond and Agapito Rey, eds., *Narratives of the Coronado Expedition* (Albuquerque, 1940). The best full biography is Herbert E. Bolton, *Coronado, Knight of Pueblos and Plains* (New York, 1949); the expedition is the subject of A. Grove Day, *Coronado's Quest* (Berkeley, Calif., 1940). These last two works will serve as guides to the extensive Coronado bibliography to be found in the historical journals.

⁹ Arthur S. Aiton, *The Muster Roll and Equipment of the Expedition of Francisco Vásquez de Coronado* (Ann Arbor, Mich., 1939).

¹⁰ The De Soto bibliography, likewise, is extensive. For the contemporary accounts of the expedition see Edward G. Bourne, ed., *Narratives of the Career of Hernando de Soto in the Conquest of Florida* (2 vols.; New York, 1904); Buckingham Smith, tr., "The Narrative of Hernando de Soto, by the Gentleman of Elvas," in F. W. Hodge and T. H. Lewis, eds., *Spanish Explorers in the Southern United States, 1528–1543* (New York, 1907); James A. Robertson, ed., *True Relation of the Hardships Suffered by Governor Fernando de Soto and Portuguese Gentlemen during the Discovery of the Province of Florida, Now Newly Set Forth by a Gentleman of Elvas* (Deland, Fla., 1932). Two biographies, neither wholly adequate, are R. B. Cunninghame-Graham, *Hernando de Soto* (London, 1903), and Theodore Maynard, *De Soto and the Conquistadores* (New York, 1930).

¹¹ Rex W. Strickland, "Moscoso's Journey through Texas," *Southwestern Historical Quarterly*, XLVI (October, 1942), 109–137, and J. W. Williams, "Moscoso's Trail in Texas," *ibid.*, 138–157.

¹² Francisco Preciado, "Diary of the Voyage of Ulloa to Baja California in 1539–1540," Hakluyt's *Principal Navigations* (many editions), Vol. III.

¹³ There are two rather good biographies of this fascinating figure of the Conquest period: J. E. Kelley, *Pedro de Alvarado, Conquistador* (New York, 1933), and M. Taylor, *Impetuous Alvarado* (New York, 1936).

[14] Henry R. Wagner, *Juan Rodríguez Cabrillo, Discoverer of the Coast of California* (San Francisco, 1941); see also Wagner, *Spanish Voyages to the Northwest Coast of America in the Sixteenth Century* (San Francisco, 1928), and *Cartography of the Northwest Coast of America to the Year 1800* (2 vols., Berkeley, Calif., 1937). The original record of the voyage has been translated and edited by Herbert E. Bolton in *Spanish Exploration in the Southwest, 1542–1706* (New York, 1916), pp. 1–40.

Chapter 3: First Settlements in the Borderlands

[1] Elias Amador, *Bosquejo histórico de Zacatecas* (Zacatecas, 1892).

[2] For a general account see Hubert Howe Bancroft, *History of the North Mexican States and Texas* (2 vols.; San Francisco, 1884–1889). A most valuable collection of documentary material on this early northern frontier is Adolph F. A. Bandelier, *Historical Documents Relating to New Mexico, Nueva Vizcaya, the Approaches Thereto, to 1773*, trans. by Charles W. Hackett (3 vols.; Washington, D. C., 1931).

[3] J. Lloyd Mecham, *Francisco de Ibarra and Nueva Vizcaya* (Durham, N. C., 1927).

[4] Excellent for the background of this frontier and its problems is Philip W. Powell, *Soldiers, Indians and Silver: The Northward Advance of New Spain, 1550–1600* (Berkeley, Calif., 1952).

[5] R. Stafford Poole, "War by Fire and Blood," *The Americas*, XXII (October 1965), 115–137.

[6] Vito Alessio Robles, *Saltillo en la historia y en la leyenda* (Mexico, 1934).

[7] George P. Hammond and Agapito Rey, eds., *Gallego's Relation of the Rodríguez Expedition to New Mexico, 1581–1582* (Sante Fe, 1927); see also by the same authors and editors *The Rediscovery of New Mexico* (Albuquerque, 1966), pp. 67–152; J. Lloyd Mecham, "Supplementary Documents Relating to the Chamuscado-Rodriguez Expedition," *Southwest Historical Quarterly*, XXIX (January, 1926), 224–232; Zephyrin Engelhardt, "El Yllustre Señor Chamuscado," *ibid.*, XXIX (April, 1926), 296–301.

[8] George P. Hammond and Agapito Rey, eds., *Expedition into New Mexico Made by Antonio Espejo, 1582–1583, as Revealed in the Journal of Diego Pérez de Luxán* (Los Angeles, 1929); see also by the same authors and editors *The Rediscovery of New Mexico* (Albuquerque, 1966), pp. 153–244; J. Lloyd Mecham, "Antonio de Espejo and His Journey to New Mexico," *Southwestern Historical Quarterly*, XXX (October, 1926), 114–139; Katherine Bartlett, "Notes upon the Routes of Espejo and Farfán to the Mines in the Sixteenth Century," *New Mexico Historical Review*, XVII (January, 1942), 21–36.

[9] See Henry R. Wagner, *Sir Francis Drake's Voyage around the World: Its Aims and Achievements* (San Francisco, 1926).

[10] At this point note might be taken of several general histories of New Mexico: Hubert Howe Bancroft, *History of Arizona and New Mexico* (San Francisco, 1889); Ralph E. Twitchell, *The Leading Facts of New Mexican History* (5 vols.; Cedar Rapids, Iowa, 1911–1917); Warren E. Beck, *New Mexico: A History of Four Centuries* (Norman, Okla., 1962); Paul Horgan, *Great River: The Rio Grande in North American History* (2 vols.; New York, 1954); and more could be noted.

[11] This background is found in the biography of the successful contender by George P. Hammond, *Don Juan de Oñate and the Founding of New Mexico* (Santa Fe, 1927); see also his *Don Juan de Oñate, Colonizer of New Mexico, 1595–1628* (Albuquerque, 1953). Documents on the unauthorized entradas into New Mexico are published in Hammond and Rey, eds., *The Rediscovery of New Mexico* (Albuquerque, 1966), pp. 245–326.

[12] A contemporary account of the founding of New Mexico is that of Gaspar Pérez de Villagrá, *History of New Mexico*, trans. and ed. by Gilberto Espinosa (Los Angeles, 1933).

[13] Irene L. Chaves, "La Ynstrucción de Don Pedro de Peralta," *New Mexico Historical Review*, IV (April, 1929), 178–187.

[14] Lansing B. Bloom, "When Was Santa Fe Founded?" *New Mexico Historical Review,* IV (April, 1929), 188–194.

[15] Lansing B. Bloom, "The Governors of New Mexico," *ibid.,* X (April, 1935), 152–157.

[16] For the general story of Florida see Woodbury Lowery, *The Spanish Settlements within the Present Limits of the United States, 1513–1561* (New York, 1901), and *The Spanish Settlements within the Present Limits of the United States, 1562–1574* (New York, 1905); Rembert W. Patrick, *Florida under Five Flags* (Gainesville, Fla., 1945); Michael Kenny, *The Romance of the Floridas* (Milwaukee, 1934); Andrés G. Barcía Carballido y Zúñiga, *Ensayo cronológico para la historia general de la Florida, 1512–1722* (Madrid, 1723), recently translated by Anthony Kerrigan; *Barcía's Chronological History of the Continent of Florida* (Gainesville, Fla., 1951); and Michael V. Gannon, *The Cross in the Sand: The Early Catholic Church in Florida, 1513–1870* (Gainesville, Fla., 1965).

[17] Victor Francis O'Daniel, *Dominicans in Early Florida* (New York, 1930).

[18] Herbert I. Priestley, *Tristán de Luna: Conquest of the Old South: A Study of Spanish Imperial Strategy* (Glendale, Calif., 1936), and *The Luna Papers* (2 vols.; Deland, Fla., 1929).

[19] Philip A. Means, *The Spanish Main—Focus of Envy, 1492–1700* (New York, 1935).

[20] Jeannette Thurber Connor, *Jean Ribaut, The True Relation of the Discovery of Terra Florida* (Deland, Fla., 1927).

[21] Jeannette Thurber Connor, trans. and ed., *Pedro Menéndez de Avilés, Adelantado, Governor and Captain-General of Florida: Memorial by Gonzalo Solís de Merás* (Deland, Fla., 1923).

[22] The Jesuit story forms a large part of Michael Kenny, *The Romance of the Floridas;* a full earlier treatment is Francisco Florencia, *Historia de la Provincia de la Compañía de Jesús en Nueva España* (Mexico, 1694).

[23] Clifford M. Lewis and Albert J. Loomie, *The Spanish Jesuit Mission in Virginia, 1570–1572* (Chapel Hill, N.C., 1953).

[24] John Tate Lanning, *The Spanish Missions of Georgia* (Chapel Hill, N.C., 1935); John Gilmary Shea, *The Catholic Church in Colonial Days* (2 vols.; New York, 1883); Maynard Geiger, *The Franciscan Conquest of Florida, 1573–1618* (Washington, D.C., 1937).

Chapter 4: First Steps on the Long Road to California, 1591–1711

[1] A fine account of this trade is found in William L. Schurz, *The Manila Galleon* (New York, 1939).

[2] A personal account of the rigors of the homebound trip, which had not changed greatly with over a century of experience, can be found in *Narrative of a Voyage on a Spanish Galleon from Manila to Acapulco in 1687–1688,* by Giovanni Francesco Gemelli Careri, translated in *Churchill's Collection of Voyages and Travels,* IV (London, 1752).

[3] Peter Gerhard, *Pirates on the West Coast of New Spain, 1575–1742* (Glendale, Calif., 1960).

[4] See Chapter 3, n. 9, of the present book.

[5] Andrew F. Rolle, *California, a History* (New York, 1963), pp. 52–53.

[6] Henry R. Wagner, "The Voyage to California of Sebastián Rodríguez Cermenho in 1595," California Historical Society *Quarterly,* III (April, 1924), 3–24; some years later Robert F. Heizer dug along the shore at Drake's Bay, uncovered remains of the cargo of the *San Agustín,* and reported the same in his article "Archeological Evidence of Sebástián Rodríguez Cermenho's California Visit," California Historical Society *Quarterly,* XX (December, 1941), 315–328.

[7] The account of this expedition is translated and edited as "Diary of Sebastián Vizcaíno," in Herbert E. Bolton, *Spanish Exploration in the Southwest, 1542–1706* (New York, 1916), pp. 52–103.

[8] *Ibid.*, pp. 91–92.

[9] "A Brief Report of the Discovery in the South Sea, by Fray Antonio de la Ascensión, 1602–1603," in Bolton, *ibid.*, pp. 104–134.

[10] Herbert E. Bolton, "The West Coast Corridor," *Proceedings* of the American Philosophical Society, Vol. 91 (December, 1947), 426–429; reprinted in John Francis Bannon, ed., *Bolton and the Spanish Borderlands* (Norman, Okla., 1964), pp. 123–130.

[11] J. Lloyd Mecham, *Francisco de Ibarra and Nueva Vizcaya* (Durham, N.C., 1927) is still the best study of this frontier figure. For the general history of the north, Hubert Howe Bancroft, *History of the North Mexican States and Texas,* (2 vols.; San Francisco, 1884–1889) is still useful.

[12] For this story see Jerome V. Jacobsen, *Educational Foundations of the Jesuits in Sixteenth Century New Spain* (Berkeley, Calif., 1938), and his shorter study in *Greater America: Essays in Honor of Herbert Eugene Bolton* (Berkeley, Calif., 1945), pp. 105–123; the early Jesuit years in New Spain were chronicled by a nearer contemporary, Francisco de Florencia, S. J., *Historia de la Provincia de la Compañía de Jesús de Nueva España* (Mexico, 1694).

[13] W. Eugene Shiels, *Gonzalo de Tapia, Founder of the First Permanent Jesuit Mission in North America* (New York, 1934); see also his summary study, "Gonzalo de Tapia (1561–1594)," in *Greater America*, pp. 125–144.

[14] The story of the mission frontier in the west-coast corridor into the 1630s is well told in Peter Masten Dunne, *Pioneer Black Robes on the West Coast* (Berkeley, Calif., 1940); a shorter study briefs these years and goes to the 1680s, John Francis Bannon, "Pioneer Jesuit Missionaries on the Pacific Slope of New Spain," in *Greater America*, pp. 181–198. One of the valuable sources for first half century of this west-coast enterprise was written by one of the participants and published in 1645: Andrés Pérez de Ribas, *Historia de los triumphos de nuestra santa fee* (Madrid, 1645); a condensed English translation has recently been published as *My Life Among the Savage Nations of New Spain, by Andrés Pérez de Ribas,* Tomas Antonio Robertson trans. and ed. (Los Angeles, 1969).

[15] John Francis Bannon, "Black Robe Frontiersman: Pedro Méndez, S.J.," *Hispanic American Historical Review,* XXVII (February, 1947), 61–86, gives the highlights of this remarkable career.

[16] A short biographical sketch of this man is Harry P. Johnson, "Diego Martínez de Hurdaide: Defender of Spain's Pacific Coast Frontier," in *Greater America*, pp. 199–218.

[17] Dunne, *Pioneer Black Robes on the West Coast*, p. 185.

[18] *Ibid.*

[19] Herbert E. Bolton and Thomas M. Marshall, *The Colonization of North America, 1492–1783* (New York, 1920), p. 240.

[20] Dunne, *Pioneer Black Robes on the West Coast*, pp. 195–197.

[21] John Francis Bannon, *The Mission Frontier in Sonora, 1620–1687* (New York, 1955).

[22] This report is summarized *ibid.*, pp. 94–96.

[23] This Zapata report is summarized *ibid.*, pp. 129–135, insofar as its information bears on Sonora. It appears in print in *Documentos para la Historia de Mexico,* 4ª ser., I, 309–419. The copy in the Archivo General de la Nación, México, *Misiones* 26, ff. 241–269, carries the imposing title: Relacion de las misiones que la Compañía tiene en el Reyno y Provincia de la Nueva España, echa el año 1678 con ocasión de la visita general della que por orden del Padre Provincial Thomas Altamirano hizo el P. Visitador Juan Ortiz Zapata de la misma Compañía.

[24] This report is from the Archivo de Parral (Mexico): Año 1686—Administrativo: Visita que practico el General Gabriel de Isturiz en la provincia de Sonora, 1685.

[25] Bolton can be said almost to have been the "discoverer" of Kino; certainly he was his earliest promoter. Bolton is responsible for the three following: *Kino's Historical Memoir of Pimería Alta* (2 vols.; Cleveland, 1919; reprinted in 1 vol., Berkeley, Calif., 1948); the short sketch, *The Padre on Horseback* (San Francisco, 1932; reprinted Chicago, 1963); and the full biography *Rim of Christendom: A Biography of Eusebio Francisco Kino, Pacific Coast Pioneer* (New York, 1936; reprinted New York, 1960). See also Rufus K. Wyllys, *Pioneer Padre: The Life and Times of Eusebio Francisco Kino* (Dallas, 1935); and Frank C. Lockwood, *With Padre Kino on the Trail* (Tucson, Ariz., 1934). The new flurry of interest in Kino has produced Charles Polzer, *A Kino Guide: His Missions—His Monuments* (Tucson, Ariz., 1968).

[26] Bolton, *The Padre on Horseback*, pp. 58–59.

[27] For long years the location of Kino's grave was a matter of interest to historians and other Kino *aficionados*. The documents told that he was buried in the chapel at Magdalena; but the problem was to find the chapel, which had long since disappeared. Spurred, and perhaps shamed, by the interest which the State of Arizona was showing in its "pioneer padre," evidenced by the nomination of Kino by that State to the Statuary Hall collection at the United States Capitol and the presentation of a statue of the padre, in February, 1965, the Mexican government ordered that diggings be made at Magdalena. The Mexican researchers in cooperation with a team from the University of Arizona uncovered the Kino grave and the Kino remains in May, 1966. Experts from both sides of the border are completely satisfied. The Mexican government is planning to erect a fitting monument, a new chapel, to house the remains. The fuller story of these searches can be found in the booklet of Father Charles Polzer, cited above (n. 25).

[28] The Kino dream, set down in a report to the viceroy, 1703, has been translated and annotated by Ernest J. Burrus and published under the title *Kino's Plan for the Development of Pimería Alta, Arizona and Lower California* (Tucson, Ariz., 1961).

[29] See Herbert E. Bolton, "The Mission as a Frontier Institution in the Spanish-American Colonies," given first as a Faculty Research Lecture at the University of California-Berkeley and originally published in *American Historical Review*, XXIII (October, 1917) and reprinted singly and in several collections, among them Herbert E. Bolton, *Wider Horizons of American History* (New York, 1939) and Bannon, *Bolton and the Spanish Borderlands* (Norman, Okla., 1964). This is one of the classics in the Borderlands historiography.

Chapter 5: The Far Northern Frontier in Danger, 1680–1700

[1] Philip Wayne Powell, *Soldiers, Indians and Silver* (Berkeley, Calif., 1952) very excellently tells the story "The Northward Advance of New Spain, 1550–1600."

[2] R. Stafford Poole, "War by Fire and Blood," *The Americas*, XXII (October, 1965), 115–137.

[3] Bolton, "The Mission as a Frontier Institution" (see Chapter 4, n. 29).

[4] Peter Masten Dunne, *Pioneer Jesuits in Northern Mexico* (Berkeley, Calif., 1944) tells the story of Jesuit activity on the eastern slope through the early decades of the seventeenth century.

[5] Dunne, *ibid.*, p. 20.

[6] See John Francis Bannon, "The Conquest of the Chínipas," *Mid-America*, XXI (January, 1939), 3–31.

[7] A short biography of this padre is given in Catherine M. McShane, "Hernando de Santarén, S.J., Pioneer and Diplomat, 1565–1616," in *Greater America*, pp. 145–162 (cited in Chapter 4, n. 12) which is a summary of a fuller study in her unpublished doctoral dissertation, University of California-Berkeley, 1940.

[8] A modern history of the State of Chihuahua, superseding the traditional account in Hubert Howe Bancroft, *History of the North Mexican States and Texas* (2 vols.; San Francisco, 1884–1889) is Florence C. and Robert H. Lister, *Chihuahua: Storehouse of Storms* (Albuquerque, 1966). The Listers have drawn heavily on the fine work of modern Chihuahua historians, such as Francisco R. Aldama, José G. Rocha, and others, who have published many colonial studies in *Boletín,* Sociedad Chihuahuaense de Estudios Históricos.

[9] Peter Masten Dunne followed his volume cited above (n. 4) with another on the Tarahumara missions: *Early Jesuit Missions in Tarahumara* (Berkeley, Calif., 1948).

[10] France V. Scholes is the authority on seventeenth-century New Mexico. His numerous studies are scattered through the indicated volumes of the *New Mexico Historical Review:* "The Supply Service of the New Mexico Missions," V (January, April, October, 1930); "Problems in the Early Ecclesiastical History of New Mexico," VII (January, 1932); "Civil Government and Society in New Mexico in the Seventeenth Century," X (January, 1935); "The First Decade of the Inquisition in New Mexico," X (July, 1935); "Church and State in New Mexico, 1610–1650," XI (January, April, July, October, 1936) and XII (January, 1937); "Troublous Times in New Mexico, 1659–1670," XII (April, October, 1937) and XIII (January, 1938) and XV (July, October, 1940) and XVI (January, July, October, 1941).

[11] "A Trade Invoice of 1638," *New Mexico Historical Review,* X (July, 1937), 242–246. The early chapters of Max L. Moorhead, *New Mexico's Royal Road* (Norman, Okla., 1958) have a short sketch of this traffic between Mexico and New Mexico; see also the Scholes study cited above (n. 10).

[12] See the Scholes study "Church and State," cited above (n. 10).

[13] Charles W. Hackett, "The Revolt of the Pueblo Indians of New Mexico in 1680," Texas State Historical Association *Quarterly,* XV (October, 1911), 93–147. Hackett has edited the major documents bearing on the revolt in his *Revolt of the Pueblo Indians of New Mexico and Otermín's Attempted Reconquest, 1680–1682* (2 vols.; Albuquerque, 1942).

[14] Angelico Chavez offers an interesting study in his article "Pohe-yemo's Representative and the Pueblo Revolt of 1680," *New Mexico Historical Review,* XLII (January, 1967), 85–126.

[15] Charles W. Hackett, "Retreat of the Spaniards from New Mexico in 1680 and the Beginnings of El Paso," *Southwestern Historical Quarterly,* XVI (October, 1912) and (January, 1913), 137–168, 259–276.

[16] Anne E. Hughes, *The Beginnings of Spanish Settlement in the El Paso District* (Berkeley, Calif., 1914).

[17] J. Manuel Espinosa is the authority on the reconquest of New Mexico; see his *Crusaders of the Rio Grande: The Story of Don Diego de Vargas and the Reconquest and Refounding of New Mexico* (Chicago, 1942), and his collection of source materials in *First Expedition of Vargas into New Mexico, 1692* (Albuquerque, 1940).

[18] Espinosa, *Crusaders,* pp. 81–82.

[19] Quoted in Espinosa, *Crusaders,* p. 109.

Chapter 6: The Borderlands Become International

[1] The most recent life of Marquette is Joseph P. Donnelly, *Jacques Marquette* (Chicago, 1968); the best study of Jolliet is Jean Delanglez, *Life and Voyages of Louis Jolliet, 1645–1700* (Chicago, 1948).

[2] Much has been written on La Salle, but a great deal is not pertinent to the present study. Francis Parkman, *La Salle and the Discovery of the Great West* (Boston, 1904) is something of a classic; Paul Chesnel, *History of Cavelier de la Salle* (New York, 1932) is later, but should be used with some caution. Many source pieces are found in Pierre

Margry, ed., *Découvertes et établissements des Français dans l'oeust et dans le sud d'Amérique Septentrionale, 1614–1698* (6 vols.; Paris, 1879).

[3] Charles W. Hackett, "New Light on Don Diego de Peñalosa," *Mississippi Valley Historical Review,* VI (December, 1919), 313–335; also C. F. Duro, *Don Diego de Peñalosa y su descubrimiento del reino de Quivira* (Madrid, 1882).

[4] A short account of La Salle in Texas is found in Henry Folmer, *Franco-Spanish Rivalry in North America, 1524–1763* (Glendale, Calif., 1953), pp. 155–188; a fuller account is William E. Dunn, *Spanish and French Rivalry in the Gulf Region of the United States, 1678–1702: The Beginnings of Texas and Pensacola* (Austin, Tex., 1917). A recent restudy is E. W. Cole, "La Salle in Texas," *Southwestern Historical Quarterly,* XLIX (April, 1946), 473–500, with maps.

[5] Herbert E. Bolton, "The Location of La Salle's Colony on the Gulf of Mexico," *Mississippi Valley Historical Review,* II (September, 1915), 165–182; reprinted in *Southwestern Historical Quarterly,* XXVII (January, 1924), 171–189.

[6] Henri Joutel, *A Journal of La Salle's Last Voyage,* ed., D. B. Rutman (New York, 1962).

[7] A short biography of this close friend and lieutenant of La Salle is Edmund R. Murphy, *Henry de Tonti* (Baltimore, 1941).

[8] *The Journal of Jean Cavelier,* trans. and ed. by Jean Delanglez (Chicago, 1938) carries the account of this trek northward.

[9] A quick overview of these activities can be found in the early pages of the article by Herbert E. Bolton, "Preliminaries to 'The Spanish Occupation of Texas, 1519–1690,' " *Southwestern Historical Quarterly,* XVI (July, 1912), 1–26; reprinted in Bannon, ed., *Bolton and the Spanish Borderlands* (Norman, Okla., 1964), pp. 96–122.

[10] The two Benavides reports have been translated and edited, the first by Peter P. Forrestal, *The Memorial of Alonso de Benavides of 1630* (Washington, D.C., 1954), and the second by F. W. Hodge, G. P. Hammond, and Agapito Rey, *Revised Memorial of Fray Alonso de Benavides, 1634* (Albuquerque, 1945).

[11] See the discussion in Carlos E. Castañeda, *Our Catholic Heritage in Texas, 1519–1936* (7 vols.; Austin, Tex., 1936–1950), I, 196–198.

[12] Hubert Howe Bancroft, *History of the North Mexican States and Texas* (2 vols.; San Francisco, 1884–1889); Vito Alessio Robles, *Coahuila y Texas en la época colonial* (Mexico, 1938).

[13] William E. Dunn, "The Spanish Search for La Salle's Colony on the Bay of Espíritu Santo," *Southwestern Historical Quarterly,* XIX (April, 1916), 323–369; see also his larger work, *Spanish and French Rivalry,* cited above, n. 4.

[14] Source materials on several of these expeditions are found in convenient form in Herbert E. Bolton, trans. and ed., *Spanish Exploration in the Southwest, 1542–1706* (New York, 1916).

[15] Robert C. Clark, *The Beginnings of Texas* (Austin, Tex., 1907).

[16] John Tate Lanning, *The Spanish Missions of Georgia* (Chapel Hill, N.C., 1935), is the best account of this missionary effort.

[17] See the short summary in John Jay TePaske, *The Governorship of Spanish Florida, 1700–1763* (Durham, N.C., 1964), pp. 5–7.

[18] The background for this Florida story can be found in a number of works. The following are worthy of note: Woodbury Lowery, *Spanish Settlements within the Present Limits of the United States, 1562–1574* (New York, 1905); Herbert E. Bolton and Mary Ross, *The Debatable Land* (Berkeley, Calif., 1925), which is really the introductory section of Bolton, *Arredondo's Historical Proof of Spain's Title to Georgia* (Berkeley, Calif., 1925); Andrés G. Barcía, *Ensayo cronológico para la historia general de la Florida, 1512–1722* (Madrid, 1723); see also Jeannette Thurber Connor, ed. and trans., *Colonial Records of Spanish Florida* (2 vols.; Deland, Fla., 1925–1930).

[19] Bolton; *Debatable Land,* p. 20.

[20] One of the better studies on this period is Verner W. Crane, *The Southern Frontier, 1670–1732* (Durham, N.C., 1932; Ann Arbor, Mich., 1956); see also Verne E. Chatelain, *The Defense of Spanish Florida, 1565–1763* (Washington, D.C., 1941).

[21] Charles Arnade, *The Siege of St. Augustine in 1702* (Gainesville, Fla., 1959).

[22] The predecessors of the stone fort are recalled in Jeannette Thurber Connor, "The Nine Old Wooden Forts of Saint Augustine," *Florida Historical Quarterly*, IV (January and April, 1926), 103–111, 171–180.

[23] Mark F. Boyd, Hale G. Smith, and John W. Griffin, *Here They Once Stood: The Tragic End of the Apalachee Missions* (Gainesville, Fla., 1951).

Chapter 7: Texas, A Defensive Borderland, 1685–1731

[1] The best biography, and the most recent, is Nellis M. Crouse, *Lemoyne Iberville: Soldier of New France* (New York, 1954). Two general studies of France in the Mississippi Valley are John Anthony Caruso, *The Mississippi Valley Frontier—The Age of French Exploration and Settlement* (Indianapolis, 1966), and Joseph H. Schlarman, *From Quebec to New Orleans* (Belleville, Ill., 1929).

[2] William E. Dunn, *Spanish and French Rivalry in the Gulf Region of the United States, 1678–1702: The Beginnings of Texas and Pensacola* (Austin, Tex., 1917), and "The Occupation of Pensacola Bay, 1689–1698," *Florida Historical Society Quarterly*, IV (July, 1925), 3–14; (October, 1925), 76–89; V (January, 1926), 140–154. Documentary materials on the years prior to the occupation of Pensacola can be found in Irving A. Leonard, trans. and ed., *Spanish Approach to Pensacola, 1689–1693* (Los Angeles, 1939).

[3] See Caruso and Schlarman, also the treatment by the Louisiana historian Charles Gayarré, *History of Louisiana* (4 vols.; New York, 1903).

[4] A biography of Cadillac is Agnes C. Laut, *Cadillac, Knight Errant of the Wilderness* (New York, 1931).

[5] Ross Phares, *Cavalier in the Wilderness: The Story of the Explorer and Trader Louis Juchereau de St. Denis* (Baton Rouge, La., 1952); Edmond J. P. Schmitt, "Who Was Juchereau de Saint Denis?" *Texas State Historical Association Quarterly*, I (January, 1898), 204–215; Lester G. Bugbee, "The Real Saint-Denis," *ibid.*, I (April, 1898), 266–281.

[6] Herbert E. Bolton and Thomas M. Marshall, *The Colonization of North America, 1492–1783* (New York, 1920), p. 292; see also Gabriel Tous, "The Espinosa-Olivares-Aguirre Expedition of 1709," *Preliminary Studies* of the Texas Catholic Historical Society, I, No. 3.

[7] Antoine Simon Le Page du Pratz, *Histoire de la Louisiane* (Paris, 1758), I, p. 10.

[8] Robert C. Clark, "Louis Juchereau de Saint-Denis and the Reestablishment of the Tejas Missions," *Texas State Historical Association Quarterly*, VI (July, 1902), 1–26.

[9] Charmion Clair Shelby, trans., "St. Denis's Declaration concerning Texas in 1717," *Southwestern Historical Quarterly*, XXVI (January, 1923), 165–183.

[10] For the early history of Texas there is the sketch in Hubert Howe Bancroft, *History of the North Mexican States and Texas* (2 vols.; San Francisco, 1884–1889), I; also Robert C. Clark, *The Beginnings of Texas, 1684–1718* (Austin, Tex., 1907), which should be controlled by the comments of Herbert E. Bolton, "Notes on Clark's 'Beginnings of Texas,'" *Texas State Historical Association Quarterly*, XII (October, 1908), 148–158. Although its title tends to be a bit misleading, one of the better general accounts of the Texas story is Carlos E. Castañeda, *Our Catholic Heritage in Texas, 1519–1936* (7 vols.; Austin, Tex., 1936–1950); Volume II treats this period 1690–1731 with great thoroughness, and the next two also bear on the colonial or Spanish period. Castañeda's translation and edition of Fray Juan Agustín Morfi, *History of Texas, 1673–1779* (2 vols.; Albuquerque, 1935) can be highly valuable, as can Antonio Bonilla, "Brief Compendium

of the Events Which Have Occurred in the Province of Texas from Its Conquest, or Reduction, to the Present [1772]," trans. by Elizabeth H. West, Texas State Historical Association *Quarterly*, VIII (July, 1904). Noteworthy too is Vito Alessio Robles, *Coahuila y Texas en la Epoca Colonial* (Mexico, 1938).

[11] Juan Domingo Arricivita, *Crónica Seráfica y Apostólica del Colegio de Propaganda Fide de la Santa Cruz de Querétaro de la Nueva España* (Mexico, 1792); more recent and excellent is Michael B. McCloskey, *The Formative Years of the Missionary College of Santa Cruz de Querétaro, 1683–1733* (Washington, D.C., 1955).

[12] Alberto Maria Carreño, "The Missionary Influence of the College of Zacatecas," *The Americas*, VII (January, 1951), 297–320. There has been quite a bit of interest in Fray Antonio Margil: Benedict Leutenegger, *Apostle of America: Fray Antonio Margil* (Chicago, 1961); Eduardo Enrique Rios, *Life of Fray Antonio Margil, O.F.M.*, trans. and rev. by Benedict Leutenegger (Washington, D.C., 1959); William H. Donahue, "The Missionary Activities of Fray Antonio de Jesús in Texas, 1716–1722," *The Americas*, XIV (July, 1957), 45–56; Paul V. Murray, "Venerable Antonio Margil de Jesús, O.F.M., Friar of the Winged Feet," *ibid.*, VII (January, 1951), 267–280.

[13] Herbert E. Bolton, "The Native Tribes about the East Texas Missions," Texas State Historical Association *Quarterly*, XI (April, 1908), 249–276.

[14] Castañeda, *Our Catholic Heritage*, II. 54–56.

[15] Angelina was an Indian woman who, having been raised in Coahuila, spoke Spanish and was able to act as interpreter.

[16] The essay by Bolton, "The Mission as a Frontier Institution," can be recalled in this connection.

[17] On the Alarcón expedition, see: Francisco Céliz, *Diary of the Alarcón Expedition into Texas, 1718–1719*, trans. and ed. by Fritz L. Hoffmann (Los Angeles, 1935); also by Hoffmann, "The Mesquía Diary of the Alarcón Expedition into Texas, 1718," *Southwestern Historical Quarterly*, XLI (April, 1938), 312–323. A running account in Castañeda, *Our Catholic Heritage*, II, pp. 33–109.

[18] Frederick C. Chabot, *San Antonio and Its Beginnings* (San Antonio, 1931).

[19] The best short sketch of the Aguayo story is Eleanor C. Buckley, "The Aguayo Expedition into Texas and Louisiana, 1719–1722," Texas State Historical Association *Quarterly*, XV (July, 1911), 1–65; see also Charles W. Hackett, "The Marquis of San Miguel de Aguayo and His Recovery of Texas from the French, 1719–1723," *Southwestern Historical Quarterly*, XLIX (October, 1945), 193–214, for some newer insights; and an interesting aspect is covered in Charmion Clair Shelby, "Efforts to Finance the Aguayo Expedition: A Study in Frontier Financial Administration in New Spain," *Hispanic American Historical Review*, XXV (February, 1945), 27–44.

[20] Buckley, *op. cit.*, pp. 60–61. "The Aguayo Expedition into Texas and Louisiana, 1719–1722."

[21] See Bancroft, *History of North Mexican States and Texas*, I, pp. 617–618.

[22] See Casteñeda, II, pp. 268–310.

[23] Retta Murphy, "The Journey of Pedro de Rivera, 1724–1728," *Southwestern Historical Quarterly*, XLI (October, 1937), 125–141.

[24] Castañeda, II, pp. 213–267; discusses the Rivera inspection of Texas at length and details its sequel, such as the removal of the Querétaran missions to the San Antonio area.

Chapter 8:   Borderland Irritants: The French and the Indians, 1700–1763

[1] See such a study as Robert M. Denhart, *The Horse of the Americas* (Norman, Okla., 1947).

[2] An overall study of the French relations with the Borderlands is Henry Folmer, *Franco-Spanish Rivalry in North America* (Glendale, Calif., 1953).

[3] Alfred Barnaby Thomas, *After Coronado* (Norman, Okla., 1935) has gathered many documents on this period and has introduced them with an excellent summary essay.

[4] See John Francis McDermott, ed., *Old Cahokia* (Saint Louis, 1949).

[5] Clarence W. Alvord, *The Illinois Country, 1673–1818* (Springfield, Ill., 1920), is still the best overall account of the French in the middle Mississippi Valley; also useful is John Anthony Caruso, *The Mississippi Valley Frontier* (Indianapolis, 1966), which updates the story.

[6] Much of this scattered data has been gathered by Noel M. Loomis and Abraham P. Nasatir, *Pedro Vial and the Roads to Santa Fe* (Norman, Okla., 1967).

[7] Thomas, *After Coronado.*

[8] On Du Tisné see Caruso and Loomis-Nasatir.

[9] See Thomas, *After Coronado.*

[10] Alfred Barnaby Thomas, "The Massacre of the Villasur Expedition at the Forks of the Platte River," *Nebraska History Magazine,* VII (July–September, 1924), 67–81.

[11] See Chapter 7 of the present book.

[12] For general coverage of Rivera, see Retta Murphy, "The Journey of Pedro Rivera, 1724–1728," *Southwestern Historical Quarterly,* XLI (October, 1937), 125–141.

[13] Henry Folmer, *Franco-Spanish Rivalry,* also "Étienne Véniard de Bourgmond in the Missouri Country," *Missouri Historical Review,* XXXVI (April, 1942), 279–298, and "Contraband Trade between Louisiana and New Mexico in the Eighteenth Century," *New Mexico Historical Review,* XVI (July, 1941), 249–274; also Marc Villiers du Terrage, *Le Découverte du Missouri* (Paris, 1925).

[14] Gilbert J. Garraghan, "Fort Orleans of the Missoury," *Missouri Historical Review,* XXXV (April, 1942), 373–384.

[15] Herbert E. Bolton, *Texas in the Middle Eighteenth Century: Studies in Spanish Colonial History and Administration* (Berkeley, Calif., 1915; reprinted New York, 1962), pp. 14–41.

[16] Besides Bolton's work cited above, the Texas story of these decades is sketched in Bancroft, *History of the North Mexican States and Texas* (2 vols.; San Francisco, 1884–1889) and much more fully told in Volumes II and III of Carlos E. Castañeda, *Our Catholic Heritage in Texas; 1519–1936* (7 vols.; Austin, Tex., 1936–1950); see also Morfí and Arricivita (Chapter 7, nn. 10 and 11, respectively).

[17] Castañeda, III, pp. 110–112.

[18] See Bolton, *Texas in the Middle Eighteenth Century,* pp. 135–378.

[19] William E. Dunn, "Apache Relations in Texas, 1718–1750," Texas State Historical Association *Quarterly,* XIV (January, 1911), 198–274, and "Missionary Activities among the Eastern Apaches Previous to the Founding of the San Sabá Mission," *ibid.,* XV (January, 1912), 186–200.

[20] Don Pedro Romero de Terreros was born in Spain, came to Mexico on the death of his eldest brother; remained and became wealthy thanks to his holdings in two Pachuca mines; very public-spirited and charitable; was founder of the National Pawn Shop in Mexico.

[21] William E. Dunn, "The Apache Mission on the San Sabá River: Its Founding and Failure," *Southwestern Historical Quarterly,* XVII (April, 1914), 379–414; a fuller and more recent study is Robert S. Weddle, *The San Sabá Mission: Spanish Pivot in Texas* (Austin, Tex., 1964).

[22] See Castañeda, *Our Catholic Heritage in Texas,* II, pp. 311–348, and III, pp. 107–240.

[23] Lawrence F. Hill, *José de Escandón and the Founding of Nuevo Santander: A Study in Spanish Colonization* (Columbus, Ohio, 1926).

[24] See Hill.

[25] Herbert E. Bolton, "Spanish Activities on the Lower Trinity River, 1746–1771,"

Southwestern Historical Quarterly, XVI (April, 1913), 339–377; also incorporated in *Texas in the Middle Eighteenth Century.* Castañeda, *Our Catholic Heritage in Texas,* has some newer materials on one or other point.

²⁶ Henry Folmer, "The Mallet Expedition of 1739 through Nebraska, Kansas, and Colorado to Santa Fe," *The Colorado Magazine,* XVI (September, 1939), 163–173.

²⁷ Herbert E. Bolton, "French Intrusions into New Mexico, 1749–1752," in *The Pacific Ocean in History,* edited by H. M. Stephens and H. E. Bolton (New York, 1917), pp. 389–407, and reprinted in Bannon, ed., *Bolton and the Spanish Borderlands* (Norman, Okla., 1964), pp. 150–171.

²⁸ See Alfred Barnaby Thomas, trans. and ed., *The Plains Indians and New Mexico* (Albuquerque, 1940).

Chapter 9: On to California, The Last Borderland, 1711–1784

¹ See the references to Kino in Chapter 4, n. 25.

² *Kino's Plan for the Development of Pimería Alta, Arizona and Upper California: A Report to the Mexican Viceroy,* translated and annotated by Ernest J. Burrus (Tucson, Ariz., 1961), pp. 32–33.

³ The best study of the Jesuit mission enterprise in Lower California is Peter Masten Dunne, *Black Robes in Lower California* (Berkeley, Calif., 1952); fuller bibliographical references can be found at the end of this volume. On Salvatierra, see Marguerite Eyer Wilbur's edition of Miguel Venegas, *Juan María Salvatierra of the Company of Jesus* (Cleveland, 1929); on Piccolo, see Ernest J. Burrus' edition of Francisco María Píccolo, *Informe de Estado de la nueva cristianidad de California, 1702, y otros documentos* (Madrid, 1962).

⁴ On the origins of the Pious Fund and its development in Jesuit days see Dunne, *Black Robes in Lower California, passim;* a note on the later history of the fund after it had been confiscated by the Mexican government is E. D. Burnett, "Pious Fund," in *The New Catholic Encyclopedia* (1966), XI, 379–380.

⁵ Peter Masten Dunne, "The Expulsion of the Jesuits from New Spain," *Mid-America,* XIX (January, 1937), 3–30.

⁶ Anton Huonder, *Deutsche Jesuiten missionäre des 17. und 18. Jahrhunderts* (Freiburg-im-Breisgau, 1899). See also Theodore E. Treutlein, "Non-Spanish Jesuits in Spain's American Colonies," in *Greater America,* pp. 219–242 (see Chapter 4, n. 12).

Dunne has a list of all the Jesuits serving in Lower California, Appendix V of his *Black Robes in Lower California.* During the decades referred to in the text there were a number of Hispanics as well as the foreigners: Arnés, Arnesto, Badillo, Díez, Barco, Escalante, Franco, García, Masariegos, Rondero, Rotea, Sotelo, two Trujillos, Ventura, and Villaviejo.

⁷ M. D. Krmpotic, *Life and Works of the Reverend Ferdinand Konščak, S.J., 1703–1759* (Boston, 1923).

⁸ *Wenceslaus Linck's Reports and Letters, 1762–1778,* trans. and ed. by Ernest J. Burrus (Los Angeles, 1967).

⁹ The early chapters of Charles E. Chapman, *The Founding of Spanish California: The Northwestward Expansion of New Spain, 1687–1783* (New York, 1916) are devoted to these decades and are drawn from a wide acquaintance with archival materials, some of which have not yet been printed. Very valuable for the period is John A. Donohue, *Jesuit Missions in Northwestern New Spain, 1711–1762* (unpublished doctoral dissertation, University of California-Berkeley, 1957; currently being readied for publication).

¹⁰ Peter Masten Dunne, *Jacobo Sedelmayr, Missionary, Frontiersman, Explorer* (Tucson, Ariz., 1955); this little volume contains four Sedelmayr narratives, translated, annotated, and with historical introduction. See also the same author's *Juan Antonio Balthasar, Padre Visitador to the Sonora Frontier, 1744–1745* (Tucson, Ariz., 1957),

whose longer historical introduction has much material on Sedelmayr and other frontier figures of the 1730s and 1740s.

[11] Russell C. Ewing, "The Pima Uprising of 1751: A Study of Spanish-Indian Relations on the Frontier of New Spain," in *Greater America,* pp. 259–280 (see Chapter 4, n. 12).

[12] Chapman, *The Founding of Spanish California,* pp. 36 ff., gives rather extensive notice to these Sánchez memorials.

[13] See Bancroft *History of California* (7 vols.; San Francisco, 1884–1890) Vol. I and Chapman.

[14] Herbert I. Priestley, *José de Gálvez, Visitor-General of New Spain* (Berkeley, Calif., 1916).

[15] This is a long story which, apart from mentioning the fact of the expulsion, is not truly germane to the Borderlands story. Charles III had his reasons of state for the decree of 1767 which expelled the Jesuits from Spain and the Spanish Indies, not all of which are evident even today. In a number of the mission areas, and Sonora-Arizona is a good example, the missions were completely stripped of their personnel. In northern New Spain and in the Peninsula of California, friars from several of the Mexican missionary colleges were called up to fill as many of the posts vacated as they could man. This decree of expulsion brought Fray Francisco Garcés to Pimería Alta and a distinguished historical career there; the same order led to the reassignment of Fray Junípero Serra from a northeast Mexico mission to Baja California.

[16] See Chapman, pp. 56 ff.

[17] Michael E. Thurman, *The Naval Department of San Blas* (Glendale, Calif., 1967).

[18] The most thorough of the Serra biographers is Maynard J. Geiger, *The Life and Times of Fray Junípero Serra* (2 vols.; Washington, D.C., 1959); Father Geiger has also translated and edited the contemporary biography by Serra's co-worker, Fray Francisco Palóu, *Life of Fray Junípero Serra* (Washington, D.C., 1955).

[19] See Priestley and Chapman for details of these preparations.

[20] Diaries and journals of the principal participants in the events of 1769 and 1770 (Portolá, Costansó, Vila, Fages) are translated and published in Academy of Pacific Coast History *Publications,* I and II (Berkeley, Calif., 1910–1911), by Robert S. Rose, Douglas S. Watson, and Frederick J. Teggart. Another earlier collection of documents in translation is Zoeth S. Eldredge, *The March of Portolá and Discovery of the Bay of San Francisco, the Log of the San Carlos, and Original Documents* (San Francisco, 1909).

[21] Herbert E. Bolton, *Fray Juan Crespi, Missionary Explorer* (Berkeley, Calif., 1927).

[22] A recent "Copley Book," an interesting combination of text (Richard F. Pourade), photographs (Harry Crosby), and paintings (Lloyd Hartung), traces the "epic journey of the Portolá-Serra expedition in 1769" in word and picture—*The Call to California* (San Diego, 1968).

[23] At this point it would seem appropriate to note some of the more important general histories of California. These have merit: H. H. Bancroft, *History of California* (n. 13 above); Irving B. Richman, *California under Spain and Mexico* (Boston, 1911); Charles E. Chapman, *The Founding of Spanish California, 1687–1783* (New York, 1916) has already been noted; the same author's *A History of California: The Spanish Period* (New York, 1921) carries the story beyond 1783; the following devote considerable space to the Spanish period: John W. Caughey, *California* (New York, 1940, and later editions); Andrew F. Rolle, *California: A History* (New York, 1963); Walton Bean, *California: An Interpretive History* (New York, 1968). The early chapters of W. H. Hutchinson's *California: Two Centuries of Man, Land, and Growth in the Golden State* (Palo Alto, Calif., 1969) are interesting.

[24] Literature on the missions is extensive; one of the better scholarly works is Zephyrin Engelhardt, *The Missions and Missionaries of California* (4 vols.; San Francisco, 1908–1915); Father Engelhardt also did shorter sketches on many of the individual

missions. A valuable contemporary source for the early California years, for civil as well as mission history, is Fray Francisco Palóu, *Noticias de la Nueva California,* which was completed in 1783 but not published until 1857; it was translated and edited by Herbert E. Bolton under the title *Historical Memoirs of New California* (4 vols.; Berkeley, Calif., 1926).

[25] See Bernard E. Bobb, *The Viceregency of Antonio María Bucareli in New Spain, 1771–1779* (Austin, Tex., 1962).

[26] Anza and his two expeditions to California have been studied and set down in most readable form by Herbert E. Bolton in his *Outpost of Empire: The Story of the Founding of San Francisco* (New York, 1931), which was substantially the introductory volume to his *Anza's California Expeditions* (5 vols.; Berkeley, Calif., 1930).

[27] Garcés, a most important later Borderlands figure, still awaits his biographer; meanwhile, see Elliott Coues, ed., *On the Trail of a Spanish Pioneer: The Diary and Itinerary of Francisco Garcés* (2 vols.; New York, 1900).

Chapter 10: Borderland Reorganization: The Provincias Internas

[1] Recall the Bolton study, "The Mission as a Frontier Institution" (cited in Chapter 4, n. 9).

[2] Robert M. Denhardt, *The Horse of the Americas* (Norman, Okla., 1947); Donald E. Worcester, "The Spread of Spanish Horses in the Southwest," *New Mexico Historical Review,* XX (January, 1945), 1–13.

[3] Charles E. Chapman, *The Founding of Spanish California* (New York, 1916). pp. 47–48 (cited in Chapter 9, n. 9).

[4] Jack D. Forbes, *Apache, Navaho, and Spaniard* (Norman, Okla., 1960); Frank M. Reeve, "The Apache Indians of Texas," *Southwestern Historical Quarterly,* L (October, 1946), 189–219.

[5] Alfred B. Thomas, *The Plains Indians and New Mexico, 1751–1778* (Albuquerque, 1940).

[6] See Herbert I. Priestley, *José de Gálvez, Visitor-General of New Spain, 1765–1771* (Berkeley, Calif., 1916).

[7] Vito Alessio Robles, *Nicolás de Lafora, Relación de Viaje que Hizo a los Presidios Internos Situados en la Frontera de la América Septentrional Perteneciente al Rey de España* (Mexico, 1939); Lawrence Kinnaird, *The Frontiers of New Spain: Nicolás de Lafora's Description, 1766–1768* (Berkeley, Calif., 1958). The following pages of the present book draw heavily on this report.

[8] An English translation of this important document can be found in Sidney B. Brinckerhoff and Odie B. Faulk, *Lancers for the King* (Phoenix, Ariz., 1965).

[9] See David M. Vigness, "Don Hugo Oconór and New Spain's Northeastern Frontier, 1764–1766," *Journal of the West,* VI (Spring, 1966), 27–40; Paige W. Christiansen, "Hugo Oconór's Inspection of Nueva Vizcaya and Coahuila, 1773," *Louisiana Studies,* II (Fall, 1963), 157–175; Enrique González Flores and Francisco R. Almada, eds., *Informe de Hugo de O'Conór Sobre el Estado de las Provincias Internas, 1771–1776* (Mexico, 1952).

[10] Alfred B. Thomas, *Teodoro de Croix and the Northern Frontier of New Spain, 1776–1783* (Norman, Okla., 1941); see also for the broader story of the Provincias Internas, Fernando Ocaranza, *Crónica de las Provincias Internas* (Mexico, 1939).

[11] Max L. Moorhead, *The Apache Frontier: Jacobo Ugarte y Loyola and Spanish-Indian Relations in Northern New Spain, 1769–1791* (Norman, Okla., 1968).

[12] Herbert E. Bolton, *Athanase de Mézières and the Louisiana-Texas Frontier, 1768–1780* (2 vols.; Cleveland, 1914).

[13] Charles E. Chapman, *The Founding of Spanish California* (see Chapter 9, n. 9), has much material on this project in the later chapters of the study.

[14] See Chapman, pp. 412–414; and Thomas (n. 10, above), pp. 59–60.

[15] Anza's career and accomplishments during his governorship in New Mexico are recorded in Alfred B. Thomas, *Forgotten Frontiers: A Study of the Indian Policy of Don Juan Bautista de Anza, Governor of New Mexico, 1777–1787* (Norman, Okla., 1932).

[16] Bernardo de Gálvez, *Instructions for Governing the Interior Provinces of New Spain, 1786* (Berkeley, Calif., 1951), trans. and ed. by Donald E. Worcester. A study by John W. Caughey, *Bernardo de Gálvez in Louisiana, 1770–1783* (Berkeley, Calif., 1934), gives his pre-New Spain career.

[17] See Moorhead, *The Apache Frontier.*

Chapter 11: Luisiana, A Quasi-Borderland, 1772–1800

[1] A short study of the so-called Second Hundred Years' War, of which the French and Indian War was the last American phase is the little work of A. H. Buffington, *The Second Hundred Years' War, 1689–1815* (New York, 1929); fuller and more specific is W. L. Dorn, *Competition for Empire, 1740–1763* (New York, 1940).

[2] See Z. E. Rashed, *The Peace of Paris, 1763* (Liverpool, 1951).

[3] For more detail see the standard histories of Louisiana, Alcée Fortier, Charles Gayarré, and others; also useful can be Marc Villiers du Terrage, *Les Dernières Années de la Louisiane Française* (Paris, 1903).

[4] Herbert E. Bolton, *Athanase de Mézières and the Louisiana-Texas Frontier, 1768–1780* (2 vols.; Cleveland, 1914), is the classic on this Borderlands figure.

[5] The Introduction of Abraham P. Nasatir, *Before Lewis and Clark* (2 vols.; Saint Louis, 1952), gives a fine summary of the history of the Mississippi Valley in the eighteenth century. Another is Clarence W. Alvord, *The Illinois Country, 1673–1818* (Springfield, Ill., 1922).

[6] See John Francis McDermott, ed., *The Early Histories of St. Louis* (Saint Louis, 1952); also Nasatir, *Before Lewis and Clark,* introduction.

[7] Abraham P. Nasatir, "Ducharme's Invasion of Missouri, an Incident in the Anglo-Spanish Rivalry for the Indian Trade of Upper Louisiana," *Missouri Historical Review,* XXIV (October, 1929), 3–25; (January, 1930), 238–260; (April, 1930), 420–429.

[8] See Nasatir, "Anglo-Spanish Rivalry on the Upper Missouri," *Mississippi Valley Historical Review,* XVI (December, 1929), 359–382; and (March, 1930), 420-429.

[9] Again, Nasatir is the pioneer in opening this story from the Spanish point of view; in the Introduction to his *Before Lewis and Clark,* he has summed up much of his research and publication in various historical journals—see especially pp. 58–115. A further reworking of these studies will be found in Noel M. Loomis and Abraham P. Nasatir, *Pedro Vial and the Roads to Santa Fe* (Norman, Okla., 1967), *passim* pp. 74–180.

[10] Abraham P. Nasatir, "Jacques d'Eglise in the Upper Missouri, 1791–1795," *Mississippi Valley Historical Review,* XIV (June, 1927), 47–56.

[11] See the Instruction of Carondelet to Trudeau, March 29, 1792, in Nasatir, *Before Lewis and Clark,* I, pp. 151–153. Other documents bearing on the sequel can be found in the same collection.

[12] The articles of incorporation of the Missouri Company are given in Nasatir, *Before Lewis and Clark,* I, pp. 217–228. See also Nasatir, "The Formation of the Missouri Company," *Missouri Historical Review,* XV (October, 1922), 10–22, and "Jacques Clamorgan: Colonial Promoter of the Northern Border of New Spain," *New Mexico Historical Review* (April, 1942), 101–112.

[13] Nasatir, "John Evans, Explorer and Surveyor," *Missouri Historical Review,* XXV (January, 1931), 219–239; (April, 1931), 432–460; (July, 1931), 585–608.

[14] On Pedro Vial see Loomis and Nasatir, *Pedro Vial and the Roads to Santa Fe,* which has the diaries of his several treks through the Borderlands which will be noticed at greater length in the sequel.

[15] This story is detailed in Chapter 9 of the present book.

[16] A full account of this expedition is found in the study by Herbert E. Bolton,

Pageant in the Wilderness: The Story of the Escalante Expedition to the Interior Basin (Salt Lake City, Utah, 1950).

[17] Bernardo de Gálvez, *Instructions for Governing the Interior Provinces of New Spain, 1786* (Berkeley, Calif., 1951), trans. and ed. by Donald E. Worcester.

[18] The best account of these years is Arthur P. Whitaker, *The Spanish-American Frontier, 1783–1795* (Boston, 1927).

[19] Samuel F. Bemis, *Pinckney's Treaty* (New Haven, Conn., rev. 1960); see also Arthur P. Whitaker, "New Light on the Treaty of San Lorenzo: An Essay in Historical Criticism," *Mississippi Valley Historical Review*, XV (March, 1929), 435–454; and "Godoy's Knowledge of the Terms of Jay's Treaty," *American Historical Review*, XXXV (July, 1930), 804–810; Whitaker's fuller study of this matter and the next years is excellent, *The Mississippi Question, 1795–1803* (New York, 1934).

[20] See Whitaker, *The Mississippi Question, 1795–1803.*

[21] James A. James, "Louisiana as a Factor in American Diplomacy, 1795–1800," *Mississippi Valley Historical Review*, I (June, 1914), 44–56.

[22] Arthur P. Whitaker, "France and the American Deposit at New Orleans," *Hispanic American Historical Review*, XI (November, 1931), 485–502.

Chapter 12: Spain's Last Years in the Borderlands, 1783-1821

[1] Arthur P. Whitaker, *The Spanish-American Frontier 1783–1795* (New York, 1927) is still the best study of this area during the years indicated.

[2] Lawrence Kinnaird, "American Penetration into Spanish Louisiana," in *New Spain and the Anglo-American West* (2 vols.; Lancaster, Pa., 1923), I, pp. 211–238.

[3] For the treaty and its diplomatic background see Samuel F. Bemis, *Pinckney's Treaty* (New Haven; revised, 1960); for the treaty and its sequel in the Mississippi Valley see Arthur P. Whitaker, *The Mississippi Question, 1795–1803* (New York, 1934).

[4] See Whitaker, *The Mississippi Question.*

[5] The threat of war with Great Britain grew out of the Nootka Sound controversy, which will be noted later in this chapter.

[6] Isaac J. Cox, *The West Florida Controversy, 1798–1813* (Baltimore, 1918).

[7] For a fuller treatment of the East Florida story see Herbert B. Fuller, *The Purchase of Florida: Its History and Diplomacy* (Cleveland, 1906).

[8] Marquis James, *Andrew Jackson, The Border Captain* (Indianapolis, 1933).

[9] Philip C. Brooks, *Diplomacy and the Borderlands: The Adams-Onís Treaty of 1819* (Berkeley, Calif., 1939).

[10] Refer again to Kinnaird (n. 2).

[11] E. E. Hale, "The Real Philip Nolan," *Publications* of the Mississippi Historical Society, IV (1901); Grace King, "The Real Philip Nolan," *Publications* of the Louisiana Historical Society, X (1917).

[12] James R. Jacobs, *Tarnished Warrior: Major General James Wilkinson* (New York, 1938).

[13] See the edition of *Pichardo's Treatise on the Limits of Louisiana and Texas*, by Charles W. Hackett (4 vols.; Austin, Tex., 1931–1946), for data on this boundary dispute.

[14] For these and subsequent events in Texas of the next years one may refer to the second volume of H. H. Bancroft, *History of the North Mexican States and Texas* (2 vols.; San Francisco, 1884–1889); to Rupert N. Richardson, *Texas: The Lone Star State* (2d ed.; New York, 1958). Two more specific period studies are Julia Kathryn Garrett, *Green Flag over Texas: A Story of the Last Years of Spain in Texas* (New York and Dallas, 1939), and Odie B. Faulk, *The Last Years of Spanish Texas, 1778–1821* (The Hague, 1964).

[15] For some help in the attempt to untangle the Burr story, reference can be made to Walter F. McCaleb, *The Aaron Burr Conspiracy* (New York, 1903), and to Thomas P. Abernathy, *The Burr Conspiracy* (New York, 1954).

[16] See Bancroft, Garrett, and Faulk for more details.

[17] Walter F. McCaleb, "The First Period of the Gutiérrez-Magee Expedition," *Texas State Historical Association Quarterly*, IV (January, 1901), 218–229; Elizabeth H. West, ed., "Diary of José Bernardo Gutiérrez de Lara, 1811–1812," *American Historical Review*, XXXIV (October, 1928), 55–77, and (January, 1929), 281–294; Harry M. Henderson, "The Magee-Gutiérrez Expedition," *Southwestern Historical Quarterly*, LV (July, 1951), 43–61; Rie Jarrett, *Gutiérrez de Lara, Mexican-Texan* (Austin, Tex., 1949).

[18] See Garrett and Faulk for a fuller treatment.

[19] The background for this venture and of the father is well told in the biography of the son, Eugene C. Barker, *The Life of Stephen F. Austin, Founder of Texas, 1793–1836* (Nashville and Dallas, 1926).

[20] Charles A. Bacarisse, "Baron de Bastrop," *Southwestern Historical Quarterly*, LVIII (January, 1955), 319–330.

[21] Much on the last Spanish years can be gleaned from Virginia H. Taylor and Juanita Hammons, *Letters of Antonio Martínez, Last Spanish Governor of Texas, 1817–1822* (Austin, Tex., 1957).

[22] On these developments of 1820–1821 in Mexico see William S. Robertson, *Iturbide of Mexico* (Durham, N. C., 1952).

[23] Louis Houck, *A History of Missouri* (3 vols.; Chicago, 1908), especially Volume I; see also Houck *The Spanish Regime in Missouri* (2 vols; Chicago, 1909); and even more valuable are several chapters of Noel M. Loomis and Abraham P. Nasatir, *Pedro Vial and the Roads to Santa Fe* (Norman, Okla., 1967), which, as noted previously, covers much more than the journeyings of Vial.

[24] Lansing B. Bloom, "The Death of Jacques d'Eglise," *New Mexico Historical Review*, II (October, 1927), 369–379.

[25] Loomis and Nasatir, *Pedro Vial*, pp. 181–204. The literature on the Lewis and Clark expedition is considerable; for refresher purposes, if needed in this connection, the very readable account by John Bakeless, *Lewis and Clark* (New York, 1947) is suggested.

[26] Clarence E. Carter, "Burr-Wilkinson Intrigues in St. Louis," *Missouri Historical Society Bulletin*, X (July, 1954).

[27] W. Eugene Hollon, *The Lost Pathfinder: Zebulon Montgomery Pike* (Norman, Okla., 1949); Elliott Coues, ed., *The Expeditions of Zebulon Montgomery Pike to the Headwaters of the Mississippi River* (3 vols.; New York, 1895) covers the earlier Pike explorations in the Mississippi Valley; Isaac J. Cox "Opening the Santa Fe Trail," *Missouri Historical Review*, XXV (January, 1930), 30–66, despite its possibly misleading title, deals with Pike.

[28] Isaac J. Cox, "Explorations of the Louisiana Frontier, 1803–1806," *American Historical Association Annual Report for 1904* (Washington, D.C., 1905).

[29] Harold A. Bierck, Jr., "Dr. John Hamilton Robinson," *Louisiana Historical Quarterly*, XXV (July, 1942), 644–669.

[30] The Pike papers were discovered a century after their confiscation by Herbert E. Bolton during one of his many forays into the Archivo General, Mexico, and in 1925 were returned to the United States government.

[31] Abraham P. Nasatir, "Jacques Clamorgan: Colonial Promoter of the Northern Border of New Spain," *New Mexico Historical Review*, XVII (April, 1942), 101–112.

[32] See Loomis and Nasatir, *Pedro Vial*, pp. 246–261.

[33] Frank B. Golley, "James Baird, Early Santa Fe Trader," *Missouri Historical Society Bulletin*, XV (April, 1959), 171–193.

[34] Thomas M. Marshall, ed., "The Journals of Jules de Mun," *Missouri Historical Society Collections*, V (1927–1928), 167–208 and 311–326.

[35] H. H. Bancroft, *History of Arizona and New Mexico* (San Francisco, 1889) has an interesting chapter "Last Years of Spanish Rule, 1801–1822"; see also Warren A.

Beck, *New Mexico* (Norman, Okla., 1962) and Paul Horgan *Great River: The Rio Grande in North American History* (2 vols.; New York, 1954), I, pp. 390–442, for these last Spanish years.

[36] Data on this dependence on the Chihuahua merchants runs through Max L. Moorhead's fine study, *New Mexico's Royal Road: Trade and Travel on the Chihuahua Trail* (Norman, Okla., 1958).

[37] For the Pino story and report see Bancroft, *History of Arizona and New Mexico* (San Francisco, 1889), pp. 287–307 *passim*.

[38] Little attention has been paid to the last Spanish years in Arizona; documentation is slim, as Bancroft, *History of Arizona and New Mexico,* noted long ago. However, the bits have been gathered into a short study by Sidney B. Brinckerhoff, "The Last Years of Spanish Arizona, 1786–1821," *Arizona and the West,* IX (Spring, 1967), 5–20.

[39] Bernardo de Gálvez, *Instructions for Governing the Interior Provinces of New Spain, 1786,* trans. and ed. by Donald E. Worcester (Berkeley, Calif., 1951)

[40] Refer to the general histories of California noted in Chapter 9 (n. 23): Bancroft, Chapman, Richman, Caughey, Rolle, Bean, Hutchinson.

[41] Maynard J. Geiger, *The Life and Times of Fray Junípero Serra* (2 vols.; Washington, D.C., 1959).

[42] Until publication of Father Francis Guest's biography of Lasuén the inquiring reader will have to be content with Finbar Kenneally, *Fermín Francisco de Lasuén: Writings* (2 vols.; Washington, D.C., 1965) and Zephyrin Engelhardt, *The Missions and Missionaries of California* (4 vols.; San Francisco, 1908–1915), and other data from the general histories.

[43] Jean François de la Pérouse, *Voyage de La Pérouse autour du Monde* (4 vols.; Paris, 1797); a recent version of the California segment is Gilbert Chinard, ed., *Le Voyage de Lapérouse sur les côtes de l'Alaska et de la Californie* (Baltimore, 1937).

[44] Donald C. Cutter, *Malaspina in California* (San Francisco, 1960); E. Boni, *Malaspina* (Rome, 1935); Edith C. Galbraith, "Malaspina's Voyage Around the World," *California Historical Society Quarterly,* III (October, 1924), 215–237.

[45] George Vancouver, *A Voyage of Discovery to the North Pacific Ocean and Round the World* (3 vols.; London, 1798); the California section has been reprinted and annotated in Marguerite Eyer Wilbur, ed., *Vancouver in California, 1792–1794* (Los Angeles, 1953). Biographical: George Godwin, *Vancouver: A Life, 1757–1798* (London, 1930); G. H. Anderson, *Vancouver and His Great Voyage* (London, 1923).

[46] For the background and the subsequent diplomatic maneuverings, see William R. Manning, "The Nootka Sound Controversy," American Historical Association *Annual Report for 1904* (Washington, D.C., 1905).

[47] Henry R. Wagner, *The Last Spanish Exploration of the Northwest Coast and the Attempt to Colonize Bodega Bay* (San Francisco, 1930).

[48] Adele Ogden, *The California Sea Otter Trade, 1784–1848* (Berkeley, Calif., 1941).

[49] Adele Ogden, "New England Traders in Spanish and Mexican California," in *Greater America: Essays in Honor of Herbert Eugene Bolton* (Berkeley, Calif., 1945), pp. 395–415.

[50] See the special issue of the California Historical Society *Quarterly,* XII (September, 1933), which contains a bibliography and articles by Adele Ogden, E. O. Essig, and Clarence J. Du Four. Also T. C. Russell, ed., *The Rezanov Voyage to Nueva California in 1806* (San Francisco, 1926); also edited by Russell is *Langsdorff's Narrative of the Rezanov Voyage to Nueva California in 1806* (San Francisco, 1927). Bibliographical: Hector Chevigny, *Lost Empire: The Life and Adventures of Nikolai Petrovich Rezanov* (New York, 1937); Gertrude Atherton, *Rezanov* (New York, 1906).

[51] For background on Bouchard, see Ricardo Caillet-Bois, *Nuestros Corsarios: Brown y Bouchard en el Pacífico, 1815–1816* (Buenos Aires, 1930); and Lewis Bealer, "Bouchard in the Islands of the Pacific," *Pacific Historical Quarterly,* IV (August, 1935), 328–342.

BIBLIOGRAPHICAL NOTES

The time span of this volume runs through three centuries, and the area covered is as broad as the United States—from Florida to California, with some of the North Mexican states thrown in for good measure. The range of materials is extensive and they themselves widely scattered. The Spaniards, it will be remembered, were great record makers, a fact which is both heartening and yet maddening to the historian.

To list the many collections of materials pertaining to the Borderlands could become a gigantic undertaking. Suffice it here simply to note a few of the principal archives and depositories. At the head of the list must come the archives of Mexico and of Spain, notably Mexico's Archivo General de la Nacion (AGN) and Spain's Archivo General de Indias (AGI). In the United States two libraries are outstanding: the Bancroft Library of the University of California at Berkeley and the Library of the University of Texas at Austin. Other libraries have valuable and important collections: by way of example, the John Carter Brown Library of Brown University and the Newberry Library (Ayer Collection) at Chicago. Note should also be made of the Hispanic Foundation holdings in the Library of Congress. State and local libraries in the Borderlands area are often proud possessors of materials for their specific region, and many are supplementing existing holdings with extensive photocopy collections.

The pages that follow are organized, generally, on a geographic basis, although in a few instances topical headings have been used. There has been no attempt to have the several sections support an individual chapter of the text, save in one or other instance. Geographical groupings seemed to be the more manageable method; however, within the regions there has often been an attempt to follow a rough chronological pattern. This bibliography makes no claim to being exhaustive, or even nearly so. It is hoped that, incomplete though it is, it may be helpful, and reasonably exact.

The Borderlands: General

The great name in the Borderlands is that of Herbert E. Bolton. He may not have been the pioneer in the strict sense; men like H. H. Bancroft, Bandelier, Lummis, were interested before him; but Bolton, more than anyone else, deserves credit for opening the field to students of "American" history. He had done considerable writing and much inspired teaching by 1921, the year in which his little volume *The Spanish Borderlands: A Chronicle of Old Florida and the Southwest* (New Haven, 1921) appeared as Volume 23 of the Chronicles of America series. This study set the name for the area. Bolton's interest continued to his death, in 1953; but it was largely through his students that Borderlands studies grew and expanded; today some of the younger writers are third-generation Boltonians. In

1939 four of Bolton's broad studies were gathered in the volume *Wider Horizons of American History* (New York, 1939); a quarter-century later John Francis Bannon chose several of these and added others, published and unpublished, in *Bolton and the Spanish Borderlands* (Norman, Okla., 1964).

Bolton was honored by his students with two *Festschrift* presentations. The senior members of the "first generation" prepared *New Spain and the Anglo-American West* (2 vols.; Lancaster, Pa.; privately printed, 1932); The junior members of the same "first generation" honored him with *Greater America—Essays in Honor of Herbert Eugene Bolton* (Berkeley, Calif., 1945). These collections have many pieces on the Borderlands; the second also contains an extensive listing of the writings of all Bolton's masters and doctors down to 1945 and can serve as the basis for a quite extensive bibliography on the Borderlands. Many of the studies from these two works are listed in proper place in the following pages of the Bibliographical Notes, but not all of them.

One recent short study which views the Borderlands in broad perspective and which deserves greater notice is Donald J. Lehmer, "The Second Frontier: The Spanish," in *The American West: An Appraisal,* edited by Robert G. Ferris (Santa Fe, 1963), pp. 141–150. The volume in which it apears is one of three published by the Western History Association in which are gathered some of the papers of the WHA annual conferences, at Santa Fe (1961), Denver (1962), and San Francisco (1967): *Probing the American West* (Santa Fe, 1962); *The American West: An Appraisal* (Santa Fe, 1963); and *Reflections of Western Historians* (Tucson, Ariz., 1968). There are some Borderlands articles in these three collections. *The American West* devoted its Summer 1966 number (III) to a series of Borderland studies; *The Journal of the West* did the same with its January 1969 number (VIII). Periodically the *Southwestern Historical Quarterly* has built numbers around a central theme, on occasion of Borderland pertinence.

Several of the regional histories of the Southwest have sizable sections on the colonial Borderlands. Worthy of note are W. Eugene Hollon, *The Southwest: Old and New* (New York, 1961); Lynn Perrigo, *Our Spanish Southwest* (Dallas, 1960); Odie B. Faulk, *Land of Many Frontiers: A History of the American Southwest* (New York, 1968); Green Peyton, *America's Heartland: The Southwest* (Norman, Okla., 1948); Rupert N. Richardson and Carl C. Rister, *The Greater Southwest* (Glendale, Calif., 1934). The state histories, too, have sections on the colonial period; these are noted in proper place later in these Notes. And it hardly seems necessary to remind the reader of the many volumes with Borderland pertinence in the *Works* of Hubert Howe Bancroft; these, too, are noted in proper place.

A valuable geographic aid to an understanding of the Borderlands is the first volume of Carl I. Wheat, *Mapping the Trans-Mississippi West* (5 vols.; San Francisco, 1957–1958), entitled "The Spanish Entrada to the Louisiana Purchase, 1540–1804."

The Borderlands: Bibliographies and Guides

The classic, listing the older works, is Henry R. Wagner, *The Spanish Southwest* (2 vols.; Albuquerque, 1937, and recent reprint). Oakah L. Jones, Jr., "The Spanish Borderlands: A Selected Reading List," *The Journal of the West,* VIII

(January, 1969), is useful and recalls many of the important works and adds a number of journal-article references. Odie B. Faulk has gathered a valuable and varied list in "A Bibliographical Note," in his *Land of Many Frontiers* (New York, 1968).

Attention should be called to some of the more restricted regional and the state bibliographies. Texas: C. W. Raines, *A Bibliography of Texas* (Austin, 1896, and reprint) is old but still useful; John H. Jenkins, *Cracker Barrel Chronicles: A Bibliography of Texas Towns and County Histories* (Austin, 1965) will have some help; the same can be said for Thomas W. Streeter, *Bibliography of Texas, 1795–1845* (Cambridge, Mass., 1955). New Mexico: Lyle Saunders, *A Guide to Materials Bearing on Cultural Relations in New Mexico* (Albuquerque, 1944). Arizona: Hector Alliot, *Bibliography of Arizona* (Los Angeles, 1914), early but helpful; Andrew Wallace, *Sources and Readings in Arizona History*. California: Robert E. and Robert G. Cowan, *A Bibliography of the History of California, 1510–1930* (3 vols.; San Francisco, 1933); Ethel Blumann and Mabel W. Thomas, *California Local History: A Centennial Bibliography* (2 vols., Stanford, 1950). Regional: Jesse L. Rader, *South of Forty, from the Mississippi to the Rio Grande: A Bibliography* (Norman, Okla., 1947); Lawrence C. Powell, *Southwestern Book Trails* (Albuquerque, 1963); J. Frank Dobie, *Guide to Life and Literature in the Southwest* (Dallas, 1965); all of these have limited value for the present study.

It seems almost superfluous to remind the interested reader that the great introduction to the Mexican archives is Herbert E. Bolton, *Guide to Materials for the History of the United States in the Principal Archives of Mexico* (Washington, 1913). Other volumes in the Carnegie Institute of Washington Guide to Materials . . . series can offer some leads to Borderland history: see Charles M. Andrews (English archives); William R. Shepherd (Spanish archives); Luis Marino Perez (Cuban archives); Carl Russell Fish (Italian archives); David W. Parker (Washington, D.C., archives); Frank A. Golder (Russian archives); and James A. Robertson (Spanish archives in print or transcript).

Note should be taken of Philip M. Hamer, *A Guide to Archives and Manuscripts in the United States* (New Haven, 1961). Two of the great libraries for Borderlands history are publishing guides to their collections: *A Guide to the Manuscript Collections of the Bancroft Library* (one volume to date) is being developed by George P. Hammond and members of the Bancroft staff; and Chester V. Kielman has compiled *The University of Texas Archives: A Guide to the Historical Manuscript Collections of the University of Texas;* this volume has 2430 entries and a very helpful index.

A somewhat unexpected source of Borderland bibliographical information, as well as biographical data on individual scholars, is the series of dedicatory sketches appearing in each number of *Arizona and the West*. A scholar is briefly memorialized and the principal of his contributions listed; also—and this is highly valuable —there is a photograph of each Borderlander so honored. In late decades the *Hispanic American Historical Review* has also published extensive obituary notices, regularly with bibliography, of Latin Americanists; a number of these qualify as Borderlanders. Another source of individual bibliographical information is the *Festschrift* volume: Bolton was honored twice; George P. Hammond was honored by the Friends of the Bancroft Library, with *GPH: An Informal Record* (Berkeley, Calif., 1965).

Indians of the Borderlands

The Indian is one of the principals in the Borderlands story. A few of the many studies will be listed here. Two fundamental works are Frederick W. Hodge, *Handbook of the American Indians North of Mexico* (2 vols.; Washington, 1907–1910), and J. R. Swanton, *The American Indian Tribes of North America* (Washington, 1952). See also Harold E. Driver, *Indians of North America* (Chicago, 1961), and Clark Wissler, *The American Indian* (New York, 1922). Elaborate is Allen M. Josephy, ed., *The American Heritage Book of Indians,* with text by William Brandon (New York, 1961). Indian life in the so-called Southwest is ancient and has won considerable scholarly attention: Edgar L. Hewitt, *Ancient Life in the American Southwest* (Indianapolis, 1930); Harold S. Gladwin, *A History of the Ancient Southwest* (Portland, Maine, 1957); Edward E. Dale, *Indians of the Southwest* (Norman, Okla., 1949).

Some studies of individual nations or families: Gordon Baldwin, *The Warrior Apaches* (Tucson, Ariz., 1966); C. L. Sonnichson, *The Mescalero Apaches* (Norman, Olka., 1958); Dan L. Thrapp, *The Conquest of the Apachería* (Norman, Okla., 1967). Rupert N. Richardson, *Comanche Barrier to South Plains Settlement* (Glendale, Calif., 1943); Ernest Wallace and E. A. Hoebel, *The Comanches: Lords of the Southern Plains* (Norman, Okla., 1952). Ruth M. Underhill, *The Navajos* (Norman, Olka., 1956). Adolph Bandelier and Edgar L. Hewitt, *Indians of the Rio Grande Valley* (Albuquerque, 1937). Jack D. Forbes, *Warriors of the Colorado* (Norman, Okla., 1956). C. D. Forde, *Ethnography of the Yuma Indians* (Berkeley, Calif., 1928). Alfred L. Kroeber, *Handbook of the Indians of California* (Washington, 1925); R. F. Heizer and M. A. Whipple, *The California Indians: A Source Book* (Berkeley, Calif., 1951); John W. Caughey, ed., *The Indians of Southern California* (San Marino, Calif., 1952); Harry C. James, *The Cahuilla Indians* (Los Angeles, 1960).

Note should be taken of two interesting and thought-provoking works on the Indians of the Borderlands: Edward H. Spicer, *Cycles of Conquest: The Impact of Spain, Mexico, and the United States on the Indians of the Southwest* (Tucson, Ariz., 1962), and Jack D. Forbes, *Apache, Navaho and Spaniard* (Norman, Okla., 1960).

No attempt has been made herein to notice the wealth of shorter studies appearing in the journals. However, in the following sections often one or other pertinent article will be listed.

The Conquistador Explorers

Interest in and the consequent bibliography on the conquistadores have become considerable. Many of the conquistadores and much of the bibliography have only marginal pertinence to the Borderlands story. Several of the men and the expeditions with which they were connected do form part of this story; only these will be recalled here in any detail.

One or two general studies can be noted, however. The volume in the Chronicles of America series, Irving B. Richman, *The Spanish Conquerors* (New Haven, 1919), sketches the careers of the principal conquistadores operating in North America; F. A. Kirkpatrick, *The Spanish Conquistadores* (London, 1934; paperback reprint, Cleveland, 1962) is broader in coverage. A perceptive analysis of the conquistador type is Jean Descola, *The Conquistadors* (trans., New York, 1957); Irwin R. Blacker and Harry M. Rosen, *The Golden Conquistadores* (Indianapolis, 1960), have made sizable selections from documents of the period and added introductions and commentaries to form a pleasantly readable account of the North American conquistadores; and John Francis Bannon has collected views, contemporary and later, to lay the basis for an answer to the question *The Conquistadores: Men or Devils?* (New York, 1960).

The recent work of Carl O. Sauer, *The Early Spanish Main* (Berkeley, Calif., 1966) can lay the background for the conquest of the mainland. Works on the conquest of Mexico and biographies of Hernán Cortés are numerous, but only marginally pertinent. Prescott's *The Conquest of Mexico* (many editions) is classic; so, too, is Bernal Díaz del Castillo's *Verdadera Historia de la Conquista de México,* which has appeared in many editions and translations. Pedro de Alvarado has some remote connection with the Borderlands; therefore, see J. E. Kelley, *Pedro de Alvarado, Conquistador* (New York, 1933); and Mack Taylor, *Impetuous Alvarado* (Dallas, 1936).

The early northward movement up the west coast of Mexico is the subject of Carl O. Sauer, *The Road to Cíbola* (Berkeley, Calif., 1932). Donald E. Chipman has done recent research on Nuño de Guzmán: *Nuño de Guzmán and the Province of Pánuco, 1518–1533* (Glendale, Calif., 1967), and "New Light on the Career of Nuño Beltrán de Guzmán," *The Americas,* XIX (April, 1963), 341–348.

The next men into the "western" Borderlands were the survivors of the Narváez expedition; Cabeza de Vaca was their historian. His *Relación* was first published, in Spain, in 1542 and another followed in 1555; it subsequently found its way into Italian, then into English (*Purchas His Pilgrimes,* in 1613), into French, and, after numerous Spanish reprintings, again into English. Buckingham Smith did the first full English translation, which was revised by John Gilmary Shea. Frederick W. Hodge included this revised version in the Original Narratives of Early American History series: Hodge and Lewis, "The Narrative of Alvar Núñez Cabeza de Vaca," *Spanish Explorers in Southern United States, 1528–1543* (New York, 1907). Fanny Bandelier did a translation which her husband Adolph edited; it was first published in 1905 and was a 1922 reissue, *The Journey of Cabeza de Vaca from Florida to the Pacific, 1528–1536.* Cleve Hallenbeck used much of the *Relación* and sought to improve on the delineation of the route as sketched by Bethel Coopwood, "The Route of Cabeza de Vaca in Texas," Texas State Historical Association *Quarterly,* III, and IV (July, 1899, to July, 1900)—Hallenbeck, *Alvar Núñez Cabeza de Vaca: The Journey and Route of the First European to Cross the Continent of North America* (Glendale, Calif., 1940). The most recent edition of the several versions and with useful notes is Cyclone Covey, *Cabeza de Vaca's Adventures in the Unknown Interior of America* (New York, 1961). Some Cabeza de Vaca materials come into the Marcos de Niza discussion and debate. Morris Bishop, *The Odyssey of Cabeza de Vaca* (New York, 1933), is a popularly written biography.

Fray Marcos de Niza a few decades back became the center of some interesting and stormy controversy. Percy M. Baldwin, "Fray Marcos de Niza's Relación," *New Mexico Historical Review,* I (April, 1926), 193–223, offered the basic document; George P. Hammond and Agapito Rey added other materials in their *Narratives of the Coronado Expedition* (Albuquerque, 1940); Father Bonaventure

Oblasser offered another translation, *Fray Marcos' Own Personal Narrative* (privately printed; Topawa, Ariz., 1939).

But in the meantime the battle had been joined. Carl O. Sauer, *The Road to Cíbola* (Berkeley, Calif., 1932), questioned Marcos' veracity in reporting; Henry R. Wagner sought to give a detailed study, "Fray Marcos de Niza," *New Mexico Historical Review,* IX (April, 1934), 184–227. Sauer came back to the question in his "Discovery of New Mexico Reconsidered," *New Mexico Historical Review,* XII (July, 1937), 270–287, and "The Credibility of the Fray Marcos Account," *ibid.,*. XVI (July, 1941), 233–243. Lansing Bloom challenged some of Sauer's contentions in "Who Discovered New Mexico?" *ibid.,* XV (April, 1940), 101–132. Mabel Farnum, *The Seven Golden Cities* (Milwaukee, 1943), was sympathetic to Fray Marcos; George J. Undreiner, "Fray Marcos de Niza and His Journey to Cíbola," *The Americas,* III (April, 1947), 415–486, also was sympathetic, and in a more scholarly fashion. Cleve Hallenbeck, *The Journey of Fray Marcos de Niza* (Dallas, 1949), strives for a balanced view.

For the viceroy who sent out both Marcos de Niza and Coronado see Arthur S. Aiton, *Antonio de Mendoza, First Viceroy of New Spain* (Durham, N.C., 1927). The first major publication of the Coronado materials was George P. Winship ed., *The Journey of Coronado, 1540–1542 From the City of Mexico to the Grand Canyon of the Colorado and the Buffalo Plains of Texas, Kansas and Nebraska* (New York, 1904); much better and with added materials is George P. Hammond and Agapito Rey, eds., *Narratives of the Coronado Expedition* (Albuquerque, 1940). The best full-dress biography is Herbert E. Bolton, *Coronado, Knight of Pueblos and Plains* (New York, 1949); A. Grove Day, *Coronado's Quest* (Berkeley, Calif., 1940), limits itself primarily to the expedition. These two works can be used as guides to the various journal articles on aspects of the expedition. Arthur S. Aiton, *The Muster Roll and Equipment of the Expedition of Francisco Vásquez de Coronado* (Ann Arbor, Mich., 1939), is an enlightening little study. Fray Angelico Chavez has published a most interesting work, *Coronado's Friars* (Washington, 1968); Paul J. Foik, "Fray Juan de Padilla," *Mid-America,* XIII (October, 1930), 132–140, sketches the story of one of them, the first martyr within the territorial boundaries of the United States, in Kansas.

The fundamental documents for the De Soto expedition can be found in the following editions: Edward G. Bourne, ed., *Narratives of the Career of Hernando de Soto in the Conquest of Florida* (2 vols.; New York, 1904); the Buckingham Smith translation, "The Narrative of Hernando de Soto, by the Gentleman of Elvas," in F. W. Hodge and T. H. Lewis, *Spanish Explorers in the Southern United States, 1528–1543* (New York, 1907); James A. Robertson, ed., *True Relation of the Hardships Suffered by Governor Fernando de Soto and Portuguese Gentlemen during the Discovery of the Province of Florida, Now Newly Set Forth by a Gentleman of Elvas* (Deland, Fla., 1932). De Soto still awaits a first-rate biography; there are two, neither of which is wholly adequate: R. B. Cunninghame-Graham, *Hernando de Soto* (London, 1903), and Theodore Maynard, *De Soto and the Conquistadores* (New York, 1930). The questions connected with the discovery of the Mississippi are studied by Jean Delanglez, "El Río del Espíritu Santo," *Mid-America,* several articles in XV (July, October, 1943) and XVI (January, April, July, 1944); see also Barbara Boston, "The 'De Soto Map'", *ibid.,* XIII (July, 1941), 236–250. Of interest is Francis Borgia Steck, "Neglected Aspects of the

De Soto Expedition," *Mid-America*, V (July, 1932), 3–26. The follow-up of the expedition is studied by Rex W. Strickland, "Moscoso's Journey through Texas," *Southwestern Historical Quarterly*, XLVI (October, 1942), and J. W. Williams, "Moscoso's Trail in Texas," *ibid.*, 138–157.

For the explorations of the Pacific side of the continent, see Maurice G. Holmes, *From New Spain by Sea to the Californias, 1519–1668* (Glendale, Calif., 1963); and especially Henry R. Wagner, *Spanish Voyages to the Northwest Coast of America in the Sixteenth Century* (San Francisco, 1928). Wagner has two volumes on *Cartography of the Northwest Coast of America to 1800* (Berkeley, Calif., 1937). Wagner also has done the biography *Juan Rodríguez Cabrillo, Discoverer of the Coast of California* (San Francisco, 1941). The original record of the Cabrillo expedition has been translated and edited by Herbert E. Bolton in *Spanish Exploration in the Southwest, 1542–1706* (New York, 1916).

At this point the little volume of Bolton, *The Spanish Borderlands* (New Haven, 1921), should again be recalled; it is a most readable survey of the main figures and principal exploits of this early period of the Borderland story.

The Floridas

Under this head will be listed the bibliography for the broader area of the southeastern United States—Florida, Georgia, South Carolina—the region which the Spaniards often designated in the plural, "Las Floridas." Two general treatments are the two volumes of Woodbury Lowery, *The Spanish Settlements within the Present Limits of the United States, 1513–1561* (New York, 1901) and *The Spanish Settlements within the Present Limits of the United States, 1562–1574* (New York, 1905); and Michael Kenny, *The Romance of the Floridas* (Milwaukee, 1934). Broad, too, in coverage is Andrés G. Barcía, *Ensayo cronológico para la historia general de la Florida, 1512–1722* (Madrid, 1723), which has recently been translated by Anthony Kerrigan as *Barcía's Chronological History of the Continent of Florida* (Gainesville, Fla., 1951).

Florida Victor F. O'Daniel, *Dominicans in Early Florida* (New York, 1930), tells the story of the evangelization attempt of Luis Cancer and his companions. Herbert I. Priestley chronicled the Luna-Villafañe venture in *Tristán de Luna: Conquest of the Old South—A Study of Spanish Imperial Strategy* (Glendale, Calif., 1936), building on his publication of *The Luna Papers* (2 vols.; Deland, Fla., 1929). For the French see Jeannette Thurber Connor, *Jean Ribaut, The True Relation of the Discovery of Terra Florida* (Deland, Fla., 1927); Jean Ribaut, *A Whole and True Discoverye of Terra Florida* (London, 1563; facsimile reprint, Gainesville, Fla., 1964); Antonine Tibesar, "A Spy's Report on the Expedition of Jean Ribaut to Florida, 1565," *The Americas*, XI (April, 1955), 589–592.

General Rembert W. Patrick, *Florida under Five Flags* (Gainesville, 1945). Ecclesiastical: Michael V. Gannon, *The Cross in the Sand: The Early Catholic Church in Florida, 1513–1870* (Gainesville, Fla., 1965); Kenny, *The Romance of the Floridas*, covers the Jesuit period; Maynard Geiger, *The Franciscan Conquest of Florida, 1573–1618* (Washington, 1937), tells the early story of the friars; John Gilmary Shea, *The Catholic Church in Colonial Days* (2 vols.; New York, 1883), has much on the Florida story. The Spanish founder: Jeannette Thurber Connor, trans. and ed., *Pedro Menéndez de Avilés, Adelantado, Governor and Captain-*

General of Florida: Memorial by Gonzalo Solís de Merás (Deland, Fla., 1923); Bartolomé Barrientos, *Pedro Menéndez de Avilés, Founder of Florida,* trans. by Anthony Kerrigan (Gainesville, Fla., 1965); even so, the Adelantado still needs a first-rate biography, in English.

Florida from the beginning was a defensive province. See Verne E. Chatelein, *The Defense of Spanish Florida, 1565–1763* (Washington, D.C., 1941); Jeannette Thurber Connor, "The Nine Old Wooden Forts of Saint Augustine," *Florida Historical Quarterly,* IV (January and April, 1926), 103–111 and 171–180; Albert C. Manucy, *The Building of Castillo de San Marcos* (Washington, D.C., 1961), and *The History of Castillo de San Marcos and Fort Matanzas;* (Washington, D.C., 1955); Mark F. Boyd, "The Siege of Saint Augustine by Governor Moore of South Carolina in 1702 as Reported to the King of Spain by Don Joseph de Zúñiga y Zerda, Governor of Florida," *Florida Historical Quarterly,* XXVI (October, 1948), 345–352; Charles W. Arnade, *The Siege of St. Augustine in 1702* (Gainesville, Fla., 1959); Verner W. Crane, *The Southern Frontier, 1670–1732* (Durham, N.C., 1932), puts Florida into a larger setting in the international rivalry picture; Charles W. Arnade, "The Failure of Spanish Florida," *The Americas,* XVI (January, 1960), 271–282, indicates his judgment by the title of his study; Mark F. Boyd has sketched several incidents in the long story "The Fortification at San Marcos, Apalachee," *Florida Historical Quarterly,* XV (January, 1936), 1–32, "The Expedition of Marcos Delgado from Apalachee to the Upper Creek Country, in 1686," *ibid.,* XVI (January, 1937), 2–32, "A Map of the Road from Pensacola to St. Augustine," *ibid.,* XVII (January, 1938), 17–23, "The Diego Peña Expedition to Apalachee and Apalachicola in 1716," *ibid.,* XXVIII (January, 1949), 1–27.

The same Mark F. Boyd has devoted much attention to the missions, especially those of Apalachee: "Spanish Mission Sites in Florida," *Florida Historical Quarterly,* XVII (July, 1939), 254–280; "Enumeration of Florida Spanish Missions in 1675," *ibid.,* XXVII (January, 1948), 101–108; "Further Considerations of the Apalachee Missions," *The Americas,* IX (April, 1953), 459–479; and with Hale G. Smith and John W. Griffin, *Here They Once Stood: The Tragic End of the Apalachee Missions* (Gainesville, Fla., 1951).

John TePaske has studied the administration of the province in his *The Governorship of Spanish Florida, 1700–1763* (Durham, N.C., 1964); data on two governors' reporting are Katherine Reding, "Letter of Gonzalo Menéndez de Conco, Governor of Florida to Philip II of Spain, June 28, 1600," *Georgia Historical Quarterly,* VIII (September, 1924), 215–229, and Charles W. Arnade, "Spanish Florida in 1643 as Seen by Its Governor," *Florida Historical Quarterly,* XXXIV (April, 1955), 172–176. Arnade has an interesting article on the capital, "The Architecture of St. Augustine," *The Americas,* XVIII (October, 1961), 149–186.

Arnade has a valuable article for researchers, "Florida History in Spanish Archives," *Florida Historical Quarterly,* XXXIV (January, 1955), 36–50; attention should be called to Jeannette Thurber Connor, trans. and ed., *Colonial Records of Spanish Florida* (2 vol.; Deland, Fla., 1925–1930); a curious historiographical piece is James G. Johnson, "Myths, Legends, Miracles and Mysteries Related by the First Historians of Florida," *Georgia Historical Quarterly,* VII (December, 1924), 292–303; and Ernest J. Burrus recalls "A Sigüenza y Góngora Contribution to the History of Florida," *The Americas,* XIX (January, 1963), 305–313.

Pensacola as a western Florida outpost was more closely tied to the Gulf of Mexico than to peninsular Florida; bibliography will be reserved for a later division of these Notes.

Georgia and South Carolina   Bolton named the area well in its Borderlands connection, when, with Mary Ross, he wrote *The Debatable Land: A Sketch of the Anglo-Spanish Contest for the Georgia Coast* (Berkeley, Calif., 1925), which was really the introduction to his edition and translation of *Arredondo's Historical Proof of Spain's Title to Georgia* (Berkeley, Calif., 1925). Spain was in this area long before England planted colonies there, as H. J. Johnson, "A Spanish Settlement in Carolina, 1526," *Georgia Historical Quarterly*, VII (December, 1923), 339–346, narrates. See also James G. Johnson, "The Spanish Period of Georgia and South Carolina History, 1566–1702," *Bulletin* of the University of Georgia, XXIII (1923), "The Spaniards in Northern Georgia during the Sixteenth Century," *Georgia Historical Quarterly*, IX (June, 1925), 159–169, "The Founding of Spanish Colonies in Georgia and South Carolina," *ibid.*, XV (December, 1931), 301–312. Another Georgian historian is J. Randolph Anderson, "The Genesis of Georgia," *ibid.*, XIII (September, 1929), 229–285, "The Spanish Era in Georgia and the English Settlement in 1733," *ibid.*, XVII (June, 1933), 91–108, "The Spanish Era in Georgian History," *ibid.*, XX (September, 1936), 210–239; Verner W. Crane, "The Origin of Georgia," *ibid.*, XIV (June, 1930), 93–111. A South Carolina venture: Mary Ross, "The Spanish Settlement of Santa Elena (Port Royal) in 1578," *ibid.*, IX (December, 1925), 353–379; later French appearances, Ross, "French Intrusions and Indian Uprisings in Georgia and South Carolina, 1577–1580," *ibid.*, VII (September, 1923), 251–281, and "The French on the Savannah, 1605," *ibid.*, VIII (September, 1924), 167–194. An overall view: James G. Johnson, "The Spanish Southeast in the Seventeenth Century," *ibid.*, XVI (March, 1932), 17–27. Bolton noted the far-ranging Carolinians in "Spanish Resistance to the Carolina Traders in Western Georgia," *ibid.*, IX (June, 1925), 115–131.

Franciscan missionary activity in Georgia is treated in John Tate Lanning, *The Spanish Missions of Georgia* (Chapel Hill, N.C., 1935); also James G. Johnson, "The Yamasee Revolt of 1597 and the Destruction of the Georgia Missions," *Georgia Historical Quarterly*, VII (March, 1923), 44–53; and the followup, Mary Ross, "The Restoration of the Spanish Missions in Georgia," *ibid.*, X (September, 1926), 171–199.

The Colonial Wars   Verner W. Crane, *The Southern Frontier, 1670–1732* (Durham, 1932), and "The Southern Frontier in Queen Anne's War," *American Historical Review*, XXIV (April, 1919), 379–395; John Tate Lanning, *The Diplomacy of Georgia* (Chapel Hill, N.C., 1936), and "The American Colonies in the Preliminaries of the War of Jenkins' Ear," *Georgia Historical Quarterly*, XI (June, 1927), 129–155; Ernest G. Hildner, "The Role of the South Sea Company in the Diplomacy Leading to the War of Jenkins' Ear, 1729–1739," *Hispanic-American Historical Review*, XVIII (August, 1938), 322–341; Trevor W. Riese, "Britain's Military Support of Georgia in the War of 1739–1748," *Georgia Historical Quarterly*, XLIII (March, 1959), 1–11; Vera Lee Brown, "Anglo-Spanish Relations in the Closing Years of the Colonial Era," *Hispanic-American Historical Review*, V (August, 1922), 325–383; W. H. Siebert, "Spanish and French Privateering in Southern Waters, July, 1762, to March, 1763," *Georgia Historical Quarterly* XVI (September, 1932), 163–179.

Nueva Vizcaya and New Mexico

The history of these two provinces is closely related; hence, the inclusion of Nueva Vizcaya (modern Mexican State of Chihuahua) in this section. The vast majority of the studies cited, however, will pertain to New Mexico.

General Hubert Howe Bancroft, *History of the North Mexican States and Texas* (2 vols., San Francisco, 1884–1889). Volume One has some pertinent chapters; Bancroft, *History of Arizona and New Mexico* (San Francisco, 1889); Warren E. Beck, *New Mexico: A History of Four Centuries* (Norman, Okla., 1962); Ralph E. Twitchell, *The Leading Facts of New Mexican History* (5 vols.; Cedar Rapids, Iowa, 1911–1917); Paul Horgan, *Great River—The Rio Grande in North American History* (2 vols.; New York, 1954), Volume One has many excellent chapters on the Indians and the Spanish period; Frank D. Reeve, *New Mexico* (Denver, 1964); Erna Fergusson, *Our Southwest* (New York, 1940); Cleve Hallenbeck, *Land of the Conquistadores* (Caldwell, Idaho, 1950). A valuable collection of documentary materials is Adolph F. A. Bandelier, *Historical Documents Relating to New Mexico, Nuevo Vizcaya, and the Approaches Thereto, to 1773*, trans. and ed. by Charles W. Hackett (3 vols.; Washington, D.C., 1931).

The problems of the early northward movement are shown in Philip W. Powell, *Soldiers, Indians and Silver: The Northward Advance of New Spain, 1550–1600* (Berkeley, Calif., 1952); and in J. Lloyd Mecham, *Francisco de Ibarra and Nueva Vizcaya* (Durham, N.C., 1927). Two regional histories: Elias Amador, *Bosquejo histórico de Zacatecas* (Zacatecas, 1892); and Florence C. and Robert H. Lister, *Chihuahua: Storehouse of Storms* (Albuquerque, 1966).

Preliminaries to Conquest First contacts with New Mexico have been documented in "The Conquistador Explorers." A new collection of documentation is found in George P. Hammond and Agapito Rey, eds., *The Rediscovery of New Mexico, 1580–1594: The Expeditions of Chamuscado, Espejo, Castaño de Sosa, Morlete, Leyva de Bonilla and Humaña* (Albuquerque, 1966); earlier publications are Hammond and Rey, *Gallegos's Relation of the Rodríguez Expedition to New Mexico, 1581–1582* (Santa Fe, 1927); J. Lloyd Mecham, "Supplementary Documents Relating to the Chamuscado-Rodríguez Expedition," *Southwestern Historical Quarterly*, XXIX (January, 1926), 224–232; Zephyrin Engelhardt, "El Yllustre Señor Chamuscado," *Southwestern Historical Quarterly*, XXIX (April, 1926), 296–301; J. Lloyd Mecham, "Antonio de Espejo and His Journey to New Mexico," *ibid.*, XXX (October, 1926), 114–139, and "The Second Spanish Expedition to New Mexico," *New Mexico Historical Review*, I (July, 1926), 265–298; Hammond and Rey, *Expedition into New Mexico Made by Antonio Espejo, 1582–1583, as Revealed in the Journal of Diego Pérez Luxán* (Los Angeles, 1929); Katherine Bartlett, "Notes upon the Route of Espejo and Farfán to the Mines in the Sixteenth Century," *New Mexico Historical Review*, XVII (January, 1942), 21–36; Albert H. Schroeder and Daniel S. Watson, *A Colony on the Move: Gaspar Castaño de Sosa's Expedition, 1590–1591* (Santa Fe, 1965).

George P. Hammond is the authority on Oñate and the occupation: *Don Juan de Oñate and the Founding of New Mexico* (Santa Fe, 1927); *Don Juan de Oñate, Colonizer of New Mexico* (Albuquerque, 1953); "Oñate's Effort to Gain Political Autonomy for New Mexico," *Hispanic American Historical Review*, XXXII (August, 1952), 321–330. A contemporary account of the founding years is Gasper Pérez de Villagrá, *History of New Mexico*, trans. and ed. by Gilberto Espinosa (Los

Angeles, 1933). On Oñate's successor, see Irene L. Chaves, "La Ynstrucción de Don Pedro de Peralta," *New Mexico Historical Review*, IV (April, 1929), 178–187; also Lansing Bloom, "The Governors of New Mexico," *ibid.*, X (April, 1935), 152–157. The last author (Bloom) attacks a moot point in New Mexican history with his "When Was Santa Fe Founded?" *ibid.*, IV (April, 1929), 188–194, which event occurred during the Peralta administration.

The Franciscans played an important role in early New Mexico and their work has attracted the attention of historians: J. Manuel Espinosa, "Our Debt to the Franciscan Missionaries of New Mexico," *The Americas*, I (July, 1944), 79–87; Charles J. G. M. Piette, "The Missions of Colonial New Mexico," *ibid.*, IV (October, 1947), 243–254, and "Three Documents Pertaining to the Colonial Missions of New Mexico," *ibid.*, 255–258; Fernando Ocaranza, *Establecimientos Franciscanos en el Misterioso Reino de Nuevo México* (Mexico, 1934), which has some interesting population figures; P. Otto Maas, *Viages de misioneros franciscanos a la conquista de Nuevo México* (Sevilla, 1915); Angelico Chavez, *Our Lady of the Conquest* (Santa Fe, 1948).

The Seventeenth Century   France V. Scholes has written extensively on the seventeenth century: "Church and State in New Mexico, 1610–1650," *New Mexico Historical Review*, XI (January, April, July, October, 1936), XII (January, 1937); "Problems in the Early Ecclesiastical History of New Mexico," *ibid.*, VII (January, 1932); "The First Decade of the Inquisition in New Mexico," *ibid.*, X (July, 1935); "Troublous Times in New Mexico, 1659–1670," XII (April, October, 1937), XIII (January, 1938), XV (July, October, 1940), XVI (January, July, October, 1941); "Civil Government and Society in New Mexico in the 17th Century, *ibid.*, X (January, 1935); "The Supply Service of the New Mexico Missions," *ibid.*, V (January, April, 1930). There are two revealing memorials of Fray Alonso de Benavides: *The Memorial of Alonso de Benavides of 1630*, trans. by Peter P. Forrestal (Washington, 1954); another edition, *The Memorial of Fray Alonso de Benavides, 1630*, annotated by F. W. Hodge and C. F. Lummis, trans. by Mrs. Edward E. Ayer (Chicago, 1916; reprinted Albuquerque, 1965); *Revised Memorial of Fray Alonso de Benavides, 1634*, trans. and ed. by F. W. Hodge, G. P. Hammond, and Agapito Rey (Albuquerque, 1945).

The Pueblo Revolt   Charles W. Hackett, *Revolt of the Pueblo Indians of New Mexico and Otermín's Attempted Reconquest, 1680–1682* (2 vols.; Albuquerque, 1942), "The Revolt of the Pueblo Indians of New Mexico in 1680," Texas State Historical Association *Quarterly*, XV (October, 1911), 93–147, "Retreat of the Spaniards from New Mexico in 1680 and the Beginnings of El Paso," *Southwestern Historical Quarterly*, XVI (October, 1912, and January, 1913), 137–168 and 259–276; Anne E. Hughes, *The Beginnings of Spanish Settlement in the El Paso District* (Berkeley, Calif., 1914); Angelico Chavez, "Pohé-yemo's Representative and the Pueblo Revolt of 1680," *New Mexico Historical Review*, XLII (January, 1967), 85–126.

The Reconquest   Jesse B. Bailey, *Diego de Vargas and the Reconquest of New Mexico* (Albuquerque, 1940); J. Manuel Espinosa, *First Expedition of Vargas into New Mexico* (Albuquerque, 1940); "New Light on the History of the Reconquest of New Mexico," *Mid-America*, XXII (October, 1940), 262–277; "The Recapture of Santa Fe, New Mexico, by the Spaniards, December 29–30, 1693," *Hispanic American Historical Review*, XIX (November, 1939), 443–463;

"Population of the El Paso District in 1692," *Mid-America,* XXIII (January, 1941), 61–84; "The Virgin of the Reconquest of New Mexico," *ibid.,* XVIII (April, 1936), 79–87. Espinosa has put much of his Reconquest research into *Crusaders of the Rio Grande: The Story of Don Diego de Vargas and the Reconquest and Refounding of New Mexico* (Chicago, 1942). A contemporary source for the Reconquest is Irving B. Leonard, trans. and ed., *The Mercurio Volante of Don Carlos Sigüenza y Góngora: An Account of the First Expedition of Diego de Vargas into New Mexico, 1692* (Los Angeles, 1932). A most enlightening study has some bearing on the Reconquest but belongs more to the following century, Oakah L. Jones, *Pueblo Warriors and Spanish Conquest* (Norman, Okla., 1966).

The Eighteenth Century Alfred B. Thomas, *After Coronado: Spanish Exploration Northeast of New Mexico, 1696–1727* (Norman, Okla., 1935), the Introduction is an excellent survey; "The Founding of Albuquerque, 1706: An Historical-Legal Problem," *New Mexico Historical Review,* XXXIX (January, 1964), 1–15; Lansing B. Bloom, "A Campaign against the Moqui Pueblos under Phelix Martínez, 1716," *ibid.,* VI (April, 1931), 158–226; Alfred B. Thomas, "The Massacre of the Villasur Expedition at the Forks of the Platte River," *Nebraska History Magazine,* VII (July-September, 1924), 67–81; Herbert E. Bolton, "French Intrusions into New Mexico, 1749–1752," in *The Pacific Ocean in History,* edited by H. M. Stephens and H. E. Bolton (New York, 1917), pp. 389–407; Max L. Moorhead, "The Presidio Supply Problem of New Mexico in the Eighteenth Century," *New Mexico Historical Review,* XXXVI (July, 1961), 210–229; Alfred B. Thomas, *Forgotten Frontiers: A Study of the Indian Policy of Don Juan Bautista de Anza, Governor of New Mexico, 1777–1787* (Norman, Okla., 1932); Adlai Feather, ed., "Colonel Don Fernando de la Concha Diary, 1788," *New Mexico Historical Review,* XXXIV (October, 1959), 285–304; Oakah L. Jones, "Pueblo Indian Auxiliaries in New Mexico, 1763–1821," *ibid.,* XXXVII (April, 1962), 81–109; Joe F. Park, "Spanish Indian Policy in New Mexico, 1765-1810," *Arizona and the West,* IV (Winter, 1962), 325–344; a work which has much on aspects of the eighteenth century is Noel M. Loomis and Abraham P. Nasatir, *Pedro Vial and the Roads to Santa Fe* (Norman, Okla., 1967). Indian problems: Jack D. Forbes, *Apache, Navaho, and Spaniard* (Norman, Okla., 1960); Frank D. Reeve, "Navaho-Spanish Wars, 1680–1720," *New Mexico Historical Review,* XXXI (July, 1958), 205–231; Alfred B. Thomas, *The Plains Indians and New Mexico, 1751–1778* (Albuquerque, 1940); Myra Ellen Jenkins, "Taos Pueblo and its Neighbors, 1540–1847," *New Mexico Historical Review,* XLI (January, 1966), 85–114.

A recent study of merit, Marc Simmons, *Spanish Government in New Mexico* (Albuquerque, 1968).

Explorations Westward Joseph J. Hill, "Spanish and Mexican Explorations and Trade Northwest from New Mexico into the Great Basin," *Utah Historical Quarterly,* III (January, 1930); and importantly, Herbert E. Bolton, *Pageant in the Wilderness: The Story of the Escalante Expedition to the Interior Basin* (Salt Lake City, 1950). Two of the principals in this exploration attempt produced historical documents of New Mexican interest; both have been translated and edited by Eleanor B. Adams; Fray Francisco Atanasio Domínguez, *The Missions of New Mexico, 1776* (Albuquerque, 1956), and Fray Silvestre Vélez de Escalante, "Letter to the Missionaries of New Mexico," *New Mexico Historical Review,* XL (October, 1965), 319–336.

Note should also be made of Eleanor B. Adams' edition of *Bishop Tamarón's Visitation of New Mexico, 1760,* Vol. IX of Publications in History of the Historical Society of New Mexico (Albuquerque, 1954), an important ecclesiastical document.

New Mexico's relations with the French will be noted under the "Louisiana-Luisiana" head; relations with the Americans, under "The Last Spanish Years."

Coahuila and Texas

Again, these two provinces are closely related during the colonial period; however, the large proportion of the bibliography will deal with Texas.

General One might start the listing of materials with Hubert Howe Bancroft, *History of the North Mexican States and Texas* (San Francisco, 1884–1889); Herbert E. Bolton and Thomas M. Marshall, *The Colonization of North America, 1492–1783* (New York, 1920), furnish the main steps in the story and mention, at least, the major figures. The Mexican historian Vito Alessio Robles has two studies which are pertinent: *Coahuila y Texas en la época colonial* (Mexico, 1938), and *Saltillo en la historia y en la leyenda* (Mexico, 1934). There is no highly satisfactory one-volume history of Texas to serve as a guide for this colonial period; however, Hodding Carter, *Doomed Road of Empire: The Spanish Trail of Conquest* (New York, 1963), is readable. The second volume of Paul Horgan, *Great River* (2 vols.; New York, 1954), has much on Texas. The extensive history of Carlos E. Castañeda, *Our Catholic Heritage in Texas* (7 vols.; Austin, Tex., 1936–1950), has scattered through the first four volumes one of the best studies of early Texas, fitted in with the Catholic story which is Castañeda's main intent; of course, down to the 1820s Texas history was largely Catholic history. There are two histories of contemporary eighteenth-century writers: Fray Juan Agustín Morfi, *History of Texas, 1673–1779,* trans. and ed. by Carlos E. Castañeda (2 vols.; Albuquerque, 1935), and Antonio Bonilla, "Brief Compendium of the Events Which Have Occurred in the Province of Texas from Its Conquest, or Reduction, to the Present [1772]," trans. by Elizabeth H. West, Texas State Historical Association *Quarterly,* VIII (July, 1904). Robert C. Clark, *The Beginning of Texas* (Austin, 1907), should be controlled by Herbert E. Bolton, "Notes on Clark's 'Beginnings of Texas,'" Texas State Historical Association *Quarterly,* XII (October, 1908), 148–158. Bolton has gathered a number of his earlier articles into the best study of the middle period, *Texas in the Middle Eighteenth Century: Studies in Spanish Colonial History and Administration* (Berkeley, Calif., 1915; reprinted New York, 1962). The beginnings of what in time came to be the Mexican State of Tamaulipas are studied in Lawrence F. Hill, *Jóse de Escandón and the Founding of Nuevo Santander: A Study in Spanish Colonization* (Columbus, Ohio, 1926).

Several Texas Indian studies: W. W. Newcomb, *The Indians of Texas: From Prehistoric to Modern Times* (Austin, 1961); Herbert E. Bolton, "The Native Tribes about the East Texas Missions," Texas State Historical Association *Quarterly,* XI (April, 1908), 249–276; Carlos E. Castañeda, "Customs and Legends of Texas Indians," *Mid-America,* XIV (July, 1931), 48–56; Marc Simmons, *Border Comanches: Seven Spanish Colonial Documents* (Santa Fe, 1967).

Pre-Spanish Texas   Herbert E. Bolton, "Preliminaries to 'The Spanish Occupation of Texas, 1519–1690'," *Southwestern Historical Quarterly,* XVI (July, 1912), 1–26; Francis Borgia Steck, *Forerunners of Captain De León's Expedition to Texas, 1670–1675* (Austin, Tex., 1932); Gabriel Tous, *The Espinosa-Olivares-Aguirre Expedition of 1709* (Texas Catholic Historical Society, Austin, Texas, 1938); contemporary accounts of the seventeenth-century contacts with Texas are published in Herbert E. Bolton, *Spanish Exploration in the Southwest, 1542–1706* (New York, 1916).

The figure of Saint-Denis intrudes into Texas history at this point: a fine biography is Ross Phares, *Cavalier in the Wilderness: The Story of the Explorer and Trader Louis Juchereau de St. Denis* (Baton Rouge, La., 1952); Lester G. Bugbee, "The Real Saint-Denis," Texas State Historical Association *Quarterly,* I (April, 1898), 266–281; Edmond J. P. Schmitt, "Who Was Juchereau de Saint Denis?" *ibid.,* I (January, 1898), 204–215, "Louis Juchereau de Saint-Denis and the Re-Establishment of the Tejas Missions," *ibid.,* VI (July, 1902), 1–26; Charmion Clair Shelby, "St. Denis's Declaration concerning Texas in 1717," *Southwestern Historical Quarterly,* XXVI (January, 1923).

Occupation and Settlement   Edward Heusinger, *Early Exploration and Mission Establishment in Texas* (San Antonio, 1936); Gabriel Tous, "Ramón Expedition: Espinosa's Diary of 1716," *Mid-America,* XII (April, 1930), 339–361; Francisco Céliz, *Diary of the Alarcón Expedition into Texas, 1718–1719,* trans, and ed. by Fritz L. Hoffmann (Los Angeles, 1935); Hoffmann, "The Mesquía Diary of the Alarcón Expedition into Texas, 1718," *Southwestern Historical Quarterly,* XLI (April, 1938), 312–323. Eleanor C. Buckley, "The Aguayo Expedition into Texas and Louisiana, 1719–1722," Texas State Historical Association *Quarterly,* XV (July, 1911), 1–65; Charles W. Hackett, "The Marquis of San Miguel de Aguayo and His Recovery of Texas from the French, 1719–1723," *Southwestern Historical Quarterly,* XLIX (October, 1945), 193–214; Charmion Clair Shelby, "Efforts to Finance the Aguayo Expedition: A Study in Frontier Financial Administration in New Spain," *Hispanic America Historical Review,* XXV (February, 1945), 27–44. Frederick C. Chabot, *San Antonio and Its Beginnings* (San Antonio, 1931); Lota M. Spell, "The Grant and First Survey of the City of San Antonio," *Southwestern Historical Quarterly,* LXVI (July, 1962), 73–89, with maps; Helen P. Norvell, *King's Highway, the Great Strategic Military Highway of America, El Camino Real, the Old San Antonio Road* (San Antonio, 1945); Richard Santos, "Proposed View of San Antonio de Valero," *Texana,* III (Fall, 1965), 197–202, and "The Quartel de San Antonio de Bexar," *ibid.,* V (Fall, 1967), 187–201; Herbert E. Bolton, "Spanish Mission Records at San Antonio," Texas State Historical Association *Quarterly,* X (April, 1907), 297–307; James M. Daniel, "The Spanish Frontier in West Texas and Northern Mexico," *Southwestern Historical Quarterly,* LXXI (April, 1968), 481–495. Damian Manzanet, "Descubrimiento de la Bahía del Espíritu Santa," Texas State Historical Association *Quarterly,* II (April, 1899), 253–312; Kathryn S. O'Connor, *Presidio la Bahía del Espíritu Santo de Zúñiga, 1721–1846* (Austin, Tex., 1966).

The Missions   Thomas P. O'Rourke, *The Franciscan Missions in Texas, 1690–1793* (Washington, 1927); Carlos E. Castañeda, "The Sons of St. Francis in Texas," *The Americas,* I (January, 1945), 289–302; R. B. Blake, "Locations of the

Early Spanish Missions and Presidios in Nacogdoches County," *Southwestern Historical Quarterly,* XLI (January, 1938), 212–224. Juan Domingo Arricivita, *Crónica Seráfica y Apostólica del Colegio de Propaganda Fide de la Santa Cruz de Querétaro de la Nueva España* (Mexico, 1792); Michael B. McCloskey, *The Formative Years of the Missionary College of Santa Cruz de Querétaro* (Washington, 1955); Fray Isidro Félix de Espinosa, *Crónica de los Colegios de propaganda fide de la Nueva España,* with notes and introduction by Lino G. Canedo (Madrid, 1964); Alberto María Carreño, "The Missionary College of Zacatecas," *The Americas,* VII (January, 1951), 297–330. Individual missions have had notice: Robert C. Weddle, "San Juan Bautista: Mother of Texas Missions," *Southwestern Historical Quarterly,* LXXI (April, 1968), which is the core theme of the larger work, *San Juan Bautista: Gateway to Spanish Texas* (Austin, Tex., 1968); William H. Obereste, *History of Refugio Mission* (Refugio, Tex., 1942); Marion A. Habig, "Mission San José y San Miguel de Aguayo," *Southwestern Historical Quarterly,* LXXI (April, 1968), 496–516; Herbert E. Bolton, "The Founding of Mission Rosario: A Chapter in the History of the Gulf Coast," *Texas State Historical Association Quarterly,* X (October, 1906), 113–139; Reginald C. Reindorf, "The Founding of Missions at La Junta de Los Rios," *Mid-America,* XX (April, 1938), 107–131. Fray Antonio Margil has attracted much attention: Eduardo Enrique Rios, *Life of Fray Antonio Margil, O.F.M.,* trans. and revised by Benedict Leutenegger (Washington, 1959); Leutenegger, *Apostle of America: Fray Antonio Margil* (Chicago, 1961); Peter P. Forrestal, "Venerable Antonio Margil de Jesús," *Mid-America,* XIV (April, 1932), 305–334; Paul V. Murray, "Venerable Antonio Margil de Jesús, O.F.M., Friar of the Winged Feet," *The Americas,* VII (January, 1951), 267–280; William H. Donahue, "The Missionary Activities of Fray Antonio Margil de Jesús in Texas, 1716–1722," *ibid.,* XIV (July, 1957), 45–56; Michael B. McCloskey, "Fray Isidro Félix de Espinosa, Companion and Biographer of Margil," *ibid.,* VII (January, 1951).

The Rivera Visita Vito Alessio Robles, *Diario y derrotero de lo caminando, visto, y observado en la visita que hizo a los presidios de Nueva España Septentrional el Brigadier Pedro de Rivera* (Mexico, 1946); Retta Murphy, "The Journey of Pedro de Rivera, 1724–1728," *Southwestern Historical Quarterly,* XLI (October, 1937), 125–141; Charles W. Hackett, "Visitador Rivera's Criticism of Aguayo's Work in Texas," *Hispanic American Historical Review,* XVI (May, 1936), 162–172.

The San Sabá Project William E. Dunn, "Apache Relations in Texas, 1718–1750," *Texas State Historical Association Quarterly,* XIV (January, 1911), 198–274, and "Missionary Activities among the Eastern Apaches Previous to the Founding of the San Sabá Mission," *ibid.,* XV (January, 1912), 186–200, and "The Apache Mission on the San Sabá River: Its Founding and Failure," *Southwestern Historical Quarterly,* XVII (April, 1914), 379–414; Robert S. Weddle, *The San Sabá Mission: Spanish Pivot in Texas* (Austin, 1964), and "The San Sabá Mission: Approach to the Great Plains," *Great Plains Journal,* IV (Spring, 1965), 29–38; Lesley B. Simpson (ed.) and Paul D. Nathan (trans.), *The San Sabá Papers: A Documentary Account of the Founding and Destruction of San Sabá Mission* (San Francisco, 1959).

A valuable study is Sandra L. Myers, "The Spanish Cattle Kingdom in the Province of Texas," *Texana,* IV (Fall, 1966), 233–246.

Later Texas bibliography will be found under "The Provincias Internas" and "The Last Spanish Years" headings.

Sinaloa and Sonora

One of the pioneering pieces is Hubert Howe Bancroft, *History of the North Mexican States and Texas* (2 vols.; San Francisco, 1884–1889). Bolton next opened this west coast story to his students and himself did a later sketch in his short article "The West Coast Corridor," *Proceedings* of the American Philosophical Society, Vol. 91 (December, 1947), 426–429, reprinted in Bannon, *Bolton and the Spanish Borderlands.*

Sinaloa J. Lloyd Mecham, *Francisco de Ibarra and Nueva Vizcaya* (Durham, N.C., 1927); W. Eugene Shiels, *Gonzalo de Tapia, Founder of the First Permanent Jesuit Mission in North America* (New York, 1934), and "Gonzalo de Tapia: Un Conquistador de Dios, 1561–1594," *Mid-America,* XIV (January, 1932), 241–252; Peter Masten Dunne, *Pioneer Black Robes on the West Coast* (Berkeley, Calif., 1940), and "Jesuits Begin the West Coast Missions," *Pacific Historical Review,* IV (June, 1935), 131–142; A contemporary's account of this mission period is Andrés Pérez de Ribas, *Historia de los triumphos de nuestra santa fee* (Madrid, 1645); the story of Sinaloa's great captain is Harry P. Johnson, "Diego Martínez de Hurdaide: Defender of the Northwestern Frontier of New Spain," *Pacific Historical Review,* XI (June, 1942), 169–186; John Francis Bannon, "Black Robe Frontiersman: Pedro Méndez, S. J.," *Hispanic American Historical Review,* XXVII (February, 1947), 61–86.

Sonora Bannon, *The Mission Frontier in Sonora, 1620–1687* (New York, 1955); Fintan Warren, "Jesuit Historians of Sinaloa-Sonora," *The Americas,* XVIII (April, 1962), 329–339. W. Eugene Shiels, "The Critical Period in Mission History," *Mid America,* XXI (April, 1939), 97–109.

Kino was and is the great Sonora figure, and the Kino bibliography is growing. Herbert E. Bolton, *Kino's Historical Memoir of Pimería Alta* (2 vols.; Cleveland, 1919; reprinted Berkeley, Calif., 1948), a translation of the Favores Celestiales of the padre, turned interest to Kino; Bolton, *The Padre on Horseback* (San Francisco, 1932; reprinted Chicago, 1963); Frank C. Lockwood, *With Padre Kino on the Trail* (Tucson, Ariz., 1934); Rufus K. Wyllys, *Pioneer Padre: The Life and Times of Eusebio Francisco Kino* (Dallas, 1935); Bolton, *Rim of Christendom: A Biography of Eusebio Francisco Kino, Pacific Coast Pioneer* (New York, 1936; reprinted New York, 1960).

Ernest Burrus has become another top authority on Kino, and his publications are many: *Kino Reports to Headquarters* (Rome, 1954); *Kino's Plan for the Development of Pimería Alta* (Tucson, Ariz., 1961); *Kino Writes to the Duchess* (Rome, 1965); *Kino and the Cartography of Northwestern New Spain* (Tucson, 1965), with many maps; "Kino, Historian's Historian," *Arizona and the West,* IV (Summer, 1962), 145–156. See also Charles Polzer, *A Kino Guide: His Missions—His Monuments* (Tucson, Ariz., 1968); Ronald L. Ives, "Navigation Methods of E. F. Kino, S.J.," *Arizona and the West,* II (Fall, 1960), 213–244; Bert M. Fireman, "Kino on the Arizona Border," *The American West,* III (Summer, 1966), 16–21; Fay Jackson Smith, John Kessel, and Francis Fox, *Father Kino in Arizona* (Phoenix, Ariz., 1966), with an extensive Kino bibliography. The work of Kino's close companion is Juan Mateo Manje, *Unknown Arizona and Sonora, 1693–1721* [Luz de Tierra Incógnita], trans. by Harry J. Karns (Tucson, Ariz., 1954).

Another study of interest is Richard J. Morrissey, "Early Agriculture in Pimería Alta," *Mid-America*, XXXI (April, 1949), 101–108; see also James R. Hastings, "People of Reason and Others: The Colonization of Sonora to 1767," *Arizona and the West*, II (Winter, 1961), 321–340.

Two interested Arizonans have visited the Sonora missions· and produced valuable studies: George B. Eckhart, "A Guide to the History of the Missions of Sonora," *Arizona and the West*, II (Summer, 1960), 165–183; more thorough and extensive and with many photographs is Paul A. Roca, *Paths of the Padres Through Sonora* (Tucson, Ariz., 1967).

Here should be noted, though not always directly pertinent to the Western Slope, the two works of Peter Masten Dunne, *Pioneer Jesuits in Northern Mexico* (Berkeley, Calif., 1944), and *Early Jesuit Missions in Tarahumara* (Berkeley, Calif., 1948). Mention should also be made of short studies by Shiels, Dunne, Bannon, Johnson, McShane, and others, bearing on the West Coast Corridor in *Greater America: Essays in Honor of Herbert Eugene Bolton* (Berkeley, Calif., 1945).

Post-Kino Sonora and Arizona

Again, begin with Hubert Howe Bancroft, *History of the North Mexican States and Texas* (2 vols.; San Francisco, 1884–1889), and add *History of Arizona and New Mexico* (San Francisco, 1889). A short sketch of this period is George P. Hammond, "Pimería Alta After Kino's Time," *New Mexico Historical Review*, IV (July, 1929), 220–238; more thorough and important will be the study of John Augustine Donohue on post-Kino Sonora and Arizona, 1711–1762, which is in prepublication stage and which is developed from his unpublished doctoral dissertation, University of California-Berkeley, 1951.

The bibliography of this period does not fall into neat packages; it will have to be listed in somewhat hit-and-miss fashion. Theodore Treutlein has produced many studies on the Jesuit missions and missionaries; noteworthy are "Jesuit Travel to New Spain, 1678–1756," *Mid-America*, XIX (April, 1937), 104–123, which is somewhat broader in its scope but pertinent here; "Father Pfefferkorn and His Description of Sonora," *ibid.*, XX (October, 1938), 229–252; "The Jesuit Missionary in the Role of Physician," *ibid.*, XXII (April, 1940), 122–141; "The Relation of Philipp Segesser," *ibid.*, XXVII (July and October, 1945), 139–187 and 257–260; "Economic Regime of the Jesuit Missions in Eighteenth Century Sonora," *Pacific Historical Review*, VIII (September, 1939), 289–300; "Non-Spanish Jesuits in Spain's American Colonies," in *Greater America: Essays in Honor of Herbert Eugene Bolton* (Berkeley, Calif., 1945), pp. 219–242; Treutlein has also translated and edited Ignaz Pfefferkorn, *Sonora, A Description of a Province* (Albuquerque, 1949), and *Missionary in Sonora: The Travel Reports of Joseph Och, S.J., 1755–1767* (San Francisco, 1965). Peter Masten Dunne has translated and edited two sets of documents, *Jacobo Sedelmayr, Missionary, Frontiersman, Explorer* (Tucson, Ariz., 1955), and *Juan Antonio Balthasar, Padre Visitador to the Sonora Frontier, 1744–1745* (Tucson, Ariz., 1957).

A miscellany of Sonora-Arizona studies: Rufus K. Wyllys, "The Historical Geography of Arizona," *Pacific Historical Review,* XXI (May, 1952), 121–128; Peter Masten Dunne, "Captain Anza and the Case of Father Campos," *Mid-America,* XXIII (January, 1941), 45–60; J. Augustine Donohue, "The Unlucky Jesuit Mission of Bac, 1732–1767," *Arizona and the West,* II (Summer, 1960), 127–139; Mary P. Torrams, "Tubac's Rightful Place in the Sun," *ibid.,* I (Winter, 1959), 368–373; John L. Kessell, "The Puzzling Presidio: San Phelipe de Guevavi, alias Terrenate," *New Mexico Historical Review,* XLI (January, 1966), 21–46; Ray H. Mattison, "Early Spanish and Mexican Settlements in Arizona," *ibid.,* XXI (October, 1946), 273–327; Sanford A. Mosk, "Economic Problems in Sonora in the Late Eighteenth Century," *Pacific Historical Review,* VIII (September, 1939), 341–346; Russell C. Ewing, "The Pima Uprising of 1751: A Study of Spanish-Indian Relations on the Frontier of New Spain," in *Greater America,* pp. 259—280, and "Investigations into the Causes of the Pima Uprisings of 1751," *Mid-America,* XXIII (April, 1941), 138–151; Henry F. Dobyns, "Fray Pedro Antonio de Arriquibar, Chaplain of the Royal Fort of Tucson," *Arizona and the West,* I (Spring, 1959), 71–79, and *Lanco Ho! Containment of the Western Apaches by the Royal Spanish Garrison at Tucson* (Lima, 1964).

The title of Charles E. Chapman, *The Founding of Spanish California* (New York, 1916), tends to be a bit misleading; the subtitle, "The Northwestward Expansion of New Spain, 1687–1783," gives a better key to the contents, for the volume has much on the post-Kino period.

Much work remains to be done on the Franciscan period, following the expulsion of the Jesuits in 1767; Zephyrin Engelhardt, *The Franciscans in Arizona* (Harbor Springs, Mich., 1899), is a preliminary sketch. Fray Francisco Garcés, too, has been too long neglected: see Elliott Coues, *On the Trail of a Spanish Pioneer* (2 vols., New York, 1900), for some of the fundamental documents; also Herbert E. Bolton, "The Early Explorations of Father Garcés on the Pacific Slope," in *The Pacific Ocean in History* (New York, 1917), pp. 317–330; Francisco Garcés, *A Record of Travels in Arizona and California, 1775–1776,* trans. and ed. by John Galvin (San Francisco, 1965).

Baja California

This was largely a Jesuit story, at least until the expulsion in 1767–1768, when the Franciscans took over; within a year or so some of the friars went on to Alta California and the history of the peninsula is tied closely to that "other" California. Peter Masten Dunne has written extensively on the Jesuit years. In *Black Robes in Lower California* (Berkeley, Calif., 1952), he uses much of the material contained in his earlier articles of which the following may be noted: "The Record Book of a Lower California Mission," *Mid-America,* XXX (July, 1947), 185–200; "Salvatierra's Legacy to Lower California," *The Americas,* VII (July, 1950), 31–50; "Lower California an Island," *Mid-America,* XXXV (January, 1953), 37–66. Mariano Cuevas, "The Missions of Lower California," *ibid.,* XVI (October, 1933), 73–78; Francis J. Weber, "Jesuit Missions in Baja California," *The Americas,* XXIII (April, 1967), 408–422; Ursula Schaefer, "Father Baegert and his *Nachrichten,*" *Mid-America,* XX (July, 1938), 151–163.

Miguel Venegas, *Juan María Salvatierra of the Company of Jesus,* trans. and ed. by Marguerite Eyer Wilbur (Cleveland, 1929). Ernest J. Burrus has recently edited Francisco María Piccolo, *Informe del Estado de la nueva cristianidad de California, 1702, y otros documentos* (Madrid, 1962); he has also translated and edited *Wenceslaus Linck's Reports and Letters, 1762–1778* (Los Angeles, 1967). One of the more thorough contemporary histories is Miguel Venegas, *Noticia de la California y de su conquista temporal y espiritual,* which was rewritten and published by Father Andrés Marcos Burriel, but without taking any credit therefor (3 vols., Madrid, 1757; Mexico, 1943–1944). M. D. Krmpotic, *Life and Works of the Reverend Ferdinand Konščak [Consag], S.J., 1703–1759* (Boston, 1923). Ugarte is still without a biographer, giant though he was of the mission enterprise and one of the founders of the famous Pious Fund.

Zephyrin Engelhardt has some notice of the Franciscan effort in Lower California in his *The Missions and Missionaries of California* (4 vols., new edition; Santa Barbara, 1929); some of the works on Serra will have short accounts of the Baja period. The Dominican enterprise is studied in Peveril Meigs, *The Dominican Mission Frontier of Lower California* (Berkeley, Calif., 1935).

Francisco Clavigero, one of the Jesuit historians expelled from New Spain in 1767 with the rest of his brethren, wrote a History of Lower California while in exile. It was first published as *Storia della California,* was subsequently translated into Spanish, and is more recently found translated in Sara E. Lake and A. A. Gray, *The History of Lower California* (Stanford, Calif., 1937).

Alta California

There are several good general histories of California, each of which devotes a good deal of space to the colonial period: John W. Caughey, *California* (New York, 1940, and later editions); Andrew F. Rolle, *California: A History* (New York, 1963); Walton Bean, *California: An Interpretive History* (New York, 1968); W. H. Hutchinson, *California: Two Centuries of Man, Land and Growth in the Golden State* (Palo Alto, Calif., 1969). More specifically on the Spanish Period: Charles E. Chapman, *The Founding of Spanish California: The Northwestward Expansion of New Spain, 1687–1783* (New York, 1916), and *A History of California: The Spanish Period* (New York, 1921); Irving B. Richman, *California under Spain and Mexico* (Boston, 1911).

The Cabrillo-Ferrelo bibliography has already been noted under the head "The Conquistador Explorers." Jack D. Forbes has an interesting story in his "Melchior Díaz and the Discovery of Alta California," *Pacific Historical Review,* XXVII (September, 1958), 351–358. The homebound route of the Galleon ties in with the next phase of California history: see William L. Schurz, *The Manila Galleon* (New York, 1939); data on an attempt to explore the California coast are Henry R. Wagner, "The Voyage to California of Sebastián Rodríguez Cermenho in 1595," *California Historical Society Quarterly,* III (April, 1924), 3–24, and Robert F. Heizer, "Archeological Evidence of Sebastián Rodríguez Cermenho's California Visit," *ibid.,* XX (December, 1941), 315–328.

The Drake visit to the California coast and its sequel has aroused much attention, particularly after the discovery of the so-called Drake Plate in 1937. See Henry R. Wagner, *Sir Francis Drake's Voyage around the World: Its Aims and Achievements* (San Francisco, 1926). Two special publications (Nos. 13 and 14) of the California Historical Society are devoted to the Drake Plate controversy: Herbert E. Bolton, *Drake's Plate of Brass: Evidence of His Visit to California in 1579* (1937), and Colin G. Fink and E. P. Polushkin, *Drake's Plate of Brass Vindicated* (1938). For the followers of Drake, see Peter Gerhard, *Pirates on the West Coast of New Spain, 1575–1742* (Glendale, Calif., 1960).

The Vizcaíno Diary and the Brief Report of Fray Antonio de la Ascensión are in Herbert E. Bolton, *Spanish Exploration in the Southwest, 1542–1706* (New York, 1916).

Two ranking Spanish officials with close ties to the California story: Herbert I. Priestley, *José de Gálvez, Visitor-General of New Spain* (Berkeley, Calif., 1916); Bernard E. Bobb, *The Viceregency of Antonio María Bucareli in New Spain, 1771–1779* (Austin, Tex., 1967).

The move into Alta California is well documented: the diaries and journals of the principal lay participants in the events of 1769 and 1770 (Portolá, Costanzó, Vila, Fages) have been translated and published in the Academy of Pacific Coast History *Publications*, I and II (Berkeley, Calif., 1910–1911); an earlier publication is Zoeth S. Eldredge, *The March of Portolá and Discovery of San Francisco, the Log of the San Carlos, and Original Documents* (San Francisco, 1909); Maynard Geiger, "The Arrival of the Franciscans in the Californias, 1768–1769," *The Americas*, VIII (October, 1951), 209–218, documents; Herbert E. Bolton, *Fray Juan Crespi, Missionary Explorer* (Berkeley, Calif., 1927); Alan K. Brown, "The Various Journals of Juan Crespi," *The Americas*, XXI (April, 1965), 375–398; Charles J. G. Maximin Piette, "An Unpublished Diary of Fray Juan Crespi, O.F.M., 1770," *ibid.*, III (July, October, 1947, and January, 1948), 102–114, 234–243, 368–381. Richard Pourade, Harry Crosby, and Lloyd Hartung collaborated on an interesting picture and text story of the move from the peninsula up to Alta California, *The Call to California* (San Diego, 1968); Pourade is also responsible for *The History of San Diego* series, published by The Union-Tribune, as "The Copley Books."

Serra is one of the giants of early California and has been the subject of many studies. He has been the subject of Maynard Geiger's research and writing over the last years; Geiger's articles are many and his extensive biography is outstanding, *The Life and Times of Fray Junípero Serra* (2 vols., Washington, 1959); Geiger has also translated and edited the Life of *Fray Junípero Serra*, by Serra's friend and contemporary Fray Francisco Palóu. Other Serra studies: Juan Hervás, "Fray Junípero Serra and Spain," *The Americas*, VI (January, 1950), 265–278; Rafael Heliodoro Valle, "Fray Junípero Serra and His Apostolate in Mexico," *ibid.*, VI (January, 1950), 279–290.

A valuable contemporary source for the early California years is Francisco Palóu, *Noticias de la Nueva California* (1783), trans. and ed. by Herbert E. Bolton as *Historical Memoirs of New California* (4 vols.; Berkeley, Calif., 1926). On Anza see Bolton, *Outpost of Empire* (New York, 1931), which is the reworking of the introductory volume of his *Anza's California Expeditions* (5 vols.; Berkeley, Calif., 1930); also on Anza, Mario Hernández Sanchez-Barba, *Juan Bautista de Anza: Un Hombre de Frontera* (Madrid, 1965). Another contemporary piece is Herbert I. Priestley, ed., *A Historical, Political and Natural Description of California by Pedro Fages* (Berkeley, Calif., 1937).

The Missions There have been a number of pictorials, with sound text and often with text less so. The pioneer mission scholar was Zephyrin Engelhardt, *The Missions and Missionaries of California* (4 vols.; San Francisco, 1908–1915); Father Engelhardt has shorter studies on many of the individual missions; Maynard Geiger has done a study of *Mission Santa Barbara* (Santa Barbara, 1965); see also Geiger, "Important California Missionary Dates Determined," *The Americas*, II (January, 1946), 287–293; J. N. Bowman, "The Birthdays of the California Missions," *ibid.*, XX (January, 1964), 289–308, and "The Names of the California Missions," *ibid.*, XXI (April, 1965), 363–374, and "The Parochial Books of the California Missions," Historical Society of Southern California *Quarterly*, XLIII (September, 1961), 303–315; George W. Beattie has an interesting topic, *California's Unbuilt Missions: Spanish Plans for an Inland Chain* (Los Angeles, 1930).

The early California bibliography could go on and on; take the following as some of the interesting items or approaches: Michael E. Thurman, *The Naval Department of San Blas: New Spain's Bastion for Alta California and Nootka Sound, 1767–1798* (Glendale, Calif., 1967), which discusses the supplying of California by sea; Edith Webb, "Agriculture in the Days of the Early California Padres," *The Americas*, IV (January, 1948), 325–344, opens a topic which needs much more research; Daniel D. McGarry, "Educational Methods of the Franciscans in Spanish California," *ibid.*, VI (January, 1950), 335–358; Kurt Baer, "Spanish Colonial Art in the California Missions," *ibid.*, XVII (July, 1961), 33–54; W. W. Robinson, *Los Angeles: From the Days of the Pueblo* (San Francisco, 1959); Ronald L. Ives, "Retracing the Route of Fages Expedition of 1781," *Arizona and the West*, VIII (Spring, Summer, 1966), 49–70, 157–170.

Explorations to the North Benito de la Sierra, "The Hezeta Expedition to the Northwest Coast in 1775," California Historical Society *Quarterly*, IX (September, 1930), 201–242; Francisco Antonio Maurelle, *Journal of a Voyage in 1775 to Explore the Coast of America, Northward of California* (London, 1781; reprinted San Francisco, 1920); Henry R. Wagner, *The Last Spanish Exploration of the Northwest Coast and the Attempt to Colonize Bodega Bay* (San Francisco, 1930).

Foreign Visitors La Pérouse: Jean François de la Pérouse, *Voyage de la Pérouse autour de Monde* (4 vols.; Paris, 1797); Gilbert Chinard has edited the California segment, *Le Voyage de Lapérouse sur les Côtes de l'Alaska et de la Californie* (Baltimore, 1937). Vancouver: George Vancouver, *A Voyage of Discovery to the North Pacific Ocean and Round the World* (3 vols.; London, 1798); the California sections have been reprinted and annotated by Marguerite Eyer Wilbur, *Vancouver in California, 1792–1794* (Los Angeles, 1953). Malaspina: Donald C. Cutter, *Malaspina in California* (San Francisco, 1960); E. Boni, *Malaspina* (Rome, 1935); Edith C. Galbraith, "Malaspina's Voyage Around the World," California Historical Society *Quarterly*, III (October, 1924), 215–237.

Explorations into the Interior Donald C. Cutter, ed., *Diary of Ensign Gabriel Moraga's Expedition of Discovery in the Sacramento Valley, 1808* (Los Angeles, 1957); S. F. Cook, *Colonial Expeditions to the Interior of California's Central Valley, 1800–1820* (Berkeley, Calif., 1960); Herbert I. Priestley, *Franciscan Explorations in California* (Glendale, Calif., 1946).

The Provincias Internas

Under this head are gathered a number of studies referring to the Provincias Internas and chief figures on the northern frontier in the latter half of the eighteenth century. Much of the story of the western provinces will be found in Charles E. Chapman, *The Founding of Spanish California* (New York, 1916), which, as previously noted, deals primarily with the background from 1687 forward. In general, more research has turned on the eastern provinces, as the sequel will indicate, in rough chronology. David M. Vigness, "Don Hugo Oconór and New Spain's Northeastern Frontier, 1764–1766," *Journal of the West*, VI (Spring, 1966), 27–40; Vito Alessio Robles, *Nicolás de Lafora, Relación de Viaje que Hizo a los Presidios Internos Situados en la Frontera de la América Septentrional Perteneciente al Rey de España* (Mexico, 1939); Lawrence Kinnaird, ed., *The Frontiers of New Spain: Nicolás de Lafora's Description, 1766–1768* (Berkeley, Calif., 1958); Enrique Gonzáles Flores and Francisco R. Almade, eds., *Informe de Hugo O'Conór sobre el Estado de las Provincias Internas, 1771–1776* (Mexico, 1952); Paige W. Christiansen, "Hugo Oconór's Inspection of Nueva Viscaya and Coahuila, 1773," *Louisiana Studies*, II (Fall, 1963), 157–175; Sidney B. Brinckerhoff and Odie B. Faulk, *Lancers for the King* (Phoenix, Ariz., 1965), which has a translation of the *Reglamento de 1772* for the reorganization of frontier defenses; these two authors have a short article, 'Soldiering at the End of the World," *The American West*, III (Summer, 1966), 29–37; Alfred B. Thomas, *Teodoro de Croix and the Northern Frontier of New Spain, 1776–1783* (Norman, Okla., 1941); Fernando Ocaranza, *Crónica de las Provincias Internas* (Mexico, 1939); Ted J. Warner, "Frontier Defense," *New Mexico Historical Review*, XLI (January, 1966), 5–20; Max L. Moorhead, "The Private Contract System of Presidial Supply in Northern New Spain," *Hispanic American Historical Review*, XLI (February, 1961), 31–54.

Indian problems were a major concern in the Provincias Internas. Herbert E. Bolton in his *Athanase de Mézières and the Louisiana-Texas Frontier, 1768–1780* (2 vols.; Cleveland, 1914), opened that field; Max L. Moorhead proved an apt disciple with his *The Apache Frontier: Jacobo Ugarte y Loyola and Spanish-Indian Relations in Northern New Spain, 1769–1791* (Norman, Okla., 1968); see also Frank M. Reeve, "The Apache Indians of Texas," *Southwestern Historical Quarterly*, L (October, 1946), 189–219; Joseph F. Park, "Spanish Indian Policy in Northern Mexico, 1765–1810," *Arizona and the West*, IV (Winter, 1962), 325–344; Odie B. Faulk, "Spanish-Comanche Relations and the Treaty of 1785," *Texana*, II (Spring, 1964), 44–53. A fascinating insight into a new Indian policy is found in Bernardo de Gálvez, *Instructions for Governing the Interior Provinces of New Spain, 1786*, trans. and ed. by Donald E. Worcester (Berkeley, Calif., 1951); the earlier career of Gálvez is studied in John W. Caughey, *Bernardo de Gálvez in Louisiana, 1770–1783* (Berkeley, Calif., 1934). An interesting study is Luis Navarro García, *Las provincias internas en el siglo XIX* (Sevilla, 1965).

Louisiana, French and Spanish

Some of the listings in this section may seem a bit arbitrary and might seem to belong more properly under another head; the French tag, however, will be the key to the choice of location—the French setting the stage for interaction with the Spaniards in the Borderlands; hence, the position of La Salle in the Texas story herein.

General works on the French in the Mississippi Valley: Joseph H. Schlarman, *From Quebec to New Orleans* (Belleville, Ill., 1929); John Anthony Caruso, *The Mississippi Valley Frontier: The Age of French Exploration and Settlement* (Indianapolis, 1966). A recent and excellent biography of one of the "discoverers" of the Mississippi is Joseph P. Donnelly, *Jacques Marquette* (Chicago, 1968); this can be blocked with Jean Delanglez, *Life and Voyages of Louis Jolliet, 1645–1700* (Chicago, 1948); see also Delanglez, "The Cartography of the Mississippi," *Mid-America,* XXX (October, 1948), 257–284, and XXXI (January, 1949), 29–52.

La Salle in the Valley and in Texas Francis Parkman, *La Salle and the Discovery of the Great West* (Boston, 1904); Paul Chesnel, *History of Cavelier de la Salle* (New York, 1932), to be used with caution; also see the La Salle materials in Pierre Margry, *Découvertes et établissements des Français dans l'oeust et dans le sud d'Amérique Septentrionale, 1614–1698* (6 vols.; Paris, 1879). On Peñalosa see C. F. Duro, *Don Diego de Peñalosa y su descubrimiento del del Reino de Quivira* (Madrid, 1882), and Charles W. Hackett, "New Light on Don Diego de Peñalosa," *Mississippi Valley Historical Review,* VI (December, 1919), 313–335. Herbert E. Bolton, "The Location of La Salle's Colony on the Gulf of Mexico," *ibid.,* II (September, 1915), 165–182, and also in *Southwestern Historical Quarterly,* XXVII (January, 1924), 171–189; Walter J. O'Donnell, "La Salle's Occupation of Texas," *Mid-America,* XVIII (April, 1936), 96–124; E. W. Cole, "La Salle in Texas," *Southwestern Historical Quarterly,* XLIX (April, 1946), 473–500; William E. Dunn, "The Spanish Search for La Salle's Colony on the Bay of Espíritu Santo," *ibid.,* XIX (April, 1916), 323–369; Henri Joutel, *A Journal of La Salle's Last Voyage,* edited by D. B. Rutman (New York, 1962); Jean Delanglez, *The Journal of Jean Cavelier* (Chicago, 1938). On La Salle's companion Tonty see Edmund R. Murphy, *Henry de Tonti* (Baltimore, 1941); Jean Delanglez, "The Voyages of Tonti in North America, 1678–1704," *Mid-America,* XXVI (July, 1944), 255–297; Mary Fletcher, "The Post of Arkansas," *Arkansas Historical Quarterly,* VII (Summer, 1948), 145–149.

One of the more recent and scholarly treatments of the early French in Louisiana is Marcel Giraud, *Histoire de la Louisiane Française* (2 vols., but still incomplete; Paris, 1953 and 1958); Nellis M. Crouse, *Lemoyne Iberville: Soldier of New France* (New York, 1954); Peter J. Hamilton, *Colonial Mobile* (Boston, 1897; revised, 1911); Agnes C. Laut, *Cadillac, Knight Errant of the Wilderness* (New York, 1931); Jean Delanglez, "Cadillac," *Mid-America,* XXVII (1945), XXX (1948), XXXII (1950), XXXIII (1951), ten articles scattered through the indicated volumes.

The Spanish reactions to French intrusions into the Gulf of Mexico: William E. Dunn, *Spanish and French Rivalry in the Gulf Region of the United States, 1678–1702* (Austin, Tex., 1917); and "The Occupation of Pensacola Bay, 1689–1698," *Florida Historical Society Quarterly,* IV (July, October, 1925), 3–14, 76–89, V (January, 1926), 140–154; Irving A. Leonard, "The Spanish Reexploration of the Gulf Coast in 1686," *Mississippi Valley Historical Review,* XXII (March, 1936), 547–557, and *Spanish Approach to Pensacola, 1689–1693*

(Los Angeles, 1939); Lawrence C. Ford, *The Triangular Struggle for Spanish Pensacola, 1689–1739* (Washington, 1937).

The Illinois Country (French)   Clarence W. Alvord, *The Illinois Country, 1673–1818* (Springfield, Ill., 1920), is a good general survey. For a study of the rivalry between the French and the Spaniards which developed following the occupation of the Mississippi Valley, see Henry Folmer, *Franco-Spanish Rivalry in North America* (Glendale, Calif., 1953). Other studies which look toward the Borderlands are Marc Villiers du Terrage, *Le Découverte du Missouri* (Paris, 1925); Ralph A. Smith, "Exploration of the Arkansas River by Bernard de la Harpe," *Arkansas Historical Quarterly,* X (Fall, 1951), 339–363; Gilbert J. Garraghan, "Fort Orleans of the Missoury," *Missouri Historical Review,* XXXV (April, 1942), 373–384; Henry Folmer, "Etienne Véniard de Bourgmond in the Missouri Country," *Missouri Historical Review,* XXXVI (April, 1942), 279–298, and "The Mallet Expedition of 1739 Through Nebraska, Kansas and Colorado to Santa Fe," *The Colorado Magazine,* XVI (September, 1939), 163–173; Herbert E. Bolton, "French Intrusions into New Mexico, 1749–1752," in *The Pacific Ocean in History,* pp. 289–407; Marc Villiers du Terrage, *Les dernières années de la Louisiane française* (Paris, 1903).

The Spaniards in Upper Louisiana   Abraham P. Nasatir, *Before Lewis and Clark* (2 vols.; Saint Louis, 1952); the long introduction to this collection of documents has a fine survey of the history of the middle Mississippi Valley. John Francis McDermott, ed., *The Early Histories of St. Louis* (Saint Louis, 1952). Nasatir is the top authority on the Spaniards in Upper Louisiana and his studies are many: "Ducharme's Invasion of Missouri, an Incident in the Anglo-Spanish Rivalry for the Indian Trade of Upper Louisiana," *Missouri Historical Review,* XXIV (October, 1929, January and April, 1930), 3–25, 238–260, 420–429; "Formation of the Missouri Company," *ibid.,* XV (October, 1922), 10–22; "Anglo-Spanish Rivalry on the Upper Missouri," *Mississippi Valley Historical Review,* VI (December, 1929; March, 1930), 359–382, 507–528; "Jacques d'Eglise in the Upper Missouri, 1791–1795," *ibid.,* XIV (June, 1927), 47–56; "Anglo-Spanish Rivalry in the Iowa Country, 1797–1798," *Iowa Journal of History and Politics,* XXVIII (July, 1930), 337–389; "The Anglo-Spanish Frontier on the Upper Mississippi, 1786–1796," *ibid.,* XXXIV (April, 1931), 155–232; "Jacques Clamorgan: Colonial Promoter of the Northern Border of New Spain," *New Mexico Historical Review,* XVII (April, 1942), 101–112; "John Evans, Explorer and Surveyor," *Missouri Historical Review,* XXV (January, April, July, 1931), 219–239, 432–460, 585–608; *Spanish War Vessels on the Mississippi, 1792–1796* (New Haven, 1968). Much of this story and more are in Noel M. Loomis and A. P. Nasatir, *Pedro Vial and the Roads to Santa Fe* (Norman, 1967), which has much more "roads to Santa Fe" than Pedro Vial. See also John Francis Bannon, "Missouri, a Borderland," *Missouri Historical Review,* LXIII (January, 1969), 227–240.

A valuable collection of documents is Lawrence Kinnaird, ed., *Spain in the Mississippi Valley, 1765–1794,* Annual Report of the American Historical Association, 1945, vols. II-IV (Washington, 1946); these materials are in the Spanish archives in the Bancroft Library, University of California-Berkeley; each volume is prefaced by an historical introduction. For this period see also, John W. Caughey, *Bernardo de Gálvez in Louisiana, 1770–1783* (Berkeley,

Calif., 1934); and several of the Louisiana histories, such as Gayarré, Martin, and others.

Attention should be called to the collection of studies, several of which have Borderland pertinence, gathered in John Francis McDermott, ed., *The French in the Mississippi Valley* (Urbana, Ill., 1965).

The Last Spanish Years in the Borderlands

During the last years of the eighteenth and through the first two decades of the nineteenth century all of the Spanish borderlands had problems with foreigners. California had its Russians; the rest of the Borderlands, with the exception of sheltered Arizona, were plagued by the *Americanos*. These foreigners figure prominently in the studies on the last years of the Spaniards in their Borderland provinces. This section will be arranged from east to west, from the Floridas to the Californias.

The Floridas The background of these late years can be found in Philip C. Brooks, *Diplomacy and the Borderlands: The Adams-Onís Treaty of 1819* (Berkeley, Calif., 1939); even before 1783, when the Floridas were returned to them, the Spaniards had plans, Kathryn Trimmer Abbey, "Spanish Projects for the Reoccupation of the Floridas during the American Revolution," *Hispanic American Historical Review*, IX (August, 1929), 265–285; then came the Anglo-Americans, Richard R. Murdoch, "Elijah Clark and Anglo-American Designs on East Florida 1797–1798," *American Historical Review*, XXXV (September, 1951), 173–191; Rufus Kay Wyllys, "The East Florida Revolution of 1812–1814," *Hispanic American Historical Review*, IX (November, 1929), 415–445; Wilbur H. Siebert, "The Loyalists in West Florida and the Natchez District," *Mississippi Valley Historical Review*, II (March, 1916), 465–484. The West Florida story is in Isaac J. Cox, *The West Florida Controversy, 1798–1813* (Baltimore, 1918).

Louisiana Arthur P. Whitaker studied the situation in the Lower Mississippi Valley extensively between 1783 and 1803: see his two works, *The Spanish-American Frontier, 1783–1795* (Boston, 1927), and *The Mississippi Question, 1795–1803* (New York, 1934), which incorporate the material of many of his earlier articles; he challenges some of the views of Samuel F. Bemis, *Pinckney's Treaty* (Baltimore, 1926), in two articles, "New Light on the Treaty of San Lorenzo: An Essay in Historical Criticism," *Mississippi Valley Historical Review*, XV (March, 1929), 435–454, and "Godoy's Knowledge of the Terms of Jay's Treaty," *American Historical Review*, XXXV (July, 1930), 804–810. James A. James studies "Louisiana as a Factor in American Diplomacy, 1795–1800," *Mississippi Valley Historical Review*, I (June, 1914), 44–56; another facet of the Louisiana frontier in those years is in Lawrence Kinnaird, "American Penetration into Spanish Louisiana," in *New Spain and the Anglo-American West*, (2 vols.; Lancaster, Pa., 1932) pp. 211–238. Burr and Wilkinson enter the story: Isaac J. Cox, "Hispanic-American Phases of the Burr Conspiracy," *Hispanic American Historical Review*, XII (May, 1932), 145–175; Clarence E. Carter, "Burr-Wilkinson Intrigues in St. Louis," Missouri Historical Society *Bulletin*, X (July, 1954), 447–464; James R. Jacobs, *Tarnished Warrior: Major General James Wilkinson* (New York, 1938).

Texas Julia Kathryn Garrett, *Green Flag over Texas: A Story of the Last*

Years of Spain in Texas (Dallas, 1939); Odie B. Faulk, *The Last Years of Spanish Texas, 1778–1821* (The Hague, 1964). E. E. Hale, "The Real Philip Nolan," *Publications* of the Mississippi Historical Society, IV (1901); Grace King, "The Real Philip Nolan," *Publications* of the Louisiana Historical Society, X (1917). Isaac J. Cox, "The Louisiana-Texas Frontier," Texas State Historical Association *Quarterly*, X (July, 1906), 1–75. There are several articles on Texas of interest: J. Autrey Dabbs, "The Texas Missions in 1785," *Mid-America*, XXII (January, 1940); Odie B. Faulk, "A Description of Texas in 1803," *Southwestern Historical Quarterly*, LXVI (April, 1963), 513–515; Jack D. L. Holmes, "The Marquis de Casa-Calvo, Nicolás de Finiels, and the 1805 Spanish Expedition through East Texas and Louisiana," *ibid.*, LXIX (January, 1966), 324–339; Nettie Lee Benson, "A Governor's Report on Texas in 1809," *ibid.*, LXXI (April, 1968), 603–616. The boundary dispute: Charles W. Hackett, ed., *Pichardo's Treatise on the Limits of Louisiana and Texas* (4 vols.; Austin, Tex., 1931–1946). Texas involvement in the Mexican Revolution of 1810: J. Villasana Haggard, "The Counter Revolution at Bexar, 1811," *Southwestern Historical Quarterly*, XLIII (October, 1939), 222–235. The Gutiérrez-Magee episode: Walter F. McCaleb, "The First Period of the Gutiérrez-Magee Expedition," Texas State Historical Association *Quarterly*, IV (January, 1901), 218–229; Elizabeth H. West, ed., "Diary of José Bernardo Gutiérrez de Lara, 1811–1812," *American Historical Review*, XXXIV (October, 1928, January, 1929), 55–77, 281–294; Rie Jarrett, *Gutiérrez de Lara, Mexican Texan* (Austin, Tex., 1949); Harry M. Henderson, "The Magee-Gutiérrez Expedition," *Southwestern Historical Quarterly*, LV (July, 1951), 43–61; Henry P. Walker, "William McLane's Narrative of the Magee-Gutiérrez Expedition, 1812–1813," *ibid.*, LXVI (October, 1962, January, 1963), 234–251, 457–479. Virginia H. Taylor and Juanita Hammons, trans. and eds., *The Letters of Antonio Martínez, Last Spanish Governor of Texas, 1817–1822* (Austin, Tex., 1957). A fascinating character is brought to life by Charles A. Bacarisse, "Baron de Bastrop," *Southwestern Historical Quarterly*, LVIII (January, 1955), 319–330; and looking toward the next period is Eugene C. Barker, *The Life of Stephen F. Austin, Founder of Texas, 1793–1836* (Nashville and Dallas, 1926).

New Mexico The early chapters of Max L. Moorhead, *New Mexico's Royal Road: Trade and Travel on the Chihuahua Trail* (Norman, Okla., 1958), deal with the Spanish period; Harold A. Bierck, "Dr. John Hamilton Robinson," *Louisiana Historical Quarterly*, XXV (July, 1942), 644–669; W. Eugene Hollon, *The Lost Pathfinder: Zebulon Montgomery Pike* (Norman, Okla., 1949); Donald Jackson, "Zebulon Pike 'Tours' Mexico," *The American West*, III (Summer, 1966), 64–71. Thomas M. Marshall, ed., "The Journals of Jules de Mun," Missouri Historical Society *Collections*, V (1927–1928), 167–208, 311–326; Frank B. Golley, "James Baird, Early Santa Fe Trader," Missouri Historical Society *Bulletin*, XV (April, 1959), 171–193; Isaac J. Cox, "Opening the Santa Fe Trail," *Missouri Historical Review*, XXV (January, 1930), 30–66; John M. Tucker, "Major Long's Route from the Arkansas to the Canadian River, 1820," *New Mexico Historical Review*, XXXVIII (July, 1963), 185–219. See also Loomis and Nasatir, *Pedro Vial and the Roads to Santa Fe* (Norman, Okla., 1967).

Arizona Sidney B. Brinckerhoff, "The Last Years of Spanish Arizona, 1786–1821," *Arizona and the West*, IX (Spring, 1967), 5–20.

California The Russians: Frank A. Golder, *Russian Expansion on the*

Pacific, 1641–1858 (Cleveland, 1914); Stuart R. Tompkins and Max L. Moorhead, "Russia's Approach to America," *The British Columbia Historical Quarterly,* (April and July-October, 1949), 55–56, 231–255; George P. Taylor, "Spanish-Russian Rivalry in the Pacific," *The Americas,* XV (October, 1958), 109–128; T. C. Russell, ed., *The Rezanov Voyage to Nueva California in 1806* (San Francisco, 1926), and *Langsdorff's Narrative of the Rezanov Voyage to Nueva California in 1806* (San Francisco, 1927); Gertrude Atherton, *Rezanov* (New York, 1906); Hector Chevigny, *Lost Empire: The Life and Adventures of Nikolai Petrovich Rezanov* (New York, 1937). The study of Adele Ogden, *The California Sea Otter Trade, 1784–1848* (Berkeley, Calif., 1941), touches many facets of California life in the last Spanish years. Maynard Geiger has dug up a most interesting late document pertaining to the missions, "Questionnaire of the Spanish Government in 1812 Concerning the Native Culture of the California Mission Indians," *The Americas,* V (April, 1949), 474–490.

The Borderlands: A Miscellany

In a bibliography organized as this one has been there are a number of studies which do not fit into regional or province patterns, at least not conveniently so. Yet they should not be overlooked. Therefore, into this catch-all section the more significant will be somewhat unceremoniously dumped.

By way of a lead-off example is that incisive study of Herbert E. Bolton, "The Mission as a Frontier Institution in the Spanish-American Colonies,"*American Historical Review,* XXIII (October, 1917), 42–61, and often reprinted. Odie B. Faulk has offered a preliminary treatment of the presidio in a similar broad setting, "The Presidio: Fortress or Farce?" *The Journal of the West,* VIII (January, 1969), 2–28; and Paige W. Christiansen follows this article with a "case study" using Janos as an example, "The Presidio and the Borderlands," *ibid.,* 29–37; and Max L. Moorhead has some thoughts on the presidial soldier, "The Soldado de Cuero: Stalwart of the Spanish Borderlands," *ibid.,* 38–55. Related to presidio studies is F. S. Curtis, "Spanish Arms and Armor in the Southwest," *New Mexico Historical Review,* II (April, 1927), 107–133.

Defying regional classification but not to be missed are Robert M. Denhart, *The Horse of the Americas* (Norman, Okla., 1947); more specifically Donald E. Worcester, "The Spread of Spanish Horses in the Southwest," *New Mexico Historical Review,* XIX (July, 1944), 225–232, and XX (January, 1945), 1–13; Francis Haines, "Horses for Western Indians," *The American West,* III (Spring, 1966), 4–15; and Floyd Ewing, "The Mule as a Factor in the Development of the Southwest," *Arizona and the West,* V (Winter, 1963), 291–314.

Again, J. Lloyd Mecham, "The *Real de Minas* as a Political Institution," *Hispanic American Historical Review,* VII (February, 1927), 45–83; Robert C. West, *The Mining Community in Northern New Spain: The Parral Mining District* (Berkeley, Calif., 1949).

Herbert E. Bolton, "The Black Robes of New Spain," *Catholic Historical Review,* XXI (October, 1935), 257–282, and "The Jesuits in America: An Opportunity for Historians," *Mid-America,* XVIII (October, 1936), 223–233.

A very interesting study is Harold C. Fritts and others, "Tree-Ring Evidence for Climatic Changes in Western North America from 1500 A.D. to 1940 A.D.,"

Annual Report of the United States Weather Bureau, 1964 (Tucson, Ariz., 1964). Jack D. Forbes crusades for the American Indian, "The Indian in the West: A Challenge for Historians," *Arizona and the West,* I (Autumn, 1959), 206–215, and, again, "The Historian and the Indian Racial Bias in American History," *The Americas,* XIX (April, 1963), 349–362. Richard J. Morrissey offers valuable economic insights with his "The Northward Expansion of Cattle Raising in New Spain, 1550–1600," *Agricultural History,* XXV (1951), 115–121.

Several studies of the advancing frontier while still in Mexico: Philip W. Powell, "Peacemaking on North America's First Frontier," *The Americas,* XVI (January, 1960), 221–250, and "Caldera of New Spain: Frontier Justice and Mestizo Symbol," *ibid.,* XVII (April, 1961), 325–342; Marc Simmons, "Tlascalans in the Spanish Borderlands," *New Mexico Historical Review,* XXXIX (April, 1964), 101–110.

Historiographical pieces: France V. Scholes, "Historiography of the Spanish Southwest: Retrospect and Prospect," in *Probing the American West* (Santa Fe, 1962), pp. 17–25; Demetrio Ramos, "The Chronicles of the Early Seventeenth Century: How They Were Written," *The Americas,* XXII (July, 1965), 41–53. Still another of pertinence is Peter Masten Dunne, "The Literature of the Jesuits of New Spain," *Catholic Historical Review,* XX (October, 1934), 248–259.

Some Unpublished Doctoral Dissertations and Master's Theses Dealing with the Borderlands

Often these studies when they do not find their way into print in their entirety are "lost"; hence, it would seem worthwhile to list some which are pertinent, even though segments have appeared in article or other form. This list is drawn from Warren F. Kuehl, *Dissertations in History: An Index to Dissertations Completed in History Departments of the United States and Canadian Universities, 1873–1960* (Lexington, Ky., 1965); some later ones have been added. Unfortunately, there is no such helpful listing of Master's theses, many of which might prove equally helpful to the student and the researcher. Harwood P. Hinton, however, has diligently gathered both doctoral and master's titles which bear on the history of Arizona in "Arizona Theses and Dissertations: A Preliminary Checklist," *Arizona and the West,* VII (Autumn, 1965), 239–264.

Beilharz, Edwin A. "Felipe de Neve, Governor of California and Commandant General of the Interior Provinces." University of California, 1951.
Bents, Doris W. "The History of Tubac, 1752–1948." University of Arizona, 1949.
Bjork, David K. "The Establishment of Spanish Rule in the Province of Louisiana, 1762–1770." University of California, 1923.
Born, John Dewey, Jr. "British Trade in West Florida, 1763–1783." University of New Mexico.
Carnes, Sister Mary Loyola. "The American Occupation of New Mexico, 1821–1852." University of California, 1925.
Carroll, Horace Bailey. "The Route of the Texas Santa Fe Expedition." University of Texas, 1935.
Castañeda, Carlos E. "Juan Agustín Morfi, 1739." University of Texas, 1932.
Caughey, John Walton. "Louisiana under Spain, 1762–1783." University of California, 1928.

Christiansen, Paige W. "Hugo Oconór: Spanish Apache Relations on the Frontiers of New Spain." University of California, 1959.

Cook, Warren L. "Spain in the Pacific Northwest, 1774–1795." Yale University, 1960.

Coon, Robin J. "The Costume of the Conquistadors, 1492–1550." University of Arizona, 1962.

Cox, Isaac Joslin. "The Early Exploration of Louisiana." University of Pennsylvania, 1904.

Cutter, Donald C. "Spanish Exploration of California's Central Valley." University of California, 1950.

Daniel, James M. "The Advance of the Spanish Frontier and the *Despoblado*." University of Texas, 1955.

Donohue, John A. "Jesuit Missions in Northwestern New Spain, 1711–1762." University of California, 1957.

Downey, Mary M. "The Expulsion of the Jesuits from Baja California." University of California, 1940.

Duell, Prentice W. "A Study of the Mission San Xavier del Bac near Tucson." University of Arizona, 1917.

DuFour, Clarence J. "John A. Sutter: His Career in California before The American Conquest." University of California, 1927.

Ewing, Russell C. "The Pima Uprising, 1751–1752." University of California, 1934.

Garrett, Kathryn. "The War of Independence in Texas, 1811–1813." University of California, 1935.

Graebner, Norman A. "The Treaty of Guadalupe-Hidalgo: Its Background and Formation." University of Chicago, 1949.

Griffith, William J. "The Spanish Occupation of the Hasinai Country, 1690–1737." University of California, 1942.

Gschaedler, Andre. "Mexico and the Pacific, 1540–1565: The Voyages of Villalobos and Legazpi." Columbia University, 1954.

Haggard, Juan V. "The Neutral Ground between Louisiana and Texas, 1806–1821." University of Texas, 1942.

Hoffmann, Fritz L. "Diary of the Alarcón Expedition into Texas, 1718–1719." University of Texas, 1935.

Holmes, Maurice G. "Some Light on the Background and Conduct of Early Spanish Nautical Exploration along the Coasts of California." University of Southern California, 1958.

Hussey, John A. "The United States and the Bear Flag Revolt." University of California, 1941.

Jimenez, Judith M. "Joaquin Arredondo, Loyalist Officer in New Spain, 1810–1821." University of Michigan, 1933.

John, Elizabeth. "Spanish Relations with the *Indios Barbaros* on the Northernmost Frontier of New Spain in the Eighteenth Century." University of Oklahoma, 1957.

Johnson, Harry P. "Diego Martinez de Hurdaide." University of California, 1940.

Kinnaird, Lawrence. "American Penetration into Spanish Territory to 1803." University of California, 1928.

Lothrop, Marian L. "Mariano Guadalupe Vallejo, Defender of the Northern Frontier of California." University of California, 1926.

Lynch, Margaret. "Colonial Texas as a Frontier Problem." Boston College, 1935.

Marcias, Albert M. "The Defense of Pimería Alta 1690–1800: A Study in Spanish-Apache Military Relations." University of Arizona, 1966.

McAlister, Lyle N. "The Army of New Spain, 1760–1800." University of California, 1950.

McCloskey, Michael B. "The Missionary College of the Holy Cross, Queretaro." Catholic University, 1952.

McShane, Catherine M. "Hernando de Santarén, Founder of the Jesuit Missions of the Sierra Madre." University of California, 1940.

Morton, Ohland. "The Life of General Don Manuel de Mier y Teran as it Affected Texas-Mexican Relations, 1821–1832." University of Texas, 1939.

Murphy, Henrietta. "Spanish Provincial Administration as Exemplified by the Inspection of Pedro de Rivera, 1724–1728." University of Texas, 1938.

Nasatir, Abraham P. "Indian Trade and Diplomacy in the Spanish Illinois, 1762–1792." University of California, 1926.

Nelson, Al B. "Juan de Ugalde and the Rio Grande Frontier, 1777–1790." University of California, 1937.

Nieser, Albert B. "The Dominican Mission Foundation in Baja California." Loyola University, 1960.

O'Callaghan, Mary A. "The Indian Policy of Carondelet in Spanish Louisiana, 1792–1797." University of California, 1942.

O'Rourke ,Thomas P. "The Franciscan Missions in Texas (1690–1793)." Catholic University, 1927.

Pockstaller, Theodore. "Juan Maria Salvatierra, S.J., and the Establishment of the First Permanent Settlements in California (1697–1708)." University of California, 1919.

Pulling, Hazel A. "A History of California's Range Cattle Industry, 1770–1912." University of Southern California, 1944.

Rowland, Donald W. "The Elizondo Expedition against the Indian Rebels of Sonora, 1765–1771." University of California, 1931.

Sirridge, Agnes T. "Spanish, British and French Activities in the Sea Otter Trade of the Far North Pacific, 1774–1790." Saint Louis University, 1954.

Stoner, Victor Rose. "The Spanish Missions of the Santa Cruz Valley." University of Arizona, 1937.

Tapia, Francisco X. "The Existence and Development of the Town Meeting *(cabildo abierto)* in Spanish Colonial America." Georgetown University.

Tate, Vernon D. "The Founding of the Port of San Blas." University of California, 1934.

Tays, George. "Revolutionary California: The Political History of the Mexican Period, 1822–1846." University of California, 1932.

Thomas, Alfred B. "Spanish Expeditions Northeast of New Mexico, 1696–1719." University of California, 1928.

Tichenor, Helen E. "The Opening of the Southern Missions of Baja California." University of California, 1941.

Tolman, Robert G. "The Spanish Mission as an Economic Institution in the Southwest." University of Arizona, 1948.

Treutlein, Theodore. "Jesuit Travel to America (1678–1756) as Recorded in the Travel Diaries of German Jesuits." University of California, 1934.

Vigness, David M. "The Republic of the Rio Grande: An Example of Separatism in Northern Mexico." University of Texas, 1951.

Walz, Vina. "A History of the El Paso Area, 1680–1692." University of New Mexico, 1951.

Warren, Harris G. "New Spain and the Filibusters." Northwestern University, 1937.

Wetzler, Lewis W. "A History of the Pima Indians." University of California, 1949.

White, Theodore I. "The Marquis de Rubí's Inspection of the Eastern Presidios on the Northern Frontier of New Spain." University of Texas, 1953.

Worcester, Donald C. "Early History of the Navaho Indians." University of California, 1947.

Wright, Doris M. "A Yankee in Mexican California: Abel Stearns, 1798–1848." Claremont, 1955.

Wright, Ione S. "Early American Voyages to the Far East, 1527–1565." University of California, 1940.

Wright, James L., Jr. "English-Spanish Rivalry in North America, 1492–1763." University of Virginia, 1958.

VICEROYS OF NEW SPAIN

1535–1550 Antonio de Mendoza
1550–1554 Luis de Velasco
1566–1567 Gastón de Peralta, Marqués de Falces
1568–1580 Martín Enríquez de Almanza
1580–1583 Lorenzo Suárez de Mendoza, Conde de la Coruña
1584–1585 Pedro Moya de Contreras, Archbishop and Visitador
1585–1590 Alvaro Manrique de Zúñiga, Marqués de Villa Manrique
1590–1595 Luis de Velasco, Marqués de Salinas
1595–1603 Gaspar de Zúñiga y Acevedo, Conde de Monterrey
1603–1607 Juan de Mendoza y Luna, Marqués de Montesclaros
1607–1611 Luis de Velasco, Marqués de Salinas
1611–1612 Fray García Guerra, Archbishop of México
1612–1621 Diego Fernández de Córdoba, Marqués de Guadalcázar
1621–1624 Diego Carrillo de Mendoza y Pimentel, Marqués de Gelves y Conde
           de Priego
1624–1635 Rodrigo Pacheco Osorio, Marqués de Cerralvo
1635–1640 Lope Díaz de Arméndariz, Marqués de Cadereyta
1640–1642 Diego López Pacheco Cabrera y Bobadilla, Marqués de Villena,
           Duque de Escalona
1642   Juan de Palafox y Mendoza, Bishop of Puebla
1642–1648 García Sarmiento de Sotomayor, Conde de Salvatierra, Marqués de
           Sobroso
1648–1649 Marcos de Torres y Rueda, Bishop of Yucatán
1650–1653 Luis Enríquez de Guzmán, Conde de Alba de Liste, Marqués de
           Villaflor
1653–1660 Francisco Fernández de la Cueva, Duque de Alburquerque
1660–1664 Juan de Leiva y de la Cerda, Marqués de Leiva y de Ladrada, Conde
           de Baños
1664   Diego Osorio de Escobar y Llamas, Bishop of Puebla
1664–1673 Antonio Sebastián de Toledo, Marqués de Mancera
1673   Pedro Nuño Colón de Portugal, Duque de Veragua, Marqués de la
           Jamaica
1673–1680 Payo Enríquez de Rivera, Archbishop of México
1680–1686 Tomás Antonio de la Cerda y Aragón, Conde de Paredes, Marqués
           de la Laguna
1686–1688 Melchor Portocarrero Lazo de la Vega, Conde de la Monclova
1688–1696 Gaspar de la Cerda Sandoval Silva y Mendoza, Conde de Galve
1696–1697 Juan de Ortega Montañez, Bishop of Michoacán
1697–1701 José Sarmiento Valladares, Conde de Moctezuma y de Tula
1701–1702 Juan de Ortega Montañez, Bishop of Michoacán
1702–1711 Francisco Fernández de la Cueva Enríquez, Duque de Alburquerque

1711–1716	Fernando de Alencastre Noreña y Silva, Duque de Linares, Marqués de Valdefuentes
1716–1722	Baltasar de Zúñiga, Marqués de Valero, Duque de Arión
1722–1734	Juan de Acuña, Marqués de Casafuerte
1734–1740	Juan Antonio de Vizarrón y Eguiarreta, Archbishop of México
1740–1741	Pedro de Castro y Figueroa, Duque de la Conquista y Marqués de Gracia Real
1742–1746	Pedro Cebrián y Agustín, Conde de Fuenclara
1746–1755	Francisco de Güemes y Horcasitas, Conde de Revilla Gigedo
1755–1760	Agustín de Ahumada y Villalón, Marqués de las Amarillas
1760	Francisco Cajigal de la Vega
1760–1766	Joaquín de Monserrat, Marqués de Cruillas
1766–1771	Carlos Francisco de Croix, Marqués de Croix
1771–1779	Fray Antonio María de Bucareli y Ursua
1779–1783	Martín de Mayorga
1783–1784	Matías de Gálvez
1785–1786	Bernardo de Gálvez, Conde de Gálvez
1787	Alonso Núñez de Haro y Peralta, Archbishop of México
1787–1789	Manuel Antonio Flores
1789–1794	Juan Vicente de Güemes Pacheco de Padilla, Conde de Revillagigedo
1794–1798	Miguel de la Grúa Talamanca y Branciforte, Marqués de Branciforte
1798–1800	Miguel José de Azanza
1800–1803	Félix Berenguer de Marquina
1803–1808	José de Iturrigaray
1808–1809	Pedro Garibay
1809–1810	Francisco Javier de Lizana y Beaumont, Archbishop of México
1810–1813	Francisco Javier Venegas, Conde de la Reunión de la Nueva España
1813–1816	Félix María Calleja del Rey, Conde de Calderón
1816–1821	Juan Ruiz de Apodaca, Conde del Venadito
1821	Francisco Novella
1821	Juan O'Donojú

INDEX